FEMINIST DISABILITY STUDIES

FEMINIST

DISABILITY

STUDIES

EDITED BY KIM Q. HALL

INDIANA UNIVERSITY PRESS

Bloomington and Indianapolis

This book is a publication of

Indiana University Press
601 North Morton Street
Bloomington, Indiana 47404-3797 USA

iupress.indiana.edu

Telephone orders   800-842-6796
Fax orders   812-855-7931

LIBRARY OF CONGRESS
CATALOGING-IN-PUBLICATION DATA

Feminist disability studies / edited by
Kim Q. Hall.
    p.   cm.
    Includes bibliographical references
and index.
    ISBN 978-0-253-35662-8 (cloth : alk.
paper) — ISBN 978-0-253-22340-1 (pbk. :
alk. paper) 1. Disability studies. 2. Feminist theory—United States. I. Hall, Kim
Q., [date]
    HV1568.2.F46 2011
    362.4082—dc22   2011012080

    1 2 3 4 5   16 15 14 13 12 11

In memory of

Paul K. Longmore

(1946–2010)

Contents

Acknowledgments

The idea for this project emerged as a result of my participation in the 2000 National Endowment for the Humanities Institute on Disability Studies. For their critical insights, work, and general brilliance, I am deeply grateful to the codirectors, Rosemarie Garland-Thomson and Paul Longmore, and all the participants who continue to inform my thinking about the body and identity. This book would not have been possible without the conversations that happened there. A couple of months after I finished the book, Paul Longmore died. Paul was a superb scholar and a powerful voice for disability rights. I hope this book would have made him proud.

Parts of this book were originally published as a special issue of the (National Women's Studies Association) and when I learned that all copies of the special issue sold out, I decided to propose it as a book with previously published articles revised as the authors deemed desirable, new essays, and a new introduction. I would like to thank all the contributors to this volume for sending me their work and for writing such interesting, thought-provoking essays. It is a privilege to make their work in feminist disability studies available to a wider audience.

So many people made possible the completion of this project. I am grateful to Kate Caras and Dee Mortensen at Indiana University Press for their enthusiasm and patience throughout the various stages of this project. Their continuous support of this project has been vital, as has been their support of me. Many friends and colleagues provided personal and intellectual community and feedback at crucial times. For asking about my progress, providing insight, and encouraging me, thanks in particular to Amy Hudnall, Beth Carroll, Chris Cuomo, Gayle Turner,

Maggie McFadden, Marilyn Smith, Pat Beaver, Robert McRuer, and Susan Staub.

Finally, I would like to thank Jill Ehnenn for reading everything that I write and for providing excellent feedback. But most especially, I want to thank her for her love. My work is better because of our many conversations, and my life is better because she is in it.

FEMINIST DISABILITY STUDIES

REIMAGINING DISABILITY AND GENDER THROUGH FEMINIST STUDIES

An Introduction

KIM Q. HALL

Feminist disability studies, like the gendered or disabled body, is more than a sum of its parts. Just as disability studies shows how disability is irreducible to bodily impairment, feminist theory shows how gender is irreducible to biological sex. However, understanding feminist disability studies as simply a combination of feminism and disability studies dulls its critical edge and lessens its potential to intervene in theoretical and social transformation. As Rosemarie Garland-Thomson observes in a recent review essay of the field, feminist disability studies reimagines disability (2005, 1557). And, I would assert, it also reimagines gender. As such, feminist disability studies does not just add disabled women's experiences to scholarship in disability studies and feminist theory. Instead, as Garland-Thomson argues in her contribution to this volume, it transforms both fields.

Two recent events illuminate the need for feminist disability analysis of race, gender, class, sexuality, and the body, and the potential of that analysis to provide crucial insights into the myriad forms of gendered oppression. In January 2007 mainstream U.S. media headlines broke the story of the "Pillow Angel." Readers learned the "Pillow Angel" was Ashley, a disabled girl whose parents in 2004 had obtained approval from doctors and the ethics committee at the Seattle Children's Hospital to pursue medical treatment that would stop her growth and sexual development. Asserting that Ashley would always have the motor and cognitive skills of a three-month-old baby, those who supported this treatment claimed the treatment would improve her quality of life by preventing future discomfort and trauma and by making it easier for her parents to take care of her.

Ashley was six years old at the time of the treatment, which consisted of high-dose estrogen therapy and fusion of bone plates to stop growth, a hysterectomy to prevent future menstruation and pregnancy, and the removal of breast buds to prevent the development of an adult woman's breasts. Ashley's parents refer to the procedures as the "Ashley Treatment" and have defended their decision as necessary to improve her quality of life. In effect, the Ashley Treatment ensures that Ashley's body will never develop the marks of womanhood. No matter how old Ashley gets, her body will remain a child's body (Carlson 2010, 3).

Ashley's story sparked the outrage of many disability rights activists and feminists. Philosopher Peter Singer weighed in with his support of the doctors' and parents' decision, asserting that the procedures minimized Ashley's suffering and was best for her and her family (2007). It should be noted that, in his arguments for euthanasia, Singer's characterizations of disability as burdensome and a mark of diminished quality of life have not, to put it mildly, made him the darling of disability rights activists and scholars. Still, it is surprising how many people remain unaware of Ashley's story. In their contribution to this book, Sharon Lamp and Carol Cleigh criticize feminists for not speaking out against what they contend is an example of contemporary eugenic treatment of disabled girls and women.

Another recent event that outraged many in queer, feminist, and disability communities was the highly publicized gender verification testing forced upon Caster Semenya, an eighteen-year-old South African runner who won the women's 800-meter race at the IAAF (International Association of Athletics Federations) World Championships in Berlin in August 2009. Her stunning victory was immediately followed by worldwide media speculation about whether she is a woman and, thus, eligible to compete in women's track events. When members of the South African government met to consider a resolution regarding Caster Semenya, Noluthando Mayende-Sibiya, the Minister of Women, Children, and Persons with Disabilities in South Africa, spoke against the violation of Semenya's human rights (Levy 2009, 50). After some deliberation, Semenya was able to keep the medal she won in Berlin in 2009; however, she was not allowed to compete in other track events until July 2010. At the time of this writing, Semenya is able to compete in women's track events, but the IAAF has not released the results of the sex determination tests it performed. Controversy continues to surround Semenya's participation in women's track events (Clarey 2010).

Semenya, who was raised as a girl, has had to endure intrusive inquiry about her muscular build, deep voice, and comportment. In their writings about this event, Alice Dreger (2009) and Ariel Levy (2009) have introduced the mainstream public in the United States to questions with which feminist and queer theorists have long been concerned: Just what makes a girl a girl and a boy a boy? Do sex characteristics provide an unproblematic, unquestionable foundation for sex and gender identity? What is the relationship between the body and gender?

At first glance it may seem strange to discuss the controversy surrounding Semenya's victory in an introduction to a book about feminist disability studies. After all, Ashley is widely perceived to be disabled; however, Caster Semenya neither self-identifies as nor is widely perceived to be disabled. In fact, dominant conceptions of disability place world-class athletes and disabled people in different categories, with the "overcoming narrative" the only place where the two overlap in dominant discourse about disability. Commentary during the Olympics is saturated with stories of athletes who have overcome disabling impairments, and various "special" Olympics are held for athletes who are disabled. In the overcoming narrative of disability, it is precisely through acts of athletic prowess that a disabled person "overcomes" disability. Eli Clare's critique of the pervasive overcoming narrative shows how it can be internalized and can influence even the most disability-politicized disabled person's embodied understanding (1999, 9).

Thinking about the treatment of Semenya and Ashley X through the lens of en- or dis-abled gender and disability enables a reimagining of disability and gender in ways that contribute further insight into the injustice against both. From a feminist disability studies perspective, both Semenya and Ashley X have extraordinary bodies,[1] and mainstream responses to both reveal the material implications of the normate. Rosemarie Garland-Thomson defines the normate as "the figure outlined by an array of deviant others whose marked bodies shore up the norm's boundaries. . . . [It] is the constructed identity of those who, by way of the bodily configurations and cultural capital they assume, can step into a position of authority and wield the power it grants them" (1997, 8). The normate's gender and sex are not challenged, and the normate's growth and development dictate how all should grow and develop. The normates against which both Ashley X and Caster Semenya are defined are the ideal woman, and thereby, the ideal man; as Simone de Beauvoir's famous and now newly translated remark, "One is not born, but rather becomes, woman" (2010, 283), explains, *woman* is defined in relation to *man* as deficiency and lack, as the Other—a point that feminist theorists such as Iris Marion Young have suggested understands *woman* as "physically handicapped" (2005, 42).[2]

Within feminist disability studies, the suggestion that "woman" is disabled by compulsory heterosexuality and patriarchy is met with ambivalence. While the claim establishes an important conceptual connection between disability and gender, it also reflects (and risks perpetuating) dominant conceptions of disability as lack and deficiency, to the extent that it is accompanied by a desire to show that the association of women with disability is unjust to women. This association leaves in place, albeit unintentionally, the idea that disability is inherently contaminating and that certain bodily conditions themselves are disabling. Thus understood, justice requires a reclamation and revaluation of *woman* at the expense of disabled people. Within feminist disability studies, exploring conceptual and lived connections between gender and disability helps to make visible the historical and ongoing interrelationship between all forms of oppression.

In her discussion of how feminist analyses of oppression would be enhanced by consideration of the lives of intellectually disabled people (particularly intellectually disabled women), Licia Carlson writes, rephrasing Elizabeth Spelman, "Does the existence of those who can be defined as complete women and mothers demand the existence of others who cannot be granted womanhood and motherhood?" (2010, 83). The Ashley Treatment provides an affirmative answer to that question. In response to the outrage many people expressed on Ashley's behalf, Ashley's parents set up a website to explain their decision and assure all concerned that they are good parents who simply want what's best for their child. Their post includes an explanation for why they think of Ashley as their "Pillow Angel": "We call her our Pillow Angel since she's so sweet and stays right where we place her, usually on a pillow" ("Ashley Treatment" 2007). Ashley's "sweetness" and staying in her place reflect cultural gendered expectations of good little girls, a point reinforced by the fact that photos accompanying media coverage have tended to feature Ashley dressed in pink. Dressed in pink and perpetually small, Ashley is presented as someone who will always be a sweet, easy-to-manage little girl.

The assumption that disabled people cannot be sexual beings is a feature of disability oppression. At the same time, cognitively disabled people are often stereotyped as hypersexual. Both assumptions inform attempts to justify the Ashley Treatment. Ashley's parents and doctors, and others who defend their decision, seem unable to reconcile the idea of being disabled with that of being a woman and a sexual being. Ashley's parents call her their "Pillow Angel" because she stays just where they put her. In fact, their decision to prevent sexual development and growth ensures that Ashley will stay just where they want her to be, literally their little girl for the rest of her life. From a feminist disability studies perspective, one might question the significance of their concern that menstruation and breast development would be particularly traumatic for Ashley. After all, such a worry seems to assume that having breasts and menstruating is not traumatic for many girls and female-bodied young people who don't identify as girls and may not think of their bodies as "female." Should we remove the breast buds and uteruses of all girls to prevent the discomfort and trauma of changing bodies and the possibility of pregnancy? Of course, this would (and should) never seriously be proposed. When confronted with criticisms of their actions as grotesque, Ashley's parents objected that "the prospect of having a full-grown fertile woman endowed with the mind of a baby" is what is really grotesque ("Ashley Treatment" 11). As Josie Byzek asks in her *New Mobility* blog post (2007), would the parents, doctors, and ethicists make a similar decision if Ashley were a boy? We ought to be deeply concerned about the decision to subject disabled girls to irreversible, unnecessary, and highly invasive surgeries and treatments in order to make caretaking easier. To be fair, Ashley's parents claim that their decision was made to preserve Ashley's dignity, not to make their caretaking easier. No doubt, their decision-making process was not easy. Nonetheless, the references to being able to lift her, keep her in her chair, and so forth reflect concerns about consequences of the Ashley Treatment for caregivers.

In *The Rejected Body: Feminist Philosophical Reflections on Disability* (1996), Susan Wendell examines how Western philosophical conceptions of the body as separate from and a hindrance to the mind inform contemporary anxieties about bodies "out of control" in general and disabled bodies in particular. The prevailing Western view, as Wendell explains, associates normalcy with the exercise of proper discipline and control over the body. Consequently, ableism is a product of long-standing Western somatophobia. As Sandra Bartky (1990) observes in her discussion of femininity and the phenomenology of oppression, disciplined bodies are also properly gendered bodies—that is, bodies whose behaviors, features, and desires flow seamlessly from binary sex characteristics.

Building on the social model of disability in disability studies and feminist theory's analysis of the naturalization of both sex and gender, feminist disability studies can suggest an avenue for critique of reductive biological understandings of both gender and disability. From a feminist disability perspective, Semenya's treatment raises questions regarding assumptions about the relationship between hormones, for example, and "true" sex. As Alice Dreger points out in her discussion of Semenya, the IAAF currently has no consistent and reliable way to ascertain an athlete's "true" sex (2009). In the midst of controversy surrounding Semenya's ambiguously sexed and gendered body, the IAAF is trying to devise a set of rules that can consistently be used. But, as Dreger points out, resolving the question of a body's sex is not merely a matter of developing the right test. There is much interpretative room when it comes to establishing the line that divides males and females. Ascertaining a body's sex is not simply a matter of looking in the right place in the body's interior or on the body's surface. For instance, Dreger notes, "The IAAF requires that transsexual women have their hormone levels kept female-typical through removal of the testes and ingestion of female-typical hormones. . . . But it allows born-females with adrenal tumors to compete as women, even though their bodies may have higher levels of testosterone than the average male" (2009).

So it would seem that not everyone who might have higher than female-typical levels of testosterone raises concerns about unfair advantage when they compete against other women in athletic events. Such concerns arise when the body's appearance and gestures seem too masculine. In Semenya's case, officials and the general public reason that this incongruity between how one's body is and the appearance and gestures expected from female bodies is a sign of gender trouble beneath the skin. Many South Africans have also commented on how Semenya's race has informed the perception of her body as gender-questionable, pointing out the parallels between fascination with Semenya's body in the media and fascination with the body of the "Hottentot Venus," Saartjie Baartman (Levy 2009, 50).

Feminist disability studies makes the body, bodily variety, and normalization central to analyses of all forms of oppression. A feminist disability studies critique of the Ashley Treatment exposes the role of gender norms in the rationalization of oppression of disabled people. And a feminist disability studies critique of questions concerning Semenya's "true" sex exposes the role of assumptions of gendered bodily norms in the oppression of gender-variant and intersexed people. In addition to critique, feminist disability studies proposes ways of rethinking and reimagining the body and embodiment, the sort of reconceptualization that Judith Butler contends is vital for making lives that have been excluded from the realm of the human and threatened with annihilation visible as lives at all (2004).

In this way, feminist disability studies moves toward reclaiming and resignifying the notion of "a life worth living" from its current place in the euthanasia debate. The question of a life worth living, from a feminist disability perspective, is not best understood as a question about whether disability impoverishes or enhances quality of life. Rather the question is, following Butler, what makes possible a life that can be lived. Moving toward that insight involves identifying and critiquing those historical, social, cultural, and political forces that have declared disabled life to be unlivable. There are many questions with which one must grapple in doing this work, including the following: What is the relationship between gender and disability? What role does gender play in the experience of disability? How is gendered disability and dis- or en-abled gender racialized? How do institutions, global economic inequalities, and ideas of citizenship and the nation produce gendered, raced, and classed disability? How does (or should) feminist disability studies address the body's materiality?

The essays in this volume represent various disciplinary contributions to feminist disability studies. While each addresses different topics, there are many interesting areas of overlap. Taken together, these essays constitute an interdisciplinary dialogue regarding the meaning of feminist disability studies and the implications of its insights regarding identity, the body, and experience. While the conversation in these pages does not by any means exhaust the range of discussion in the field, each essay offers a significant contribution to feminist disability studies scholarship and opens the door to important future work.

The first section, "Toward a Theoretical Framework for Feminist Disability Studies," reflects ongoing efforts to define the nature and scope of feminist disability studies and begins, appropriately, with Rosemarie Garland-Thomson, a major feminist disability theorist whose work inaugurated the field. Her contribution to this book, first published in the *NWSA Journal* special issue on feminist disability studies, has become a classic article and continues to provide a useful overview and introduction to major issues with which feminist disability studies is concerned. Garland-Thomson focuses on four "domains" of feminist theory (the body, representation, identity, and activism) and shows how feminist disability studies transforms feminist inquiry in each domain. The version of her essay in this book includes a postscript in which she discusses the implications of and her subsequent thoughts about what she says in this essay. Ellen Samuels's essay explores how Judith Butler's theory of the body and gender performativity has been taken up within feminist disability studies. Samuels stresses the important place of *real* bodies and *lived* disability in theory and argues against approaches that fail to meaningfully distinguish between lived experiences of sex/gender from lived experiences of ability/disability. Her essay raises important questions about how far feminist disability studies can go in its understanding of the interrelatedness of gender and disability before it erases the specificity of disability experience.

"Refiguring Literature" features essays that use feminist disability studies to reconsider literary works and raise questions about foundational assumptions that define genres. Contending that Georgina Kleege's memoir, *Sight Unseen*, is not just a story about becoming blind, Susannah Mintz demonstrates how Kleege critiques the centrality of vision in

Western culture, feminism, and the genre of autobiography. Mintz shows how Kleege's text contributes to understanding the gendering of disability, the en- or dis-abling of gender, and the gendering and dis-abling of the conventions of autobiography. In her essay, Elizabeth Donaldson questions several thematic issues in both feminist and disability studies, including distinctions between impairment and disability and critiques of the medical model of disability that are so central to the social model of disability. Ultimately, Donaldson is concerned that feminist tendencies to reclaim women's madness as a form of resistance to patriarchal oppression risk denying that mental illness is an impairment, which in turn erases real bodies in ways that hinder effective advocacy for mentally ill people. Donaldson's discussion focuses on *Jane Eyre*'s Bertha Mason and offers a fresh, important reading of that text.

This collection's third section is "Interrogating Fitness: Nation, Identity, and Citizenship." Both Nirmala Erevelles and Jennifer James focus specifically on disability, race, and gender in the context of war. Erevelles argues that feminist disability studies has ignored poor people in the third world, especially poor women of color, and that third world feminism has ignored the lives of disabled people in the third world. To correct these gaps, Erevelles defines and defends "transnational feminist disability studies" as an approach that attends to the global unequal distribution of wealth and the harmful consequences of war. As Erevelles points out, it is only by attending to global material inequalities that third world feminism and feminist disability studies can adequately understand the realities of disability and gender in the economic South. Jennifer James's essay turns to the tradition of African American war writing and Gwendolyn Brooks's critical interventions into that tradition. Ultimately, James seeks to reclaim Brooks's war writing as a "black womanist poetics of rehabilitation" that resists efforts to repair, normalize, and erase the injured black body. At stake for James is the meaning and status of the gendered black body in efforts to advocate for the full citizenship of African Americans.

In their contributions to this section, Cindy LaCom and Sharon Lamp and Carol Cleigh pay particular attention to fitness, national identity, and citizenship, especially how those ideas figure in resistance to exclusion and oppression. LaCom examines these issues in the postcolonial context, focusing specifically on the novel *Clear Light of Day* and the play *You Have Come Back*; her essay contends that the disabled characters play an important role in postcolonial nation-building and have the potential to disrupt expectations and norms of both gender and national identity. In their essay, Lamp and Cleigh critique the eugenic roots of contemporary feminism. They demonstrate the ableism in Margaret Sanger's and

Charlotte Perkins Gilman's work and argue the same ableist assumptions continue to inform contemporary feminist understanding of disability.

The essays in "Sexual Agency and Queer Feminist Futures" investigate how feminist disability studies can transform queer and feminist analyses of sexual agency, reproductive choice, and the future. Abby Wilkerson provides a much-needed discussion of sexual autonomy and disability. Despite their path-forging analyses of sexuality, shame, and desire, Wilkerson argues that neither feminist nor disability studies has sufficiently understood how denial of sexual autonomy plays a key role in disabled people's oppression. Alison Kafer's essay analyzes Marge Piercy's classic feminist text, *Woman on the Edge of Time* (especially its current prominence in women's studies classrooms), and the controversy surrounding the case of two deaf lesbians who desired a deaf child. Kafer compares these two seemingly unrelated events in order to explore unexamined assumptions about disability that inform feminist conceptions of the future. Kafer critiques Piercy's feminist utopia as a future without disability and contends that imagining a future with disability is crucial for countering the dominant emphasis on curing disability.

Essays in the final section, "Inclusions, Exclusions, and Transformations," use a feminist disability studies framework to question institutional power and accommodation, the definition of disability, and theater. In her contribution, April Herndon makes the case for understanding fatness as a disability. Drawing similarities between fat and deaf identities, Herndon argues that reframing fatness as disability makes visible the politics of size in ways that make it possible to recognize fat as a political group identity, not an impairment or disease. Karen Jung's essay draws on interviews with chronically ill women students to question the effects of accommodation policies in universities. In particular, Jung focuses on the meanings of disability and accommodation in institutional settings for women with invisible disabilities and illuminates how the meaning and experience of disability is shaped by institutional policies. Finally, in their collaborative contribution to the book, Ann Fox and Joan Lipkin explore the possibilities of an alliance between feminist theater and an emergent disability theater. They consider the meaning and possibility of a "disability aesthetic," critique the metaphor of disability in feminist theater, and seek to contribute to constructive conversation about alliances between feminist and disability concerns. In order to illustrate the possibilities of a "disability aesthetic" and a feminist disability theater, the essay includes three scripts by Joan Lipkin and the DisAbility Project, a grassroots theater group in St. Louis, Missouri.

In their essay, Fox and Lipkin ask readers (and spectators) to "go figure" the possibilities of connections between feminist critiques of gender normativity and disability studies critiques of normative embodiment. *Feminist Disability Studies* offers an interdisciplinary contribution to that figuring. It is my hope that these essays will inspire readers to rethink the meanings of disability and its relation to gender, race, class, sexuality, and nation in ways that move toward a transformative feminist disability theory and practice.

NOTES

1. Thanks to Megan Lease for putting it this way.
2. See also Rosemarie Garland-Thomson's discussion of this issue in her contribution to this volume.

REFERENCES

"The Ashley Treatment: Towards a Better Quality of Life for 'Pillow Angels.'" 2007. Ashley's Mom and Dad. http://pillowangel.org/Ashley%20Treatment%20v7.pdf.

Bartky, Sandra. 1990. *Femininity and Domination: Studies in the Phenomenology of Oppression*. New York: Routledge.

Butler, Judith. 2004. *Undoing Gender*. New York: Routledge.

Byzek, Josie. 2007. "Tremors of Intent: More Thoughts on the Ashley Treatment." *New Mobility.* http://www.newmobility.com/browse_thread.cfm?blogid=10&id=42&srch=Spirituality%20Religion.

Carlson, Licia. 2010. *The Faces of Intellectual Disability: Philosophical Reflections.* Bloomington: Indiana University Press.

Clare, Eli. 1999. *Exile and Pride: Disability, Queerness, and Liberation.* Cambridge, Mass.: South End Press.

Clarey, Christopher. 2010. "Semenya Returns and So Do Questions." *New York Times,* 23 August.

de Beauvoir, Simone. (1949) 2010. *The Second Sex.* Translated by Constance Borde and Sheila Malovany-Chevallier. New York: Knopf.

Dreger, Alice. 2009. "Seeking Simple Rules in Complex Gender Realities." *New York Times,* 25 October.

Garland-Thomson, Rosemarie. 1997. *Extraordinary Bodies: Figuring Physical Disability in American Culture and Literature.* New York: Columbia University Press.

———. 2005. "Feminist Disability Studies." *Signs* 20 (2): 1557–87.

Levy, Ariel. 2009. "Either/Or: Sports, Sex, and the Case of Caster Semenya." *New Yorker,* 30 November, 47–59.

Singer, Peter. 2007. "A Convenient Truth." *New York Times,* 26 January.

Wendell, Susan. 1996. *The Rejected Body: Feminist Philosophical Reflections on Disability.* New York: Routledge.

Young, Iris Marion. 2005. "Throwing Like a Girl: A Phenomenology of Feminine Body Comportment, Motility, and Spatiality." *On Female Body Experience: Throwing Like a Girl and Other Essays,* 27–45. New York: Oxford University Press.

PART ONE

TOWARD A

THEORETICAL FRAMEWORK

FOR FEMINIST

DISABILITY STUDIES

One

INTEGRATING DISABILITY, TRANSFORMING FEMINIST THEORY

ROSEMARIE GARLAND-THOMSON

Over the last several years, disability studies has moved out of the applied fields of medicine, social work, and rehabilitation to become a vibrant new field of inquiry within the critical genre of identity studies. Charged with the residual fervor of the civil rights movement, women's studies and race studies established a model in the academy for identity-based critical enterprises that followed, such as gender studies, queer studies, disability studies, and a proliferation of ethnic studies, all of which have enriched and complicated our understandings of social justice, subject formation, subjugated knowledges, and collective action.

Even though disability studies is now flourishing in disciplines such as history, literature, religion, theater, and philosophy in precisely the same way feminist studies did twenty-five years ago, many of its practitioners do not recognize that disability studies is part of this larger undertaking that can be called identity studies. Indeed, I must wearily conclude that much of current disability studies does a great deal of wheel reinventing. This is largely because many disability studies scholars simply do not know either feminist theory or the institutional history of women's studies. All too often the pronouncements in disability studies of what we need to start addressing are precisely issues that feminist theory has been grappling with for years. This is not to say that feminist theory can be transferred wholly and intact to the study of disability studies, but to suggest that feminist theory can offer profound insights, methods, and perspectives that would deepen disability studies.

Conversely, feminist theories all too often do not recognize disability in their litanies of identities that inflect the category of woman. Repeatedly, feminist issues that are intricately entangled with disability—such as reproductive technology, the place of bodily differences, the particularities of oppression, the ethics of care, the construction of the subject—are discussed without reference to disability. Like disability studies practitioners who are unaware of feminism, feminist scholars are often simply unacquainted with disability studies' perspectives. The most sophisticated and nuanced analyses of disability, in my view, come from scholars who are conversant with feminist theory. And the most compelling and complex analyses of gender intersectionality take into consideration what I call the ability/disability system—along with race, ethnicity, sexuality, and class.

I want to give the omissions I am describing here the most generous interpretation I can. The archive, Michel Foucault has shown us, determines what we can know. There has been no archive, no template for understanding disability as a category of analysis and knowledge, as a cultural trope, and as a historical community. So just as the now widely recognized centrality of gender and race analyses to all knowledge was unthinkable thirty years ago, disability is still not an icon on many critical desktops. I think, however, that feminist theory's omission of disability differs from disability studies' ignorance of feminist theory. I find feminist theory and those who are familiar with it quick to grasp the broad outlines of disability theory and eager to consider its implications. This, of course, is because feminist theory itself has undertaken internal critiques and proved to be porous and flexible. Disability studies is news, but feminist theory is not. Nevertheless, feminist theory is still resisted for exactly the same reasons that scholars might resist disability studies: the assumption that it is narrow, particular, and has little to do with the mainstream of academic practice and knowledge (or with themselves). This reductive notion that identity studies are intellectual ghettos limited to a narrow constituency demanding special pleading is the persistent obstacle that both feminist theory and disability studies must surmount.

Disability studies can benefit from feminist theory, and feminist theory can benefit from disability studies. Both feminism and disability studies are comparative and concurrent academic enterprises. Just as feminism has expanded the lexicon of what we imagine as womanly, has sought to understand and destigmatize what we call the subject position of woman, so has disability studies examined the identity *disabled* in the service of integrating people with disabilities more fully into our society. As such, both are insurgencies that are becoming institutionalized, underpinning inquiries outside and inside the academy. A feminist disability theory builds on the strengths of both.

My title here, "Integrating Disability, Transforming Feminist Theory," invokes and links two notions, integration and transformation, both of which are fundamental to the feminist project and to the larger civil rights movement that informed it. Integration suggests achieving parity by fully including that which has been excluded and subordinated. Transformation suggests reimagining established knowledge and the order of things. By alluding to integration and transformation, I set my own modest project of integrating disability into feminist theory in the politicized context of the civil rights movement in order to gesture toward the explicit relation that feminism supposes between intellectual work and a commitment to creating a more just, equitable, and integrated society.

This essay aims to amplify feminist theory by articulating and fostering feminist disability theory. In naming feminist disability studies here as an academic field of inquiry, I am sometimes describing work already under way, some of which explicitly addresses disability and some of which gestures implicitly to the topic. At other times I am calling for study that needs to be done to better illuminate feminist thought. In other words, this essay, in part, sets an agenda for future work in feminist disability theory. Most fundamentally, though, the goal of feminist disability studies, as I lay it out in this essay, is to augment the terms and confront the limits of how we understand human diversity, the materiality of the body, multiculturalism, and the social formations that interpret bodily differences. The fundamental point I will make here is that integrating disability as a category of analysis and a system of representation deepens, expands, and challenges feminist theory.

Academic feminism is a complex and contradictory matrix of theories, strategies, pedagogies, and practices. One way to think about feminist theory is to say that it investigates how culture saturates the particularities of bodies with meanings and probes the consequences of those meanings. Feminist theory is a collaborative, interdisciplinary inquiry and a self-conscious cultural critique that interrogates how subjects are multiply interpellated—in other words, how the representational systems of gender, race, ethnicity, ability, sexuality, and class mutually construct, inflect, and contradict one another. These systems intersect to produce and sustain ascribed, achieved, and acquired identities—both those that claim us and those that we claim for ourselves. A feminist disability theory introduces the ability/disability system as a category of analysis into this diverse and diffuse enterprise. It aims to extend current notions of cultural diversity and to more fully integrate the academy and the larger world it helps shape.

A feminist disability approach fosters complex understandings of the cultural history of the body. By considering the ability/disability system, feminist disability theory goes beyond explicit disability topics such as illness, health, beauty, genetics, eugenics, aging, reproductive technologies, prosthetics, and access issues. Feminist disability theory addresses such broad feminist concerns as the unity of the category *woman*, the status of the lived body, the politics of appearance, the medicalization of the body, the privilege of normalcy, multiculturalism, sexuality, the social construction of identity, and the commitment to integration. To borrow Toni Morrison's notion that blackness is an idea that permeates American culture, disability, too, is a pervasive, often unarticulated ideology informing our cultural notions of self and other (1992). Disability—like gender—is a concept that pervades all aspects of culture: its structuring institutions, social identities, cultural practices, political positions, historical communities, and the shared human experience of embodiment.

Integrating disability into feminist theory is generative, broadening our collective inquiries, questioning our assumptions, and contributing to feminism's intersectionality. Introducing a disability analysis does not narrow the inquiry, limit the focus to women with disabilities, or preclude engaging other manifestations of feminisms. Indeed, the multiplicity of foci we now call feminisms is not a group of fragmented, competing subfields, but rather a vibrant, complex conversation. In talking about feminist disability theory, I am not proposing yet another discrete feminism, but suggesting instead some ways that thinking about disability transforms feminist theory. Integrating disability does not obscure our critical focus on the registers of race, sexuality, ethnicity, or gender, nor is it additive. Rather, considering disability shifts the conceptual framework to strengthen our understanding of how these multiple systems intertwine, redefine, and mutually constitute one another. Integrating disability clarifies how this aggregate of systems operate together, yet distinctly, to support an imaginary norm and structure of the relations that grant power, privilege, and status to that norm. Indeed, the cultural function of the disabled figure is to act as a synecdoche for all forms that culture deems nonnormative.

We need to study disability in a feminist context to direct our highly honed critical skills toward the dual scholarly tasks of unmasking and reimagining disability, not only for people with disabilities, but for everyone. As Simi Linton puts it, studying disability is "a prism through which one can gain a broader understanding of society and human experience" (1998, 118). It deepens our understanding of gender and sexuality, individualism and equality, minority group definitions, autonomy, wholeness, independence, dependence, health, physical appearance, aesthetics, the integrity of the body, community, and ideas of progress and perfection in every aspect of cultures. A feminist disability theory introduces what Eve Sedgwick has called a "universalizing view" of disability that will replace an often persisting "minoritizing view." Such a view will cast disability as "an issue of continuing, determinative importance in the lives of people across the spectrum" (1990, 1). In other words, understanding how disability operates as an identity category and cultural concept will enhance how we understand what it is to be human, our relationships with one another, and the experience of embodiment. The constituency for feminist disability studies is all of us, not only women with disabilities: disability is the most human of experiences, touching every family and—if we live long enough—touching us all.

THE ABILITY/DISABILITY SYSTEM

Feminist disability theory's radical critique hinges on a broad understanding of disability as a pervasive cultural system that stigmatizes certain kinds of bodily variations. At the same time, this system has the potential to incite a critical politics. The informing premise of feminist disability theory is that disability, like femaleness, is not a natural state of corporeal inferiority, inadequacy, excess, or a stroke of misfortune. Rather, disability is a culturally fabricated narrative of the body, similar to what we understand as the fictions of race and gender. The ability/disability system produces subjects by differentiating and marking bodies. Although this comparison of bodies is ideological rather than biological, it nevertheless penetrates into the formation of culture, legitimating an unequal distribution of resources, status, and power within a biased social and architectural environment. As such, disability has four aspects: first, it is a system for interpreting and disciplining bodily variations; second, it is a relationship between bodies and their environments; third, it is a set of practices that produce both the able-bodied and the disabled; fourth, it is a way of describing the inherent instability of the embodied self. The disability system excludes the kinds of bodily forms, functions, impairments, changes, or ambiguities that call into question our cultural fantasy of the body as a neutral, compliant instrument of some transcendent will. Moreover, *disability* is a broad term within which cluster ideological categories as varied as *sick, deformed, crazy, ugly, old, maimed, afflicted, mad, abnormal,* or *debilitated*—all of which disadvantage people by devaluing bodies that do not conform to cultural standards. Thus, the disability system functions to preserve and validate such privileged designations as *beautiful, healthy, normal, fit, competent, intelligent*—all of which provide cultural capital to those who can claim such status, who can reside within these subject positions. It is, then, the various interactions between bodies and world that materialize disability from the stuff of human variation and precariousness.

A feminist disability theory denaturalizes disability by unseating the dominant assumption that disability is something that is wrong with someone. By this I mean, of course, that it mobilizes feminism's highly developed and complex critique of gender, class, race, ethnicity, and sexuality as exclusionary and oppressive systems rather than as the natural and appropriate order of things. To do this, feminist disability theory engages several of the fundamental premises of critical theory: (1) that representation structures reality, (2) that the margins define the center, (3) that gender (or disability) is a way of signifying relationships of power, (4) that human identity is multiple and unstable, and (5) that all analysis and evaluation has political implications.

In order to elaborate on these premises, I discuss here four fundamental and interpenetrating domains of feminist theory and suggest some of the kinds of critical inquiries that considering disability can generate within these theoretical arenas. These domains are representation, the body, identity, and activism. While I have disentangled these domains here for the purposes of setting up a schematic organization for my analysis, they are, of course, not discrete in either concept or practice, but rather tend to be synchronic.

REPRESENTATION

The first domain of feminist theory that can be deepened by a disability analysis is representation. Western thought has long conflated femaleness and disability, understanding both as defective departures from a valued standard. Aristotle, for example, defined women as "mutilated males." Women, for Aristotle, have "improper form"; we are "monstrosit[ies]" (1944, 27–28, 8–9). As what Nancy Tuana calls "misbegotten men," women thus become the primal freaks in Western history, envisioned as what we might now call *congenitally deformed* as a result of what we might now term *genetic disability* (1993, 18). More recently, feminist theorists have argued that female embodiment is a disabling condition in sexist culture. Iris Marion Young, for instance, examines how enforced feminine comportment delimits women's sense of embodied agency, restricting them to "throwing like a girl" (1990b, 141). Young concludes, "Women in a sexist society are physically handicapped" (153). Even the general American public associates femininity with disability. A recent study on stereotyping showed that housewives, disabled people, blind people, so-called retarded people, and the elderly were all judged as being similarly incompetent. Such a study suggests that intensely normatively feminine positions—such as a housewife—are aligned with negative attitudes about people with disabilities (Fiske, Cuddy, and Glick 2001).[1]

Recognizing how the concept of disability has been used to cast the form and functioning of female bodies as nonnormative can extend feminist critiques. Take, for example, the exploitation of Saartjie Baartman, the African woman exhibited as a freak in nineteenth-century Europe (Fausto-Sterling 1995; Gilman 1985). Known as the Hottentot Venus, Baartman's treatment has come to represent the most egregious form of racial and gendered degradation. What goes unremarked in studies of her display, however, are the ways that the language and assumptions of the ability/disability system were implemented to pathologize and exoticize Baartman. Her display invoked disability by presenting as deformities or abnormalities the characteristics that marked her as raced and gendered. I am not suggesting that Baartman was disabled, but rather that the concepts of disability discourse framed her presentation to the Western eye. Using *disability* as a category of analysis allows us to see that what was normative embodiment in her native context became abnormal to the Western mind. More important, rather than simply supposing that being labeled as a freak is a slander, a disability analysis presses our critique further by challenging the premise that unusual embodiment is inherently inferior. The feminist interrogation of gender since Simone de Beauvoir (1974) has revealed how women are assigned a cluster of ascriptions, like Aristotle's, that mark us as Other. What is less widely recognized, however, is that this collection of interrelated characterizations is precisely the same set of supposed attributes affixed to people with disabilities.

The gender, race, and ability systems intertwine further in representing subjugated people as pure body, unredeemed by mind or spirit. This sentence of embodiment is conceived as either a lack or an excess. Women, for example, are considered castrated or, to use Marge Piercy's wonderful term, "penis-poor" (1969). They are thought to be hysterical or to have overactive hormones. Women have been cast as alternately having insatiable appetites in some eras and as pathologically self-denying in other times. Similarly, disabled people have supposedly extra chromosomes or limb deficiencies. The differences of disability are cast as *atrophy,* meaning degeneration, or *hypertrophy,* meaning enlargement. People with disabilities are described as having *aplasia,* meaning absence or failure of formation, or *hypoplasia,* meaning underdevelopment. All of these terms police

Fig, 128. LOVE DEFICIENT.

FIG. 1.1. Physiognometric drawing of a supposedly
pathologically "love deficient" woman (1885).

variation and reference a hidden norm from which the bodies of people
with disabilities and women are imagined to depart.

Female, disabled, and dark bodies are supposed to be dependent,
incomplete, vulnerable, and incompetent bodies. Femininity and race
are performances of disability. Women and the disabled are portrayed as
helpless, dependent, weak, vulnerable, and incapable bodies. Women, the
disabled, and people of color are always ready occasions for the aggran-
dizement of benevolent rescuers, whether strong males, distinguished
doctors, abolitionists, or Jerry Lewis hosting his telethons. For example,
an 1885 medical illustration of a pathologically "love deficient" woman—that is, the cultural stereotype of the ugly woman or perhaps the
lesbian—suggests how sexuality and appearance slide into the terms of
disability (fig. 1.1). This illustration shows that the language of deficiency
and abnormality is used simultaneously to devalue women who depart
from the mandates of femininity by equating them with disabled bodies.
Such an interpretive move economically invokes the subjugating effect of
one oppressive system to deprecate people marked by another system of
representation.

Subjugated bodies are pictured as either deficient or as profligate. For instance, what Susan Bordo describes as the too-muchness of women also haunts disability and racial discourses, marking subjugated bodies as ungovernable, intemperate, or threatening (1993). The historical figure of the monster, too, invokes disability, often to serve racism and sexism. Although the term has expanded to encompass all forms of social and corporeal aberration, *monster* originally described people with congenital impairments. As departures from the normatively human, monsters were seen as category violations or grotesque hybrids. The semantics of monstrosity are recruited to explain gender violations like Julia Pastrana, for example, the Mexican Indian "bearded woman" whose body was displayed in nineteenth-century freak shows both during her lifetime and after her death. Pastrana's life, and later her embalmed body, spectacularly confused and transgressed established cultural categories. Race, gender, disability, and sexuality augmented one another in Pastrana's display to produce a spectacle of embodied otherness that is simultaneously sensational, sentimental, and pathological (Garland-Thomson 1999). Furthermore, much current feminist work theorizes figures of hybridity and excess such as monsters, grotesques, and cyborgs to suggest their transgressive potential for a feminist politics (Haraway 1991; Braidotti 1994; Russo 1994). However, this metaphorical invocation seldom acknowledges that these figures often refer to the actual bodies of people with disabilities. Erasing real disabled bodies from the history of these terms compromises the very critique they intend to launch and misses an opportunity to use disability as a feminist critical category.

Such representations ultimately portray subjugated bodies not only as inadequate or unrestrained but at the same time as redundant and expendable. Bodies marked and selected by such systems are targeted for elimination by varying historical and cross-cultural practices. Women, people with disabilities or appearance impairments, ethnic Others, gays and lesbians, and people of color are variously the objects of infanticide, selective abortion, eugenic programs, hate crimes, mercy killing, assisted suicide, lynching, bride burning, honor killings, forced conversion, coercive rehabilitation, domestic violence, genocide, normalizing surgical procedures, racial profiling, and neglect. All of these discriminatory practices are legitimated by systems of representation, by collective cultural stories that shape the material world, underwrite exclusionary attitudes, inform human relations, and mold our senses of who we are. Understanding how disability functions along with other systems of representation clarifies how all the systems intersect and mutually constitute one another.

The second domain of feminist theory that a disability analysis can illuminate is the investigation of the body: its materiality, its politics, its lived experience, and its relation to subjectivity and identity. Confronting issues of representation is certainly crucial to the cultural critique of feminist disability theory. But we should not focus exclusively on the discursive realm. What distinguishes a feminist disability theory from other critical paradigms is that it scrutinizes a wide range of material practices involving the lived body. Perhaps because women and the disabled are cultural signifiers for the body, their actual bodies have been subjected relentlessly to what Foucault calls "discipline" (1979). Together, the gender, race, ethnicity, sexuality, class, and ability systems exert tremendous social pressures to shape, regulate, and normalize subjugated bodies. Such disciplining is enacted primarily through the two interrelated cultural discourses of medicine and appearance.

Feminist disability theory offers a particularly trenchant analysis of how the female body has been medicalized in modernity. As I have already suggested, both women and the disabled have been imagined as medically abnormal—as the quintessential sick ones. Sickness is gendered feminine. This gendering of illness has entailed distinct consequences in everything from epidemiology and diagnosis to prophylaxis and therapeutics.

Perhaps feminist disability theory's most incisive critique is revealing the intersections between the politics of appearance and the medicalization of subjugated bodies. Appearance norms have a long history in Western culture, as is witnessed by the anthropometric composite figures of ideal male and female bodies made by Dudley Sargent in 1893 (fig. 1.2). The classical ideal was to be worshiped rather than imitated, but increasingly in modernity the ideal has migrated to become the paradigm that is to be attained. As many feminist critics have pointed out, the beauty system's mandated standard of the female body has become a goal to be achieved through self-regulation and consumerism (Wolf 1991; Haiken 1997). Feminist disability theory suggests that appearance and health norms often have similar disciplinary goals. For example, body braces that were developed in the 1930s, ostensibly to correct scoliosis, discipline the body to conform to dictates of both the gender and the ability systems by enforcing a standardized female form similarly to the nineteenth-century corset, which, ironically, often disabled female bodies. Although both devices normalize bodies, the brace is part of medical discourse, whereas the corset is cast as a fashion practice.

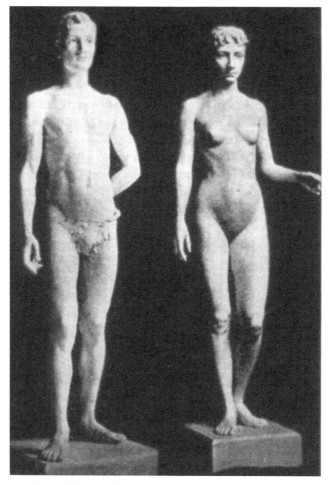

FIG. 1.2. Anthropometric composite figures by Dudley Sargent
of normative man and woman in European culture (1893).
Courtesy of the National Museum of American History.

Similarly, a feminist disability theory calls into question the separation of
reconstructive and cosmetic surgery, recognizing their essentially normalizing function as what Sander L. Gilman calls "aesthetic surgery" (1998). Cosmetic surgery, driven by gender ideology and market demand, now enforces
feminine body standards and standardizes female bodies toward what I
have called the *normate*—the corporeal incarnation of culture's collective,
unmarked, normative characteristics (Garland-Thomson 1997, 8). Cosmetic
surgery's twin, reconstructive surgery, eliminates disability and enforces the
ideals of what might be thought of as the normalcy system. Both cosmetic
and reconstructive procedures commodify the body and parade mutilations

as enhancements that correct flaws to improve the psychological well-being of the patient. The conception of the body as what Bordo terms "cultural plastic" (1993, 246) through surgical and medical interventions increasingly pressures people with disabilities or appearance impairments to become what Foucault calls "docile bodies" (1979, 135). The twin ideologies of normalcy and beauty posit female and disabled bodies, particularly, as not only spectacles to be looked at, but as pliable bodies to be shaped infinitely so as to conform to a set of standards called *normal* and *beautiful*.

Normal has inflected beautiful in modernity. What is imagined as excess body fat, the effects of aging, marks of ethnicity such as supposedly Jewish noses, bodily particularities thought of as blemishes or deformities, and marks of history such as scarring and impairments are now expected to be surgically erased to produce an unmarked body. This visually unobtrusive body may then pass unnoticed within the milieu of anonymity that is the hallmark of social relations beyond the personal in modernity. The purpose of aesthetic surgery, as well as the costuming of power, is not to appear unique—or to "be yourself," as the ads endlessly promise—but rather not to be conspicuous, not to look different. This flight from the nonconforming body translates into individual efforts to look normal, neutral, unmarked, to *not* look disabled, queer, ugly, fat, ethnic, or raced. Beauty, then, dictates corporeal standards that create not distinction but utter conformity to a bland look that is at the same time unachievable so as to leash us to consumer practices that promise to deliver such sameness. In the language of contemporary cosmetic surgery, the unreconstructed female body is persistently cast as having abnormalities that can be corrected by surgical procedures that supposedly improve one's appearance by producing ostensibly natural-looking noses, thighs, breasts, chins, and so on. Thus, our unmodified bodies are presented as unnatural and abnormal, whereas the surgically altered bodies are portrayed as normal and natural. The beautiful woman of the twenty-first century is sculpted surgically from top to bottom, generically neutral, all irregularities regularized, all particularities expunged. She is thus nondisabled, deracialized, and de-ethnicized.

In addition, the politics of prosthetics enters the purview of feminism when we consider the contested use of breast implants and prostheses for breast cancer survivors. The famous 1993 *New York Times* cover photo of the fashion model Matushka baring her mastectomy scar or Audre Lorde's account of breast cancer in *The Cancer Journals* challenges the sexist assumption that the amputated breast must always pass for the normative, sexualized one either through concealment or prosthetics (1980). A vibrant feminist conversation has emerged about the politics of the surgically altered, the disabled breast. Diane Price Herndl (2002) challenges

FIG. 1.3. Obsessed with Breasts poster. "It's No Secret."
Courtesy of the Breast Cancer Fund.

Audre Lorde's refusal of a breast prosthesis after mastectomy, and Iris Marion Young's classic essay "Breasted Experience" queries the cultural meanings of breasts under the knife (1990a).

Another entanglement of appearance and medicine involves the spectacle of the female breast, both normative and disabled. In January 2000 the San Francisco-based Breast Cancer Fund mounted a public-awareness poster campaign called Obsessed with Breasts, which showed women boldly displaying mastectomy scars. The posters parodied familiar commercial media sites—a Calvin Klein perfume ad, a *Cosmopolitan* magazine cover, and a Victoria's Secret catalog cover—that routinely represent women's breasts as only sexual in nature. The posters replace the now unremarkable eroticized breast with the forbidden image of the amputated breast (fig. 1.3). In doing so, they disrupt the visual convention of the female breast as sexualized object for male appropriation and pleasure. The posters thus produce a powerful visual violation by exchanging the spectacle of the eroticized breast, which has been desensationalized by its endless circulation, with the medicalized image of the scarred breast, which has been concealed from public view. The Breast Cancer Fund used these remarkable images to challenge both sexism in medical research and treatment for breast cancer as well as the oppressive representational practices that make everyday erotic spectacles of women's breasts while erasing the fact of the amputated breast.

Feminist disability theory can press far its critique of the pervasive will to normalize the nonstandard body. Take two related examples: first, the surgical separation of conjoined twins and, second, the surgical assignment of gender for the intersexed, people with ambiguous genitalia and gender characteristics. Both forms of embodiment are regularly—if infrequently—occurring, congenital bodily variations that spectacularly violate sacred ideologies of Western culture. Conjoined twins contradict our notion of the individual as discrete and autonomous quite similarly to the way pregnancy does. Intersexed infants challenge our insistence that biological gender is unequivocally binary. So threatening to the order of things is the natural embodiment of conjoined twins and intersexed people that they are almost always surgically normalized through amputation and mutilation immediately after birth (Clark and Myser 1996; Dreger 1998a; Kessler 1990; Fausto-Sterling 2000). Not infrequently, one conjoined twin is sacrificed to save the other from the supposed abnormality of their embodiment. Such mutilations are justified as preventing suffering and creating well-adjusted individuals. So intolerable is their insult to dominant ideologies about who patriarchal culture insists we are that the testimonies of adults with these forms of embodiment who say they do not want to be separated is routinely ignored in establishing the rationale for medical treatment (Dreger 1998b). In truth, these procedures do not benefit the affected individuals, but rather they expunge the kinds of corporeal human variations that contradict the ideologies the dominant order depends upon to anchor truths that it insists are unequivocally encoded in bodies.

I do not want to oversimplify here by suggesting that women and disabled people should not use modern medicine to improve their lives or help their bodies function more fully. But the critical issues are complex and provocative. A feminist disability theory should illuminate and explain, not become ideological policing or set orthodoxy. The kinds of critical analyses I am discussing offer a counter-logic to the overdetermined cultural mandates to comply with normal and beautiful at any cost. The medical commitment to healing, when coupled with modernity's faith in technology and interventions that control outcomes, has increasingly shifted toward an aggressive intent to fix, regulate, or eradicate ostensibly deviant bodies. Such a program of elimination has often been at the expense of creating a more accessible environment or providing better support services for people with disabilities. The privileging of medical technology over less ambitious programs, such as rehabilitation, has

FIG. 1.4. March of Dimes poster child (1949).
Courtesy of the March of Dimes.

encouraged the cultural conviction that disability can be extirpated; inviting the belief that life with a disability is intolerable. As charity campaigns and telethons repeatedly affirm, cure, rather than adjustment or accommodation, is the overdetermined cultural response to disability (Longmore 1997). For instance, a 1949 March of Dimes poster shows an appealing little girl stepping out of her wheelchair into the supposed redemption of walking. "Look, I Can Walk Again!" the text proclaims, while at once charging the viewers with the responsibility of assuring her future ambulation (fig. 1.4). Nowhere do we find posters suggesting that life as a wheelchair user might be full and satisfying, as many people who actually use them find their lives to be. This ideology of cure is not isolated in medical texts or charity campaigns, but in fact permeates the entire cultural conversation about disability and illness. Take, for example, the discourse of cure in get-well cards. A 1950 card, for instance, urges its recipient to "snap out of it." Fusing racist, sexist, and ableist discourses, the card recruits the Mammy figure to insist on cure. The stereotypical racist figure asks, "Is you sick, Honey?" and then exhorts the recipient of her care to "jes hoodoo all dat illness out o you."

The ideology of cure directed at disabled people focuses on changing bodies imagined as abnormal and dysfunctional rather than on exclusionary attitudinal, environmental, and economic barriers. The emphasis on cure reduces the cultural tolerance for human variation and vulnerability by locating disability in bodies imagined as flawed rather than social systems in need of fixing. A feminist disability studies would draw an important distinction between prevention and elimination. Preventing illness, suffering, and injury is a humane social objective. Eliminating the range of unacceptable and devalued bodily forms and functions the dominant order calls disability is, on the other hand, a eugenic undertaking. The ostensibly progressive socio-medical project of eradicating disability all too often is enacted as a program to eliminate people with disabilities through such practices as forced sterilization, so-called physician-assisted suicide and mercy killing, selective abortion, institutionalization, and segregation policies.

A feminist disability theory extends its critique of the normalization of bodies and the medicalization of appearance to challenge some widely held assumptions about reproductive issues as well. The cultural mandate to eliminate the variations in form and function that we consider disabilities has undergirded the reproductive practices of genetic testing and selective abortion (Saxton 1998; Parens and Asch 2000; Rapp 1999). Some disability activists argue that the "choice" to abort fetuses with disabilities is a coercive form of genocide against the disabled (Hubbard 1990). A more nuanced argument against selective abortion comes from Adrienne Asch and Gail Geller, who wish to preserve a woman's right to choose whether to bear a child but at the same time object to the ethics of selectively aborting a wanted fetus because it will become a person with a disability (1996). Asch and Geller counter the quality-of-life and prevention-of-suffering arguments that are so readily invoked to justify selective abortion, as well as physician-assisted suicide, by pointing out that we cannot predict or, more precisely, control in advance such equivocal human states as happiness, suffering, or success. Neither is any amount of prenatal engineering going to produce the life that any of us desire and value. Indeed, both hubris and a lack of imagination characterize the prejudicial and reductive assumption that having a disability ruins lives. A vague notion of suffering and its potential deterrence drives much of the logic of elimination that rationalizes selective abortion (Kittay 2000). Life chances and quality are simply far too contingent to justify prenatal prediction.

Similarly, genetic testing and applications of the Human Genome Project as the key to expunging disability are often critiqued as enactments of eugenic ideology, what the feminist biologist Evelyn Fox Keller calls a "eugenics of normalcy" (1992). The popular utopian belief that all forms of disability can be eliminated through prophylactic manipulation of genetics will only serve to intensify prejudice against those who inevitably will acquire disabilities through aging and encounters with the environment. In the popular celebrations of the Human Genome Project as the quixotic pinnacle of technological progress, seldom do we hear cautionary logic about the eugenic implications of this drive toward what Priscilla Wald calls "future perfect" (2000, 1). Disability scholars have entered the debate over so-called physician-assisted suicide as well, by arguing that oppressive attitudes toward disability distort the possibility of unbiased free choice (Battin, Rhodes, and Silvers 1998). The practices of genetic and prenatal testing as well as physician-administered euthanasia, then, become potentially eugenic practices within the context of a culture that is deeply intolerant of disability. Both the rhetoric and the enactment of this kind of disability discrimination create a hostile and exclusionary environment for people with disabilities that perhaps exceed the less virulent architectural barriers that keep them out of the workforce and the public sphere.

Integrating disability into feminism's conversation about the place of the body in equality and difference debates produces fresh insights as well. Whereas liberal feminism emphasizes sameness, choice, and autonomy, cultural feminism critiques the premises of liberalism. Out of cultural feminism's insistence on difference and its positive interpretation of feminine culture comes the affirmation of a feminist ethic of care. This ethic of care contends that caregiving is a moral benefit for its practitioners and for humankind. Feminist disability studies complicates both the feminist ethic of care and liberal feminism in regard to the politics of care and dependency.

A disability perspective nuances feminist theory's consideration of the ethics of care by examining the power relations between the givers and receivers of care. Anita Silvers has argued strongly that being the object of care precludes the equality that a liberal democracy depends upon and undermines the claim to justice as equality that undergirds a civil rights approach used to counter discrimination (1995). Eva Kittay, on the other hand, formulates a "dependency critique of equality," which asserts that the ideal of equality under liberalism repudiates the fact of human dependency, the need for mutual care, and the asymmetries of care relations (1999, 4). Similarly, Barbara Hillyer has called attention to dependency in order to critique a liberal tendency in the rhetoric of disability rights (1993). Disability itself demands that human interdependence and the universal need for assistance be figured into our dialogues about rights and subjectivity.

IDENTITY

The third domain of feminist theory that a disability analysis complicates is identity. Feminist theory has productively and rigorously critiqued the identity category of woman, on which the entire feminist enterprise seemed to rest. Feminism increasingly recognizes that no woman is ever *only* a woman, that she occupies multiple subject positions and is claimed by several cultural identity categories (Spelman 1988). This complication of *woman* compelled feminist theory to turn from an exclusively male/ female focus to look more fully at the exclusionary, essentialist, oppressive, and binary aspects of the category *woman* itself. Disability is one such identity vector that disrupts the unity of the classification *woman* and challenges the primacy of *gender* as a monolithic category.

Disabled women are, of course, a marked and excluded—albeit quite varied—group within the larger social class of women. The relative privileges of normative femininity are often denied to disabled women (Fine and Asch 1988). Cultural stereotypes imagine disabled women as asexual, unfit to reproduce, overly dependent, unattractive—as generally removed from the sphere of true womanhood and feminine beauty. Women with disabilities often must struggle to have their sexuality and rights to bear children recognized (Finger 1990). Disability thus both intensifies and attenuates cultural scripts of femininity. Aging is a form of disablement that disqualifies older women from the limited power allotted females who are young and meet the criteria for attracting men. Depression, anorexia, and agoraphobia are female-dominant, psychophysical disabilities that exaggerate normative gendered roles. Feminine cultural practices such as foot-binding, clitorectomies, and corseting—as well as their less hyperbolic costuming rituals such as stiletto high heels, girdles, and chastity belts—impair women's bodies and restrict their physical agency, imposing disability on them.

Banishment from femininity can be both a liability and a benefit. Let me offer, with some irony, an instructive example from popular culture. Barbie, that cultural icon of femininity, offers a disability analysis that clarifies how multiple identity and diversity are commodified and how the commercial realm might offer politically useful feminist counter-images. Perhaps the measure of a group's arrival into the mainstream of multiculturalism is to be represented in the Barbie pantheon. While Barbie herself still identifies as able-bodied—despite her severely deformed body—we now have several incarnations of Barbie's "friend" Share-a-Smile Becky. One Becky

FIG. 1.5. Barbie's friend Becky, the School Photographer.

uses a cool hot-pink wheelchair; another is Paralympic Champion Becky, brought out for the 2000 Sydney Olympics in a chic red-white-and-blue warm-up suit with matching chair. Most interesting, however, is Becky the school photographer, clad in a preppy outfit, complete with camera and red high-top sneakers (fig. 1.5). As she perkily gazes at an alluring Barbie in her camera's viewfinder, this Becky may be the incarnation of what Erica Rand has called "Barbie's queer accessories" (1995).

A disabled, queer Becky is certainly a provocative and subversive fusion of stigmatized identities, but more important is that Becky challenges notions of normalcy in feminist ways. The disabled Becky, for example, wears comfortable clothes: pants with elastic waists, no doubt; sensible shoes; and roomy shirts. Becky is also one of the few dolls with flat feet and legs that bend at the knee. The disabled Becky is dressed and poised for agency, action, and creative engagement with the world. In contrast, the prototypical Barbie performs excessive femininity in her restrictive sequined gowns, crowns, and push-up bras. So while Becky implies on the one hand that disabled girls are purged from the feminine economy, on the other hand she also suggests that disabled girls might be liberated from those oppressive and debilitating scripts. The last word on Barbies comes from a disability activist who quipped that he would like to outfit a disabled doll with a power wheelchair and a briefcase to make her a civil rights lawyer who enforces the Americans with Disabilities Act (1990). He wants to call her "Sue-Your-Ass-Becky."[2] I think she would make a very good role model.

The paradox of Barbie and Becky, of course, is that the ultra-feminized Barbie is a target for sexual appropriation both by men and beauty practices, whereas the disabled Becky escapes such sexual objectification at the potential cost of losing her sense of identity as a feminine sexual being. Some disabled women negotiate this possible identity crisis by developing alternate sexualities, such as lesbianism (Brownworth and Raffo 1999). However, what Harlan Hahn calls the "asexual objectification" of people with disabilities complicates the feminist critique of normative sexual objectification (1988). Consider the 1987 *Playboy* magazine photos of the paraplegic actress Ellen Stohl. After becoming disabled, Stohl wrote to editor Hugh Hefner that she wanted to pose nude for *Playboy* because "sexuality is the hardest thing for disabled persons to hold onto" ("Meet Ellen Stohl" 1987, 68). For Stohl, it would seem that the performance of excessive feminine sexuality was necessary to counter the social interpretation that disability cancels out sexuality. For Stohl, then, this confirmation of normative heterosexuality was no Butlerian parody, but rather the affirmation she needed as a disabled woman to be sexual at all.

Ellen Stohl's presentation by way of the sexist conventions of the porn magazine illuminates the relation between identity and the body, an aspect of subject formation that disability analysis can offer. Although binary identities are conferred from outside through social relations, these identities are nevertheless inscribed on the body as either manifest or incipient visual traces. Identity's social meaning turns on this play of visibility. The photos of Stohl in *Playboy* both refuse to and insist on marking her impairment. The centerfold spread—so to speak—of Stohl nude and masturbating erases her impairment to conform to the sexualized conventions of the centerfold. This photo expunges her wheelchair and any other visual clues to her impairment. In other words, to avoid the cultural contradiction of a sexual, disabled woman, the pornographic photos must offer up Stohl visually as nondisabled. But appealing to the cultural narrative of overcoming disability that sells so well seems novel and capitalizes on sentimental interest; Stohl must be visually dramatized as disabled at the same time. So *Playboy* includes several shots of Stohl that mark her as disabled by picturing her in her wheelchair, entirely without the typical porn conventions. In fact, the photos of her using her wheelchair invoke the asexual poster child. Thus, the affirmation of sexuality that Stohl sought by posing nude in the porn magazine came at the expense of denying, through the powerful visual register, her identity as a woman with a disability, even while she attempted to claim that identity textually.

Another aspect of subject formation that disability confirms is that identity is always in transition. Disability reminds us that the body is, as Denise Riley asserts, "an unsteady mark, scarred in its long decay" (1999, 224). As Caroline Walker Bynum's intriguing work on werewolf narratives suggests, the body is in a perpetual state of transformation (1999). Caring for her father for more than twenty years of Alzheimer's disease prompted Bynum to investigate how we can understand individual identity as continuous even though both body and mind can and do change dramatically, certainly over a lifetime and sometimes quite suddenly. Disability invites us to query what the continuity of the self might depend upon if the body perpetually metamorphoses. We envision our racial, gender, or ethnic identities as tethered to bodily traits that are relatively secure. Disability and sexual identity, however, seem more fluid, although sexual mutability is imagined as elective, where disability is seldom conceived of as a choice. *Disability* is an identity category that anyone can enter at any time, and we will all join it if we live long enough. As such, disability reveals the essential dynamism of identity. Thus, disability attenuates the cherished cultural belief that the body is the unchanging anchor of identity. Moreover, it undermines our fantasies of stable, enduring identities in ways that may illuminate the fluidity of all identity.

Disability's clarification of the body's corporeal truths also suggests that the body/self materializes—in Judith Butler's sense—not so much through discourse, but through history (1993). The self materializes in response to an embodied engagement with its environment, both social and concrete. The disabled body is a body whose variations or transformations have rendered it out of sync with its environment, both the physical and the attitudinal environments. In other words, the body becomes disabled when it is incongruent both in space and in the milieu of expectations. Furthermore, a feminist disability theory presses us to ask what kinds of knowledge might be produced through having a body radically marked by its own particularity, a body that materializes at the ends of the curve of human variation. For example, an alternative epistemology that emerges from the lived experience of disability is nicely summed up in Nancy Mairs's book title *Waist-High in the World* (1996), which she irreverently considered calling "cock high in the world."[3] What perspectives or politics arise from encountering the world from such an atypical position? Perhaps Mairs's epistemology can offer us a critical positionality called *sitpoint theory*, a neologism I offer to interrogate the ableist assumptions underlying the notion of standpoint theory (Harstock 1983).

Our collective cultural consciousness emphatically denies the knowledge of vulnerability, contingency, and mortality. Disability insists otherwise, contradicting such phallic ideology. I would argue that disability is perhaps the essential characteristic of being human. The body is dynamic, constantly interactive with history and environment. We evolve into disability. Our bodies need care; we all need assistance to live. An equality model of feminist theory sometimes prizes individualistic autonomy as the key to women's liberation. A feminist disability theory, however, suggests that we are better off learning to individually and collectively accommodate bodily limits and evolutions than trying to eliminate or deny them.

Identity formation is at the center of feminist theory. Disability can complicate feminist theory often quite succinctly by invoking established theoretical paradigms. This kind of theoretical intertextuality inflects familiar feminist concepts with new resonance. Let me offer several examples: the idea of "compulsory able-bodiedness," which Robert McRuer (1999) has coined, extends Adrienne Rich's famous analysis of "compulsory heterosexuality" (1986). Joan Wallach Scott's germinal work on gender is recruited when we discuss disability as "a useful category of analysis" (1988, 1). The feminist elaboration of the gender system informs my use of the term *disability system*. Lennard Davis suggests that the term *normalcy studies* supplants the name *disability studies* in the way that *gender studies* sometimes succeeds *feminism* (1995). The oft-invoked distinction between sex and gender clarifies a differentiation between impairment and disability, even though both binaries are fraught. The concept of performing disability cites, as it were, Judith Butler's vigorous critique of essentialism (1990). Reading disabled bodies as exemplary instances of "docile bodies" invokes Foucault (1979). To suggest that identity is lodged in the body, I propose that the body haunts the subject, alluding to Susan Bordo's notion regarding masculinity that "the penis haunts the phallus"(1994, 1). My own work has complicated the familiar discourse of the gaze to theorize what I call the stare, which, I argue, produces disability identity. Such theoretical shorthand impels us to reconsider how identity categories cut across and redefine one another, pressuring both the terms *woman* and *disabled*.

A feminist disability theory can also highlight intersections and convergences with other identity-based critical perspectives, such as queer and ethnic studies. Disability coming-out stories, for example, borrow from gay and lesbian identity narratives to expose what previously was hidden, privatized, and medicalized in order to enter into a political community. The politicized sphere into which many scholars come out is feminist disability studies, which enables critique, claims disability identity, and creates affirming counter-narratives. Disability coming-out narratives raise questions about the body's role in identity by asking how markers so conspicuous as crutches, wheelchairs, hearing aids, guide dogs, white canes, or empty sleeves can be closeted.

Passing as nondisabled complicates ethnic and queer studies' analyses of how this seductive but psychically estranging access to privilege operates. Some of my friends, for example, have measured their regard for me by saying, "But I don't think of you as disabled." What they point to in such a compliment is the contradiction they find between their perception of me as a valuable, capable, lovable person and the cultural figure of the disabled person whom they take to be precisely my opposite: worthless, incapable, and unlovable. People with disabilities routinely announce that they do not consider themselves as disabled. Although they are often repudiating the literal meaning of the word *disabled,* their words nevertheless serve to disassociate them from the identity group of the disabled. Our culture offers profound disincentives and few rewards to identifying as disabled. The trouble with such statements is that they leave intact, without challenge, the oppressive stereotypes that permit, among other things, the unexamined use of disability terms such as *crippled, lame, dumb, idiot,* and *moron* as verbal gestures of derision. The refusal to claim disability identity is in part due to a lack of ways to understand or talk about disability that are not oppressive. People with disabilities and those who care about them flee from the language of *crippled* or *deformed* and have no other alternatives. Yet, the civil rights movement and the accompanying black-is-beautiful identity politics have generally shown white culture what is problematic with saying to black friends, "I don't think of you as black." Nonetheless, by disavowing disability identity, many of us learned to save ourselves from devaluation by a complicity that perpetuates oppressive notions about ostensibly real disabled people. Thus, together we help to make the alternately menacing and pathetic cultural figures who rattle tin cups or rave on street corners become figures from whom we with impairments often flee more surely than those who imagine themselves as nondisabled.

ACTIVISM

The final domain of feminist theory that a disability analysis expands is activism. There are many arenas of what can be seen as feminist disability activism: marches; protests; the Breast Cancer Fund poster campaign I discussed above; and action groups such as the Intersex Society of North America (ISNA), Not Dead Yet, who oppose physician-assisted suicide, and the American Disabled for Accessible Public Transit (ADAPT). What counts as activism cuts a wide swath through U.S. society and the academy. I want to suggest here two unlikely, even quirky, cultural practices that function in activist ways but are seldom considered as potentially transformative. One practice is the use of disabled fashion models, and the other is academic tolerance. Both are different genres of activism from the more traditional marching-on-Washington or chaining-yourself-to-a-bus modes. Both are less theatrical but perhaps fresher and more interestingly controversial ways to change the social landscape and to promote equality, which I take to be the goal of activism.

The theologian and sociologist Nancy Eiseland has argued that in addition to legislative, economic, and social changes, achieving equality for people with disabilities depends upon cultural "resymbolization" (1994, 98). Eiseland asserts that we must shift the way we imagine disability and disabled people in order for real social change to occur. Whereas Eiseland's work resymbolizes our conceptions of disability in religious iconography, my own examinations of disabled fashion models do similar cultural work in the popular sphere, introducing some interesting complications into her notion of resymbolization.

Images of disabled fashion models in the media can shake up established categories and expectations. Because commercial visual media are the most widespread and commanding source of images in modern, image-saturated culture, they have great potential for shaping public consciousness, as feminist cultural critics are well aware. Fashion imagery is the visual distillation of the normative gilded with the chic and the luxurious to render it desirable. The commercial sphere is completely amoral, driven as it is by the single logic of the bottom line. As we know, it sweeps through culture, seizing with alarming neutrality anything it senses will sell. This value-free aspect of advertising produces a kind of pliable potency that sometimes can yield unexpected results.

Take, for example, a shot from the monthly fashion feature in *WE Magazine*, a *Cosmopolitan* knock-off targeted at the disabled consumer market (fig. 1.6). In this conventional, stylized, high-fashion shot, a typical female model—slender, white, blonde, clad in a black evening gown—is accompanied by her service dog. My argument is that public images such as this are radical because they fuse two previously antithetical visual discourses: the chic high-fashion shot and the earnest charity campaign. Public representations of disability have traditionally been contained within the conventions of sentimental charity images, exotic freak-show portraits,

HI, SOCIETY

Photography by Alberto Rizzo
W's Fashion Editor Lori Frisher

YOU'VE GOT A SLEW OF INVITATIONS
TO HOLIDAY GATHERINGS AND
THAT MEANS EVERY NIGHT
YOU'RE GOING TO BE DRESSED
TO THE NINES FOR COCKTAILS
DINNER, DANCING AND BEYOND

FIG. 1.6. Blind model with service dog.
Alberto Rizzo, photographer, Courtesy of WeMedia.Inc.

medical illustrations, or sensational and forbidden pictures. Indeed, people with disabilities have been excluded most fully from the dominant, public world of the marketplace. Before the civil rights initiatives of the mid-twentieth century began to transform the public architectural and institutional environment, disabled people were segregated to the private and medical spheres. Until recently the only available public image of a woman with a service dog that shaped the public imagination was a street-corner beggar or a charity poster. By juxtaposing the elite body of a visually normative fashion model with the mark of disability, this image shakes up our assumptions about the normal and the abnormal, the public and the private, the chic and the desolate, the compelling and the repelling. Introducing a service dog—a standard prop of indigents and poster children—into the conventional composition of an upscale fashion photo forces the viewer to reconfigure her assumptions about what constitutes the attractive and the desirable.

I am arguing that the emergence of disabled fashion models is inadvertent activism without any legitimate agent for positive social change. Their appearance is simply a result of market forces. This both troubling and empowering form of entry into democratic capitalism produces a kind of instrumental form of equality: the freedom to be appropriated by consumer culture. In a democracy, to reject this paradoxical liberty is one thing; not to be granted such liberty is another. Ever straining for novelty and capitalizing on titillation, the fashion-advertising world promptly appropriated the power of disabled figures to provoke responses. Diversity appeals to an upscale liberal sensibility these days, making consumers feel good about buying from companies that are charitable toward the traditionally disadvantaged. More important, the disability market is burgeoning. At 54 million people and quickly growing as baby boomers age, the spending power of disabled consumers was estimated to have reached the trillion-dollar mark in 2000 (Williams 1999).

For the most part, commercial advertising presents disabled models in the same way as it does nondisabled models, simply because all models look essentially the same. The physical markings of gender, race, ethnicity, and disability are muted to the level of gesture, subordinated to the overall normativity of the models' appearance. Thus, commercial visual media cast disabled consumers as simply one of many variations that compose the market to which they appeal. Such routinization of disability imagery—however stylized and unrealistic it may be—nevertheless brings disability as a human experience out of the closet and into the normative public sphere. Images of disabled fashion models enable people with disabilities, especially those who acquire impairments as adults, to imagine themselves as a part of the ordinary, albeit consumerist, world rather than as a special class of excluded untouchables and unviewables. Images of impairment as a familiar, even mundane, experience in the lives of seemingly successful, happy, well-adjusted people can reduce the identifying against oneself that is the overwhelming effect of oppressive and discriminatory attitudes toward people with disabilities. Such images, then, are at once liberatory and oppressive. They do the cultural work of integrating a previously excluded group into the dominant order—for better or worse—much like the inclusion of women in the military.

This form of popular resymbolization produces counter-images that have activist potential. A clearer example of disability activism might be Aimee Mullins, who is a fashion model, celebrity, champion runner, Georgetown University student, and double amputee. Mullins was also one of *People* magazine's "50 Most Beautiful People" of 1999. An icon of disability pride and equality, Mullins exposes—in fact, calls attention to—the mark of her disability in most photos, refusing to normalize or hide her disability in order to pass for nondisabled. Indeed, the public version of her career is that her disability has been a benefit: she has several sets of legs, both cosmetic and functional, and so is able to choose how tall she wants to be. Photographed in her prosthetic legs, she embodies the sexualized jock look that demands women be both slender and fit (fig. 1.7). In her cosmetic legs, she captures the look of the high-fashion beauty in the controversial shoot by Nick Knight called "Accessible," showcasing outfits created by designers such as Alexander McQueen (fig. 1.8). But this is high fashion with a difference. In the jock shot, her functional legs are brazenly displayed, and even in the voguishly costumed shot, the knee joints of her artificial legs are exposed. Never is there an attempt to disguise her prosthetic legs; rather, all of the photos thematically echo her prostheses and render the whole image chic. Mullins's prosthetic legs, whether cosmetic or functional, parody—indeed proudly mock—the fantasy of the perfect body that is the mark of fashion, even while the rest of her body conforms precisely to fashion's impossible standards. So rather than concealing, normalizing, or erasing disability, these photos use the hyperbole and stigmata traditionally associated with disability to quench postmodernity's perpetual search for the new and arresting image. Such a narrative of advantage works against oppressive narratives and practices that are usually invoked about disabilities. First, Mullins counters the insistent narrative that one must overcome an impairment rather than incorporating it into one's life and self, even perhaps as a benefit. Second, Mullins counters the practice of passing for nondisabled that people with disabilities are often obliged to enact in the public sphere. Mullins uses her conformity with beauty standards to assert her disability's violation of those very standards. As legless and beautiful, she is an embodied paradox, asserting an inherently disruptive potential.

What my analysis of these images reveals is that feminist cultural critiques are complex. On the one hand, feminists have rightly unmasked consumer capitalism's appropriation of women as sexual objects for male gratification. On the other hand, these images imply that in its drive to harvest new markets the same capitalist system can produce politically progressive counter-images and counter-narratives, however fraught they may be in their entanglement with consumer culture. Images of disabled fashion models are both complicit and critical of the beauty system that oppresses all women. Nevertheless, they suggest that consumer culture can provide the raw material for its own critique.

FIG. 1.7. Aimee Mullins using functional legs. *Courtesy of Nick Knight.*

The concluding version of activism I offer is less controversial and subtler than glitzy fashion spreads. It is what I call academic activism, the activism of integrating *education*, in the very broadest sense of that term. The academy is no ivory tower, but rather it is the grass roots of the educational enterprise. Scholars and teachers shape the communal knowledge and the pedagogical archive that is disseminated from kindergarten to the university. Academic activism is most self-consciously vibrant in the aggregate of interdisciplinary identity studies—of which women's studies is exemplary—that strive to expose the workings of oppression, examine subject formation, and offer counter-narratives for subjugated groups. Their cultural work is building an archive through historical and textual retrieval, canon reformation, role modeling, mentoring, curricular reform, and course and program development.

A specific form of feminist academic activism can be deepened through the complication of a disability analysis. I call this academic activism the methodology of intellectual tolerance. By this I do not mean tolerance in the more usual sense of tolerating each other, although that would

FIG. 1.8. Aimee Mullins using cosmetic legs. *Courtesy of Nick Knight.*

be useful as well. What I mean is the intellectual position of tolerating what has been thought of as incoherence. As feminism has embraced the paradoxes that have emerged from its challenge to the gender system, it has not collapsed into chaos, but instead has developed a methodology that tolerates internal conflict and contradiction. This method asks difficult questions but accepts provisional answers. This method recognizes the power of identity at the same time that it reveals identity as a fiction. This method both seeks equality and claims difference. This method allows us to teach with authority at the same time that we reject notions of pedagogical mastery. This method establishes institutional presences even while it acknowledges the limitations of institutions. This method validates the personal but implements disinterested inquiry. This method both writes new stories and recovers traditional ones. Considering disability as a vector of identity that intersects gender is one more internal challenge that threatens the coherence of woman, of course. But feminism can accommodate such complication and the contradictions it cultivates. Indeed the intellectual tolerance I am arguing for espouses the partial, the provisional, the particular. Such an intellectual habit can be informed by disability experience and acceptance. To embrace the supposedly flawed body of disability is to critique the normalizing phallic fantasies of wholeness, unity, coherence, and completeness. The disabled body is contradiction, ambiguity, and partiality incarnate.

My claim here has been that integrating disability as a category of analysis, a historical community, a set of material practices, a social identity, a political position, and a representational system into the content of feminist—indeed into all inquiry—can strengthen the critique that is feminism. Disability, like gender and race, is everywhere, once we know how to look for it. Integrating disability analyses will enrich and deepen all of our teaching and scholarship. Moreover, such critical intellectual work facilitates a fuller integration of the sociopolitical world—for the benefit of everyone. As with gender, race, sexuality, and class, to understand how disability operates is to understand what it is to be fully human.

A POSTSCRIPT

My admittedly corny joke about our efforts to develop disability studies as a "new field" in the liberal arts is to quip that "if it quacks like a duck . . ." This colloquialization of Foucault's point that knowledge depends on the archive for its materialization grew from a slow anecdotal realization on my part. I came to understand that if talked about often enough in print and in institutional settings, "the new field of disability studies" became a reality. Naming what we were doing heralded it into being in the academic community. The *Chronicle of Higher Education* wrote articles about it, forums and interest groups burgeoned, and university press editors spoke of it with assurance.

My purpose in publishing "Integrating Disability, Transforming Feminist Theory" in the *National Women's Studies Association Journal* was to make "feminist disability theory" quack. I wanted to fuse feminist theory with disability studies to produce a quacking critter that my academic colleagues could take up with the confidence that it was something. I wrote about feminist disability theory as if it were an extant critical discourse that I was hailing rather than something I was working out for myself sentence by sentence. More than defining the term, I wanted to call up in print the many conversations I have had with colleagues about the intersections of disability and femininity, of the theories we have developed to understand both systems. I wanted my colleagues to put feminist disability theory on their CVs as one of their academic specializations; I wanted departments to list it in job descriptions; I wanted it to be an academic keyword.

I followed the announcement of feminist disability theory in the *NWSA Journal* with another article that augmented this initial quack. In 2005 I published "Feminist Disability Studies: A Review Essay" in *Signs: Journal of Women and Culture in Society*. In this extended review essay, I tried to show where we can find feminist disability theory. In other words, my purpose was to demonstrate that there was a field called feminist disability studies and that it was a substantial, vital academic duck. My aim was to show that disability theory was everywhere in feminist studies if we just knew how to look for it. I called my method in that review essay "recruitment" because many of the texts I reviewed would not have known to call themselves feminist disability studies. The review essay thus established an archive, even a canon, of feminist disability studies and set an agenda for future scholarship. I wanted this review essay to yield syllabi and bibliographies across the humanities and social sciences. I wanted fellow scholars to be able to enter a vibrant, established conversation.

Because I am a humanist who deals in bold speculation at the expense of empirical study, I have no reliable data to support the success or failure of my endeavor. I can say that versions of "Integrating Disability, Transforming Feminist Theory" have been reprinted in feminist theory readers and collections such as this one. I can only hope that my colleagues toss around the term *feminist disability studies* in their conference papers, publication hopefuls, and professional self-descriptions. But I do have the kind of evidence that scholars like me put much stock in. Most of the time we send our words into the world as an act of faith that they will do the cultural work we intend them to do. My experience is that only occasionally do we get verification of our aspirations. I conclude this postscript by offering you two responses I received about feminist disability theory/studies that affirm the work we do as scholars and feminists. The first is from a colleague in response to my review essay. She writes generous comments such as "superb essay" and "a wonderful theoretical and political piece laying out extremely clearly." But more important than this gratifying praise is her confirmation of my critical aims: for her, this article was a "reminder of real-life effects of representation." Moreover, my colleague puts that reminder to scholarly use: "There is a lot of work here that I am not familiar with," she writes to me, "and so this is also an extremely useful introduction to and analysis of this literature. . . . This piece actually is extremely helpful to me right now in framing the book I am trying to finish." This is precisely what we hope all of our scholarly work does.

The most significant thing I want to include in this postscript is an e-mail message I received from a student I have never met. This is exactly the scene I hope my scholarly work stages. Let me leave you with this without further comment from me, because it speaks so eloquently for itself:

As a woman with Cerebral Palsy, I was deeply moved and changed in my sophomore year, while reading your piece [from the *NWSA Journal*] in Wendy Kolmar's "Feminist Theory: A Reader," during my Gender and Feminist Theory class. I vividly remember sitting on a Greyhound bus going from Canton, New York to Syracuse, on a weekend home to visit my family. As I sat on the bus, surrounded by people, I remember reading your words and nodding my head in agreement as I more often than not audibly voiced "Yes," because I connected so much with your work. Upon returning to class later the next week, I excitedly discussed with my professor the possibility of making a change to the syllabus, including your piece and simultaneously incorporating my own experience as a Disabled woman into the following class.

I consider the reading of your work for the first time (and several times afterwards, on my own) a pivotal moment in my academic career and my life more generally. Reading your analysis and observations influenced me significantly and upon graduation from St. Lawrence in May of this coming year, I am excited to pursue a PhD in order to become a college professor in Women's Studies and Disability Studies.

NOTES

1. Interestingly, in Fiske's study, feminists, businesswomen, Asians, northerners, and black professionals were stereotyped as highly competent, thus envied. In addition to having very low competence, housewives, disabled people, blind people, so-called retarded people, and the elderly were rated as warm, thus pitied.

2. Personal conversation with Paul Longmore, San Francisco, California, June 2000.

3. Personal conversation with Nancy Mairs, Columbus, Ohio, 17 April 1998.

REFERENCES

Americans with Disabilities Act of 1990. http://www.ada.gov/pubs/ada.htm.
Aristotle. 1944. *Generation of Animals.* Translated by A. L. Peck. Cambridge, Mass.: Harvard University Press.
Asch, Adrienne, and Gail Geller. 1996. "Feminism, Bioethics and Genetics." In *Feminism, Bioethics: Beyond Reproduction,* edited by S. M. Wolf, 318–50. Oxford, UK: Oxford University Press.
Battin Margaret P., Rosamond Rhodes, and Anita Silvers, eds. 1998. *Physician Assisted Suicide: Expanding the Debate.* New York: Routledge.

Bordo, Susan. 1993. *Unbearable Weight: Feminism, Western Culture, and the Body.* Berkeley: University of California Press.

———. 1994. "Reading the Male Body." In *The Male Body,* edited by Laurence Goldstein, 265–306. Ann Arbor: University of Michigan Press.

Braidotti, Rosi. 1994. *Nomadic Subjects: Embodiment and Sexual Difference in Contemporary Feminist Thought.* New York: Columbia University Press.

Brownworth, Victoria A., and Susan Raffo, eds. 1999. *Restricted Access: Lesbians on Disability.* Seattle: Seal Press.

Butler, Judith. 1990. *Gender Trouble.* New York: Routledge.

———. 1993. *Bodies That Matter.* New York: Routledge.

Bynum, Caroline Walker. 1999. "Shape and Story: Metamorphosis in the Western Tradition." Paper presented at the National Endowment for the Humanities Jefferson Lecture, 22 March, Washington, D.C.

Clark, David L., and Catherine Myser. 1996. "Being Humaned: Medical Documentaries and the Hyperrealization of Conjoined Twins." In *Freakery: Cultural Spectacles of the Extraordinary Body,* edited by Rosemarie Garland-Thomson, 338–55. New York: New York University Press.

Davis, Lennard J. 1995. *Enforcing Normalcy: Disability, Deafness, and the Body.* New York: Verso.

de Beauvoir, Simone. (1952) 1974. *The Second Sex.* Translated by H. M. Parshley. New York: Vintage Books.

Dreger, Alice Domurat. 1998a. *Hermaphrodites and the Medical Invention of Sex.* Cambridge, Mass.: Harvard University Press.

———. 1998b. "The Limits of Individuality: Ritual and Sacrifice in the Lives and Medical Treatment of Conjoined Twins." In *Freakery: Cultural Spectacles of the Extraordinary Body,* edited by Rosemarie Garland-Thomson, 338–55. New York: New York University Press.

Eiesland, Nancy. 1994. *The Disabled God: Toward a Liberatory Theology of Disability.* Nashville, Tenn.: Abingdon Press.

Fausto-Sterling, Anne. 1995. "Gender, Race, and Nation: The Comparative Anatomy of Hottentot Women in Europe, 1815–1817." In *Deviant Bodies: Cultural Perspectives in Science and Popular Culture,* edited by Jennifer Terry and Jacqueline Urla, 19–48. Bloomington: Indiana University Press.

——— 2000. *Sexing the Body: Gender Politics and the Construction of Sexuality.* New York: Basic Books.

Fine, Michelle, and Adrienne Asch, eds. 1988. *Women with Disabilities: Essays in Psychology, Culture, and Politics.* Philadelphia: Temple University Press.

Finger, Anne. 1990. *Past Due: A Story of Disability, Pregnancy, and Birth.* Seattle: Seal Press.

Fiske, Susan T., Amy J. C. Cuddy, and Peter Glick. 2001. "A Model of (Often Mixed) Stereotype Content: Competence and Warmth Respectively Follow from Perceived Status and Competition." Unpublished study.

Foucault, Michel. 1979. *Discipline and Punish: The Birth of the Prison.* Translated by Alan M. Sheridan-Smith. New York: Vintage Books.

Garland-Thomson, Rosemarie. 1997. *Extraordinary Bodies: Figuring Physical*

Disability in American Culture and Literature. New York: Columbia University Press.

———. 1999. "Narratives of Deviance and Delight: Staring at Julia Pastrana, 'The Extraordinary Lady.'" In *Beyond the Binary,* edited by Timothy Powell, 81–106. New Brunswick, N.J.: Rutgers University Press.

———. 2005. "Feminist Disability Studies: A Review Essay." *Signs* 30 (2): 1557–87.

Gilman, Sander L. 1985. *Difference and Pathology: Stereotypes of Sexuality, Race, and Madness.* Ithaca, N.Y.: Cornell University Press.

———. 1998. *Creating Beauty to Cure the Soul.* Durham, N.C.: Duke University Press.

———. 1999. *Making the Body Beautiful.* Princeton, N.J.: Princeton University Press.

Hahn, Harlan. 1988. "Can Disability Be Beautiful?" *Social Policy* 18 (Winter): 26–31.

Haiken, Elizabeth. 1997. *Venus Envy: A History of Cosmetic Surgery.* Baltimore: Johns Hopkins University Press.

Haraway, Donna. 1991. *Simians, Cyborgs, and Women.* New York: Routledge.

Harstock, Nancy. 1983. "The Feminist Standpoint: Developing Their Ground for a Specifically Feminist Historical Materialism." In *Discovering Reality: Feminist Perspectives on Epistemology, Metaphysics, Methodology, and Philosophy of Science,* edited by Sandra Harding and Merrell Hintikka, 283–305. Dortrecht, Holland: Reidel Publishing.

Herndl, Diane Price. 2002. "Reconstructing the Posthuman Feminist Body: Twenty Years after Audre Lorde's *Cancer Journals.*" In *Disability Studies: Enabling the Humanities,* edited by Brenda Brueggemann, Rosemarie Garland-Thomson, and Sharon Snyder, 144–55. New York: MLA Press.

Hillyer, Barbara. 1993. *Feminism and Disability.* Norman: University of Oklahoma Press.

Hubbard, Ruth. 1990. "Who Should and Who Should Not Inhabit the World?" *The Politics of Women's Biology,* 179–98. New Brunswick, N.J.: Rutgers University Press.

Keller, Evelyn Fox. 1992. "Nature, Nurture and the Human Genome Project." In *The Code of Codes: Scientific and Social Issues in the Human Genome Project,* edited by Daniel J. Kevles and Leroy Hood, 281–99. Cambridge, Mass.: Harvard University Press.

Kessler, Suzanne J. 1990. *Lessons from the Intersexed.* New Brunswick, N.J.: Rutgers University Press.

Kittay, Eva Feder. 1999. *Love's Labor: Essays on Women, Equality, and Dependency.* New York: Routledge.

Kittay, Eva, with Leo Kittay. 2000. " On the Expressivity and Ethics of Selective Abortion for Disability: Conversations with My Son." In Parens and Asch, *Prenatal Testing and Disability Rights,* 165–95.

Linton, Simi. 1998. *Claiming Disability: Knowledge and Identity.* New York: New York University Press.

Longmore, Paul K. 1997. "Conspicuous Contribution and American Cultural Dilemmas: Telethon Rituals of Cleansing and Renewal." In *The Body and Physical Difference: Discourses of Disability,* edited by David Mitchell and Sharon Snyder, 134–58. Ann Arbor: University of Michigan Press.

Lorde, Audre. 1980. *The Cancer Journals.* San Francisco, Calif.: Spinsters Ink.

Mairs, Nancy. 1996. *Waist-High in the World: A Life among the Nondisabled.* Boston: Beacon Press.

McRuer, Robert. 1999. "Compulsory Able-Bodiedness and Queer/Disabled Existence." Paper presented at Modern Language Association Convention, 28 December, Chicago, Illinois.

"Meet Ellen Stohl." 1987. *Playboy* (July): 68–74.

Morrison, Toni. 1992. *Playing in the Dark: Whiteness and the Literary Imagination.* Cambridge, Mass.: Harvard University Press.

Parens, Erik, and Adrienne Asch. 2000. *Prenatal Testing and Disability Rights.* Washington, D.C.: Georgetown University Press.

Piercy, Marge. 1969. "Unlearning Not to Speak." *Circles on Water,* 97. New York: Doubleday.

Rand, Erica. 1995. *Barbie's Queer Accessories.* Durham, N.C.: Duke University Press.

Rapp, Rayna. 1999. *Testing Women, Testing the Fetus: The Social Impact of Amniocentesis in America.* New York: Routledge.

Rich, Adrienne. 1986. "Compulsory Heterosexuality and Lesbian Existence." *Blood, Bread, and Poetry,* 23–75. New York: Norton.

Riley, Denise. 1999. "Bodies, Identities, Feminisms." In *Feminist Theory and the Body: A Reader,* edited by Janet Price and Margrit Shildrick, 220–26. Edinburgh, Scotland: Edinburgh University Press.

Russo, Mary. 1994. *The Female Grotesque: Risk, Excess, and Modernity.* New York: Routledge.

Saxton, Marsha. 1998. "Disability Rights and Selective Abortion." In *Abortion Wars: A Half Century of Struggle (1950–2000),* edited by Ricky Solinger, 374–93. Berkeley: University of California Press.

Scott, Joan Wallach. 1988. "Gender as Useful Category of Analysis." *Gender and the Politics of History,* 29–50. New York: Columbia University Press.

Sedgwick, Eve Kosofsky. 1990. *Epistemology of the Closet.* Berkeley: University of California Press.

Silvers, Anita. 1995. "Reconciling Equality to Difference: Caring (F)or Justice for People with Disabilities." *Hypatia* 10 (1): 30–55.

Spelman, Elizabeth, V. 1988. *Inessential Woman: Problems of Exclusion in Feminist Thought.* Boston: Beacon Press.

Tuana, Nancy. 1994. *The Less Noble Sex: Scientific, Religious, and Philosophical Conceptions of Woman's Nature.* Bloomington: Indiana University Press.

Wald, Priscilla. 2000. "Future Perfect: Grammar, Genes, and Geography." *New Literary History* 31 (4): 681–708.

Williams, John M. 1999. "And Here's the Pitch: Madison Avenue Discovers the 'Invisible Consumer.'" *WE Magazine* (July/August): 28–31.

Wolf, Naomi. 1991. *The Beauty Myth: How Images of Beauty Are Used against Women.* New York: William Morrow.

Young, Iris Marion. 1990a. "Breasted Experience." *Throwing Like a Girl and Other Essays in Feminist Philosophy and Social Theory,* 189–209. Bloomington: Indiana University Press.

———. 1990b. "Throwing Like a Girl." *Throwing Like a Girl,* 141–59.

Two

CRITICAL DIVIDES

Judith Butler's Body Theory and the Question of Disability

ELLEN SAMUELS

Marginality thus means something altogether different to me from what it means to social theorists. It is no metaphor for the power relations between one group of human beings and another but a literal description of where I stand (figuratively speaking): over here, on the edge, out of bounds, beneath your notice. I embody the metaphors. Only whether or not I like doing so is immaterial.   —NANCY MAIRS

The push to expose physical difference as an ideological phantasm has, ironically, resulted in the further reification of disability as the term absented from our social models.

—DAVID T. MITCHELL AND SHARON L. SNYDER

How can one read a text for what does *not* appear within its own terms, but which nevertheless constitutes the illegible conditions of its own legibility?   —JUDITH BUTLER

To invoke disability as a category of critical analysis is, at the present time, a fairly radical endeavor. Unlike other identity categories such as gender, race, and sexuality, (dis)ability is not yet widely recognized as a legitimate or relevant position from which to address such broad subjects as literature, philosophy, and the arts. Even well-known disability theorist Michael Bérubé admits he once considered disability too specialized a category to apply to general education: "I was kind to people who used wheelchairs . . . and respectful of all persons regardless of their mental abilities, but when it came to whether disability should be a major academic subject, I just couldn't see the point of another 'additive' studies program in the curriculum" (1998, ix). Even assuming most contemporary scholars have the relatively benign view of people with disabilities that Bérubé once espoused, and that they will listen tolerantly to the arguments of scholars and critics with disabilities, such uneasy patronage is still a far cry from achieving for disability even the embattled legitimacy that gender, race, and sexuality have achieved in the academic and critical worlds.

This context is crucial for my discussion of the relation between, on the one hand, Judith Butler's immensely influential critical work on gender, sexuality, and the body, and, on the other, the question of disability. In formulating the goals of such an inquiry, I am concerned not only with elucidating the usefulness and limitations of applying Butler's work to disability but also with this inquiry's relevance to the larger struggle for legitimacy and power by the emerging field of disability studies. For the purpose of this essay, I am focusing upon Butler's 1993 text, *Bodies That Matter: On the Discursive Limits of "Sex,"* because it is the text most often cited by scholars writing about disabled or ill bodies, and also because it represents Butler's attempt to extend her earlier argument concerning the performativity of gender to include other embodied social identities, most notably race. This extension of Butler's analysis beyond gender makes *Bodies That Matter,* among Butler's many works, at once the most vulnerable to criticism regarding the exclusion of disability and (conversely) the most easily adapted to the subjects and goals of disability studies.

Butler does not explicitly address the issue of disability in *Bodies That Matter.* The words *disabled* and *disability* never appear, and we find only fleeting references to bodies that "endure illness." When Butler deploys terms such as *deformation* or *blindness,* it is unclear if they refer to physical matters or textual ones—or to the blurred area between the two that is her primary realm of analysis. However, it seems clear she is not referring to actual disabled people or bodies, and the texts and characters she analyzes are consistently discussed in terms of their sexed, gendered, and racial formations, not their physical or mental abilities.

But why should we expect Butler to account for the disabled body in her work? As she wryly observes in her introduction,

> any analysis which foregrounds one vector of power over another will doubtless become vulnerable to criticisms that it not only ignores or devalues the others, but that its own constructions depend on the exclusion of the others in order to proceed. On the other hand, any analysis which pretends to be able to encompass every vector of power runs the risk of a certain epistemological imperialism which consists in the

presupposition that any given writer might explain the complexities of contemporary power. (18–19)

It is difficult to argue with Butler's point that "no author or text" can claim to offer a fully inclusive and cohesive analysis of every power structure that shapes the cultural landscape, and the purpose of this essay is not to lambaste Butler for her exclusions. Setting aside the question of the critic's culpability, however, an investigation of how Butler constructs her idea of a body, sans (dis)ability, can open up two vital and important questions: First, what happens when we attempt to graft Butler's body theory onto an inquiry that does foreground (dis)ability? And second, is there a funda-mental dissonance between postmodern feminist body theory, as exem-plified by Butler, and the existence/analysis of the disabled body? Both of these questions have far-reaching implications for the intellectual and logistical challenges inherent in integrating disability into contemporary critical paradigms.[1]

NOT JUST FOR GENDER ANYMORE: THE INCREASING USE OF BUTLER IN DISABILITY STUDIES

How does that materialization of the norm in bodily formation produce a domain of abjected bodies, a field of deformation, which in failing to qualify as the fully human, fortifies those regulatory norms? What chal-lenge does that excluded and abjected realm produce to a symbolic he-gemony that might force a radical rearticulation of what qualifies as bod-ies that matter, ways of living that count as "life," lives worth protecting, lives worth saving, lives worth grieving?   —JUDITH BUTLER

Bodies That Matter extends Butler's concern with body performativity to focus upon a "domain of abjected bodies," as she repeatedly inquires which physical and discursive conditions render bodies *legible* or *livable*. Such an inquiry appears tailor-made for the disabled body that, in its lit-eral deformations, has historically occupied the center of Western specu-lations as to what constitutes the *human*.[2] Disability rights advocates fight-ing against the routine abortion or euthanasia of congenitally disabled infants and of severely disabled children and adults may hear a particu-larly urgent resonance in Butler's concern with "lives worth protecting, lives worth saving, lives worth grieving."

Despite the obvious applicability of many of Butler's insights to the cen-tral questions of disability studies, however, her work was largely absent from the seminal published works of disability studies, even in the writings of scholars who explicitly drew upon and aligned themselves with feminist and gender theory. Butler's most influential works of body theory, *Gender Trouble* and *Bodies That Matter,* were published in 1990 and 1993 respectively. However, there is not a single reference to Butler in the American anthology *The Disability Studies Reader* (Davis 1997) or its British counterpart *The Disability Reader* (Shakespeare 1998), nor in such founding texts as Lennard Davis's *Enforcing Normalcy* (1995), Susan Wendell's *The Rejected Body* (1996), Rosemarie Garland-Thomson's *Extraordinary Bodies* (1997), and Simi Linton's *Claiming Disability* (1998).[3] Butler is mentioned once in a footnote to David Mitchell and Sharon Snyder's introduction to their edited volume *The Body and Physical Difference* (1997; a note to which I will return below), but is not cited by any of the book's fourteen contributors.

Since early 1999, when I first began investigating the use, and dis-use, of Butler's work in the field, disability scholars have begun utilizing Butler's work much more widely. Between 1999 and 2001 a number of important works in disability studies that utilize Butler's theories have appeared (Corker 1999; McRuer 2002; Price and Shildrick 1999a; Sandahl 1999; Stocker 2001). And since 2002, when this essay was first published, those numbers have continued to increase (McRuer 2006, Siebers 2008). In addition, routine references to Butler as an important conceptual source for social theories of disability have become much more common than in the early and mid-1990s (Corker 2001; Erevelles 2001; Schriempf 2001; Wilson and Lewiecki-Wilson 2001). These new developments, however, do not render the present inquiry outdated; rather, I would suggest that it becomes even more important to look critically at how and when disability studies and Butler's theories intersect.

Additionally, the intriguing question remains: why did so many fundamental works in the field originally omit or deliberately reject Butler? By contrast, and as a sign of Butler's general influence, a recently published volume on "feminist theory and the body," which collects writings from the 1980s and 1990s, includes more indexed references to Butler than to any other theorist except the ubiquitous Foucault—more than Freud, Irigaray, or de Beauvoir (Price and Shildrick 1999a, 485–87). We are left, then, with the question: why did these pioneering disability scholars, writing and publishing during the exact years in which Butler's theories rose to prominence, essentially leave Butler out? Dismissing the unlikely idea that these scholars were unaware of Butler's work, and setting aside for the moment the issue of her notoriously obtuse writing style, we are left with two real possibilities: (1) they (we) saw Butler's work as irrelevant to their (our) scholarly goals; and (2) they (we) saw Butler's work as contrary to those goals. Disability scholars are not a monolithic group, of course, and writers may have different reasons for excluding Butler. Yet the existence of a broad tendency such as that demonstrated by the examples cited above invites further inquiry as to the original tendency of the field of disability studies as a whole and suggests the pertinence of interrogating how Butler has now become more commonly used in the "second wave" of disability studies publications.

One way to begin such an inquiry is to examine those works that, with varying degrees of success, attempt to integrate Butler into a disability studies framework and to proceed from that examination to a closer engagement with Butler's own text. In my original research I could locate only a handful of works that mentioned Butler in relation to disability, several of which were unpublished conference presentations. The comparative proliferation of disability studies texts referencing Butler that were published between 1999 and 2001 naturally transforms and expands my original inquiry in important ways; however, I have found that most of these new publications fit quite well into the original categories of analysis I had based on my pre-1999 research. To wit, several of these works merely reference Butler in passing, as an important or exemplary source of postmodern feminist and psychoanalytic thought (Kafer 1998; Quayson 1999; Schriempf 2001; Corker 2001). Others draw upon her theories to enable an analysis of disability in specific relation to queer identity (Bender 2000; McRuer 2002). Finally, a number of writers transpose Butler's theories wholeheartedly into a disability studies framework, either analogizing disability to gender/sex (Cho 1997; Corker 1999; Price and Shildrick 1999b; Sandahl 1999; Wilson and Lewiecki-Wilson 2001) or engaging directly with Butler's works to interrogate their usefulness for social theories of disability (Erevelles 2001; Stocker 2001). These engagements with Butler indicate future directions for disability theory, but certain transpositions that adopt Butler's terms while substituting *disability* for *gender* indicate some of the potential pitfalls to beware as we embrace that future.

Although most of the writers I address below are located within the field of disability studies, I would like first to discuss the work of one writer who attempts to integrate the consideration of disability into a gender studies framework. This writer's work is not particularly well known or influential, but it is useful as a cautionary tale for all feminist and gender theorists (and I include myself in this group) as we work toward an integrated feminist disability praxis. Julia Cho's essay "Sideshow Freaks and Sexualized Children: Abject Bodies on Display" (1997) explicitly links Butler's ideas in *Bodies That Matter* with current disability theory, exemplified by the work of Rosemarie Garland-Thomson (1996; 1997). In the opening paragraph of her essay, Cho depicts Garland-Thomson's work on "freakish" bodies as supplying "one answer" to the question posed by Butler: "Are certain constructions of the body constitutive in this sense: that we could not operate without them, that without them there would be no 'I,' no 'we'?" (Cho 1997, 18). Thus, she extends an observation Butler had originally applied to sex/gender to include other "regulatory schemas" (Butler 1993, ix) that serve to materialize the abject body (in this case, childhood and freak shows) and proceeds to merge the critical approaches of Butler and Thomson: "both Butler and Thomson emphasize the ways in which, far from being agentless objects of the norms which regulate the articulation of normal 'bodies' as such, these abject bodies inform those very norms" (Cho 1997, 19). Such a move is certainly critically defensible, as one of Garland-Thomson's central theoretical terms is *normate,* her neologism for "the veiled subject position of cultural self, the figure outlined by the array of deviant others whose marked bodies shore up the normate's boundaries" (1997, 6). Yet Cho's enfolding of Garland-Thomson's work into Butler's also enacts a troubling enfolding of the freakishly disabled body into the freakishly gendered body, in which the gendered body emerges as a realized subject while the disabled body remains a reflective trope.

In order to develop her primary argument regarding the use of the freakish body to reflect the feminine, Cho first analyzes the fiction of Carson McCullers and Flannery O'Connor and then examines contemporary media portrayals of conjoined twin girls Ashley and Brittany Hensel and murdered child model JonBenét Ramsey. In her intriguing discussion of scenes from McCullers's and O'Connor's fiction in which a young female character views a carnival freak: "the confused and ambiguous sexuality of young female characters is mirrored by hermaphrodite characters" (1997, 22). Such an argument still relies upon the physically deviant body as a trope, rather than a body in its own right, and thus, like the majority of current social and literary criticism, remains confined within the limitations of its assumptions. What Cho's essay suggests about the possibility of integrating Butler's theories with the work of a disability theorist is that their very compatibility may lead to a disturbing slippage between the terms of the inquiry: from *gender* to *disability* and beyond.

This problem arises in a different form in works by authors more closely associated with disability studies. In a philosophical essay that examines the usefulness of Butler's "genealogical" approach to disability studies praxis, Susan Stocker uses an intriguing financial metaphor to explain her use of Butler's theory: "Butler's subversion of contingent discursive regimes may be used to contest any received norms. She emphasizes sexual norms, but the cash value of her scheme is such that we can apply it to able-bodied norms" (2001, 39). Stocker's "cash value" approach suggests an essential value or meaning within Butler's work that can be separated from the specific identity categories to which it was originally attached. As I observed above, because much of Butler's work appears highly applicable to disability, one is certainly tempted to draw upon her important critical insights while exchanging the term *disability* for the original term *sex/gender*. However, I would like to suggest the need for rigorous critical scrutiny of the implications of such an exchange. In its most extreme forms, this exchange can become an apparent substitution that suggests a direct correspondence or equation between two very different realms of social and bodily existence.

For example, in Janet Price and Margrit Shildrick's essay "Breaking the Boundaries of the Broken Body" (1999b), the authors admit to "brazenly paraphras[ing]" Butler's work on gender and sexuality to apply to disability: they begin with an excerpt from Butler; remove the terms *gender, sex,* or *homosexuality;* and attach the remaining quotation to a sentence about disability, thus creating Butlerian assertions such as "disability itself 'is performative in the sense that it constitutes as an effect the very subject that it appears to express'" (442), and "disability 'secures its self-identity and shores up its ontological boundaries by protecting itself from what it sees as the continual predatory encroachments of its contaminated other,' ability" (442–43). Similarly, in his insightful article "Compulsory Able-Bodiedness and Queer/Disabled Existence," Robert McRuer excerpts a paragraph from *Gender Trouble* and inserts the words *able-bodiedness, able-bodied identity,* and *disabled* in brackets where Butler had originally used *heterosexuality* and *gay/lesbian* (McRuer 2002, 93–94; Butler 1990, 122).[4] Mairian Corker provides another intriguing twist on this strategy by suggesting a parallel correspondence between Butler's critique of the sex/gender binary and the social model's critique of impairment/disability (1999, 636). However, Corker provides more contexts for this exchange by interrogating the "biological foundationalism" that undermines both sets of terms and by proposing Butler's work as a model for challenging binary oppositions within disability studies.[5]

To a certain extent, all of these critics' appropriations of Butler succeed in theoretically grounding and extending their positions. However, there would seem to be an element of imprecision, at the least, in merely substituting one term for another in a given piece of theory and then citing it as such. One can certainly understand the substitutive impulse, since, as discussed in the beginning of this section, there are many passages in Butler that beg the question of disability, and her primary theoretical concerns appear deeply relevant as well. Yet the question remains: what meaning, or intention, is lost through the wholesale adoption of Butler's theoretical framework inflected only by a mere substitution of terms? In making such substitutions, do we lose sight of the fact that Butler is quite explicitly discussing *not* (dis)ability, *but* gender/sex—that the abject domain she delineates is specifically produced by "certain highly *gendered* regulatory schemas" (1999, ix; my emphasis)? Is it not necessary to at least ask if there is a difference between disability/impairment and gender/sex, and, since there obviously is, how that difference operates in the present situation?

We are generally accustomed to marshaling such terms as *race, class,* and *gender,* and we may someday become used to including *disability* in that lineup, but perhaps we too often lose sight of the profound differences between those social designations. Each may function to materialize norms and their constitutive others, but those functions are neither parallel nor discrete. What we risk losing sight of when we substitute one term for the other in our analytical framework is the necessary evolution of those frameworks beyond a single-term approach. This is a particularly important point in the case of *disability,* since, as Bérubé observes, "disability is perhaps the most unstable designation of them all" (1998, xi). It is certainly true that many of Butler's most compelling conclusions about how bodies are sexed can inform our analysis of how bodies are "abled"; however, her work itself is en-abled by its own reliance upon a stable, functional body that is able to walk, talk, give birth, see, and be seen. When we utilize Butler's work without addressing these limitations, we incorporate the limitations into our own critique, and the problem compounds itself.

NECESSARY INTERLUDE: DISABILITY AND FEMININITY

The above critique relies upon the assumption that disability and gender are distinctly different concepts. Yet before we can rest easily upon the solid "obviousness" of that statement, we must at least take account of the fact that Western thought has historically claimed, not a difference, but a correspondence between disability and *femininity,* which Garland-Thomson traces to the Aristotelian assertion that "'the female is as it were a deformed male' . . . not only does this definition of the female as a 'mutilated male' inform later depictions of woman as diminished man, but it also arranges somatic diversity into a hierarchy of value that assigns completeness to some bodies and deficiency to others" (1997, 20). The notion that the disabled body stands in a similar relationship to the nondisabled body as the female does to the male has contributed, on the one hand, to the development of sexist medical models that pathologize female bodily functions such as pregnancy and menopause and exclude women from research studies, and on the other hand, to the de-masculinization of disabled men, who are then lumped together with women, children, and the elderly in the realm of abject and dependent bodies. Thus, Garland-Thomson and others argue, feminists fighting to reclaim the "normalcy" of the female body should claim common cause with disability rights advocates of both genders.[6]

In further support of this point, Garland-Thomson observes:

> Many parallels exist between the social meanings attributed to female bodies and those assigned to disabled bodies. Both the female and the disabled body are cast as deviant and inferior; both are excluded from full participation in public as well as economic life; both are defined in opposition to a norm that is assumed to possess natural physical superiority. Indeed, the discursive equation of femaleness with disability is common, sometimes to denigrate women and sometimes to defend them. (19)

On the other hand, nondisabled feminists may actually distance themselves from the disabled body, to prove that the female body is *not* diseased or deformed. Garland-Thomson also laments, "Even feminists today invoke negative images of disability to describe the oppression of women; for example Jane Flax asserts that women are 'mutilated and deformed' by sexist ideology and practices" (19).

On which side of this debate do we find Butler? In the first chapter of *Bodies That Matter,* Butler interprets Luce Irigaray's version of the Platonic/Aristotelian cosmogony (female equals deformed male) to exclude the possibility of *any* resemblance between woman and man, through the introduction of the feminized receptacle (1997, 43). Yet, contradictorily,

> the receptacle is not simply a figure *for* the excluded, but, taken as figure, stands for the excluded and thus performs or enacts yet another set of exclusions of all that remains unfigurable under the sign of the feminine— that in the feminine which resists the figure of the nurse-receptacle. In other words, taken as a figure, the nurse-receptacle freezes the feminine as that which is necessary for the reproduction of the human, but which itself is not human, and which is in no way to be construed as the formative principle of the human form that is, as it were, produced through it. (42)

Thus, in Butler we find the development of two versions of femininity: one is containable and figurable, and functions to reproduce form, while the other is uncontained and unfigurable, and functions to reproduce alterity—the free space against which the form is realized. These two versions correspond to Butler's notion of a performativity that simultaneously reinscribes and calls into question matters of embodied identity such as gender. One might then contend that Butler's work could be used to argue either for or against an alliance between feminism and disability, depending upon which version of femininity one chose to extract from Butler's writings—that which reinforces form or that which contests it.

Yet here again the question is not so simple, for Butler is clearly writing an intentionally liberatory text aimed at destabilizing gendered and sexualized norms—in that sense, it seems she clearly privileges the second version of femininity described above. Finally, it appears that femininity per se is simply not Butler's main concern. Ultimately, her work is not directed at furthering the sort of feminist analysis that seeks to stabilize the female body in opposition to the oppressive male, but at liberating *all* bodies from the oppressions of gender hierarchy. She analyzes femininity, like masculinity, heterosexuality, and homosexuality, to inform her inquiry into how bodies are materialized through sex.

Every attempt, in fact, to determine just what Butler means or intends in her writing is liable to the same sort of destabilization and phantasmic haunting that she describes as shaping our every word and interaction, our very bodies and selves. If one is indeed concerned with defining and defending "bodies that matter," does it matter that it is so difficult to locate the exact, determinable body within Butler's writing itself? Butler is quite aware of this critique and responds by emphasizing the role of language in conceiving and apprehending materiality:

> It must be possible to concede and affirm an array of "materialities" that pertain to the body, that which is signified by the domain of biology, anatomy, physiology, hormonal and chemical composition, illness, age, weight, metabolism, life and death. None of this can be denied. But the undeniability of these "materialities" in no way implies what it means to affirm them, indeed, what interpretive matrices condition, enable and limit that necessary affirmation. . . . We might want to claim that what persists . . . is the "materiality" of the body. But perhaps we will have fulfilled the same function, and opened up some others, if we claim that what persists here is *a demand in and for language.* (1993, 66–77)

Although Butler's point is well taken, and indeed constitutes one of her most important critical insights, her astonishingly quick and seemingly facile rundown of the body's material substance, as "hormonal and chemical composition, illness, age, weight, metabolism, life and death"—each of which are terms that could occupy (and have occupied) whole lifetimes of theorizing about the body, not to mention living as one—does suggest a certain disinterest on her part regarding those aspects of the body that are firmly rooted in the physical realm. Thus, many scholars who focus on the cultural negotiations of the physical body find Butler's work inapplicable and perhaps dangerous to their own critical concerns.

CRITICS AND CHIMPS: THE QUESTION OF INCOMPATIBILITY

So much of left criticism has devoted itself to the issue of the body, of the social construction of sexuality and gender. Alternative bodies people this discourse: gay, lesbian, hermaphrodite, criminal, medical, and so on. But lurking behind these images of transgression and deviance is a much more transgressive and deviant figure: the disabled body.

—LENNARD J. DAVIS

All of my discussion above may be for naught if the tendency continues among many prominent disability studies scholars to disregard or disdain theorists, such as Butler, who fail to account for the disabled body in their work—and despite the recent spate of publications utilizing Butler's theories, this tendency remains a phenomenon to be reckoned with. As my introduction suggests, this persistent rejection appears to proceed not merely from annoyance at the exclusion of disability, but also from the belief that an edifice of theory built upon a presumably nondisabled body cannot be brought to bear upon the disabled body without collapsing under its own exclusionary weight. Thus, we must critically question whether the disabled body is the abject Other that haunts and enables Butler's work as she would claim the sexually deviant body haunts and enables the sexually normative body of everyday use.[7] Can we adopt her work usefully to help elucidate the meanings and materialization of disability? If theorists like Butler have already developed complex apparatus with which to examine the abject body, are we "emerging field" critics reinventing the wheel just to spite her for leaving us out?

Among many of the most prominent disability studies scholars, one finds a common tendency to critique the larger world of scholars—variously figured as literary critics, postmodernists, feminist theorists, and so on—for their refusal to engage disability, even as tropes and figures of disability pervade and underpin both their subjects and modes of discourse.[8] Simi Linton notes, "Although the so-called reflective disciplines, such as philosophy, literature . . . rhetoric, art, and history, evoke disability everywhere, they seem unable to reflect upon it" (1998, 87). Certainly Western culture is filled with disabled figures, from Shakespeare's Richard III and

Herman Melville's Ahab to the nineteenth-century female invalid and the twentieth-century cyborg, and it is equally true that the push for multicultural curricula in the past thirty years has rarely, if ever, included disability as an essential component of such revisions. Discussing feminist theory in particular, Rosemarie Garland-Thomson points out that "although ethnicity, race, and sexuality are frequently knitted into current feminist analysis, the logical leap toward seeing disability as a stigmatized social identity and a reading of the body remains largely untaken" (1994, 585). Lennard Davis suggests that this phenomenon is not a matter of benign neglect or ignorance, but a result of a deeper ideological contradiction:

> The disabled body is a nightmare for the fashionable discourse of theory because that discourse has been limited by the very predilection of the dominant, ableist culture. The body is seen as a site of *jouissance*, a native ground of pleasure, the scene of an excess that defies reason, that takes dominant culture and its rigid, power-laden vision of the body to task. . . . Observations of chimpanzees reveal that they fly in terror from a decapitated chimp; dogs, by contrast, will just sniff at the remains of a fellow dog. That image of the screaming chimpanzee facing the mutilated corpse is the image of the critic of *jouissance* contemplating the paraplegic, the disfigured, the mutilated, the deaf, the blind. Rather than face this ragged image, the critic turns to the fluids of sexuality, the gloss of lubrication, the glossary of the body as text, the heteroglossia of the intertext, the glossolalia of the schizophrenic. But almost never the body of the differently abled. (1995, 5)

My question, then, is whether we can draw evidence from Butler's work that she would respond like the critic-of-*jouissance*/chimp if the disabled body were integrated into her critical universe. Do her theories presume able-bodiedness as a prerequisite of subjectivity, or do they offer liberatory models that can further the work of separating supposedly material identities from the social matrices that bring them into being?

In a note to their introduction to *The Body and Physical Difference*, David Mitchell and Sharon Snyder specifically cite Butler as one of two "influential philosophers" (the other is Sander Gilman) whose constructivist approaches run contradictory to a disability studies paradigm, since

> undergirding their rhetoric of constructed deviancy is that they strategically distance their interest in "abject communities" from the tangible evidence of physical aberrancy. Subsequently, disabled communities that

are defined by virtue of the presence of physical differences will be hard pressed to utilize the same rhetorical tactic. (1997, 27n27)

One reading of Butler would suggest her sustained concern with the normative criteria that form legible, bounded, human bodies versus illegible, uncontrolled, inhuman bodies attempts to recuperate sexuality at the expense of disability. By exposing and explicating the cultural processes at work, Butler aims to demonstrate the unfixed and constructed nature of sexuality/gender, thus destabilizing the hierarchy of normal (hetero) versus abnormal (homo) forms. However, in doing so she must necessarily acknowledge and discursively materialize a realm of abnormal bodies, only to rescue queer bodies from inside it. But what remains?

Butler's discussion of Freudian hypochondria offers some clues; here, the physically ill body emerges as the product of inappropriately abjected sexuality, forced into psychosomatic emergence through sociopsychological prohibition (1993, 58–64). The ill body and the homosexual body emerge, in Butler's paradigm, as ontological opposites whose coexistence is the product of oppressive social schemas. It naturally follows for Butler to oppose the "metaphorics of illness that pervade the description of sexuality," especially in the context of AIDS and the subsequent re-pathologization of homosexuality (64). To question Butler on this point is not to endorse the pathologization of gayness or to imply that queer and ill/disabled bodies have any natural or presumed commonalties. It is, however, to point out that Butler's liberatory approach to sexuality takes as a matter of course that "metaphorics of illness" are always negative and that somewhere, somehow, bodies *do* exist that deserve pathologization based upon the very material, biological "realities" she seeks to destabilize.

Mitchell and Snyder describe this problem as the "representational double bind of disability" in which, "while disabled populations are firmly entrenched on the outer margins of social power and cultural value, the disabled body also serves as the raw material out of which other socially disempowered communities make themselves visible" (1997, 6). Thus, "any attempt to distance disenfranchised communities from the fantasy of deformity further entrenches the disabled as the 'real' abnormality from which all other nonnormative groups must be distanced" (6). This "double bind" also emerges in Garland-Thomson's critique, cited earlier, of feminist theories that attempt to de-pathologize the normative female body at the expense of the physically deviant or ill body. Whereas Mitchell, Snyder, and Garland-Thomson focus their critique of postmodern body theory on that theory's reliance upon the disabled body as a constitutive Other, Susan Wendell is concerned that postmodern theories focus too exclusively upon the body-as-construction and thus elide the lived experience of "actual" bodies, particularly the "negative body"—that is, the body that is disabled, ill, or suffering (1996, 166–68).

We see in Butler's work many examples of such apparently "disembodied bodies." In particular, body parts separated from their original, intact bodies populate Butler's work in a strangely impersonal fashion that certainly seems divorced from any literally fragmented bodies—meaning amputees, congenitally "deformed" persons, and so forth. To elucidate her idea of the imagined phallus versus the physical penis, Butler extends Freudian theory on hypochondria to suggest that the "ambiguity between a real and conjured pain . . . is sustained in the analogy with erotogenicity, which seems defined as the very vacillation between real and imagined body parts" (1993, 59). This idea is then extended to include the Lacanian "partitioned body," "the body 'in pieces' before the mirror," which comes to stand for the whole, thus creating a "phantasm of control" (80). These concepts form the basis for Butler's analysis of Willa Cather's fiction, in which, she claims, "body parts disengage from any common center, pull away from each other, lead separate lives, become sites of phantasmic investments that refuse to reduce to singular sexualities" (140). As in Cho's essay discussed above, the disabled body becomes a disinvested symbolic medium for the display and mediation of sexuality, which then apparently constitutes "real" and primary subjectivity. In addition, the fragmented body parts littering the landscape are so firmly located within the imaginary that it is not even necessary for Butler to clarify at any point that she is not talking about actual bodies, that no characters in Cather's fiction suffer the loss of limbs. Yet, once versed in the rudiments of the social construction of disability, one cannot help but perceive the incompleteness of Butler's argument, because "the disabled body is a direct *imago* of the repressed fragmented body. The disabled body causes a kind of hallucination of the mirror phase gone wrong" (Davis 1995, 139).

Not only disability studies scholars have challenged Butler for her elision of the lived experience of the physical body. Butler tells us that she wrote *Bodies That Matter* in part to respond to such critiques of *Gender Trouble,* which she parrots into her introduction in the form of the oft-repeated question "What about the materiality of the body, Judy?" (1993, ix). Her consistent response is that, of course, she is not arguing that bodies or gender are *only* constructions, but that construction is an integral part of their being and thus must be elucidated:

For surely bodies live and die; eat and sleep; feel pain, pleasure; endure illness and violence; and these "facts" one might skeptically proclaim, cannot be dismissed as mere constructions. Surely there must be some kind of necessity that accompanies these primary and irrefutable experiences. And surely there is. But their irrefutability in no way implies what it might mean to affirm them and through what discursive means. (xi)

Butler's point is well taken, but so are those of her critics. The concerns of disability studies scholars, such as Wendell, who worry about "approaches to cultural construction of 'the body' that . . . deny or ignore bodily experience in favor of fascination with bodily representations" echo those of some transgender activists regarding *pomo* gender theory (1996, 44). In her book *Read My Lips*, Riki Ann Wilchins (1997), cofounder of the political action group Transsexual Menace, robustly critiques the academic field of gender studies as a voyeuristic anthropology of transgender experience. Gender studies in the academy, says Wilchins, too often "escalate[s] the politicization of our bodies, choices, and desires, so that, with each new book, while their audience enjoys the illusion of knowing more about us, we find ourselves more disempowered, disembodied, and exploited than before" (22). Wilchins cites the extremely high incidence of physical violence and abuse in transpeople's lives, as well as their painful struggles for self-determination, and then notes "you won't find any of this in the next trans or gender studies book because the real challenges of our lives aren't perceived as relevant. . . . It is far easier to invest *us* as a topic of study than the depredations of the gender regime that marginalizes and preys upon us" (24).

This critique is powerful and necessary, yet it jibes oddly with Wilchins's citations of Butler and Foucault in her book and with her description of Butler's *Gender Trouble* as "the most far-reaching and penetrating critique of feminism, sexuality, and binary sex from a postmodern viewpoint to date" (224). One can reasonably be left confused as to Wilchins's ultimate feelings about gender theory in general and Butler in particular. Yet, perhaps her contradictory attitude can actually provide a useful model for disability theorists as we begin to formulate more nuanced and liberatory ways to integrate Butler and her fellow constructivists into our own scholarship. I find a very similar moment in Carrie Sandahl's wonderfully unresolved interrogation of her own attempt to deconstruct both disability and femininity while directing a production of Joan Schenkar's play *Signs of Life*. Like other critics of postmodern body theory, Sandahl observes, "Butler's theory of performativity . . . relies on a metaphorical association between gender 'freakishness' and deformed bodies. . . . In a sense, then, Butler uses disability (or the deformed, abject body) as a metaphor for gender and sex difference, and . . . ignores the identities and concerns of actual people with disabilities" (1999, 15). Yet on the very next page, Sandahl decides to use Butler anyway, because "Butler's theory . . . allows us to see the performative parallel between gender and disability" (16). It seems that Butler's work exerts a powerful influence, not only on our academic discourse, but perhaps also on our minds and hearts. Her insights have the potential to be so far-reaching and liberatory that even as we formulate critiques of her theories, we are also drawn in to the possibilities those theories offer.

CONCLUSION: CAN'T THINK WITH HER, CAN'T THINK WITHOUT HER

Writing the disabled body will mean that our most basic conceptions of the body will need to be rewritten. . . . Like the normative ideologies of the body to which they often stand opposed, theoretical discourses of the body already contain within themselves a series of unacknowledged and/ or disavowed assumptions and theories about disability. Bringing these out for inspection is one way that body theory can begin to learn something from disability studies and can intervene in them in turn.

—JAMES I. PORTER

Judith Butler's theories already have had wide and far-reaching influence on contemporary critical work on the body, gender, sexuality, and identity. Disability studies scholars cannot afford to ignore or dismiss Butler's work, but neither should we adopt it uncritically. As I have suggested, merely inserting disability into the mix without thoroughly examining the meaning and implications of the new ideas we thus create is not only inaccurate, but it also falls short of pushing Butler's work as the necessary next step to fully account for the not-always-able body. Such wholesale adoptions treat Butler's theories as more fixed and final than even she, with her emphasis on unfixed, ever-shifting, and irreducible meanings, would likely endorse.

There is no ideal blueprint of how future work in disability studies should integrate Butler's theories, and I will not pretend to offer one. But ultimately the groundbreaking nature of Butler's work means it represents the first steps of a new body of thought that will necessarily become more nuanced, comprehensive, and accountable as it grows with time, and I believe disability studies must and should be an active participant in that growth—not only to enhance our own work, but also to provide the necessary apparatus to evolve those theories beyond their original limitations. As postmodern body theory and disability theory continue to develop and expand, they are certain to pursue parallel, if not corresponding, tracks: I have already noted that as our understanding of disability as visually constructed has begun to evolve toward a more complex analysis of the role of language in forming discursive bodily identities, Butler has also moved from focusing upon the performativity of the body to inquire more deeply into the ways in which "language sustains the body" (1997, 5). Critics such as Mairian Corker develop this parallel to its logical and fruitful next step by integrating Butler's insights with a disability framework (1999; 2001). But this integration will have limited success if it works in only one direction. So I would like to end on a note of challenge to all body theorists working within Butler's framework (not to mention Butler herself) to include and account for the disabled body in your work, not as a metaphor or sign for gender but in all its real complexity. Only then can we begin to cross our divide.

NOTES

I am grateful for generous feedback and support at various stages of this essay's writing from Alison Kafer, Colleen Lye, Susan Schweik, and Kim Q. Hall.

1. Since my analysis is necessarily influenced by my own frame of reference, I feel it is important to note that I am both a disability studies scholar and a person with a disability. My perspective is also influenced by my grounding in the humanities and the study of American culture.

2. For discussion of this history, see Garland-Thomson (1997), Wendell (1996), and Mitchell and Snyder (1997).

3. Garland-Thomson does include Butler in her bibliography but makes no direct reference to Butler in her text or notes.

4. Although he makes a very similar rhetorical move to Cho (1997) and Price and Shildrick (1999), I find McRuer's substitutions somewhat less disturbing, since he explicitly addresses queer identity in his piece rather than eliding it fully under the sign of *disability*.

5. "If impairment is positioned in place of sex and disability in place of gender, it is possible to see how a separate sociology of impairment, most especially one which is grounded in medical sociology, might end up working against a social theory of disability, rather than enhancing our understanding of the relationship between disability and impairment" (Corker 1999, 636). Corker uses Butler, then, in a contextualized fashion to engage with important debates about impairment's role in developing feminist disability theory. See also Schriempf (2001) and Wendell (2001).

6. See also Wendell (1996, chap. 7).

7. "Given this understanding of construction as constitutive constraint, is it still possible to raise the critical question of how such constraints not only produce the domain of intelligible bodies, but produce as well a domain of unthinkable, abject, unlivable bodies? This latter domain is not the opposite of the former . . . the latter is the excluded and illegible domain that haunts the former domain as the specter of its own impossibility, the very limit to intelligibility, its constitutive outside" (Butler 1993, xi).

8. See Davis (1995; 1999, xi, 4–5); Linton (1998, 87–91, 110–16); Mitchell and Snyder (1997, 5); Porter (1997, xii–xiv); Wendell (1996, 45, 166–68).

REFERENCES

Bender, Emily. 2000. "The Queer Body, the Disabled Body, and Social Anxiety."
Paper presented at the Disability, Sexuality, and Culture: Societal and Experien-
tial Perspectives on Multiple Identities Conference, 17 March, San Francisco State
University, San Francisco, California.

Bérubé, Michael. 1998. "Pressing the Claim." Foreword to Linton, *Claiming Disability*, vii–ix.

Butler, Judith. 1990. *Gender Trouble: Feminism and the Subversion of Identity*. New
York: Routledge.

———. 1993. *Bodies That Matter: On the Discursive Limits of "Sex."* New York:
Routledge.

———. 1997. *Excitable Speech: A Politics of the Performative*. New York: Routledge.

Cho, Julia. 1997. "Sideshow Freaks and Sexualized Children: Abject Bodies on Display." *Critical Sense* 5 (2): 18–52.

Corker, Mairian. 1999. "Differences, Conflations and Foundations: the Limits to
'Accurate' Theoretical Representation of Disabled People's Experience?" *Disability and Society* 14 (5): 627–42.

———. 2001. "Sensing Disability." *Hypatia* 16 (4): 34–52.

Davis, Lennard J. 1995. *Enforcing Normalcy: Disability, Deafness and the Body*. New
York: Verso.

———, ed. 1997. *The Disability Studies Reader*. New York: Routledge.

———. 1999. "Crips Strike Back: The Rise of Disability Studies." *American Literary
History* 11 (3): 500–12.

Erevelles, Nirmala. 2001. "In Search of the Disabled Subject." In Wilson and Lewiecki-Wilson, *Embodied Rhetorics*, 92–111.

Garland-Thomson, Rosemarie. 1994. "Redrawing the Boundaries of Feminist Disability Studies." *Feminist Studies* 20 (3): 583–96.

———, ed. 1996. *Freakery: Cultural Spectacles of the Extraordinary Body*. New York:
New York University Press.

———. 1997. *Extraordinary Bodies: Figuring Physical Disability in American Culture
and Literature*. New York: Columbia University Press.

Kafer, Alison. 1998. "Resistant Bodies: Physical Illness and Disability as Sites of Resistance." Paper presented at the Women's Studies Conference "Fulfilling Possibilities: Women and Girls with Disabilities," 3 October, Southern Connecticut State
University, New Haven, Connecticut.

Linton, Simi. 1998. *Claiming Disability: Knowledge and Identity*. New York: New York
University Press.

Mairs, Nancy. 1996. *Waist-High in the World: A Life among the Nondisabled*. Boston:
Beacon Press.

McRuer, Robert. 2002. "Compulsory Able-Bodiedness and Queer/Disabled Exi-
stence." In *Disability Studies: Enabling the Humanities*, edited by Sharon Snyder,
Brenda Jo Brueggemann, and Rosemarie Garland-Thomson, 88–99. New York:
MLA Press.

————. 2006. *Crip Theory: Cultural Signs of Disability and Queerness*. New York: NYU Press.

Mitchell, David T., and Sharon Snyder, eds. 1997. *The Body and Physical Difference: Discourses of Disability in the Humanities*. Ann Arbor: University of Michigan Press.

Porter, James I. 1997. Foreword to Mitchell and Snyder, *Body and Physical Difference*, xiii–xiv.

Price, Janet, and Margrit Shildrick, eds. 1999a. *Feminist Theory and the Body: A Reader*. New York: Routledge.

————. 1999b. "Breaking the Boundaries of the Broken Body." *Feminist Theory and the Body: A Reader*, 432–44. New York: Routledge.

Quayson, Ato. 1999. "Looking Awry: Tropes of Disability in Post-Colonial Writing." In *Introduction to Contemporary Fiction*, edited by Rod Menghan, 53–68. Cambridge, UK: Cambridge University Press.

Sandahl, Carrie. 1999. "Ahhhh Freak Out! Metaphors of Disability and Femaleness in Performance." *Theatre Topics* 9 (1): 11–30.

Schriempf, Alexa. 2001. "(Re)fusing the Amputated Body: An Interactionist Bridge for Feminism and Disability." *Hypatia* 16 (4):52–79.

Shakespeare, Tom, ed. 1998. *The Disability Reader: Social Science Perspectives*. New York: Cassell.

Siebers, Tobin. 2008. *Disability Theory*. Ann Arbor: University of Michigan Press.

Stocker, Susan S. 2001. "Problems of Embodiment and Problematic Embodiment." *Hypatia* 16 (3): 30–55.

Wendell, Susan. 1996. *The Rejected Body: Feminist Philosophical Reflections on Disability*. New York: Routledge.

————. 2001. "Unhealthy Disabled: Treating Chronic Illnesses as Disabilities." *Hypatia* 16 (4): 17–33.

Wilchins, Riki Anne. 1997. *Read My Lips: Sexual Subversion and the End of Gender*. Ithaca, N.Y.: Firebrand Books.

Wilson, James C., and Cynthia Lewiecki-Wilson. 2001. "Disability, Rhetoric, and the Body." *Embodied Rhetorics: Disability in Language and Culture*, 1–24. Carbondale: Southern Illinois University Press.

PART TWO

REFIGURING

LITERATURE

Three

INVISIBLE DISABILITY
Georgina Kleege's Sight Unseen

SUSANNAH B. MINTZ

In a short piece titled "Autobiography as Performative Utterance," Michael Bérubé writes, "the conditions under which certain authors claim the authority of autobiography are sometimes exceptionally hostile to the claim" (2000, 341). Making a link between slave narrative and the life writing of people with cognitive disabilities, Bérubé argues that self-representation serves the radical and political function of declaring a self worthy to be named—asserting, in effect, that it *does* matter who speaks and that the speaker is a legitimate self—which in turn disrupts the kinds of dehumanizing ideologies that equate difference with unworthiness, inferiority, and lack.[1] For a woman with some form of disability, the act of writing herself into a textual identity entails combating a triple erasure—from the long history of autobiography in the West, which has typically excluded women's experience from the kinds of life stories deemed worthy of recording, as well as from able-bodied culture and feminist theory, in which disability has tended to be stigmatized as a sign of failure and inadequacy, or ignored altogether as a meaningful component of identity. It is from a position of cultural invisibility, then, that the female writer of disability narrative struggles toward a "performative utterance" that will announce the authority of her multiply unspeakable self.

What follows is a reading of Georgina Kleege's *Sight Unseen,* a recent collection of autobiographical essays that "do not pretend to offer a definitive view of anyone's blindness" but her own (1999, 5). Yet Kleege's text is far from solipsistically narrow in its discussion of vision. To the contrary, *Sight Unseen* is more an indictment of negative representations of the blind, and of cultural mythologies about perception, eye contact, and "normal" behavior, than it is the story of one woman's experience of losing her sight. Indeed, *Sight Unseen* minimizes autobiographical detail in favor of cultural and semiotic analysis. Kleege's investment lies more in deciphering how people see than in telling her own story, and she thus subordinates her childhood and "interior" experience to her adult, active participation in a sighted world. Arguing that the linear structure of conventional blindness autobiographies reaffirms the idea that blindness can be separated from the "self" as an affliction one overcomes—a narrative of transcendence and resolution that "presupposes that blindness is somehow outside oneself" (4)—Kleege suggests that the radical intent of *Sight Unseen* is to claim blindness as constitutive of identity in ways that are surprisingly, unfamiliarly positive. In this sense, her own book is a "'coming out' narrative" (5) that also "renegotiate[s]," in Caren Kaplan's words, "the relationship between personal identity and the world, between personal and social history" (1998, 212).

The three sections of *Sight Unseen* proceed from an opening discussion of "Blindness and Culture" through "Blind Phenomenology" to final essays on "Voice, Texture, [and] Identity." In one way this sequence seems to move steadily "inward," ever closer to some "authentic" Kleege. But I would argue that the trajectory of Kleege's text is in fact deliberately anti-linear, nonprogressive, and fragmentary in ways that underscore the discontinuity between normative parameters for gendered subjectivity and the lived particulars of anomalous corporeality.[2] *Sight Unseen* charts a mock journey or quest that presents the self not as an isolate individual triumphing over cultural forces, but rather as something one accumulates in contact with the stuff of culture. Gesturing toward, and subsequently rupturing, the typical life-path structure of men's self-writing, *Sight Unseen* exposes what is usually left out of canonical autobiographies—influences of cultural mythology, expectations of a "normal" body, triumphs of mind and will over the body and the circumstances of birth. Culture is thus not so much a secondary background against which Kleege's singular subjectivity stands out in high relief, but rather the very material from which she explicitly fashions a sense of self.

Feminist disability scholars have pointed out that mainstream feminism's critique of patriarchal myths of women as essentially sexual and maternal ignores the fact that ableist culture also deems women with disabilities to be essentially asexual and non-maternal. From this perspective, when a woman represents herself in terms of the confluence of disability and erotic and/or maternal experience, her narrative can be openly resistant in ways that an ableist, feminist reading may mistakenly disregard. Compared to recent work by such writers as Nancy Mairs, Lucy Grealy, Cheryl Marie Wade, and Anne Finger, however, *Sight Unseen* is striking for its exclusion of any direct discussion of how Kleege feels about her sexuality or "femininity," or about how her blindness might intersect with traditional female roles of mother or caretaker.[3] *Sight Unseen* follows a different path: its parameters are neither a masculinist public domain, a feminized domestic sphere, nor the explicitly contestatory and sexualized space carved out by many women writers of disability.

Yet Kleege's suppression of personal revelation serves an equally gendered argument highlighting the dynamics of gazing. Whereas performative displays of disability and sexuality in work by other women force reevaluation of normative conceptions of beauty, desire, and "legitimate" female identity, Kleege makes specularity the spectacle, putting vision itself, rather than her body, on display. Implicitly invoking women's cultural position as passive and preoccupied with their own appearance—what other disabled women might deconstruct by actively examining their bodies in terms of the social relations that define them as abnormal—Kleege authorizes her blind gaze to wrench apart the equation of seeing with knowing, exploding conventional binaries of male and female, subject and object, seer and seen. When she asks, "Incompetent, dependent, potentially unruly, sexually deviant—is this really how the sighted see the blind?" (1999, 57), Kleege might also be speaking of how patriarchal culture views women. Her project thus becomes a doubled act of dismantling what Susan Wendell has referred to as the "disciplines of normality" (1996, 88).

If inhabiting a world that privileges sighted men requires Kleege to disidentify with herself as blind and as a woman, then writing herself into a blind identity means having to create new and acceptable versions of blindness that contest inhibiting stereotypes—or as Wendell puts it, the "young, healthy, professionally successful blind woman who has 'overcome' her handicap with education" (1996, 12). To an extent, Kleege actually conforms to this image. Yet her exploration of blindness and vision seeks not to prove equality with the sighted nor to announce her triumph over impairment, but rather to dislocate her readers, to complicate the grounds on which dominant assumptions about blindness are constructed, and to provoke readers toward a more subtle awareness of the gendered relationship between vision and power.

In the first sentence of *Sight Unseen,* Kleege announces, "Writing this book made me blind" (1999, 1). Such a proclamation establishes an important framework for this collection of personal essays, which investigate representations of blindness and sight through the conceptual lens of Kleege's own partial vision. The book's opening gambit invokes an entrenched cultural prejudice that reads illness as a kind of punishment, a sign of mental weakness or moral lapse. The implication that Kleege might have "made herself sick" by writing links her visual impairment with the unfeminine self-indulgence of art, even as it seems designed to instigate readers' pity for her diminished capacity. The author's physical limitation becomes the mark of her psychological overreaching and the proof of her audience's difference from her. Yet Kleege summons the myth of disability as otherness and failure only to disrupt it. Declared legally blind after experiencing macular degeneration at the age of eleven, Kleege did not literally "go blind" during the composition of the book, but her statement underscores the relationship between self-creation and writing that is a key component of disability narratives by women. Kleege suggests that only through the construction of *Sight Unseen* was she able to discover new, positive meanings for blindness and thus to claim a blind identity on her own definitional terms. Calling herself "blind" is not a capitulation to enfeeblement or helplessness, but rather an act of defiant self-re-creation.

Kleege's story foregrounds the conflictedness of female disabled subjectivity in a culture that privileges male able-bodied independence, the paradox of having to accept marginalized status along with the pressure to conform and perform "normally." The internalized stigma of blindness, Kleege argues—the "burden of negative connotations and dreaded associations"—encourages blind people "to sham sight" through technology and adaptation (19), even as those very efforts are reminders of their failure to meet culturally agreed-upon designations of normality. Kleege writes that as her own vision began to deteriorate as a child, she learned quickly to disguise her difficulty with reading books and blackboards and recognizing distant objects by mimicking the body gestures, the tone of voice, even the facial expressions associated with sightedness. She thus raises questions about how a culture determines the limits of "normal" behavior, appearance, or physical ability and about how we understand and experience illnesses that do not render a person obviously or visibly disabled. Though Kleege's visual acuity is less than 20/200 (the barrier of legal blindness), she is nonetheless able to "pas[s] as sighted" in certain social situations (12); at the same time, she calls herself "imperfectly blind" (150), suggesting that what sight she has actually debars her from full participation in the category of blindness. In this way Kleege's liminal condition shows us how the boundaries of identity are both highly arbitrary and easily disturbed.

Perhaps more importantly, *Sight Unseen* confronts a sighted reader's complacent trust in certitudes of perception by situating the so-called norm on the margins of Kleege's own visual experience. Her descriptions of what her eyes perceive and how she actually looks at an object challenge a normative sense of the "right way" (96) to see. Because her form of macular degeneration leaves a very large "blind spot" in the middle of her vision, Kleege must "move [her] attention off center, viewing the world askance" (104). She holds objects an inch from her face, sliding her eyes from one edge to another in order to see with her peripheral vision. She stands "a foot" away from (93), then edges "closer and closer" to (94), huge canvasses in museums. Her "flawed vision" (147) necessitates a kind of literal "close reading" or Nietzschean slow seeing—two of the text's controlling metaphors. All of this slowing down and moving in defies the notion that "seeing is both instantaneous and absolute" or that "[s]ight provides instantaneous access to reality" (96). If the only proper way to see "is to take something in at a glance and possess it whole, comprehending all its complexities" (96), Kleege suggests, then her sidelong way of looking, "circumambulat[ing]" (104) objects, becomes an ideological metaphor for displacing the eyes as the source of power and eyesight as a guarantor of knowledge and identity.

Kleege's description of various ways of seeing calls attention to the gendered dynamics of looking. The objectifying gaze that purports to guarantee wholeness—long associated with the mechanisms of patriarchal power and manifested in the blazons of Petrarchan poets, in the Renaissance penchant for dissection, and in the scopophilic certitudes of Enlightenment philosophy, Freudian, and later Lacanian, psychoanalysis—occludes even as it anticipates a woman's returning look. So thoroughly is subjectivity bound up with vision that the possibility of a woman looking back has provoked fears of castration, a dismantling or disabling of coherent male identity, even as the so-called female gaze has been said to reclaim the power to determine subjectivity. But Kleege goes beyond merely inverting a gendered specular exchange. Introducing herself as the legitimate subject of a manner of looking that Slavoj Žižek might define as "awry,"[4] Kleege achieves something more complex than simply authorizing herself as a viewer; instead, she tears down patriarchal *and* feminist trust in vision.

Neither the freak-show spectacle who must protest her basic humanity to readers (what Kleege describes as the "conventional goal of blind autobiography" [1999, 3]) nor a hero whose will and fortitude defeat the defects of the body, Kleege repeatedly focuses her attention on her readers, as if staring directly at them: "Look at me when I'm talking to you," she demands. "Do you really see all that you say? . . . Aren't you projecting your own expectations, interpretations, or desires onto my blank eyes?" (138). In one way such provocations empower Kleege as the origin of language and meaning: her vision is panoptical (she knows where one's gaze is directed) and capable of undetected spying; she can control where one looks and even what impression one might have of the view. But the display of monological—and perhaps Medusan—visual power is deceptive; Kleege's manner of looking moves her, and her readers, to the margins, where meanings are discovered rather than imposed. *Sight Unseen* redefines the meaning of blindness not so much by attempting to establish an equivalency between vision and blindness, but rather by "disabling" sightedness itself, undermining its epistemological stability. Kleege uses her gradual, tactile, relational way of seeing to illustrate that "there is no one way to look . . . no optimum vantage point or viewing condition" (147). Hers is a gaze transformed, a look whose approach to the stuff of the world, and whose sense of its own power, contests both masculinist and feminist formulations of the gaze.

In the first several essays of *Sight Unseen,* Kleege complicates gendered stereotypes about blindness and vision by demonstrating her facility for a variety of "sighted" activities. In "Blind Nightmares" and "In Oedipus' Shadow," Kleege presents herself as a skilled semiotician, deftly unpacking representations of blindness in literature and film. In "The Mind's Eye" she details her penchant for art museums and her unusual way of looking at paintings. In each of these instances, Kleege transforms a conventional understanding of what it means to be blind or sighted: How has a "legally blind" woman seen the movies and read the books she describes? What exactly does she "see" at the museum? Where other women writers tend to generate a critique of dominant paradigms of disability strictly through personal experience, Kleege begins her story with an extended interpretation of culture's stories about blindness and vision. Beginning with Oedipus and ranging through visual media as divergent as the novel *Jane Eyre,* the 1967 film *Wait until Dark,* and Monet's *Water Lilies,* Kleege situates herself as just another looker, a participant in the visual world, a teacher as well as a partner in the project of "seeing." In short, she makes us viewers *together,* eliding herself as the object of our attention while simultaneously using her visual perspective to argue for the limitations of sight as one's sole or primary means of knowing the world. Kleege stretches the limits of identification with her readers, avoiding the dual seductions of voyeurism and sympathy; indeed, for much of *Sight Unseen* we are not looking at Georgina Kleege at all, but rather at habits of looking themselves.

The cumulative and strategic effect of Kleege's discussion of movies and literature through two chapters clearly dissociates her from characterizations of the blind as "supernatural or subhuman, alien or animal," "different" and "dangerous" (28), and of blindness as symbolic of "fragility and helplessness" (55), "divine retribution" (71), or "the complete loss of personal, sexual, and political power" (69). But displaying her dexterity as a cultural critic allows Kleege not simply to protest the invalidity of such negative stereotypes; more to the point, she *proves* through her own performance of intellectual analysis their single-minded and reductive attitudes about loss of sight. Kleege makes her case less through personal outcry than through a scholarly marshaling of evidence, dismantling "facile assumptions about blindness" (65) by exposing the underlying cultural anxieties that motivate those assumptions in the first place.

Narratives about blindness "are not about blindness at all," Kleege suggests (58), but rather about a need to guarantee the privileged status of the sighted—a need that in turn emerges from fears about the fragility and unpredictability of embodied identity. In what Susan Wendell calls "the flight from the rejected body," disability signifies all that must be carefully guarded against by normative corporeality: "tragic loss, weakness, passivity, dependency, helplessness, shame, and global incompetence" (1996, 85, 63). Kleege's staging of herself as an interpreter of myths of blindness thus serves as a specific refutation of the kinds of associations Wendell enumerates; far from weak, passive, or incompetent, Kleege takes charge—she surveys the ideological territory, she infiltrates, she squares off against an imagined reader's resistance to any suggestion that sightedness is less than immediate and unfailing. "Why not break this absolute dependence you have on your eyesight?" Kleege queries (1999, 32). "The sighted can be so touchingly naive about vision" (96).

Positioned as *Sight Unseen*'s beginning, Kleege's deconstructive examination of blindness in film and literature deflects attention away from Kleege herself—from the "personal" or intimate details one tends to associate with the autobiographical mode for women—to such an extent that we lose "sight" of Kleege altogether, at least temporarily. We may forget that her own vision is at stake here, too—even that she herself is "blind," so thoroughly do we associate reading and moviegoing with sightedness. Not only do these chapters demand, therefore, that we reexamine stereotypes about the blind; perhaps more pointedly, Kleege also puts pressure on the category of *sightedness*. "Blindness"—as a trope, a symbol, an event that must be interpreted and invested with meaning—is situated in the culture rather than the individual author, and Kleege further insists that whatever diminishment a blind person experiences is a function of social relations rather than personal insufficiency. Rejecting sustained autobiographical narrative at the start of her text, Kleege thus enacts on the page the sort of "favorable depiction" of blind people she fantasizes might someday be possible in film: "blindness would become invisible," Kleege writes, because "a 'realistic' blind person on screen would have so mastered the skills of blindness that there would be no need to draw attention to them" (57). Kleege's phrasing here—the "skills of blindness"—dissolves impaired vision into just another form of normal behavior. To speak of the skills of blindness rather than the skills of seeing disturbs the hierarchical binary, figuring blindness not as tragic diminishment but as something anyone could learn to do, even as a kind of expertise or virtuosity. Indeed, Kleege encourages her readers to "practice" blindness, as a way of decentering sight and relinquishing their monological—and ultimately anxiety-driven—grip on vision as one's primary mode of contact with, and sense of rootedness within, one's environment.

Something more overtly gendered is also at work in Kleege's display of her proficiency as a reader of text. Comparing male and female blind characters, she writes, "While movies occasionally allow blind men some instructive wit and wisdom, blind women are nothing but need. . . . Their helplessness is surpassed only by their passivity and desperation" (51). What's more, the "obsessive self-preoccupation" expected of blind women in cinema would "label a sighted woman as a dangerous vamp" (55). Such statements remind us that if patriarchal ideology tends to pinion women generally in the paradox of emotional immaturity and sexual threat, blind women may have an even more vexed relationship to the self-appraisal of autobiography. At the start of the book, Kleege recounts the behavior of her students when she first informs them that she's blind: they stare at her, "Eyeing [her] askance," gazes "intent" (9–10). Identifying herself as blind, as she does in the first sentence of *Sight Unseen,* invites and perhaps amplifies the objectifying looks of an ableist, male-centered culture. That Kleege looks so consistently *outward* frustrates readers' desire to "see" her, thus refusing the kinds of stereotypes that encode blind women in film as at once frail and childlike, egotistical and sexually voracious. The blind characters Kleege explores (most often the creations of male writers and directors) may require the assistance of male heroes to rescue and protect them, but it is Kleege herself in *Sight Unseen* who seeks to "save" sighted readers from cultural misapprehensions about blind identity. Kleege is thus a woman who sees much more than herself being seen. Keenly aware that blindness makes women both "unsightly" (54) and "tempting to men" precisely because they can't "look back" (56), Kleege-as-author looks awry, eyes the world askance, and deprives her readers of any sure position from which to ascertain the "truth" of her gendered and disabled experience.

When we enter a Matisse exhibit with Kleege, her unique way of seeing comes more fully to the fore of her narrative. Kleege describes her behavior in museums in highly physical terms, as a kind of dance: "I perform a slow minuet before each painting, stepping forward and back, sweeping my gaze from edge to edge" (95). Such a procedure seems sequential and partial, resulting not in the instant intake, the global impression that the sighted claim to experience, but something more interactive, involving the whole body's motion in the process of looking. As such, Kleege's sight is neither complacently unquestioned nor singular, but rather follows feminist theorizing about embodied identity toward a more partial and relational form of vision. Because she proceeds so methodically, Kleege forces us to slow down, too, and to reconsider the process of making meaning out of what we see. To see slowly resists the idea that we "see" wholly and instinctively, that through seeing we achieve mastery over the phenomena of the world. From up close, Kleege observes details that casual viewing "overlooks"—texture, thickness, size, color. "The most 'realistic' eye" in a painting "may be no more than a swirl of brown with a thin comma of white laid over," Monet's water lilies are "crusty" rather than "liquid," and abstract paintings have "depth and form" from two inches away (94). Reading such descriptions, we begin to imagine what Kleege sees and to remember our own impressions of what painting looks like, an overlap that serves less to reify Kleege's identity as "impaired" than to upend our belief in a single, correct way of looking—always to be understood as a correct way of "being."

Kleege, then, is what Shakespeare might have called the master-mistress of vision and blindness alike, both instructor and student of the dynamics of looking and interpreting what can be seen. Cautious about positioning herself as an "instructive spectacle, useful to everyone but [her]self" (90), she keeps readerly attention focused on the ambiguities and deceptions of sight generally, not the anguish or struggle of losing her sight in particular.[5] Yet there is one "sighted" activity in which Kleege emphatically cannot participate: eye contact. Where *Sight Unseen* starts from the premise that Kleege "find[s] it easy to imagine what it's like to be sighted" (3) because the dominant culture—from infrastructure to ideology—is so fully oriented toward the sighted, the chapter titled "Here's Looking at You" admits to feeling "confus[ed]" (122) by the "mystery" (124) of eye contact. Macular degeneration makes it impossible for Kleege to pick up facial details or even to perceive the totality of a person's face in a single glance. "When I try to look someone in the eyes," she explains, "he disappears" (124). Since the same "off-center gaze" that troubles her fellow museum-goers makes her appear "shy, distracted, suspicious, bored, or untrustworthy" (124), Kleege "fake[s]" eye contact (138), aiming her eyes and face in the right direction, "perform[ing] tricks" (126) with her eyes that mimic the concentrated intimacy, the assertiveness or honesty associated with a direct look.[6]

That Kleege's experience of seeing and feeling "nothing" could be interpreted as "the most significant visual exchange" (125) with another person throws into question the privileged cultural and theoretical status accorded an exchange of looks. "Here's Looking at You" repudiates the idea that because they are "excluded from [the] constant, kinetic interchange" of eye contact, the blind "must take the sighted's word" for its importance and trustworthiness (131). Kleege focuses her discussion on what eye contact is believed to reveal—the "truth" of a person's psychical or ontological state—as well as on the contextual data that contribute to our assessment of the "genuine" emotion allegedly communicated by the eyes. What the sighted attribute solely to eye-to-eye understanding, for instance, Kleege explains as a function of the entire face and body: stretched skin, widened eyelids, light reflected off of the eyeballs, furrowed brows and twitching lips. Again, the effect shifts the reader's perspective away from the eyes and onto what surrounds them. Compared to the specular exactness claimed by the sighted, Kleege admits she "focus[es] too much on the peripheral details" (128) to appreciate fully the significance of eye contact. Yet what lies at the periphery of vision is precisely Kleege's concern in *Sight Unseen*. Calling attention to the stage of looking—all the details from body posture to setting to desire and projection—Kleege suggests the presumed guarantees of visual contact are, on the one hand, partial and gradual and, on the other, comprised of myriad pieces of information that *supplement* what the eyes alone exhibit. Thus, by conveying to her readers all that presses into a scene of looking from the surround, Kleege explodes any idea that we have access to, that we can "know," the other's "interior" just by looking into his or her eyes.

As a result of what Kleege can't see, the essay concentrates on what she knows, transforming a putative lack into a cognitive advantage. "Here's Looking at You" ranges from the physiology of "the visual system" (128), to the artificial strategies (air-brushing, dilating eye drops) employed by actors and fashion models to maximize the specular effects of their appearance on film, to the sighted habit of employing metaphors that "point to the eyes . . . as the site of all significant experience" (131). At the same time, however, Kleege also repeats such words and phrases as "apparently" (134, 137), "I assume" (133), "I'd like to see" (132), "I'm not sure" (134), "I've heard tell" (136), even "I miss the point" (129). These terms seem to emphasize the cultural displacement of a disabled woman who is assumed to be "not in full possession of [her] reasoning powers" (Keith 1996, 86); as one who can't make eye contact, Kleege doesn't "get it," and thus she speaks tentatively and seems intellectually blunted, out of the social loop.

The fundamental pressure point here is less blindness than sighted arrogance about eye contact, with all the psychological, erotic, epistemological charge of that phrase held under scrutiny. Kleege situates herself in a sighted milieu where stories are trafficked as truth, a world where people uncritically "tell" the appropriate narratives of cultural myth. The doubt and uncertainty implied by "apparently" or "assume" pertains not at all to Kleege's limited understanding, but instead levels the author's skepticism against what people insist they can discern from the eyes. By figuring the certitudes of eye contact as the product of a kind of rumor mill, Kleege interrogates one of sighted culture's most sacred forms of accessing another's true self, refusing to take for granted—to take anyone's word for—what constitutes meaning, significant experience, or identity.

A discussion of the local, interpersonal event of eye contact, then, becomes a critique of patriarchal technologies of understanding, of culturally sanctioned mechanisms of interpretation and assessment. Kleege foregrounds the way in which sighted ideology reduces knowledge and meaning to the single action of seeing, wholly subsuming the participation of bodies, expectations, and desires into the mythologized behavior of eyes. She concedes an evolutionary and biological basis for the importance of vision (citing, for example, mother-infant mirroring and the predatory advantage of forward-directed eyes), but she refutes the symbolized, romanticized, poeticized assumptions about eye contact that deny legitimacy to other forms of making contact with the world. The sheer "diversity" (1999, 136) of the stories Kleege recounts about the impact of eye contact reveals more, finally, about sighted people's belief in its authority than about any real access it has to "reality." Perhaps more pointedly, Kleege makes clear that social codes governing visual interaction are embedded in patriarchal mythology: whether she is looking at photographs of fashion models, reading self-defense literature that cautions women against eye contact with strangers, or pondering romantic clichés about love at first sight, Kleege links the cultural privileging of vision with both physical and discursive violence. Yet if power cannot be said to reside in one's ability to see, as *Sight Unseen* endeavors to prove, then power itself must become open to reclamation, and identities constructed within certain cultural configurations of power are available for rewriting, revision. Kleege performs her own version of eye contact in this chapter. "Pull the wool off your eyes," she commands her readers. "Tell me what you see" (138).

If it is possible to see in a different manner—off center, askew, up close, and side-to-side—*Sight Unseen* also argues we can "see" with a different part of the body. To contest sight as culture's dominant mode of knowing (a structure that necessarily assumes the blind as less than fully human or grants them supererogatory and highly idealized "insight"), Kleege defocuses the eyes entirely and shifts to the hands, examining various forms of touch as an additional metaphor for relating to the world. Describing her father, for example, an artist known for large-scale sculpture, Kleege relates an early memory of him helping her weld together pieces of metal: "My hand moves inside my father's hand. His index finger lifts and points. I look where he points. I draw the flame to the point. . . . Like most of our conversations, this one was essentially wordless, conducted hand-to-hand, my small hand inside his" (163). The scene accumulates images of both real and symbolic connection—the fused scraps of metal, one small hand clasped within another, daughter to father, human to metal, idea to "form and dimension" (163)—that reflect a central preoccupation in *Sight Unseen*. Being "hand in hand" with the world refuses a subject position defined by static hierarchies of gender and health that equate women with receptive passivity, physical difference with helplessness.

Though she was not yet blind in the scene above, the metaphor of welding shapes one of *Sight Unseen's* central propositions: American cultural myths of self-reliance and isolate identity privilege male able-bodiedness and condemn intersubjective relations, caretaking, and disability as signs of—or thresholds onto—regressive dependency. In contrast, Kleege argues for reciprocity and mutuality, for "conversations" between people and between people and things in the world that unite body and idea, hands and eyes, words and movement. Kleege suggests that communication does not derive solely from sight (indeed, it may not even require sight) and that it is only through the mutual interaction of embodied selves that the myriad seams of reality and identity stay "fast and lasting" (163). Relationality, then, for Kleege, informs everything she does—from seeing and reading to teaching, writing, making art—but in a way that challenges reductive models of female identity as selflessly oriented toward others and others' feelings.[7] Importantly, the scene of welding with her father emblematizes a relational experience in which meaning emerges from active partnership rather than domination or mastery.

The quintessential manifestation of this dialectical phenomenology, the most potent instance of "hand in hand" contact with information and meaning, is Kleege's decision to learn braille, a process she begins only as an adult. Reading braille is profoundly physical, involving the whole self from fingertips and arms, through the shoulders and into the head, brain, and mind. Reading this way, Kleege reactivates her body in communication with the world, empowering her hands in the place of her eyes. But she does more than propose hand reading as secondary compensation for the loss of sight, and she "returns" to a body that is signified not only as different, but also, in fact, *deviant* (this move is at once literal, textual, and theoretical, as Kleege turns from the more intellectualized chapters of the first part of *Sight Unseen* to chapters that foreground her corporeal self).[8] "Close reading" had once signified Kleege's literal proximity to a computer screen or a printed page—she describes herself as "the physical embodiment of close reading" (198)—and therefore measured the distance between Kleege and "normally" sighted individuals, whose eyes "process as many as a dozen [characters] at a time" compared to Kleege's three (199).

But despite her wry analogy to the habit of "dwell[ing]" (197) closely over textual detail (Kleege was a Yale undergraduate and writes that she "felt physically well-suited, if not predestined, to be a close reader" [198]), the liberating possibilities afforded her by braille have little to do with New Critical interpretive practice or ideology. The tactile reading of braille allows Kleege to rediscover a way of being in the body that struggling to read with her eyes had forced her to relinquish. With her eyes, Kleege is an inefficient reader; with braille she reads more quickly, with less strain and greater mobility. With her hands at work, Kleege can move *away* from the page, letting her body uncoil, stretch out and relax: "The frantic uncertainty of reading print was gone. And there was no pain. . . . I was serene, floating" (204). Moreover, hand reading has the unexpected effect of disguising Kleege's visual impairment. Comparing the logistical problems of giving public readings by sight to the ease of reading by braille, Kleege writes that "[her] blindness is less visible to [her] audience" (227). In a paradoxical way, reading braille makes Kleege both more and less "blind"; it is one of the "skills" of blindness that indicates her difference from the sighted world even as it strenuously resists negative connotations of failure or inadequacy.

Reading braille carries an even more political valence in that it marks identity: "the way we read defines who we are" (217). To choose braille—reading with the fingers, not the eyes—is to seem to regress to a benighted state of incapacity and to openly identify oneself as disabled, to repudiate the promise of low-vision aids and thus of "progress"; but it is also to reject sightedness altogether and to defiantly claim disinterest in trying to be or seem "normal." Particularly because Kleege does have some sight, because she can, however "imperfectly," read with her eyes, her decision to learn braille inspires resistance and anxiety from those who are threatened by her apparent indifference to a sighted way of life: "braille is a part of the dim and dire past, not the desirable present," Kleege explains. "My desire to learn braille cast me as an eccentric Luddite" (215). The issue is less old-fashioned recalcitrance about technology, of course, than it is the choice of "blind" behavior over sighted, a willingness to "be seen" as blind when gadgets and machinery could allow her to mimic the practices of the sighted.

Kleege makes the point that reading braille has to do with more than just convenience, physical comfort, access to materials, or lower costs; a far more confrontational desire to challenge the dominance of the norm is at stake here, a call to widen the array of ways of being in the world and of articulating subjectivity. "The first time I read my name in braille," Kleege remarks, "made me muse on identity again: 'This is me in braille'" (217–18). Reading braille thus effects a shift in Kleege's sense of herself as a person and as blind; far from confining her to a state of diminishment, braille is generative, creating new possibilities, surprising her with the discovery of an unfamiliar but no less legitimate self. Braille enables Kleege to move back and forth across the divide between ability and disability, to transgress and thus to destabilize that boundary. "Me in braille" is just one more self, one more version of Georgina Kleege.

The intersection of feminist and disability theory seems obvious here. Kleege "respells" her name, and thus herself, both in braille and then in the pages of *Sight Unseen*. Layering text on text, she claims multiple identities that depend on particular languages she knows, some of which exclude her sighted readers; "she" becomes mobile and elusive.[9] But at the same time, her braille identity, no less than the self she creates in her book, has no meaning apart from her physical condition: the material reality of the body produces the discursive play. Kleege's representation of herself in a language she must reclaim from the margins of sighted culture effects a breach with what Leigh Gilmore has called "a patriarchal regime of names" (2001, 124); but unlike writers whose self-representational project indulges the ambiguity of signification at the expense of bodily specificity, Kleege's act of naming and identifying herself ("This is me in braille") is rooted in the material condition of her eyes. Despite its origin in the gradual loss of her sight, reading herself in braille is thus a form of gain for Kleege, one further implement with which she can traverse, and thereby denaturalize, the boundaries of disability and health, passivity and agency, patriarchal authority and the silencing of women.

There *is* a kind of patrilineal narrative at work in *Sight Unseen,* but it is a revisionary one that problematizes fatherly law. "Up Close, In Touch" recounts Kleege's pursuit not only of braille but also of the life of Louis Braille himself, including an odyssey to the Braille museum at his birthplace in Coupvray, France. Kleege details the accident that blinded Braille as a child and his later perfection, as a teenager at the Paris Institute for the Young Blind, of a system of coded dots, and acknowledges her admiration for Braille's "strength of character" (1999, 225), his willingness to take enormous risks in the face of institutional resistance to adopting his new system (a resistance ultimately due, Kleege implies, to sighted fear about the ramifications of empowering the blind with the ability to read). Identifying with Braille because he "stood up to sighted authority and said, 'What you offer is good. What I offer is better'" (225), Kleege in turn indicts her own culture's oppressive myths of normalcy and impairment. And by ending with Braille's story, *Sight Unseen* wraps itself back to the rhetorical mode with which it began: making use of cultural representations of blindness in order to uncover the power dynamics and ideological anxieties that contribute to their perpetuation.

Braille's life narrative becomes significant at this particular juncture in the text for several reasons. By emphasizing Braille's inventiveness, lingering over the crafty subterfuge whereby students utilized his system despite the threat of expulsion from the school, Kleege implicitly counters the stereotypes of blind helplessness that hindered Louis Braille and his peers. The story also provides a historical context for Kleege's insistence on learning braille, her own refusal to fully accommodate herself to the dominance of the visual. Braille's system, and his insistence on its usefulness, resonates with Kleege's own project in *Sight Unseen;* she, too, defies cultural authority by telling an alternative story of blind identity, by creating a new language with which to articulate a blind and female subject. As we read Kleege's discovery of Braille and his refusal to accept defeat in the face of cultural pressures against his new language, we have been situated in Kleege's own position, witnessing *her* invention of a new vocabulary that spells the world and herself within it.[10] And she powerfully reminds us that no identity is ever unattached to others in the world; far from superseding her voice or story, Braille's narrative is adamantly Kleege's—she is the mediator, translator, bilingual interpreter, legatee of the freedom of braille and creator thereby of her own new story.

Kleege's effort to locate this alternative father figure is juxtaposed to what she reveals about her relationship with her own father, the only intimate one to figure prominently in *Sight Unseen.* The text devotes a chapter to him, titled "A Portrait of the Artist by His Blind Daughter." Given that Kleege is so circumspect about other significant relationships (her husband, Nick, and her mother, also an artist, are mentioned but do not factor as "characters" to nearly the same degree), this singling out of the father seems noteworthy and motivated by two important and intertwined thematic issues: patriarchal authority and the broken body of the father. Kleege states that she "inherited [her] flawed vision" (149) from her grandmother, who developed the more common form of age-related macular degeneration, and that the linchpin of this connection is her father, through whom the "defective gene" passes (150). These two other impaired bodies establish a familial legacy of responding to illness in ways that reinforce the agon of mind and body, defining consciousness as if it were at the mercy of an unruly body—unless it can be subdued through enormous force of will.

Kleege explicitly describes her grandmother as a hypochondriac who used illness "to manipulate the people around her" (149). Partially sighted, like Kleege—or "imperfectly blind"—the grandmother was suspected of "faking" incapacity, of disguising how *capable* she actually was, so that her health problems became a sign of what was assumed to be psychological weakness. The father had "doubts about the severity of his mother's blindness" and read physical impairment as proof that she was "dependent, fearful, and needy" (150). This resentment of and resistance to his mother's ailments is bound up with Kleege's father's own childhood infirmities—asthma and other respiratory problems—and his mother's anxiety about the severity of these conditions, which Kleege describes as "almost completely debilitating" (151). Not only did Kleege's father learn to suspect sickness in his mother as deceptive and manipulative, then, but also to deny physical limitation in himself. Kleege writes that he deliberately transformed himself into "an extremely athletic adolescent" (151) and specifically links the scale and muscularity of her father's artwork to his determination to overcome any vestige of the "sickly" child that his mother feared he was (and, we are to assume, very nearly produced in him).

Kleege's own vision problems are thus shaped by an environment in which women's bodies are viewed as traitorous, their illnesses doubted as inherently fraudulent, and in which men learn to define selfhood as a triumphant transcendence of physical limitation. In the Kleege family, the body becomes a source of falsehood and denial, demonized as an instrument of interpersonal treachery or suppressed as an obstruction to proper gendered behavior and parental approval. Kleege admits that she internalized a sense of guilt about her "flawed vision" (150) and exaggerated her self-sufficiency to protect her father from the bad feelings associated with her "defect" (150), as well as his sense of personal inadequacy or defectiveness: "If I could preserve the illusion of normalcy, I would remain unflawed" (150).[11] If Kleege's father's relationship with his mother is inflected by suspicion, Kleege's with her father serves as an index of how disabled women often experience their anomalous bodies as obstacles to specifically *male* approval and desire.

Whereas her father's effort to deny bodily weakness merely reiterates masculinist norms of singularity and strength, Kleege's similar effort signifies a problematic association between denial of self and the need to please an authoritative father. Kleege's father renounces his illness to move away from his mother (presumably heightening her worry and therefore linking health and autonomy with repudiation of the mother); Kleege disguises her illness to move *toward* her father, assuaging *his* feelings of guilt and subsuming her needs into his. When she says her father "resisted any impulse he might have felt to disable [her] with paternal protection," or her blindness "never limited his expectations of what [she] could do or become" (151), such claims seem somehow disingenuous, particularly because Kleege also says her father had a kind of morbid curiosity about her ability to "mask [her] lack of sight" (151). Although the father may have respected and stimulated Kleege's intellect, his fascination for her ability to "fake" sight—for the "artifice" of healthiness—nonetheless imposes on Kleege an explicit association between intimacy and normalcy. Kleege writes that because "complaining" about her condition "would only make [her] more troublesome and less lovable" (207), she impersonates sightedness: "it was . . . easier to pretend that I saw what they did" (208); "I could only draw a version of what he saw" (151).[12]

Disability repeats itself not only genetically, then, but also ideologically, circulating in families who take their cues from cultural attitudes toward gender, illness, and generational conflict. "A Portrait of the Artist" shows us that art is similarly relational; it is created not by the "vision" of the solitary genius but rather by the many layerings of social dynamic. The chapter begins by announcing that Kleege and her father "disagree[d]" (139) about eye contact, suggesting again that "Visual experience is relative" (139) and thereby initiating an extended meditation on the various connections between seeing, disability, and art.[13] The father's giant sculptures take shape in direct reaction to Kleege's grandmother's attitudes about bodily ailment. In turn, Kleege's art signifies an explicit break from her father's denial of both his own illness and her blindness. Her way of writing—the fact that she *is* a writer, and not, say, a dancer—emerges from her need to tell the story of what she sees, to intervene into familial and cultural tale-telling about blindness and gender. In its discussion of art, family, and illness, the chapter actively blurs a series of binary oppositions, deconstructing boundaries that separate father from daughter, the disabled from the norm, the literal from the representational. Kleege's "portrait of the artist" is thus also a self-portrait, exploring the familial and social constructions of blindness, health, and gender roles that ultimately inform her identity as a writer.

When Kleege tries to describe exactly what she sees, she paints in words, passages as clearly and lyrically rendered as if she were describing an actual painting or writing poetry.[14] Yet she confesses, "Words are only the restless prowl around and around the thing I want to name, a spiral search from the periphery toward the center. But words are at least a point of departure" (153). In a parallel movement, Kleege describes her father's return to painting late in his life (too weakened from cancer, emphysema, and tuberculosis to continue his metalwork) and the small abstracted pieces that resemble the "splinters of color," the "pulsating shimmer" of Kleege's own vision (159). Words and painting: each is instigated by physical collapse and by a desire to acknowledge both the simultaneous failures and continuity of the body. Kleege writes of one of her father's paintings: "I could hold it over any image and say, 'This is what I see.' It's not quite right. . . . But it's close enough. A point of departure" (159).

The repeated phrase—"a point of departure"—joins words and painting in a shared understanding that no medium can make stable and solid what is ever threatening to come apart. The polysemic swirl around an absent center—words that only haunt the edges, "slashes of color" that "spiral" inward as if into the depths of a "cone" (159)—invoke the same "central black hole" (153) of Kleege's vision, the "frayed" cells of her retinas (155). These metaphorical eddies are precisely the point: there is no transcendental signified, no "truth" at the center that writing, painting, sculpting, or "perfect" vision could ever hold firm. All forms of storytelling, Kleege implies, from family legends to cultural mythology, are only a point of departure, endless beginnings that initiate inconclusive journeys. It is the attempt to travel that matters, Kleege has us understand, and the willingness to keep one's head turned toward the margins, toward the vibrant colors and shapes that occupy the periphery of our vision.[15]

Sight Unseen recounts a profound desire to escape the confines of the body through the performance of "normalcy," and it describes internalizing tenacious cultural messages that link social acceptance with an absence of identifiable difference. Kleege writes, "Offered no means of coping with my condition (the word 'blindness' was to be avoided), I did everything I could to conceal it" (206–207). Importantly, the text also mounts a revolt against the tyranny of the visual, articulating new ways of seeing that, instead of wrenching the afflicted body to culture's limited narratives of gendered or disabled experience, make that body itself the very ground of narrative and subjective authority. *Sight Unseen* at once identifies its author as "disabled" and resists the stigma associated with disability, pointing out how Kleege's physical condition is "different" while calling attention to how difference is embedded in cultural signification, and questioning the fictional and discursive terms by which we understand sameness. In effect, Kleege articulates both sides of the subject-object dynamic, complicating our understanding of what it means to be seen and to look, to be the object of derisive or even appreciative gazes as well as the subject of a presumably masterful vision. Even as she claims a disabled surface (braille, cane), she unravels the binary that would marginalize her as defective. Transforming disability into a meaningful vantage point, Kleege "announce[s] [her] blindness without apology" (227).

NOTES

1. Following Bérubé, I am referring to the end of Foucault's "What Is an Author," in which he asks, "What difference does it make who is speaking?" (qtd. in Bérubé 2000, 343n3). A piece by Kleege on Helen Keller's memoir, *The Story of My Life*, also appears in this special issue of *American Quarterly*. Kleege's work is titled "Helen Keller and 'The Empire of the Normal.'"

2. On the discontinuities of female experience and autobiography, see Shari Benstock (1988). Nancy Mairs writes, "A collection of personal essays stutters—begins, halts, shifts, begins anew," in a way that reflects but also resists the cultural disenfranchisement of the women writer (1994, 79). Also, G. Thomas Couser (1997) discusses various narrative strategies that frame personal stories of disability and illness.

3. I am thinking particularly of Nancy Mairs (1986) and Lucy Grealy (1994), who engage in a far more relentless anatomization of their shame, sexual longings, and acquiescence to patriarchal lessons. See also Anne Finger (1986).

4. Žižek claims, "If we look at a thing straight on, i.e., matter-of-factly, disinterestedly, objectively, we see nothing but a formless spot; the object assumes clear and distinctive features only if we look at it 'at an angle,' i.e., with an 'interested' view, supported, permeated, and 'distorted' by *desire*" (1992, 11–12).

5. A point of comparison may be Jim Knipfel's memoir *Slackjaw* (1999), in which the author's "stupid little story" (xi) about losing his vision to retinitis pigmentosa takes precedence over a cultural analysis of blindness as both a material and discursive condition. Knipfel presents his narrative as an "honest" depiction of how blindness is "a big pain in the ass" (231), a self-consciously ironized send-up not only of his own stubborn resistance to the accoutrements of blindness, but also of nearly everyone else who appears in the book—other blind people, those who assist the blind, women, academics, and so on. While *Slackjaw* was enthusiastically received for its apparently unsentimental depiction of disease, it is nonetheless a troublingly aggressive text that does not, in contrast to *Sight Unseen,* encourage its readers to participate in a thoughtful reevaluation of their own assumptions about vision. Where Kleege ascribes a lyrical and fundamentally intersubjective basis to her (diminished) way of looking, Knipfel's relation to the world seems violent and mean, his descriptions of women often blithely disparaging, and his representation of his own blindness marked by dichotomies of enraged failure and mythic control.

6. Kleege's language of "faking"—like her assertion of "passing"—seems aimed at provoking deep-seated anxieties about "others" breaking down or infiltrating the hegemonic power structure of Western culture. If women can fake orgasm and racial minorities can pass as white, how are stable relationships of sexual and racial mastery to be maintained? The fact that Kleege can "fake" eye contact and thus "pass" as sighted makes her social position a threateningly liminal one, which she rhetorically

maximizes. In a slightly different way, her claim that *Sight Unseen* is a "coming out" story emphasizes not only her solidarity with a group blind identity but also the potential affront that such allegiance might constitute for sighted readers. In each case, Kleege subtly undermines sighted complacency about knowing who Kleege "is" or being able to keep her put.

7. In defense of listening to books on tape, for example, Kleege writes that "reading this way almost always feels like a shared experience. I feel myself not merely a passive audience but engaged in a kind of exchange. Readers are not reading to me; we are reading together. I have a sense of a continuous back-and-forth commentary. . . . This is precisely what confounds the sighted reader who thinks of reading as a private and intensely personal act, a solo flight" (1999, 181). Kleege claims that reading aloud to someone is an "act of generosity that should never be underesteemed" (191).

8. Rosemarie Garland-Thomson distinguishes between "different" and "deviant" (1997, 23).

9. Consider Audre Lorde, offering a "new spelling of [her] name" in her biomythography, *Zami*. Jeanne Perreault's (1995) introductory chapter also discusses the indeterminate "I" of women's autobiography and the political intersections of self-naming and group identification.

10. *Sight Unseen* is available in both braille and on cassette, recorded by Terry Sales.

11. In discussing the intertwinings of her father's art, the family's various ailments, and her relationship with her parents, Kleege repeats the words *flaw, flaws,* and *flawed* seven times in just three pages, as if unwittingly articulating a worry that her father's awareness of her blindness might impede their closeness.

12. A similar sentiment recurs throughout Lucy Grealy's *Autobiography of a Face,* which links the atypical shape of Grealy's face (a sizable portion of her jaw having been removed due to cancer) to being ugly and therefore "unlovable." In contrast, Jim Knipfel's efforts to mask his decreasing eyesight seem directed at guarding his autonomy rather than at retaining affection. Grealy and Kleege discuss their experiences in specifically relational terms; Knipfel speaks in terms of "pride and self-sufficiency," "determination and cold viciousness" (1999, 225, 227), presenting himself as a solitary individual whose encroaching blindness exposes him to the vulnerability of neediness.

13. Kleege reveals ambivalence about whether her father's vision can be relied upon; she both appreciates the "unfailing accuracy" of his artist's gaze (1999, 143) and acknowledges his inability to perceive the extent of her impairment. She writes, "I had to believe that my father was someone who could read the language of the eyes" (139). Yet the "language" of the eyes is under erasure throughout *Sight Unseen*, its validity—or at least its stability—thoroughly contested. In fact, as the ensuing essay makes clear, Kleege and her father share an understanding that seeing has as much to do with touch, preexisting beliefs, and a priori conceptions of reality, as anything like pure vision.

14. Training her writerly vision on the politics, physics, and symbolics of seeing, Kleege travels back and forth between scientific and symbolic discourse. At times

with clinical precision she describes what her eyes can see and how she actually goes about seeing. Disability scholars might point out that Kleege's ability to penetrate to the core of her own eyeballs so technically is a sign of her capitulation to a "medical model" of disability. But Kleege achieves two important representational goals: First, she complicates the authority of medical discourse by setting it against her own—*she* still has epistemic authority in her story. Second, Kleege uses scientific language as an antidote (anecdote?) to the literary and mythological connotations of blindness that comprise the first two chapters of her text. Despite the problems of attending to the so-called medical model (that we view our bodies largely through medical language and thus as unrelated parts or things, disconnected from a controlling consciousness), Kleege has a great deal of cultural baggage about vision to cut through. Her descriptions of what happens during fear or eye contact (the skin stretching or certain parts of the brain being activated) move these activities away from the realm of popular belief, superstition, and myth and into something more mundane, less charged with mystery and entrenched assumptions.

15. Compare Kleege's concern to make disability an alternative (and rebellious) vantage point from which the nondisabled might think more critically about themselves with Knipfel's remark, toward the end of *Slackjaw:* "Going blind . . . has been my salvation . . . or my karmic retribution" (1999, 231).

REFERENCES

Benstock, Shari. 1988. "Authorizing the Autobiographical." In *The Private Self: Theory and Practice of Women's Autobiographical Writings,* edited by Shari Benstock. Chapel Hill: University of North Carolina Press.

Bérubé, Michael. 2000. "Autobiography as Performative Utterance." *American Quarterly* 52 (2): 339–43.

Couser, G. Thomas. 1997. *Recovering Bodies: Illness, Disability, and Life Writing.* Madison: University of Wisconsin Press.

Finger, Anne. 1986. *Past Due: A Story of Disability, Pregnancy and Birth.* Seattle: Seal Press.

Garland-Thomson, Rosemarie. 1997. *Extraordinary Bodies: Figuring Physical Disability in American Culture and Literature.* New York: Columbia University Press.

Gilmore, Leigh. 2001. *The Limits of Autobiography: Trauma and Testimony.* Ithaca, N.Y.: Cornell University Press.

Grealy, Lucy. 1994. *Autobiography of a Face.* Boston: Houghton Mifflin.

Kaplan, Caren. 1998. "Resisting Autobiography: Out-Law Genres and Transnational Feminist Subjects." In *Women, Autobiography, Theory: A Reader,* edited by Sidonie Smith and Julia Watson, 208–16. Madison: University of Wisconsin Press.

Keith, Lois. 1996. "Encounters with Strangers." In *Encounters with Strangers: Feminism and Disability,* edited by Jenny Morris, 69–88. London: Women's Press.

Kleege, Georgina. 1999. *Sight Unseen.* New Haven, Conn.: Yale University Press.

———. 2000. "Helen Keller and 'The Empire of the Normal.'" *American Quarterly* 52 (2): 322–25.

Knipfel, Jim. 1999. *Slackjaw*. New York: Berkley Books.

Lorde, Audre. 1982. *Zami: A New Spelling of My Name*. Freedom, Calf.: Crossing Press.

Mairs, Nancy. 1986. *Plaintext*. Tucson: University of Arizona Press.

———. 1994. "Essaying the Feminine." *Voice Writers: On Becoming a (Woman) Writer*. Boston: Beacon Press.

Perreault, Jeanne. 1995. *Writing Selves: Contemporary Feminist Autobiography*. Minneapolis: University of Minnesota Press.

Wendell, Susan. 1996. *The Rejected Body: Feminist Philosophical Reflections on Disability*. New York: Routledge.

Žižek, Slavoj. 1992. *Looking Awry: An Introduction to Jacques Lacan through Popular Culture*. Boston: MIT Press.

Four

REVISITING THE CORPUS OF THE MADWOMAN

Further Notes toward a
Feminist Disability Studies Theory of Mental Illness

ELIZABETH J. DONALDSON

More than thirty years ago, Sandra Gilbert and Susan Gubar published *The Madwoman in the Attic* (1978), a now classic text of early feminist literary criticism. Basing their title on the character of Bertha Mason, a madwoman secretly imprisoned in her husband's attic in Charlotte Brontë's *Jane Eyre* ([1847] 1981), Gilbert and Gubar argued that the "maddened doubles" in texts by nineteenth- and twentieth-century women writers "function as social surrogates," projecting women writers' anxiety of authorship in a male-dominated literary tradition (1978, xi). Much like the determined women who fueled feminism in the 1960s and 1970s, these madwomen rebel against the strictures of patriarchal authority. Since then, the figure of the madwoman as feminist rebel has had a sustained cultural currency. As Elaine Showalter notes, "To contemporary feminist critics, Bertha Mason has become a paradigmatic figure" (1985, 68). Furthermore, as Showalter also points out, feminist critics have sympathy for Bertha Mason that, ironically, Charlotte Brontë does not seem to share (68–69).

Many factors, not the least of which is the proliferation of feminist criticism and reading practices, have contributed to Bertha Mason's paradigmatic status and to contemporary readers' newfound sympathy. Perhaps most notably, Jean Rhys's *Wide Sargasso Sea* ([1966] 1985), a prequel to *Jane Eyre,* has influenced a generation of readers' responses to Brontë's character. Rhys's novel tells the story of Bertha "Antoinette" Mason's life in Jamaica before she marries Edward Rochester and moves to England.[1] The novel gives voice to the previously silent madwoman and depicts what some might consider the causes of her madness: a difficult childhood, a dangerous social climate, and her husband's ultimate betrayal. In depicting the events preceding Antoinette's attic imprisonment, Rhys departs in important ways from *Jane Eyre*'s configuration of madness, which I will discuss in greater detail below. By stressing the causal factors that contribute to Antoinette's emotional state, Rhys also makes it easier for readers to understand and identify with the originally enigmatic and inarticulate character.

Another factor significantly affecting contemporary readers' sympathy for Bertha Mason is the changing cultural thinking about psychiatry, mental illness, and the asylum from the late 1960s to the present. Psychiatry, feminist critics pointed out, unfairly pathologizes women.[2] Mental illness, according to the anti-psychiatry movement, is a myth.[3] The asylum, Michel Foucault (1988) explained, is primarily a form of institutional control.[4] The reception of Rhys's reevaluation of Bertha Antoinette Mason is in part a product of this particular historical moment in England and the United States. In this context, Bertha Mason, and the figure of the madwoman in general, became a compelling metaphor for women's rebellion.

Yet this metaphor for rebellion has problematic implications. Although Gilbert and Gubar warn readers against romanticizing madness, the figure of Bertha Mason as a rebellious woman subverting the patriarchal order by burning down her husband's estate has a certain irresistible appeal. Gilbert and Gubar's text and Rhys's novel are, of course, not the only texts that figure madness as rebellion. In *Women and Madness* Phyllis Chesler views women's madness as a journey of mythic proportions: "women have already been bitterly and totally repressed sexually; many may be reacting to or trying to escape from just such repression, and the powerlessness it signifies, by 'going mad'" (1972, 37). In the face of such repression, "going mad" might be considered the only sane response to an insane world (Deleuze and Guattari 1977). The ability to "go mad" also functions as a class marker of a higher sensibility: this sort of psychological depth has "the glow of transgressive glamour" (Pfister 1997, 176). For example, in *Mockingbird Years,* Emily Fox Gordon describes her stay at a mental hospital as "the fulfillment of an adolescent fantasy":

> The status of mental patient would invest me with significance. . . . We had seen the movie *David and Lisa* [Perry and Heller 1962], a tearjerker about a love affair between two adolescent mental patients, and we were smitten with the romance of madness. I think we believed that if we cultivated dissociation we would become as beautiful as Lisa: our complexions would turn luminous, our faces grow expressive hollows, our hair lie flat and glossy. We spent our days edging cautiously around the grounds, taking drags on shared cigarettes and muttering "a touch can kill," hoping to be noticed by the patients, drawn into their glamorous orbit by the magic of proximity. (2000, 5)

Oprah Winfrey's new production of *David and Lisa,* more than thirty years after the original, illustrates the enduring romantic appeal of madness (Winfrey and Kramer 1998).[5] Even more recently, in a film version of Susanna Kaysen's memoir, *Girl, Interrupted* (1999), Angelina Jolie's portrayal of a mental patient reinforces this linkage of mental illness and transgressive glamour for a new generation of young women. Similarly, in *Gothika* (2003), a film that shares the sensibilities of *Wide Sargasso Sea's* version of the post-Brontë madwoman tale, model/actress Halle Berry plays Dr. Miranda Grey, a former psychiatrist turned mental patient, who is incarcerated after murdering her husband, a psychiatrist who conceals his madwomen victims in a barn basement rather than an attic. In keeping with the contemporary madwoman tradition in fiction, Dr. Grey's madness is not actually mental illness: her body is possessed by the angry spirit of a woman her husband had abused.

However it is romanticized, madness itself offers women little possibility for true resistance or productive rebellion. As Marta Caminero-Santangelo argues in her aptly titled *The Madwoman Can't Speak; or, Why Insanity Is Not Subversive,* Bertha Mason's madness only "offers the illusion of power" (1998, 3). Using both fictional madwomen and women's biographical accounts of asylum experiences, Caminero-Santangelo reveals the limited political efficacy of the mad subject. Similarly, Shoshana Felman writes:

> Depressed and terrified women are not about to seize the means of production and reproduction: quite the opposite of rebellion, madness is the impasse confronting those whom cultural conditioning has deprived of the very means of protest or self-affirmation. Far from being a form of contestation, "mental illness" is a request for help, a manifestation both of cultural impotence and of political castration. (1997, 8)

Furthermore—and this is a crucial point for my argument here—using madness to represent women's rebellion has undesirable effects due primarily to the inevitable slippage, as the previous quotation illustrates, between "madness" and "mental illness." Although Gilbert and Gubar make it clear that their discussion concerns madness as a metaphor, not mental illness in the clinical sense, this distinction proves impossible to maintain. Fictional representations of madness have a way of influencing clinical discourses of mental illness and vice versa. As Showalter demonstrates, the figure of Bertha Mason circulated in precisely this way during Brontë's time: "Bertha's violence, dangerousness and rage, her regression to an inhuman condition and her sequestration became such a powerful model for Victorian readers, including psychiatrists, that it influenced even medical accounts of female insanity" (1985, 68).

Why is the association between women's rebellion/madness and mental illness undesirable? In some ways it isn't. Beginning in part with this insight, feminist critiques of psychiatry and psychology provide us with necessary and important analyses of the gendered politics of psychiatric diagnoses: it is certainly true that women have been disproportionately and in some cases even falsely diagnosed as mentally ill. And it is certainly true that psychiatry and psychiatric hospitals were in dire need of outside critics in the early days before deinstitutionalization and the patient rights movement transformed the mental health care system. However, at this particular historical moment, when disability studies and feminist disability studies are coming of age, I believe that the madness/rebellion configuration subtly reinforces what has become an almost monolithic way of reading mental illness within feminist literary criticism and perhaps in the larger culture of women's studies scholarship.[6] This is undesirable, I would argue, because this configuration of madness, if it remains widely accepted and uncontested, may limit our inquiry into madness/mental illness.

Indeed, one could argue, when madness is used as a metaphor for feminist rebellion, mental illness itself is erased. In *Illness as Metaphor*, Susan Sontag describes "the punitive or sentimental fantasies concocted" about tuberculosis and cancer and attempts to counteract stereotyped conceptions of these diseases (1977, 3). In comparison, the madness-as-feminist-rebellion metaphor might at first seem like a positive strategy for combating the stigma traditionally associated with mental illness. However, this metaphor indirectly diminishes the lived experience of many people who are disabled by mental illness, just as the metaphoric use of terms like *lame, blind,* and *deaf* can misrepresent, in ways that have ultimately harmful political effects, the experiences of living with those physical conditions. For example, during the first trial of Andrea Yates, who was diagnosed with schizophrenia and depression, the prosecution argued that Yates, though mentally ill, was rebelling against her domineering husband when she drowned their five children and was therefore culpable for these deaths (Parker 2002). The defense's attempts to explain Yates's medical condition and the delusional systems of thought caused by her mental illness failed to convince the jury, who were most likely influenced not only by the argument that Yates was a rebellious woman but also by the popular suspicions and misconceptions surrounding mental illness and by the state of Texas's slippery definition of legal insanity.[7] In Yates's case the prosecution's use of the figure of the rebellious madwoman in her trial illustrates the cultural currency of this feminist configuration of madness, our obligation to rigorously examine and complicate this model, and the need for new theories of mental illness and disability from feminist perspectives.

In my experience, theories that pay attention exclusively to the social causes and construction of mad identity while overlooking the material conditions of the body, and the body as a material condition, have a limited political scope.[8] In the United States today, the largest single mental health institution is not a psychiatric hospital but the Los Angeles County Jail. Legislation such as Kendra's Law, a New York state law that authorizes forced outpatient treatment for people with severe mental illnesses, reinforces the linkage between mental illness and violence in the public imagination. Ironically, this law is named after a young woman who was killed by Andrew Goldstein, a man with schizophrenia who sought but was denied treatment at a local hospital shortly before the incident; though the law is ostensibly about mandated treatment, it is inspired by an event caused by lack of access to voluntary treatment. Growing numbers of people lack health insurance, and, for those who are insured, health insurance policies rarely provide "parity" or equivalent coverage for mental illnesses in comparison to coverage for physical ailments. Changing conditions of psychiatric care and mental health policy demand new and alternate methods of critical engagement, methods that can strategically depart from the conventional feminist assumptions regarding madness. A feminist disability studies theory of mental illness that includes the body, one that theorizes bodies as "material-semiotic generative nodes" and mental illnesses as physical impairments, would be a timely and productive way of developing the discussion of madness/mental illness within women's studies scholarship (Haraway 1999, 208).[9] Perhaps the most appropriate way to begin thinking through a new feminist theory of embodiment and mental illness is with the paradigmatic figure of women's madness, *Jane Eyre*'s Bertha Mason.

REREADING THE MADWOMAN IN THE ATTIC

A feminist disability studies reading that stresses the connections between madness and physiognomy, between mind and body, provides us with an alternate way of conceptualizing madness in *Jane Eyre*. This alternative view restores the novel's original emphasis on the physical basis of mental illness, and in so doing seeks to complicate current constructions of madness within feminist theory. In this reading, Bertha Mason's madness is a socio-medical condition, a secret family history of mental illness. This family history precedes and supersedes Bertha Mason's marriage. *Jane Eyre*'s plot rests on a structure not exactly of mad doubles, but of juxtapositions between normative and nonnormative bodies, between the accidental and the congenital, between masculine rationality and femi-nine embodiment, and between melancholy and raving madness. Reading the body is a central practice in *Jane Eyre*: madness gets its meaning from the novel's underlying logic of physiognomy.

While the novel, to a certain extent, deconstructs ideals of beauty and the perfect body, it simultaneously is heavily invested in the notion of phys-iognomy, of reading moral character through facial features.[10] Jane Eyre's rival for Rochester's affection, the "beautiful Miss Ingram," for example, is described as "moulded like a Diana. . . . The noble bust, the sloping shoul-ders, the graceful neck, the dark eyes and black ringlets were all there" (Brontë 1981, 161). Edward Rochester describes his supposed rival for Jane's affection, St. John, as "a graceful Apollo . . . tall, fair, blue-eyed, and with a Grecian profile" (422). Yet these classically beautiful bodies enclose flawed characters who are not successful in their matches. St. John rejects the perfect beauty of Rosamond and is in turn rejected by *plain* Jane. Blanche Ingram's face and her facial expressions contradict her perfect form: "but her face? Her face was like her mother's; a youthful unfurrowed likeness: the same low brow, the same high features, the same pride. . . . Her laugh was satirical, and so was the habitual expression of her arched and haughty lip" (161). Beauty may be skin deep; but expression and gesture are visually evident on and through the surface of the body and, if read correctly, are accurate manifestations of inner moral character and identity.

The narrator herself cannot escape becoming the object of the structur-ing narrative of physiognomy. As Miss Ingram's mother remarks, "I am a judge of physiognomy, and in [Jane's] I see all the faults of her class" (166). Rochester, a much more sensitive reader than the Ingrams, also reads Jane's body, more precisely her head and face. Borrowing from the terms of phre-nology, the study of character based on the shape of the head, Rochester at one point describes Jane as having "a good deal of the organ of Adhesive-ness" (236; see fig. 4.1). According to phrenology, the brain's inner organs are associated with specific personality traits and cognitive skills. The over- or underdevelopment of these inner organs can be read through the external shape of the skull and its protrusions and recesses (Davies 1955, 4). Adhesiveness, sometimes depicted as two sisters embracing (fig. 4.2), signifies social bonds and friendship.[11] The offhand reference to "the organ of Adhesiveness" is never explained in *Jane Eyre,* which seems to suggest the audience's familiarity with this term. In keeping with this emphasis on the continuity between the external head and the internal mind, Rochester, while posing as a gypsy fortune-teller, quickly throws aside the pretense of reading Jane's palm in favor of reading her countenance: "what is in a palm?

Destiny is not written there . . . it is in the face: on the forehead, about the eyes, and in the eyes themselves, in the lines of the mouth" (Brontë 1981, 185–86).[12] Jane, previously skeptical of the gypsy's powers, replies, "Ah! Now you are coming to reality. . . . I shall begin to put some faith in you presently" (186). Both Jane and *Jane Eyre* the novel partake in a deep abiding faith in the discerning powers of physiognomy.

Physiognomy was also used to discern madness and idiocy, two mental states that were commonly discussed in tandem. John Caspar Lavatar's *Essays on Physiognomy* (1789) introduced to many English readers a connection between facial expressions and insanity. By the time Brontë was writing *Jane Eyre*, Alexander Morison's depictions of madness in texts like *The Physiognomy of Mental Disease* (1840) were familiar and "greatly influential" (Gilman 1982, 100).[13] When Jane first sees Richard Mason, the madwoman's brother, she notes,

> he was a fine-looking man, at first sight especially. On closer examination, you detected something in his face that displeased; or rather, that failed to please. His features were regular, but too relaxed: his eye was large and well cut, but the life looking out of it was a tame, vacant life—at least so I thought. (Brontë 1981, 178)

On second sight, Jane, who fittingly has a distinctive talent for sketching revealing portraits, remarks, "I liked his physiognomy even less than before. . . . For a handsome and not unamiable-looking man, he repelled me exceedingly" (178–79). Immediately juxtaposed with Jane's examination, the Ingrams' perceptions of Richard's features differ significantly: "a beautiful man," "a pretty little mouth," "what a sweet-tempered forehead," "such a placid eye and smile!" (179). The Ingrams, of course, are not good judges of character. Jane's more accurate evaluation of Richard's physiognomy is verified later when we learn about Richard's congenital legacy. Richard is Bertha's brother, a Mason, and as such, according to Rochester, is more than likely destined to hereditary madness or idiocy: "he has some grains of affection in his feeble mind . . . [but he] will probably be in the same state [as his siblings] one day" (291).

The novel's assumptions about biological destiny are also explicitly reinforced in the discussions about Rochester's ward, Adèle, "the illegitimate offspring of a French opera-girl [Céline]" (135). Once Rochester discovers that his mistress Céline is having an affair, Adèle's paternity is cast forever in doubt: "the Varens, six months before, had given me this fillette Adèle, who she affirmed, was my daughter; and perhaps she may be, though I see no proofs of such grim paternity written in her countenance: Pilot

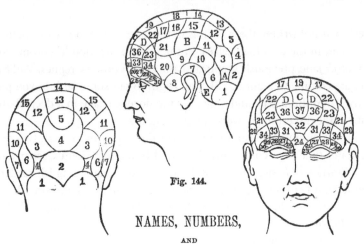

Fig. 144.

NAMES, NUMBERS,

AND

LOCATION OF THE ORGANS.

1. AMATIVENESS.	13. SELF-ESTEEM.	26. SIZE.
A. CONJUGAL LOVE.	14. FIRMNESS.	27. WEIGHT.
2. PARENTAL LOVE.	15. CONSCIENTIOUSNESS.	28. COLOR.
3. FRIENDSHIP.	16. HOPE.	29. ORDER.
4. INHABITIVENESS.	17. SPIRITUALITY.	30. CALCULATION.
5. CONTINUITY.	18. VENERATION.	31. LOCALITY.
E. VITATIVENESS.	19. BENEVOLENCE.	32. EVENTUALITY.
6. COMBATIVENESS.	20. CONSTRUCTIVENESS.	33. TIME.
7. DESTRUCTIVENESS.	21. IDEALITY.	34. TUNE.
8. ALIMENTIVENESS.	B. SUBLIMITY.	35. LANGUAGE.
9. ACQUISITIVENESS.	22. IMITATION.	36. CAUSALITY.
10. SECRETIVENESS.	23. MIRTH.	37. COMPARISON.
11. CAUTIOUSNESS.	24. INDIVIDUALITY	C. HUMAN NATURE.
12. APPROBATIVENESS.	25. FORM.	D. SUAVITY.

FIG. 4.1. Numbered and listed phrenological organs. From Samuel R. Wells's *New Physiognomy* (1871). *Courtesy of the Library Company of Philadelphia.*

[my dog] is more like me than she" (135). Though Jane searches Adèle's face for a resemblance to Mr. Rochester, she "found none; no trait, no turn of expression announced relationship" (136). In the absence of a confirmed, legitimate paternity, Adèle is defined by her matrilineal origins— and she is indelibly, innately French. Jane sees in Adèle "a superficiality of character, inherited probably from her mother, hardly congenial to an English mind" (136); "there was something ludicrous as well as painful in the little Parisienne's earnest and innate devotion to dress" (160). Rochester explains: "I am not her father; but hearing that she was quite destitute, I e'en took the poor thing out of the slime and mud of Paris, and transplanted it here, to grow up clean in the wholesome soil of an English country garden" (135). Adèle's French nature is checked by her English nurture: "As she grew up, a sound English education corrected in a great measure her French defects" (431). For Adèle, female is to male as nature is to nation. And the nation is always England.[14] Embodiment and the imperatives of the physical are a matrilineal legacy. Enculturation

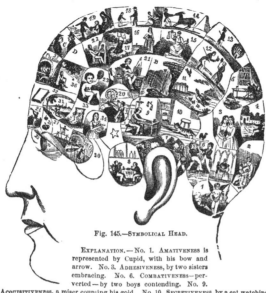

Fig. 145.—Symbolical Head.

Explanation.—No. 1. Amativeness is represented by Cupid, with his bow and arrow. No. 3. Adhesiveness, by two sisters embracing. No. 6. Combativeness—perverted—by two boys contending. No. 9. Acquisitiveness, a miser counting his gold. No. 10. Secretiveness, by a cat watching for a mouse. B. Sublimity, Niagara Falls. 24. Individuality, a boy with a telescope. 31. Locality, by a traveler consulting a guide-board. 36. Causality, Newton studying the laws of gravity by the falling of an apple. 18. Veneration, devotion, and deference, respect, and prayer. 19. Benevolence, the Good Samaritan bestowing charity. No. 17. Spirituality, Moses, on Mount Sinai, receiving the tables from Heaven on which were engraved the Ten Commandments. 16. Hope, the anchor, and a ship at sea. 15. Conscientiousness, Justice, with the scales in one hand and the sword in the other, and so forth. Each organ is represented by a symbol, which in some cases may show the appropriate, and in others the perverted action. The latter is shown in case of the miser, the gluttons, and the fighting boys. It is used as a means of indicating both the location of the organs and to show their natural action as frequently exhibited in life.

FIG. 4.2. Illustrated phrenological organs. From Samuel R. Wells's *New Physiognomy* (1871). *Courtesy of the Library Company of Philadelphia.*

and Englishness become patrilineal prerogatives. That Adèle is somehow tainted by her mother is in keeping with the novel's anxious relationship to female and to disabled bodies.

The madness of Bertha Mason, "the true daughter of an infamous mother," is similarly congenital (291). Grounded in her body, her madness is contextualized as a matrilineal legacy of national, ethnic identity and physical disorder: "Bertha Mason is mad; and she came of a mad family; idiots and maniacs through three generations! Her mother, the Creole, was both a madwoman and a drunkard!—as I found out after I had wed the daughter: for they were silent on family secrets before" (277). Yet at the same time, the gestation of her madness is specifically linked to her drinking and to her sexual appetites—failures of the will, not the body, in Rochester's opinion. Therefore, despite Bertha Mason's fated madness, Rochester still holds her morally accountable for her illness. For example, at one point Jane upbraids Rochester for speaking of his wife with contempt: "Sir . . . you are inexorable for that unfortunate lady: you speak of her with hate—with vindictive antipathy. It is cruel—she cannot help being mad" (286). However, according to Rochester, Bertha Mason can help being mad, although to a limited extent: "her excesses had prematurely developed the germs of insanity" (292). Rochester also, for what it is worth, distinguishes the source of his hatred: he claims not to hate her for being mad, but for those excesses.

Bertha Mason would be recognizable to Victorian readers as an exemplar of "raving madness," depicted by Cauis Gabriel Cibber's well-known sculpted figure over the gates of Bethlem "Bedlam" Hospital (Gilman 1982, 17–19; see fig. 4.3, figure on the right). Cibber's figure is restrained by chains, a common image in connection with raving madness or mania. Rochester himself mimes key features of this image in a game of charades earlier in the novel: "Amidst this sordid scene, sat a man with his clenched hands resting on his knees, and his eyes bent on the ground. . . . As he moved, a chain clanked; to his wrists were attached fetters. 'Bridewell!' exclaimed Colonel Dent, and the charade was solved" (Brontë 1981, 172–73). "Bridewell" refers simultaneously to the infamous prison and to the secretly imprisoned bride, Bertha, as well as to Rochester, who is bound to her by marriage. Paraphernalia of the prison, the fetters and chains, were all-too-common paraphernalia of the asylum, despite the attempts of reformers to ameliorate the treatment of patients. For example, Edward Wakefield's influential 1815 broadside publicized the case of William Norris, who had been fastened to a short, foot-long chain by the neck and warehoused in Bethlem Hospital for more than ten years (Gilman 1982, 153–55). However, by the time *Jane Eyre* was first published in 1847, only a handful of English asylums had discontinued the practice of mechanically restraining patients (Shortt 1986, 128).[15] In the novel, restraint and isolation are presented as necessary conditions of raving madness. Once Bertha is declared mad, she, "of course," must be sequestered: "since the medical men had pronounced her mad, she had, of course, been shut up" (Brontë 1981, 292). When Rochester publicly reveals Bertha's existence, he restrains her while Jane and others watch: "he mastered her arms; Grace Poole gave him a cord, and he pinioned them behind her: with more rope, which was at hand, he bound her to a chair" (279). Even if Jane Eyre should happen to go mad, she will not escape the requirements of restraint, as Rochester explains:

> Your mind is my treasure, and if it were broken, it would be my treasure still: if you raved, my arms should confine you, and not a strait waist-coat—your grasp, even in fury would have a charm for me: if you flew at me as wildly as that woman did this morning, I should receive you in an embrace, at least as fond as it would be restrictive. (286)

FIG. 4.3. Cauis Gabriel Cibber's sculpted figures of "raving madness"
(*right*) and "melancholy madness" (*left*) over the gates of
Bethlam "Bedlam" Hospital, London. *Courtesy of the
Harvey Cushing/John Jay Whitney Medical Library at Yale University.*

Whether confined by a straitjacket, also known as an "English camisole,"
or by Rochester's fond embrace, the mad and manic body appears to war-
rant physical restraint (Gilman 1982, 153).

Above the gates of Bedlam, Cibber's sculpture of raving madness faced
its counterpart, melancholy madness (see fig. 4.3, figure on the left). Similarly, once Bertha dies in the fire that she begins, Rochester becomes her
would-be mirror image, the second half of Cibber's mad dyad. After the
fire, Rochester is "blind, and a cripple": he is missing one eye, has limited sight in the remaining eye, and has had one hand amputated (Brontë
1981, 410). Though Rochester's blindness and missing hand might have
seemingly little to do with Bertha's madness, these physical alterations
mark him as an icon of melancholy madness.[16] In Cibber's sculpture the
clenched hands and chained wrists of the raving madness figure are juxtaposed with the melancholic's hidden hands, which almost seem to disappear at the wrist. In *Seeing the Insane,* Sander Gilman identifies hidden
or obscured hands as a conventional element in the iconography of mel-
ancholia. Symbolizing "the melancholic's ineffectuality," the hidden hands
are also a common gesture of grieving (1982, 14). When Rochester shows
Jane his amputation, his missing hand alludes to this tradition of images:

"'On this arm I have neither hand nor nails,' he said, drawing the muti-lated limb from his breast, and showing it to me" (Brontë 1981, 417). Not only is the hand missing, permanently obscured, but the blinded Roches-ter also draws his hand from his breast. The gesture of hiding this absence further marks him as melancholic. Jane recognizes this quickly: "I will be . . . eyes and hands to you. Cease to look so melancholy" (416).

At her death, Bertha's disabling mental illness is transferred to the body of her husband as physical impairment and blindness, which in turn are deployed by Brontë to depict melancholy madness. Paradoxically, Roch-ester's blindness helps to make madness visible. Rochester, because of his blindness, invokes a notion of the inescapable predominance of interior vision, an interiority that threatens to separate the self from the exterior world, just as a severe mental illness might. After his impairment, Roch-ester retreats to the desolate Ferndean manor house, and his self-imposed exile there parallels the seclusion of Bertha Mason:

> One saw that all to him was void darkness. He stretched his right hand
> (the left arm, the mutilated one, he kept hidden in his bosom): he seemed
> to wish by touch to gain an idea of what lay around him: he met but
> vacancy still. . . . He relinquished the endeavor, folded his arms, and stood
> quiet and mute in the rain. (413)

Like an asylum yard inmate, Rochester's folded arms, mute gestures, and inability to seek cover from the rain illustrate the self-neglect and social isolation associated with melancholy madness.

In a text so occupied with looking and the way faces look, Roches-ter's blindness and his "cicatrized visage" threaten to place him outside the novel's prevailing visual economy (417). Yet the vision of Jane keeps him firmly placed within this purview. After the fire, Rochester becomes a safely specular object, and the invisible Jane can now gaze at Rochester whenever she wishes: "in his countenance I saw a change . . . that looked desperate and brooding" (412). Jane's narrative encourages readers not to stare but to gaze with pity upon Rochester's newly disabled body: "It is a pity to see it; and a pity to see your eyes—and the scar of fire on your fore-head: and the worst of it is, one is in danger of loving you too well for all this; and making too much of you" (417).[17]

Despite the continuity between Bertha's raving madness and Roches-ter's melancholy, Rochester's impairments differ in significant ways. While Bertha's madness is congenital and chronic, Rochester's is coincidental and curable. In addition to the associations with melancholy, Jane also com-pares Rochester's impairments to Nebuchadnezzar's temporary madness:

It is time some one undertook to rehumanize you . . . for I see that you are being metamorphosed into a lion, or something of that sort. You have a *faux air* of Nebuchadnezzar in the fields about you, that is certain: your hair reminds me of eagles' feathers; whether your nails are grown like bird's claws or not, I have not yet noticed. (417)

After Nebuchadnezzar has a prophetic dream of a blasted tree and his kingdom's dissolution, he undergoes a brief period of madness that transforms him into an animal-like, subhuman figure: "he was driven from men, and did eat grass as oxen, and his . . . hairs were grown like eagles' feathers, and his nails like bird claws" (Dan. 4:33).[18] Later, Nebuchadnezzar's reason returns to him. Similarly, Rochester's first marriage proposal to Jane is followed by a lightning blast that destroys a tree, foreshadowing Rochester's future punishment and paralleling Nebuchadnezzar's dream. Just as Nebuchadnezzar returns to reason, Rochester wakes from the dream of blindness and of disability. The closed eyes of the sleeping dreamer seem temporarily blinded. Imprisoning and isolating the dreamer, the dream state represents the threat of inescapable interiority, or madness. Rochester wakes—regains his sight—in time to see his newborn son and, more importantly, his resemblance in his son's eyes: "When his first-born was put into his arms, he could see that the boy had inherited his own eyes, as they once were—large, brilliant, and black" (Brontë 1981, 432). Rochester can therefore verify his son's paternity by sight, in direct contrast to the inscrutable paternity of Adèle. His son's eyes reinforce the logic of physiognomy and disability in *Jane Eyre:* a legitimate patrilineal succession corrects the female-based legacy of disability. Rochester's restored vision and the exchanged gaze between Rochester and his son confirms the primacy of hereditary traits and is presented as Rochester's triumph over madness, disability, and the disabling female body. "Normalcy," Lennard Davis notes, "has to protect itself by looking into the maw of disability and then recovering from that glance" (1997, 26).[19]

TOWARD A FEMINIST DISABILITY STUDIES THEORY OF EMBODIMENT AND MENTAL ILLNESS

Jane Eyre's Bertha Rochester is mental illness incarnate; however, the embodied nature of Bertha's madness, and the novel's insistent physiognomy, often fails to register in a critical climate occupied with the notions of mental illness as primarily socially produced and of madness as feminist rebellion. A feminist disability studies reading, in contrast, demands closer attention to physical bodies and to the theories of embodiment that structure the novel. Moreover, feminist disability studies provides a framework for new and alternate ways of theorizing about mental illness from a feminist perspective.

Victorian notions of physiognomy and madness might seem far removed from the neuroscience and psychopharmacology that comprise scientific thinking about mental illness today. Yet all share a basic understanding of the brain as a territory to be mapped. Phrenologists drew comparisons between the occurrence of mental disease and the development of organs of the brain. Today magnetic resonance imaging (MRI) scans depict the enlarged brain ventricles of people diagnosed with schizophrenia, positron emission tomography (PET) scans show increased glucose metabolism in people diagnosed with obsessive compulsive disorder, and on the cellular level neuropharmacology targets dopamine receptors between nerve cells to alleviate the symptoms of severe mental illness. Although there is a certain continuity between the medical imaging processes of phrenology and modern neuroscience, there are also crucial differences, and the types of pharmaceutical interventions that psychiatry practices today are a marked departure from the moral treatment advocated in the nineteenth century.

Nevertheless, I do want to suggest that the enduring importance of medical imaging and madness might be productively linked to what Donna Haraway would call the "tropic" nature of corporealization: "bodies are perfectly 'real,' and nothing about corporealization is 'merely' fiction. But corporealization is tropic and historically specific at every layer of its tissues" (1997, 142).[20] Though Bertha Rochester is merely fiction, the system of phrenology and physiognomy in which *Jane Eyre* participates is part of the corporealization of mad bodies in the nineteenth century. One of the goals of a feminist disability studies theory of mental illness should be to examine these scientific tropes of the mad body. Furthermore, as Haraway suggests, it is possible to accept the "tropic and historically specific" nature of corporealization (and of medical language) while simultaneously thinking of bodies (and of mental illness) as *real*.

Beginning to think through mental illness using this notion of corporealization will necessitate a pivotal shift from the model of madness-as-rebellion currently in circulation within women's studies scholarship, and it will require a more detailed analysis of some of the central terms and concepts of disability studies. More specifically, a theory of the corporealization of mental illness demands a closer examination of the relationship between *impairment* and *disability*. The distinction between impairment and disability, the material body and the socially constructed body, has been a crucial one within disability studies. As Lennard Davis explains: "An impairment involves a loss . . . of sight, hearing, mobility, mental ability, and so on. But an impairment only becomes a disability when the ambient society creates environments with barriers—affective, sensory, cognitive, or architectural" (1997, 506–507). What Davis describes here may be termed the impairment-disability system. Like Gayle Rubin's configuration of the sex-gender system—the process by which biological sex is transformed into cultural gender—the impairment-disability system is the process by which biological impairment is transformed into cultural disability (1975). This configuration of the impairment-disability system has been particularly useful for people in the disability rights movement, who combat stigma and who protect the civil rights of people with disabilities: by shifting attention away from the biological (impairment) to the social (disability), one can effectively identify and address discrimination.

However, while the politically strategic split between impairment and disability has been particularly useful, it also has limits as it is currently conceived. The impairment-disability system appropriately distinguishes between physical conditions of the body (impairment) and the body's barriers in public space (disability). Since most disability scholars begin with issues related to physical impairment, this is a useful, compelling distinction to make. Yet, when one begins with issues related to mental impairment, the boundary between impairment and disability becomes harder to maintain, primarily because of unexamined assumptions about the body and the self within this current configuration. The assumptions are that impairment and disability occur in and through the body, and that the body's self or mind is a transcendent civil identity that exists above and beyond the body: this abstract, symbolically disembodied civil self remains intact, unaltered, even normal, despite physical impairment. The language of the Americans with Disabilities Act of 1990 evokes this false ideal: the subject ("American") is the seemingly stable core that exists independently from the accidental body ("with a disability"). However, the impairments of severe mental illness challenge the normalizing logic of this model. Using a wheelchair does not disrupt the notion of *American* quite so much as being delusional does. For example, although the physical barriers that exist for wheelchair users are very real and pervasive, they are quite different in nature from mental competency requirements that restrict the rights to vote or to refuse medication. The barriers confronting people with severe mental illnesses and cognitive disabilities are more complicated because they involve the concept of the self that is the very foundation of our political system.

Theorizing about mental illness from a feminist disability studies perspective, I argue, demands a different focus on impairment. Because it requires a shift toward medical models of illness, this repositioning is not without risks. As Simi Linton correctly observes, medical definitions of disability in the past have functioned to keep disability "within the purview of the medical establishment, to keep it a personal matter and 'treat' the condition and the person with the condition rather than 'treating' the social processes and policies that constrict disabled people's lives" (1998, 11). Borrowing a term from Eve Sedgwick's *Epistemology of the Closet,* Rosemarie Garland-Thomson also points out that medical definitions of impairments have fostered a "minoritizing" view of disability as private tragedy rather than positioning disability as a universal problem affecting everyone (1997b, 282).

Adopting a medical model also poses other risks. Thinking about physical impairment—in particular, congenital physical impairment—is often characterized by concomitant reductive assumptions about biological bodies. This is the case, for example, with Bertha Mason's madness in *Jane Eyre* and with the definitive powers attributed to pathological genes today. In order to steer clear of the pitfalls of essentialism and biological determinism when conceptualizing mental illness as physical impairment, it is useful to begin with the understanding that bodies are not simply born, but made. As Haraway explains, "bodies as subjects of knowledge are material-semiotic generative nodes. Their boundaries materialize in social interactions; 'objects' like bodies do not pre-exist as such" (1999, 208). Feminist science studies and feminist examinations of the body can offer us the conceptual modes and the critical language to begin a rigorous denaturalization of impairment within disability studies. In *Bodies That Matter,* Judith Butler revised how we think of the sex-gender system—arguing in part that *sex* is not the static, natural category out of which the social construction of gender emerges (1993). Similarly, reexamining the impairment-disability system, and, moreover, repositioning mental illness as a physical impairment, seems appropriate and particularly necessary when we speak of severe and chronic mental illnesses within the disability studies rubric.

It is possible to begin with the premise that mental illness is a neurobiological disorder and still remain committed to a feminist and a disability studies agenda—an agenda that fights discrimination, advocates for the rights of women and people with disabilities, seeks to dismantle ideologies of oppression, critiques medical discourses of mental illness, and demands equal access to social services and medical treatment—and it is important that feminists and disability scholars begin to think about mental illness in these medical and physical terms.[21] The elision of the physical component of Bertha Rochester's madness in contemporary criticism is not coincidental, but is symptomatic of a larger, cultural anxiety surrounding mental illness. This anxiety, I suspect, emerges from the impossible task of reconciling medical discourses of mental illness, which describe the symbolic failure of the self-determined individual, and the competing discourses of democratic citizenship, in which will and self are imagined as inviolable—a tension that lies at the heart of both liberal individualism and the impairment-disability system. "Democracy," Lennard Davis writes, "needs the illusion of equality, and equality needs the fiction of the equal or average citizen" (2002, 110). In *Frontiers of Justice* Martha Nussbaum begins her examination of John Rawls's social contract theory, which is based on the assumption that citizens are "free, equal, and independent," with a similar insight: "We cannot extend the core idea of inviolability and the related idea of reciprocity to people with severe physical and mental impairments without calling these features into question, thus severing ties with the classical social contract tradition" (2006, 119). Of course, if one insists that mental illness is a myth, that mental illness does not exist as a material, physical impairment, then one avoids such thorny problems. In this sense, anti-psychiatry and conceptions of madness as feminist rebellion are essentially conservative: they do not require a radical rethinking of our central political principles. Tempting though it may be to fall back on concepts that imagine mental illness as purely socially produced, the true radical challenge that Bertha Rochester represents is far more complex. Ideally, this is a challenge that a next wave of madwoman theory, one based on the insights of both feminism and disability studies theory, will begin to address.

NOTES

1. In *Jane Eyre* the madwoman's maiden name is Bertha Antoinette Mason. In Rhys's novel (1985), the parallel character's maiden name is Antoinette Mason, née Cosway; the name "Bertha" is her husband Edward Rochester's invention, and this renaming emphasizes the formative role the husband has in forging her mad identity in Rhys's text. I use "Bertha" to refer to Brontë's character and "Antoinette" to distinguish Rhys's character, although, for those who have read both texts, a hybrid of the two—Bertha Antoinette Cosway Mason Rochester—might best describe the composite character who emerges.

2. Showalter (1985) details the gendered nature of ideas about insanity, and Chesler (1972) describes a similar phenomenon. For data on the predominance of women patients in the mental health care system, see Guttentag, Salasin, and Belle (1980) and Howell and Bayes (1981). See also Ehrenreich and English (1973).

3. For very explicit statements of this position, see Thomas Szaz (1974; 1991). Szaz is influenced by the work—and in particular, the psychiatric labeling theory—of R. D. Laing (1967; 1976).

4. For American versions of this form of institutional critique, see Goffman (1961), Rothman (1971; 1980), and Grob (1983).

5. The original film *David and Lisa* (Perry and Heller 1962) is based on the study by psychoanalyst Theodore Rubin (1961). See the novel *One Flew over the Cuckoo's Nest* (Kesey 1962) and the subsequent film (Forman and Douglas 1975) for the masculinized counterpart of the glamorization of madness, which ironically also trivializes and denigrates the experience of people with mental illness. In *Cuckoo's Nest* the patients fall into two categories: those in therapy who appear to suffer from socially produced ailments and chronic, or "real," patients who fall outside the realm of discourse, sympathy, and redemption. This is a point that Mitchell and Snyder also discuss (2000, 173–74) and that I explore in greater detail in another essay (Donaldson 2005).

6. The impressive body of work by feminist historian Nancy Tomes is a notable exception here (1990; 1994b). Tomes was an early critic of female malady interpretations of insanity and of the madness-as-feminist-rebellion configuration.

7. As the appeal process revealed, these were probably not the only factors influencing the jury's decision. In her second trial, Yates's defense argued that the prosecution's star expert witness, psychiatrist Park Dietz, allowed his religious beliefs to color his testimony (Parker 2006). During the first trial, Dietz was the only mental health expert to testify that Yates was legally sane and the only mental health specialist employed by the prosecution. Several years later at a similar trial, Dietz testified that Deanna Laney was legally insane when she killed her children, because she believed she was following directions from God at the time (Parker 2006). Yates, on the other hand, believed that she was under the direction of Satan during her psychosis but also believed she was saving her five children from eternal damnation when she killed them. In an interview, Dietz stated, "Let's assume both of them understand that killing is against the law. Mrs. Laney believed herself to be doing the right thing at God's direction. Mrs. Yates believed herself to be doing the wrong thing, with Satan's prompting, and that it was sinful" (Parker 2006). For Dietz, who considered both women to be delusional and psychotic, Laney's Abrahamic insanity seems to be compatible with Texas's definition of legal insanity, the inability to tell right from wrong; Yates's directives from Satan do not. Laney is obedient to God and, like Abraham, submits to the ultimate test of faith; Yates is rebellious, follows Satan, and is therefore legally culpable. At her second trial in 2006, the jury found Yates not guilty by reason of insanity.

8. My mother has had schizophrenia for as long as I can remember. Her emotional distress, hallucinations, and other symptoms were formative parts of my childhood, and these symptoms continue to affect her life and mine in important ways. My brother was diagnosed with schizophrenia in his mid-twenties. After several arrests, periods of homelessness, and forced hospitalizations, he became part of an assertive community treatment program where he received discounted housing, medical treatment and medication, and the much-needed help of a team of overworked and underpaid social workers. My thinking about mental illness reflects this past personal history and my more recent experiences as my brother's legal guardian (or, as he says, his "personal secretary").

9. In the time since this essay was originally researched and published, other scholars have made similar remarks. Regarding mental illness and disability studies theories, Anna Mollow writes, "Analyses that privilege disability over impairment deflect attention from the political nature of impairment itself" (2006, 288). She also notes that framing disability primarily in terms of social oppression may "sacrifice . . . a way of thinking in political terms about the suffering some impairments cause" (287). Andrea Nicki also stresses a movement away from an exclusively social model of psychiatric disability: "In order for mental illnesses to be conceived as real illnesses and those afflicted to be treated appropriately, mental illnesses must not be seen purely in terms of their cultural and social components" (2001, 83). She notes, "a social constructionist approach to mental illness . . . may be used to undermine mental illness as a legitimate illness and disability," which may in turn harm women disabled by psychiatric illnesses (84). See also Squier (2004).

10. Lennard Davis (1998) observes that Jane's unconventional plainness marks her as an abnormal heroine for a novel. Cora Kaplan also notes, "Jane's constellation of defects . . . works as a defensive counterdiscourse" (2000, 309).

11. Walt Whitman was particularly proud of the development of his organ of adhesiveness. See Whitman's phrenological chart in the second edition of *Leaves of Grass* (1856), which was published by the American phrenologists Orson Squire Fowler and Samuel Wells (reprinted in Stern 1982, 76–77). The image of the two sisters embracing recalls Brontë's relationship to her sisters as well as the many references in *Jane Eyre* to the likeness between Jane and Rochester, "familiar to me as my own face in a glass" (Brontë 1981, 190).

12. Although palmistry as a science is discounted in this scene, the gesture of hands is quite significant in *Jane Eyre,* a point I discuss in greater detail later.

13. In *Seeing the Insane* (1982), Sander Gilman has compiled an extensive collection of the icons of madness, including Lavatar's and Morison's illustrations. My discussion here owes much to Gilman's work. Also see Hartley (2001) for a history of physiognomic thinking in the nineteenth century.

14. Female bodies are often identified in tellingly reductive ways in *Jane Eyre.* Blanche Ingram, whose body is said to resemble Bertha Mason's, is "dark as a Spaniard" (Brontë 1981, 162), and Bertha Mason's mother is simply "the Creole" (277). After Bertha Mason's madness manifests itself, Rochester embarks on a geographic search "for the antipodes of the Creole" and chooses an international menu of mistresses—an Italian, a German, and finally the Frenchwoman who is Adèle's mother (296). See also Spivak (1985).

15. In addition to Shortt (1986), other helpful histories of asylum life and mental illness in nineteenth-century England and America include Scull (1979), Tomes (1994a), Dwyer (1987), and Wright (2001).

16. Admittedly, when Jane learns that Rochester is blind, she thinks to herself, "I had dreaded worse. I had dreaded he was mad" (Brontë 1981, 410). While this statement makes a clear distinction between blindness and madness, I would argue that the madness Brontë distinguishes from blindness here is raving madness, not melancholy. Jane's fear or dread of raving madness is evident from her previous reactions to

Bertha and to Rochester's earlier threat to "try violence," which she prevents in part by repositioning his hand: "I took hold of his clenched hand, loosened the contorted fingers" (286–87). In *Jane Eyre,* though Bertha's raving madness is certainly "worse" than Rochester's blind melancholy, they share a symbiotic relationship.

17. See Garland-Thomson for the distinction between the gaze and the stare— "the gaze intensified" that frames the body as "an icon of deviance" (1997a, 26). See also Shapiro's *No Pity* for a critique of the politics of pity regarding the disabled body (1993).

18. Although both Rochester's and Bertha's madness are presented as animal-like states, Rochester's madness is nevertheless nobler. Bertha crouches on all fours like a "clothed hyena" (Brontë 1981, 279). Rochester resembles "some wronged and fettered wild beast or bird, dangerous to approach in his sullen woe. The caged eagle, whose gold-ringed eyes cruelty has extinguished, might look as looked that sightless Samson" (412).

19. See also Mitchell and Snyder's recent work on "narrative prosthesis": a narrative's "need to restore a disabled body to some semblance of an originary wholeness" (2001). The birth of Rochester's son at the conclusion of *Jane Eyre,* and this resemblance in and of Rochester's eyes, is in keeping with Mitchell and Snyder's notion of "prosthetic intervention."

20. Similarly James Wilson and Cynthia Lewiecki-Wilson have also previously noted the potential contributions that corporeal feminism might make to rhetorical studies of disability (2001, 3).

21. For many reasons, this is a difficult but necessary statement to make. In a poignant essay about a close friend who has schizophrenia, Catherine Prendergast characterizes this dilemma well when she writes, "For an academic like myself with generally poststructuralist leanings, to think of schizophrenia as a 'disease' makes me sound at best conservative and at worst theoretically unsound. I am therefore left wandering far from my usual terrain to find language with which I can address the dilemmas and gaps in understanding that mental illness presents" (2001, 46). As Prendergast's essay illustrates, to conceive of schizophrenia as a "disease," or of severe mental illness as a physically based impairment, does not necessarily result in a conservative, biologically reductive theory of mental illness: on the contrary, to be unable to theorize mental illness as a disease unduly limits our strategies of political and philosophical engagement.

REFERENCES

Americans with Disabilities Act of 1990. http://www.ada.gov/pubs/ada.htm.
Brontë, Charlotte. (1847) 1981. *Jane Eyre.* New York: Bantam.
Butler, Judith. 1993. *Bodies That Matter: On the Discursive Limits of "Sex."* New York: Routledge.
Caminero-Santangelo, Marta. 1998. *The Madwoman Can't Speak; or, Why Insanity Is Not Subversive.* Ithaca, N.Y.: Cornell University Press.
Chesler, Phyllis. 1972. *Women and Madness.* Garden City, N.J.: Doubleday.

Davies, John D. 1955. *Phrenology, Fad, and Science: A 19th-Century Crusade.* New Haven, Conn.: Yale University Press.

Davis, Lennard J. 1997. "Constructing Normalcy: The Bell Curve, the Novel, and the Invention of the Disabled Body in the Nineteenth Century." In *The Disability Studies Reader,* edited by Lennard Davis, 9–28. New York: Routledge.

———. 1998. "Who Put the 'The' in the Novel? Identity Politics and Disability in Novel Studies." *Novel* 31(3): 317–34.

———. 2002. *Bending over Backwards: Disability, Dismodernism, and other Difficult Positions.* New York: New York University Press.

Deleuze, Gilles, and Félix Guattari. 1977. *Anti-Oedipus: Capitalism and Schizophrenia.* Translated by Robert Hurley, Mark Seem, and Helen R. Lane. New York: Viking Press.

Donaldson, Elizabeth J. 2005. "The Psychiatric Gaze: Deviance and Disability in Film." In "The Discourse of Disability," special issue of *Atenea* 25 (1): 31–48.

Dwyer, Ellen. 1987. *Homes for the Mad: Life Inside Two Nineteenth-Century Asylums.* New Brunswick, N.J.: Rutgers University Press.

Ehrenreich, Barbara, and Deirdre English. 1973. *Complaints and Disorders: The Sexual Politics of Sickness.* Old Westbury, Conn.: Feminist Press.

Felman, Shoshana. 1997. "Women and Madness: The Critical Phallacy." In *Feminisms: An Anthology of Literary Theory and Criticism,* edited by Robyn R. Warhol and Diane Price Herndl, 7–20. New Brunswick, N.J.: Rutgers University Press.

Forman, Milos, dir., and Michael Douglas, prod. 1975. *One Flew over the Cuckoo's Nest.* Burbank, Calif.: Warner Studios. Motion picture.

Foucault, Michel. (1965) 1988. *Madness and Civilization: A History of Insanity in the Age of Reason.* Translated by Richard Howard. New York: Random House.

Garland-Thomson, Rosemarie. 1997a. *Extraordinary Bodies: Figuring Physical Disability in American Culture and Literature.* New York: Columbia University Press.

———. 1997b. "Feminist Theory, the Body, and the Disabled Figure." In Davis, *Disability Studies Reader,* 279–92.

Gilbert, Sandra M., and Susan Gubar. 1978. *The Madwoman in the Attic: The Woman Writer and the Nineteenth-Century Literary Imagination.* New Haven, Conn.: Yale University Press.

Gilman, Sander. 1982. *Seeing the Insane.* New York: John Wiley.

Girl, Interrupted. 1999. Dir. James Mangold. Prods., Cathy Konrad and Douglass Wick. Columbia Pictures. Motion picture.

Goffman, Erving. 1961. *Asylums: Essays on the Social Situation of Asylum Patients and other Inmates.* Garden City, N.J.: Anchor Books.

Gordon, Emily Fox. 2000. *Mockingbird Years: A Life in and out of Therapy.* New York: Basic Books.

Gothika. 2003. Dirs., Mathieu Kassovitz and Thom Oliphant. Prod., Susan Downey. Dark Castle Entertainment. Motion picture.

Grob, Gerald. 1983. *Mental Illness and American Society, 1875–1940.* Princeton, N.J.: Princeton University Press.

Guttentag, Marcia, Susan Salasin, and Deborah Belle. 1980. *The Mental Health of Women*. New York: Academic Press.

Haraway, Donna. 1997. *Modest_Witness@Second_Millennium. FemaleMan©_Meets _OncoMouse*TM: *Feminism and Technoscience*. New York: Routledge.

———. 1999. "The Biopolitics of Postmodern Bodies: Determinations of Self in Immune System Discourse." In *Feminist Theory and the Body: A Reader*, edited by Janet Price and Margrit Shildrick, 203–14. New York: Routledge.

Hartley, Lucy. 2001. *Physiognomy and the Meaning of Expression in Nineteenth-Century Culture*. Cambridge, Mass.: Cambridge University Press.

Howell, Elizabeth, and Marjorie Bayes, eds. 1981. *Women and Mental Health*. New York: Basic Books.

Kaplan, Cora. 2000. "Liberalism, Feminism, and Defect." Afterword to *"Defects": Engendering the Modern Body*, edited by Helen Deutsch and Felicity Nussbaum, 301–18. Ann Arbor: University of Michigan Press.

Kesey, Ken. 1962. *One Flew over the Cuckoo's Nest*. New York: Signet Books.

Laing, R. D. 1967. *The Politics of Experience*. New York: Ballantine Books.

———. 1976. *The Divided Self*. Harmondsworth, UK: Penguin Books.

Lavatar, John Caspar. 1789. *Essays on Physiognomy*. Translated by Henry Hunter. London: John Murray.

Linton, Simi. 1998. *Claiming Disability: Knowledge and Identity*. New York: New York University Press.

Mitchell, David T., and Sharon Snyder. 2000. *Narrative Prosthesis: Disability and the Dependencies of Discourse*. Ann Arbor: University of Michigan Press.

Mollow, Anna. 2006. "When *Black* Women Start Going on Prozac . . .": The Politics of Race, Gender, and Emotional Distress in Meri Nana-Ama Danquah's *Willow Weep for Me*." In Davis, *Disability Studies Reader*, 2nd ed., 283–99.

Morison, Alexander. 1840. *The Physiognomy of Mental Disease*. London: Longman.

Nicki, Andrea. 2001. "The Abused Mind: Feminist Theory, Psychiatric Disability, and Trauma." *Hypatia* 16 (4): 80–104.

Nussbaum, Martha C. 2006. *Frontiers of Justice: Disability, Nationality, Species Membership*. Cambridge, Mass.: Harvard University Press.

Parker, Laura. 2002. "Insanity Law Helped Doom Yates' Defense." *USA Today*, 14 March, 3A.

———. 2006. "Yates Trial Highlights Power of an Expert Witness." *USA Today*, 20 June. http://www.usatoday.com/news/nation/2006-06-20-expert-witnesses_x.htm.

Perry, Frank, dir., and Paul M. Heller, prod. 1962. *David and Lisa*. United States: Continental Distributing. Motion picture.

Pfister, Joel. 1997. "Glamorizing the Psychological: The Politics of the Performances of Modern Psychological Identities." In *Inventing the Psychological: Toward a Cultural History of Emotional Life in America*, edited by Joel Pfister and Nancy Schnog, 167–213. New Haven, Conn.: Yale University Press.

Prendergast, Catherine. 2001. "On the Rhetorics of Mental Disability." In Wilson and Lewiecki-Wilson, *Embodied Rhetorics*, 45–60.

Rhys, Jean. (1966) 1985. *Wide Sargasso Sea*. In *The Complete Novels of Jean Rhys*, 465–574. New York: W. W. Norton.

Rothman, David. 1971. *The Discovery of the Asylum: Social Order and Disorder in the New Republic*. Boston: Little, Brown.

———. 1980. *Conscience and Convenience: The Asylum and its Alternatives in Progressive America*. Boston: Little, Brown.

Rubin, Gayle. 1975. "The Traffic in Women: Notes on the Political Economy of Sex." In *Toward an Anthropology of Women*, edited by Rayna Reiter, 157–210. New York: Monthly Review Press.

Rubin, Theodore I. 1961. *Lisa and David*. New York: Macmillan.

Scull, Andrew T. 1979. *Museums of Madness: The Social Organization of Insanity in Nineteenth-Century England*. New York: St. Martin's Press.

Shapiro, Joseph P. 1993. *No Pity: People with Disabilities Forging a New Civil Rights Movement*. New York: Random House.

Shortt, S. E. D. 1986. *Victorian Lunacy: Richard M. Bucke and the Practice of Late Nineteenth-Century Psychiatry*. New York: Cambridge University Press.

Showalter, Elaine. 1985. *The Female Malady: Women, Madness, and English Culture, 1830–1980*. New York: Pantheon.

Sontag, Susan. 1977. *Illness as Metaphor*. New York: Farrar, Straus, and Giroux.

Spivak, Gayatri. 1985. "Three Women's Texts and a Critique of Imperialism." *Critical Inquiry* 12 (1): 243–61.

Squier, Susan. 2004. "Meditation, Disability, and Identity." *Literature and Medicine* 23 (1): 23–45.

Stern, Madeleine, comp. 1982. *A Phrenological Dictionary of Nineteenth-Century Americans*. Westport, Conn.: Greenwood Press.

Szaz, Thomas R. 1974. *The Myth of Mental Illness: Foundations of a Theory of Personal Conduct*. New York: Harper and Row.

———. 1991. *Ideology and Insanity: Essays on the Psychiatric Dehumanization of Man*. New York: Syracuse University Press.

Tomes, Nancy. 1990. "Historical Perspectives on Women and Mental Illness." In *Women, Health, and Medicine in America: A Historical Handbook*, edited by Rima Apple, 143–71. New York: Garland.

———. 1994a. *The Art of Asylum-Keeping: Thomas Story Kirkbride and the Origins of American Psychiatry*. Philadelphia: University of Pennsylvania Press.

———. 1994b. "Feminist Histories of Psychiatry." In *Discovering the History of Psychiatry*, edited by Mark S. Micale and Roy Porter, 348–83. New York: Oxford University Press.

Whitman, Walt. 1856. *Leaves of Grass*. 2nd ed. New York: Fowler and Wells.

Wilson, James C., and Cynthia Lewiecki-Wilson. 2001. "Disability, Rhetoric, and the Body." In *Embodied Rhetorics: Disability in Language and Culture*, 1–24. Carbondale: Southern Illinois University Press.

Winfrey, Oprah, prod., and Lloyd Kramer, dir. 1998. *David and Lisa*. Chicago: Harpo Productions. Teleplay.

Wright, David. 2001. *Mental Disability in Victorian England: The Earlswood Asylum 1847–1901*. Oxford, UK: Oxford University Press.

PART THREE

INTERROGATING FITNESS

Nation, Identity, and Citizenship

Five

THE COLOR OF VIOLENCE

Reflecting on Gender, Race, and Disability in Wartime

NIRMALA EREVELLES

As I write this chapter, I am very conscious I am writing in a time of war. Almost daily there are reports of roadside bombs detonating; the launching of military offensives; power failures; and shortages of food, drinking water, and fuel in the "postwar" contexts of a devastated Afghanistan and an occupied Iraq. Not much has changed since President Obama announced the complete pull-out of U.S. troops from Iraq and Afghanistan in the near future. Here, in the United States, a few news media organizations keep diligent count of U.S. soldiers killed in the war. Even more infrequently, and almost always as a passing note, we hear a rare report of disabled war veterans returning from combat. While there are some reports of civilian deaths in Afghanistan and Iraq, I have been unable to find reports of Afghan and Iraqi civilians and members of the military (and now the insurgency) who have become disabled as a result of the war and the postwar conflict. I find this extremely troubling, but neither the alternative press nor radical scholars in the academy seem perturbed by these omissions.

It is not just the missing reports about disability that are troubling in this time of war. What is more troubling are the missing analyses of "disability and war" in the otherwise radical scholarship of both feminist disability studies and third world feminism, especially given the relevance of this topic for both analytical frameworks.[1] War is one of the largest producers of disability in a world still inhospitable to disabled people and their predominantly female caregivers (Russell 1998; Charlton 1998; Nakano-Glenn 1992; Parker 1993; Chang 2000). While upper- and middle-class disabled people may enjoy a certain level of social and economic accessibility in advanced industrialized nations in Europe and the Americas, poor disabled people, particularly poor disabled people of color, experience both social and economic oppression. This oppression is exacerbated in the third world. Thus, while disabled U.S. war veterans may be able to anticipate at least a minimal level of services and social support when they return from war, disabled veterans and civilians in war-torn areas of the third world face an inadequate, overburdened, and/or nonexistent infrastructure in service provision for disabled people. In contexts where subsistence is a struggle, third world disabled people in general, and third world women who are themselves disabled and/or caregivers for disabled family members/clients, face the social, political, and economic consequences of invisibility (Erevelles 1996; Chang 2000; Ghai 2003).

In this essay I explore an often ignored area in both feminist disability studies and third world feminism—the intersection of war, disability, and gender in the third world. In the first section I identify both feminist disability studies and third world feminism as radical perspectives within feminist theory that are nevertheless analytically limited regarding gender and disability in post/neocolonial contexts. Drawing on the contemporary political context of the "war on terror," I argue that the violence of imperialism is instrumental not only in the creation of disability but also in the absence of public recognition of the impact of disability in the third world. Furthermore, I contend it is possible to map historical continuities and discontinuities between racism, sexism, and ableism in the eugenics practices in both the early twentieth century and in contemporary neocolonialist wars in the third world. I aim to foreground the repercussions of the invisibility of disability in radical analyses and to outline the theory and practice of what I term a *transnational feminist disability studies perspective.*

KEEPING IT REAL: FEMINIST DISABILITY STUDIES VERSUS THIRD WORLD FEMINISM

In an essay that makes the case for the inclusion of feminist disability studies in mainstream feminist discourse, Rosemarie Garland-Thomson provocatively describes such scholarship as "academic cultural work with a sharp political edge and a vigorous political punch" (2005, 1557). Judy Rohrer echoes Garland-Thomson's vision when she asks feminists to formulate a "disability theory of feminism," a theory that "upsets old frameworks and allows new questions to be asked" (2005, 40–41). According to both Garland-Thomson and Rohrer, disability analysis deepens feminist analyses of the simultaneity of oppression, body politics, interdependency and agency, and the possibility of transformation.

As a feminist who also works in disability studies, I agree that feminist disability studies has radical potential, potential that has been unrealized in contemporary feminist disability scholarship. Feminist disability studies has effectively critiqued the category of "woman" upheld by mainstream feminism (notwithstanding critiques from poor women, lesbians, women of color, and third world women). Nonetheless, it falls prey to its own critique of normativity by failing to seriously engage "difference" along the axes of race, class, ethnicity, sexuality, and nationality. Thus, although I agree with Garland-Thomson that the analytic category of disability is useful in destabilizing static notions of identity, exploring intersectionality, and investigating embodiment, I argue that the effectiveness of much of feminist disability studies remains limited because of its overreliance on metaphor at the expense of materiality. By *materiality* I mean the actual historical, social, and economic conditions that influence (disabled) people's lives, conditions further mediated by race, ethnic, gender, class, and sexual politics. To a certain extent, I concur with disability studies scholars who characterize disability as a "heterogeneous and fluid category" that embodies the "ultimate postmodern subjectivity" in a "dismodern" post-identity world (Davis 2002; Rohrer 2005, 41–42).[2] However, I propose that this subjectivity's radical potential can be harnessed only within certain privileged material contexts that many disability studies scholars appear to take for granted.

In order for feminist disability studies to realize its transformational potential, it must move from mere discursive intervention to deep interrogation of the material constraints that give rise to the oppressive binaries of self/other, normal/abnormal, able/disabled, us/them. In her discussion of disabled identity from a feminist disability studies perspective, Garland-Thomson explains that disability is often presented "as an exceptional and escapable calamity, rather than as what is perhaps the most universal of human conditions" (2005, 1568). Thus, she asserts that disability should be presented as "an integral part of one's embodiment, character, life, and way of relating to the world . . . , as part of the spectrum of human variation" (1568). While Garland-Thomson fundamentally challenges feminist concepts of the (ab)normal body, her argument relies on an unexamined assumption that disabled identity always occurs outside of historical, social, and economic contexts. This assumption is especially problematic given the intersection of race, class, gender, sexuality, ethnicity, nationality, and disability.

How can acquiring a disability be celebrated as "the most universal of human conditions" if it is acquired under the oppressive conditions of poverty, economic exploitation, police brutality, neocolonial violence, and lack of access to adequate health care and education? What happens when human variation (e.g., race) is deployed in the construction of disabled identities for purely oppressive purposes (e.g., slavery, colonialism, and immigration law)? What does it mean to celebrate cyborg subjectivities when the manufacture of prostheses and assistive technology is dependent on an exploitative international division of labor? How does one "value interdependence" within imperialist/neocolonial contexts that locate consumers and producers of goods and services within a network of fundamentally unequal social relationships (Erevelles 1996)?[3] And finally, how do we build solidarity across difference even while we negotiate the disstances that simultaneously separate and divide us within the contemporary context of transnational capitalism? Unfortunately, feminist disability studies has provided few responses to these questions.

Like feminist disability studies, third world feminism critiques normative tendencies in (Western) mainstream feminism. Here, *Western* describes a certain normative construction of *woman* (read: educated, modern, having control of one's body, and the freedom to make one's own decisions) against whom the "average third world woman" is compared and found to be lacking. The "average third world woman" is generally represented as leading an "essentially truncated life on account of her gender (read: sexually constrained) and her being 'third world' (read: ignorant, poor, uneducated, tradition-bound, domestic, family-oriented, victimized, etc.)" (Mohanty 1991b , 56). These images constitute third world women as an embodiment of lack and mirror ableist representations of disabled women, who also struggle against the stereotypical images of pathetic victimized femininity that justify patriarchal, imperialist, and ableist interventions (Fine and Asch 1988; Morris 1991; Garland-Thomson 1997; Thomas 1999; Ghai 2003). Yet, despite a potentially common platform of resistance, disability is conspicuously missing in third world feminist analyses of difference. For example, disabled Indian feminist Anita Ghai reports that although more than thirty-five million disabled women inhabit India, the National Women's Commission testifies that "disability is not an issue which attracts the feminists" (2003, 25).

Omitting disability in third world feminism is costly, especially given (disabled) women's experiences in the patriarchal postcolonial state (Mohanty 1991; Rai 1996; Kaplan, Alarcon and Moallem 1999). Third world feminists argue that the postcolonial state is "the central site of 'hegemonic masculinity' . . . [and is responsible for monitoring] the defining lines of citizenship for women, racialized ethnicities, and sexualities in the construction of a socially stratified society" (Kaplan et al. 1999, 1). In fact, the state "looms large in women's lives *only* when women transgress the boundaries set by the state in various areas of public and private life over which it has jurisdiction" (Rai 1996, 36; my emphasis). Because disabled women have been characterized historically as dangerous, the patriarchal and ableist state closely patrols the boundaries of female bodily difference (Morris 1991; Garland-Thomson 1997; Thomas 1999; Ghai 2003). This policing of female bodily variation is evident in state practices that seek to control (disabled) women's reproduction (Ghai 2004; Molina 2006); (disabled) women's immigration and citizenship rights (Molina 2006); and (disabled) women's economic (in)dependence (Chang 2000; Livingston 2006; Erevelles 2006).

Notwithstanding "different histories with respect to the particular inheritance of post-fifteenth-century Euro-American hegemony: the inheritance of slavery, enforced migration, plantation and indentured labor, colonialism, imperial conquest, and genocide" (Mohanty 1991a, 10), third world feminists should have common cause around the issue of disability, an inevitable repercussion of the violence of oppressive practices and structures. So in which spaces do disabled third women claim sisterhood? How do they relate to their disabled sisters who derive certain privileges from residing in the imperialist states that facilitated their becoming disabled in the first place? More urgently, how do disabled third world feminists challenge their invisibility among their third world sisters who, while critiquing the imperialist state, leave unexamined the ableist assumptions that ultimately work against all third world women?

DISABILITY AS IMPERIALIST DISCOURSE: THE POLITICS OF GENDER, RACE, AND NATION

Intersections of gender, disability, and race within the neocolonial state are especially relevant in war's context because nationalist discourses use war to rally support for a contradictory stance in which difference is simultaneously denied and universalized (Kaplan et al. 1999). However, it is not only in times of war that the gendered nature of the nation-state becomes apparent (Mohanty 1991b; Afshar 1996; Kaplan et al. 1999). Even in peacetime, women mediate their relationship to the state through their role as biological reproducers (mothers of the nation); as members of ethnic collectives; as participants in the ideological reproduction of the national collectivity; as transmitters of culture; and as participants in national, economic, political, and military struggles (Waylen 1996, 15). Seen as essential to the biological, social, and cultural reproduction of national identity, women are often subject to the close scrutiny of the normalizing regime of the nation-state.

The disciplinary and regulatory functions of this normalizing regime are manifested in state policies that both feminist disability studies and third world feminism would find familiar. Georgina Waylen (1996) separates these policies into three categories: (1) so-called protective policies aimed at women (abortion and maternity leave); (2) policies mediating relationships between men and women (property rights, sexuality, family relations); and (3) policies assuming and reinforcing a gendered distinction between public and private sphere (policies pertaining to war, foreign policy, international trade, resource extraction versus those pertaining to welfare and reproduction). Women and children are both providers and recipients of state services, and often women are forced to liaison with welfare services on behalf of their family members. Women who fail to adhere to the ideological norms of the state face severe material costs and are designated as deviant/abnormal citizens. I offer two examples to illustrate this point.

The question of who may give birth to citizens has been central in the intersecting context of immigration legislation and reproductive rights (Molina 2006). Natalia Molina notes that before the U.S. Immigration Act of 1924, despite the fact that the number of Mexicans who died of tuberculosis were almost double that of all other immigrant groups, Mexican male laborers were not regarded as "diseased," because their bodies were deemed uniquely equipped to perform physical labor in the agricultural, mining, and railroad industries. On the other hand, high infant mortality rates in Mexican communities were perceived as evidence of Mexican women's ill health, lack of education, and poor parenting skills, not as a consequence of poor economic conditions and inadequate prenatal care. In this way, Mexican women were cast as diseased reproducers of unfit citizens and, thus, as undeserving of the privilege of legal immigration.

Similarly, M. Jacqui Alexander and Chandra Talapade Mohanty (1997) describe how the colonial/postcolonial/neocolonial nation-state conflates (white)(hetero)sexuality with citizenship and organizes a "citizenship machinery" that renders suspect all who deviate from white heterosexual norms of citizenship. For example, although their sexuality was used for the reproduction of slavery in the colonial state, African American women were deemed fit only for "a dehumanized reproduction" (Price and Shildrick 1999, 80). This construction of African American women's sexuality and reproductive capacity continues to manifest itself in policies representing African American women with HIV/AIDS as both dependent and diseased and, thus, ineligible for resources needed for survival. Evelynn M. Hammonds (1997) describes how although African American women's voices are not heard in discussions of HIV/AIDS, the intimate details of the lives of African American women with HIV/AIDS are widely exposed in efforts to blame them for their HIV/AIDS status. In this way African

American women living with HIV/AIDS are represented as "the victims that are the 'other' of the 'other,' the deviants of the deviant, irrespective of their sexual identities or practices" (179).

In both of these examples, "disability" is a political and analytical category deployed by the colonialist state to patrol the boundaries of citizenship. Yet, both third world feminist theory and feminist disability studies fail to explore the implications of interpreting disability in this way. Perhaps this omission stems from the fact that many third world feminists accept disability as an individual pathology or tragedy rather than a state responsibility (Stienstra 2002). To perceive disability as an individual's plight problematically (re)locates disability in the "private" sphere. Similarly, despite their argument that disability is not a "private" issue but a "public" social category, feminist disability theorists often fail to offer a sustained critique of how the neocolonial state is implicated in the pathologization of disability, race, gender, and sexuality.

MILITARIZING/MATERIALIZING DIFFERENCE: GENDER, RACE, AND DISABILITY IN WARTIME

Alexander and Mohanty argue that "militarized [hyper]masculinity" plays a strategic role in the reproduction of (neo)colonialism and the (re)-organization of gendered hierarchies in the nation-state (1997, xxv). For example, in the "patriotic" context of war, men's military service is both paid and honored, whereas women's service to their families is unpaid (Haslanger 2003). Similarly, during war nationalist popular media glorifies tough, aggressive, and robustly masculine soldiers (Myrttinen 2004) while ignoring women unless they appear in "recognizable and traditional roles such as the mourning widow or the all-feeling mother" (Lidinsky 2005, 142). Moreover, the military exists in persistent terror of being emasculated (Pin-Fat and Stern 2005), fearful that an "effeminate masculinity" may undermine loyalty and defense of the nation-state (Alexander and Mohanty 1997, xxvi). Thus, gay men and lesbians who serve in the U.S. military (and who are stereotyped as "feminine men" and "masculine women" in popular imagination) were required to maintain a silent presence in order to sustain the mythical image of the hypermasculine, heteronormative imperialist army. It is only recently, under the Obama administration, that the "Don't Ask, Don't Tell" policy in the U.S. military has been rescinded after much debate and opposition.

Nonetheless, the realities of war humble even the toughest and most aggressive soldiers. War injuries produce disability—another threat to the hypermasculine imagery. Many male soldiers diagnosed with depression, posttraumatic stress, and mental illness are afraid to admit their vulnerability and dependence on others—traits that appear contradictory to the ideal of masculinity (Glasser 2005). In Operation Iraqi Freedom, soldiers purportedly had access to the best emergency medical attention and technology immediately after acquiring their injuries, especially prosthetics.[4] Proud of such technology, the U.S. military announced new efforts to keep certain disabled personnel on active duty if they can regain their fitness after being fitted with a prosthetic (Hull 2004). For example, David Rozelle, who was fitted with a prosthetic leg and scheduled to be deployed to Iraq as commander of the Third Armored Cavalry Regiment, was one of the few disabled soldiers celebrated in the mass media. Rozelle is seen as the embodiment of the saying, "once a soldier, always a soldier"—the epitome of the U.S. military's fabled toughness and manliness.

Disabled soldiers like Rozelle represent a new identity in contemporary military discourses—"the cyborg soldier . . . the juncture of ideals, metals, chemicals, and people who make weapons of computers and computers of weapons and soldiers" (Masters 2005, 113). The cyborg soldier is a new post-human subject who is intimately interconnected with modern technologies of war (e.g., the Patriot missile, smart bombs) that are infused with the ability to reason and think without being interrupted by emotions, guilt, or bodily limitations. The body of the human soldier is the weakest link in this new cyborg militarism. In almost every way, the cyborg soldier constantly battles against the human body using "technological prostheses that replicate biological senses while circumventing human biological limitations: poor eyesight, hearing and discernment" (122). Masters describes this cyborg soldier as "a much more resilient subject, a hegemonic technological subject animated by masculine subjectivity, effectively mitigating against the imperfections of the human body while simultaneously [forging] a close identification with white, heterosexual, masculine subjectivity" (121).

From a feminist disability studies perspective, the cyborg soldier may appear a cause for celebration. As a post-human subject, the cyborg subject troubles the boundaries of normal/abnormal humanity, creating a transgressive image of disabled subjectivity. Whereas disabled subjectivity has been categorized historically as effeminate, the disability of the hypermasculine cyborg soldier challenges oppressive images of weak, pitiable, broken, and wounded human flesh and offers an empowering and transgressive image of possibility. In fact, advanced technologies developed during war often trickle down to domestic markets (cell phones, video games, and high-tech prostheses) and enhance the quality of (disabled) civilian life. Thus, some feminist disability theorists could argue that the cyborg soldier, discursively and materially, presents transgressive possibilities for disabled people.

However, the social, political, and economic context of an imperialist war highlights a more sobering scenario of violence, invisibility, and dehumanization. For example, Cristina Masters argues that the modern battlefield can embrace the cyborg soldier only because the cyborg soldier may never have to actually be in the battlefield and therefore may "never have to lay human eyes on the enemy because to kill in a battle is to aim at a blip in a radar screen or a heat-sensored image" (123). Thus, there is little space to distinguish between simulation and reality. This, Masters contends, produces a distance from the material reality of the battlefield by making the body disappear from war. Masters reports that twenty-three thousand cyborg-guided bombs were dropped in the early phases of Operation Iraqi Freedom as compared to ninety-five hundred in Operation Desert Storm, an observation often omitted in popular depictions of the war as "shock and awe" with limited collateral damage. Within cyborg discourse, the other (enemy) is dehumanized and reconstituted as a "code problem in need of techno-scientific solutions" (124).

What happens when we actually look at the "other" face of disability, one that, as a result of actual social, political, and economic deprivation, resists being classified as cyborg? As mentioned earlier, war produces disabilities that include loss of limbs, paralysis, and emotional trauma—disabilities that challenge families, communities, and government agencies (Safran 2001). In Afghanistan vast numbers of people have physical disabilities arising from polio, blast injuries, and untreated eye diseases; mental disabilities associated with malnutrition, iodine deficiency disorders, and trauma; and epilepsy associated with trauma or untreated malaria (Miles 2002). Moreover, Afghan refugees who have been wounded and/or disabled by "friendly fire" must depend on their families' meager resources for survival. M. Miles (2002) reports that already-limited access to disability services for women ceased functioning completely during Taliban rule. In addition, access to community rehabilitation is restricted for women and children in Afghanistan. Notably, restricting Afghan women's mobility has resulted in fewer women being killed or disabled by fighting, landmines, and unexploded bombs. Women also participate disproportionately in informal home care and assistance, a major source of disability services in Afghanistan. Given these material realities, neither feminist disability studies nor third world feminism can dismiss disability in the third world as either a troublesome trope or an irritating detail.

Iraq's situation is even more sobering. Like Afghanistan, Iraq has suffered years of war, economic sanctions, and a U.S. invasion and ongoing occupation. A recent study by the United Nations Development Program (UNDP) contains the following indexes of what they term the "social misery" in Iraq (Walsh 2005):

- Nearly a quarter of Iraq's children suffer from chronic malnutrition.
- The probability of dying before age forty for Iraqi children born between 2000 and 2004 is approximately three times the level found in neighboring countries.
- More than 722,000 Iraqi families have no access to either safe or stable drinking water.
- Forty percent of families in urban areas live in neighborhoods with sewage on the streets.
- More than 200,000 Iraqis have "chronic" disabilities caused by war.

In addition, lessons learned from other war-torn countries like Bosnia, Sierra Leone, and Kosovo reveal the proliferation of invisible disabilities. For example, Susan McKay (2004) reports that in Sierra Leone children who have participated in war return to rural communities with daily suffering and memories of terror. Children exposed to war experience post-traumatic stress, anxiety and depressive symptoms, psychophysiological disturbances, behavioral problems and personality changes, as well as physical traumas resulting from injury, physical deformities, and diseases such as tuberculosis, malaria, and parasites (Kuterovac-Jagodic 2003; McKay 2004; Al-Ali 2005).

Hazem Adam Ghobarah, Paul Huth, and Bruce Russett (2004) describe some major influences wars have on public health infrastructures. First, as mentioned earlier, wars increase the civilian population's risk of disease, injury, and death as a result of displacement. Bad food, water, sanitation, and housing turn refugee camps into vectors for infectious disease. With the destruction of the health care infrastructure occasioned by war, prevention and treatment programs are weakened, and in these circumstances new drug-resistant strains of diseases (e.g., tuberculosis, HIV/AIDS) evolve. Second, wars reduce the pool of available resources for civilian health care and constrain the level of resources allocated to the public health care system. Third, wartime destruction of the transportation infrastructure weakens the distribution of clean water, food, medicine, and relief supplies to both refugees and those who remain behind in war-torn areas.

As these material realities of war reveal, the proliferation of disability in war gives rise to positive and negative meanings that are attributed to disability. In the third world, international organizations like the World Bank and the International Monetary Fund are often instrumental in organizing programs that support particularly oppressive definitions of disability to aid in administering these programs. One such example is the concept of the DALY (disability adjusted life years). According to the World Bank's 1993 report on health, the DALY is

> a unit used for measuring both the global burden of disease and the effectiveness of health interventions, as indicated by reductions in the disease burden. It is calculated as the present value of the future years of disability-free life that are lost as the result of the premature deaths or cases of disability occurring in a particular year.[5]

Put more simply, using the DALY, the World Bank prioritizes health interventions by calculating their relative cost-effectiveness. Cost-effectiveness is measured by the number of DALYs saved through each intervention, and the cost of each intervention is weighed against the person's potential "productivity" (contribution to economic growth) (Werner 1995). Each disease, ailment, or disability is classified according to how many years of "productive" (disability-free) life the individual loses and is weighted against age and work potential. As a result, children and the elderly are assigned lower value than young adults, and, presumably, disabled persons who are unable to work are awarded zero value and therefore have little or no entitlement to health services at public expense.

From a transnational feminist disability studies perspective, such calculations are simply preposterous. In fact, disability studies scholars have critiqued the construction of disabled people as defective citizens who are incapable of contributing anything to society (Ferguson 1987; Garland-Thomson 1997; Russell 1998; Charlton 1998; Kittay 2000). However, productivity is not a transhistorical category. Under current demands of global capitalism and U.S. imperialism, an individual's productivity is not measured by his or her ability to produce goods and services that satisfy social/human needs; rather, individual productivity is based solely on capitalist exploitative demands for increasing profits. The logic under which capitalism and imperialism operate has deleterious consequences for disabled individuals. Since most disabled individuals have physiological complications that prevent the efficient extraction of surplus value from their labor power, their labor power is accorded little value within the competitive marketplace. As a result, disabled people are constructed as unemployable. DALY constitutes disabled people as a liability to the state rather than as a valued investment.

It is not only the representational violence of DALY that is significant. From a transnational feminist disability studies perspective, the material implications of these representations on third world women's lives cannot be ignored. For example, disability policies implemented by international organizations like the World Bank and the International Monetary Fund as part of their proposed "structural adjustment programs" have sought increased privatization of health care and user-financed health services— and thereby transferred resources from poor clients to the wealthy investors in health care. This is evident in community-based rehabilitation programs (CBRs) that are actively supported by the World Bank and other international organizations, like ActionAid, and are perceived to be one of the most cost-efficient means to reduce mounting staff costs, manpower, and services (M. Thomas 1992). Seeking maximum cost-efficiency, policy makers assume that the primary support for these programs will come from the community. For instance, they assume disabled community members will receive more specialized services from parents and workers in the community under the supervision of a village rehabilitation worker (VRW) and a multipurpose rehabilitation worker (MRW), (female) health volunteers living in the community.

CBRs transfer service costs to the community. Even Maya Thomas, CBR advocate and director of the disability division of ActionAid India, has admitted "the trend of progressive impoverishment of rural dwellings and the growing abandonment of extended family systems leave little economic and man-power resources in families that continue to look after the needs of their disabled members" (1992, 9). In patriarchal contexts, family provision of rehabilitation services predominantly implies that women will provide these services. Thus, the rural housewife caught up in her daily struggle for economic survival shoulders another burden. Additionally, rehabilitation aides, who are low in the occupational hierarchy and receive pitiably low wages, are predominantly poor women from the community. State-initiated policies lauded for their cost-effectiveness actually "[mobilize] . . . people's resources for government programs" (Kalyanpur 1996, 125), and low-paid and unpaid labor of poor third world women continue to absorb the costs of these services. In a context where war creates the proliferation of disability, it is critical that third world feminists and feminist disability theorists examine the impact of disability on (both nondisabled and disabled) third world women's lives as they struggle against the oppressive policies and practices of the imperialist/ neocolonial state.

So far I have demonstrated why both feminist disability studies and third world feminism must critically engage disability within postcolonialism/ neocolonialism, especially in the context of war. In this section I make the case for a *transnational feminist disability studies perspective*—a perspective that engages gender and disability and their intersections with race, class, and sexuality within the postcolonial/neocolonial state. This perspective is neither ahistorical nor limited by national or ethnic boundaries. It is neither burdened by narrow class interests nor restricted by normative modes of being. Rather, this perspective maps both the continuities and discontinuities between women along the axes of race, class, disability, sexuality, ethnicity, and nationality by foregrounding both discursive representations and the material (i.e., actual) conditions of their lives.

To provide an example of a transnational feminist disability studies perspective, I link the discussion of disability and war to the oppressive practices of eugenics within the broader transnational context of colonialism/neocolonialism. I contend it is possible to map the historical continuities and discontinuities between racism, sexism, and ableism embodied in the eugenics practices of the early twentieth century and the contemporary context of neocolonialist wars and their impact on disability, race, and gender in the third world.

In Britain in 1883, Francis Galton coined the term *eugenics* to describe a program of selective breeding. Within the imperialistic context of colonialism, eugenics thrived on the fear of racialized Others fueled by racist associations of genetic degeneration and disease. J. Edward Chamberlin and Sander Gilman (1985) define degeneration as loss of the properties of the genus, and the fear of this loss encouraged unscientific stereotyping of physiological differences. Degeneration became a compelling racial metaphor that positioned colonized races as intrinsically degenerate and incapable of improvement. By hinting that society would decay if these degenerate "bodies" were not brought under control, the segregation and/ or the destruction of the colonized races was presented as necessary for the public good.

The association of degeneracy, disease, and racial difference also translated into assumptions that nonwhite people had diminished cognitive capacities. Labels such as "feeble-mindedness" and "mental illness" were often seen as synonymous with nonwhite bodies. Fearing that such characteristics could be passed down from generation to generation and pose a threat to the dominant white race, eugenicists proposed and implemented "protective" policies such as forced sterilizations; rigid miscegenation laws; residential segregation in ghettoes, barrios, and reservations; institutionalization; and sometimes even genocide (e.g., the Holocaust). David Mitchell and Sharon Snyder (2003) adapted race theorist Paul Gilroy's concept of the black Atlantic to describe what they term a "eugenic Atlantic" to demonstrate the role of parallel race and disability discourses in the dehumanizing practices of eugenics. They argue that eugenics needs to be understood as a transatlantic ideology that used the social category of disability to produce constructs such as IQ (intelligent quotients), and practices such as institutionalization, sterilization, segregated education, and restrictive immigration policies to the detriment of both people of color and disabled people. Eugenics grouped disabled people and people of color under the category of "defect."

While Mitchell and Snyder's argument foregrounds the discursive import of disability and race in eugenic ideologies, their analysis fails to address gender and to explore *why* these ideologies gained credence within particular historical moments. I argue that their failure to engage these concerns stems from an assumption that disability, race, and gender are constituted outside of historical, social, and economic structures. Their analysis of the eugenic Atlantic needs to be expanded to consider how the project of colonialism and nation-building was intimately intertwined with eugenics policies that marked people of color and people with disabilities as "unfit bodies" and "unworthy citizens" (Roman 2003).

The history of eugenics cannot be separated from war. Wars produce scarcity, and those who suffer the most are society's most vulnerable populations. For example, according to Mark P. Mostert (2002), the material and logistic requirements of fighting during World War I had both social and material repercussions for asylum inmates. The wartime rationing of food resulted in decreased caloric intake for inmates as well as less heat, clothing, and medication. These shortages, along with overcrowding and poor sanitary conditions, led to an increase in communicable diseases and mortality rates among asylum inmates. Thus, even though caregivers acknowledged the deplorable conditions in asylums, these conditions were generally accepted as a necessary transfer of resources from those deemed unable to support the war effort to those considered able to do so. These ideas characterized disabled people as "useless eaters" and justified the violent practice of euthanasia as the right to alleviate suffering for disabled people. Aided and abetted by sociobiological interpretations of Darwin, eugenics practices like sterilization also became commonplace, and the lives of disabled people in general (and disabled women in particular) came to be viewed as lives of little value. Mostert's argument demonstrates how macro-political and social forces harnessed by eugenics ideologies are detrimental to disabled people and people of color in wartime.

While some would argue that eugenics was an oppressive practice in the colonialist past, I contend that eugenics ideology continues to inform oppression in the contemporary context of the imperialist/neocolonialist war on terror. By foregrounding the imperialist ideological use of disability to mark certain racialized, gendered, sexual, and class differences as "defective," it is possible to name and analyze the eugenic impulses articulated in the war on terror.

As I have already discussed, the war on terror has had violent, oppressive consequences for both poor nondisabled and disabled women in both the first and third worlds, and I am troubled by the absence of analyses of this violence in the otherwise radical analyses of feminist disability studies and third world feminism. The disproportionate surge of death and destruction in Afghanistan is not the only by-product of the war on terror. The war has also disproportionately increased the numbers of disabled children and adults as a result of war-related injuries, military torture, civil war, economic scarcity, and psychological trauma.

The sheer scope of this violence should be difficult to ignore, and yet it is ignored; its invisibility is justified by the imperialist/neocolonial state that aims to regulate and control differences seen as disruptive to the "natural" order of global civil society. This is where the echoes of eugenics policies of the late nineteenth and early twentieth centuries resonate in contemporary times. For example, Iraqis and Afghans who are killed or disabled in their "occupied" countries are not thought of as *civilians* resisting an imperialist force but as *terrorists* and *insurgents*—terms that negate any right to enfranchised citizenship. Even when civilian deaths and disabilities caused by war are acknowledged, they are dismissed as collateral damage. The meager pensions and lack of disability benefits made available to widows, mothers, and caregivers who have lost family members are rationalized as a luxury that did not exist before the occupation. Additionally, decisions about who has access to health care deploy concepts like DALY to the detriment of the thousands of civilians disabled by war and their caregivers, most of whom are poor women of color. In the war on terror eugenic ideologies that associate race, gender, and disability with disease, degeneracy, biological inferiority, and dependence shape ideas about legitimate citizenship and justify representational and material violence against both disabled and nondisabled people of color, especially women.

Invisibility is costly. Recognition, on the other hand, can inspire action. By foregrounding the critical discussion of disability, gender, race, and war, a transnational feminist disability studies will enable solidarity across differences and foster transformative scholarship and radical action that will disrupt the oppressive structures that make bodily variation meaningful. Only then can we ever really give peace a chance.

NOTES

1. I do not use the term *third world* to merely denote geographical difference or allude to hierarchies of economic development. Rather, I use the term, following Chandra Mohanty, as "an analytical and political category [that represents an] 'imagined community' . . . [that] links . . . the histories and struggles of third world women against racism, sexism, colonialism, imperialism, and monopoly capital. 'Imagined' not because it is not 'real' but because it suggests potential alliances and collaborations across divisive boundaries, and 'community' because in spite of internal hierarchies within third world contexts, it nevertheless suggests a significant, deep commitment to what Benedict Anderson . . . calls horizontal comradeship" (1991a, 4).

2. Lennard Davis distinguishes "dismodern" from "postmodern" by arguing that the "postmodern" is still based on humanist notions of the subject. The dismodern subject is "partial and incomplete . . . [and its] realization is not autonomy and independence but dependency and interdependence" (Davis 2002, 30). This is a good example of a disability studies perspective that privileges the metaphorical without really examining the material conditions within which such metaphors gain prominence.

3. For more on valuing interdependence, see Rohrer 2005, 47.

4. Here I refer only to the emergency care soldiers receive at military bases and hospitals like Walter Reed in Bethesda, Maryland. Follow-up medical care in Veterans Administration hospitals is reported to be far from satisfactory.

5. International Bank for Reconstruction and Development/World Bank. *World Development Report 1993*, x.

REFERENCES

Afshar, Haleh. 1996. *Women and Politics in the Third World*. New York: Routledge.

Al-Ali, Nadje. 2005. "Reconstructing Gender: Iraqi Women between Dictatorship, War, Sanctions, and Occupation." *Third World Quarterly* 26 (4–5): 739–58.

Alexander, M. Jacqui, and Chandra Talpade Mohanty, eds. 1997. "Geneaologies, Legacies, Movements." Introduction to *Feminist Geneaologies, Colonial Legacies, Democratic Futures*, xii–xlii. New York: Routledge.

Anderson, Benedict. 1983. *Imagined Communities: Reflections on the Origins and Spread of Nationalism*. London: Verso.

Beresford, Peter, and Chris Holden. 2000. "We Have Choices: Globalization and Welfare User Movements." *Disability and Society* 15 (7): 973–89.

Chamberlin, J. Edward, and Sander Gilman, eds. 1985. *Degeneration: The Dark Side of Progress*. New York: Columbia University Press.

Chang, Grace. 2000. *Disposable Domestics: Immigrant Women Workers in the Global Economy*. Boston: South End Press.

Charlton, James I. 1998. *Nothing about Us without Us: Disability, Oppression, and Empowerment*. Berkeley: University of California Press.

Davis, Lennard J. 2002. *Bending over Backwards: Disability, Dismodernism, and Other Difficult Positions*. New York: New York University Press.

Erevelles, Nirmala. 1996. "Disability and the Dialectics of Difference." *Disability and Society* 11 (4): 519–37.

———. 2006. "Disability in the New World Order: The Political Economy of World Bank Intervention in (Post/Neo)colonial Context." In *Color of Violence: The INCITE Anthology,* edited by A. Smith, B. E. Richie, and J. Sudbury, 25–31. Boston: South End Press.

Ferguson, Phillip. 1987. "The Social Construction of Mental Retardation." *Social Policy* 18(1): 51–56.

Fine, Michelle, and Adrienne Asch, eds. 1988. *Women with Disabilities: Essays in Psychology, Culture, and Politics*. Philadelphia: Temple University Press.

Garland-Thomson, Rosemarie. 1994. "Redrawing the Boundaries of Feminist Disability Studies." *Feminist Studies* 20 (3): 582–97.

———. 1997. *Extraordinary Bodies: Figuring Physical Disability in American Culture and Literature*. New York: Columbia University Press.

———. 2005. "Feminist Disability Studies." *Signs* 30 (2): 1557–87.

Ghai, Anita. 2003. *(Dis)embodied Form: Issues of Disabled Women*. New Delhi: Har-Anand Publications.

Ghobarah, Hazem Adam, Paul Huth, and Bruce Russett. 2004. "The Post-war Health Effects of Civil Conflict." *Social Science and Medicine* 59: 869–84.

Glasser, R. J. 2005. "A War of Disabilities." *Harper's* (July): 59–62.

Hammonds, Evelynn M. 1997. "Toward a Genealogy of Black Female Sexuality: The Problematic of Silence." In Alexander and Mohanty, *Feminist Geneaologies, Colonial Legacies,* 170–82.

Haslanger, Sally. 2003. "Gender, Patriotism, and the Events of 9/11." *Peace Review* 15 (4): 457–61.

Hoglund, Anna, T. 2003. "Justice for Women in War? Feminist Ethics and Human Rights for Women." *Feminist Theology* 11 (3): 346–61.

Hughes, Bill, Linda McKie, Debra Hopkins, and Nick Watson. 2005. "Love's Labor Lost? Feminism, the Disabled People's Movement, and an Ethic of Care." *Sociology* 39 (2): 259–75.

Hull, Anne. 2004. "Wounded or Disabled but Still on Active Duty." *Washington Post,* 1 December, A23.

Hussain, Yasmin. 2005. "South Asian Disabled Women: Negotiating Identities." *Sociological Review* 53 (3): 522–38.

International Bank for Reconstruction and Development/World Bank. *World Development Report 1993. Investing in Health: World Development Indicators*. Oxford: Oxford University Press, 1993. http://files.dcp2.org/pdf/WorldDevelopment Report1993.pdf.

Jaggar, Alison. M. 1998. "Globalizing Feminist Ethics." *Hypatia: A Journal of Feminist Philosophy* 13 (2): 7–31.

Kalyanpur, Maya. 1996. "The Influence of Western Special Education on Community Based Services in India." *Disability and Society* 11 (2): 249–70.

Kaplan, Caren, Norma Alarcon, and Minoo Moallem, eds. 1999. *Between Women and Nation: Nationalisms, Transnational Feminism, and the State.* Durham, N.C.: Duke University Press.

Khan, Ayesha. 2003. "Gendering War Talk." *International Feminist Journal of Politics* 5 (3): 448–55.

Kittay, Eva Feder. 1998. *Love's Labor: Essays on Women, Equality, and Dependency.* New York: Routledge.

Kuterovac-Jagodic, Gordana. 2003. "Posttraumatic Stress Symptoms in Croatian Children Exposed to War: A Prospective Study." *Journal of Clinical Psychology* 59 (1): 9–25.

Lansdown, Gerison, 1998. "The Rights of Disabled Children." *International Journal of Children's Rights* 6: 221–27.

Lidinsky, April. 2005. "The Gender of War: What *Fahrenheit 9/11*'s Women Don't Say." *International Feminist Journal of Politics* 7 (1): 142–46.

Livingston, Julie. 2006. "Insights from an African History of Disability." *Radical Review of History* 94: 111–26.

Masters, Cristina. 2005. "Bodies of Technology: Cyborg Soldiers and Militarized Masculinities." *International Feminist Journal of Politics* 7 (1): 112–32.

McKay, Susan. 2004. "Reconstructing Fragile Lives: Girls' Social Reintegration in Northern Uganda and Sierra Leone." *Gender and Development* 12 (3): 19–30.

McRuer, Robert. 2006. "We Were Never Identified: Feminism, Queer Theory, and a Disabled World." *Radical History Review* 94: 148–54.

Miles, M. 2002. "Formal and Informal Disability Resources for Afghan Reconstruction." *Third World Quarterly* 23 (5): 945–59.

Mitchell, David, and Sharon Snyder. 2003. "The Eugenic Atlantic: Race, Disability, and the Making of an International Eugenic Science, 1800–1945." *Disability and Society* 18 (7): 843–64.

Mohanty, Chandra Talpade. 1991a. "Cartographies of Struggle: Third World Women and the Politics of Feminism." Introduction to *Third World Women and the Politics of Feminism,* edited by Chandra Talpade Mohanty, Ann Russo, and Lourdes Torres, 1–47. Bloomington: Indiana University Press.

———. (1986) 1991b . "Under Western Eyes: Feminist Scholarship and Colonial Discourse." In Mohanty et al., *Third World Women,* 51–80.

Molina, Natalia. 2006. "Immigration, Race, and Disability in Early 20th Century America." *Radical History Review* 94: 167–201.

Morris, Jenny. 1991. *Pride against Prejudice.* London: Women's Press.

Mostert, Mark P. 2002. "Useless Eaters: Disability as Genocidal Marker in Nazi Germany." *Journal of Special Education* 36 (3): 155–68.

Myrttinen, Henri. 2004. "'Pack Your Heat and Work the Streets': Weapons and the Active Construction of Violent Masculinities." *Women and Language* 27 (2): 29–34.

Nakano-Glenn, Evelyn. 1992. "From Servitude to Service Work: Historical Continuities in the Racial Division of Paid Reproductive Work." *Signs* 18 (1): 1–18.

Narayan, Uma. 1998. "Essence of Culture and a Sense of History: A Feminist Critique of Cultural Essentialism." *Hypatia* 13 (2): 86–106.

Parker, Gillian. 1993. *With This Body: Caring and Disability in Marriage*. Philadelphia: Open University Press.

Pin-Fat, Veronique, and Maria Stern. 2005. "The Scripting of Private Jessica Lynch: Biopolitics, Gender, and the 'Feminization' of the U. S. Military." *Alternatives* 30: 25–53.

Price, Janet, and Margaret Shildrick, eds. 1999. *Feminist Theory and the Body: A Reader*. New York: Routledge.

Rai, Shirin. 1996. "Women and the State in the Third World." In *Women and Politics in the Third World*, edited by Haleh Afshar, 25–39. New York: Routledge.

Renzetti, Claire M. 2005. "Gender-based Violence." *Lancet*, 19 March.

Rohrer, Judy. 2005. "Towards a Full-inclusion Feminism: A Feminist Deployment of Disability Analysis." *Feminist Studies* 31 (1): 34–61.

Roman, Leslie. 2003. "Education and the Contested Meanings of 'Global Citizenship.'" *Journal of Educational Change* 4 (3): 269–93.

Russell, M. 1998. *Beyond Ramps: Disability at the End of the Racial Contract*. Monroe, Maine: Common Courage Press.

Safran, Stephen P. 2001. "Movie Images of Disability and War: Framing History and Political Ideology." *Remedial and Special Education* 22 (4): 223–32.

Schutte, Ofelia. 1998. "Cultural Alterity: Cross-cultural Communication and Feminist Theory in North-South Contexts." *Hypatia* 13 (2): 53–72.

Silber, Irina Carlotta. 2004. "Mothers/Fighters/Citizens: Violence and Disillusionment in Post-war El Salvador." *Gender and History* 16 (3): 561–87.

Stienstra, Deborah. 2002. "DisAbling Globalization: Rethinking Global Political Economy with a Disability Lens." *Global Society* 16 (2): 109–21.

Stone-Mediatore, Shari. 1998. "Chandra Mohanty and the Revaluing of Experience." *Hypatia* 13 (2): 116–33.

Thomas, Carol. 1999. *Female Forms: Experiencing and Understanding Disability*. London: Open University Press.

Thomas, Maya. 1992. "Community Based Rehabilitation in India: An Emerging Trend." *Indian Journal of Pediatrics* 59 (4): 401–406.

Walsh, David. 2005. "US War in Iraq Yields a Social 'Tragedy.'" World Socialist Web Site. http://www.wsws.org/articles/2005/may2005/iraq-m18.shtml.

Waylen, Georgina. 1996. "Analyzing Women in the Politics of the Third World." In Afshar, *Women and Politics*, 7–24.

Werner, D. 1995. "Turning Health into an Investment: Assaults on Third World Health Care." *Economic and Political Weekly*, 21 January, 147–51.

Six

GWENDOLYN BROOKS, WORLD WAR II, AND THE POLITICS OF REHABILITATION

JENNIFER C. JAMES

The final chapter of Gwendolyn Brooks's 1953 novel *Maud Martha*, titled "back from the wars!" begins with the heroine rejoicing in her brother's return from World War II: "There was Peace, and her brother Harry was back from the wars, and well. And it was such a beautiful day!" (1993, 177).[1] It was for Maud Martha a long-awaited moment of relief; however, her respite will prove brief. Just as she dashes out of her kitchenette in "exhilaration," her mind is invaded by brutal images of bodies transformed by war: "They 'marched,' they battled behind her brain . . . the men with two arms off and two legs off, the men with the parts of faces. Then her guts divided" (179). These descriptions openly refuse any glamorization of war, serving as bodily reminders of war's inevitable consequences. This frank corporeal imagery also structures Brooks's presentation of war in an earlier twelve-poem meditation on World War II, "gay chaps at the bar," published in *A Street in Bronzeville* (1945). Initially labeled the "Soldier Sonnets,"[2] these poems were based on letters Brooks received from servicemen abroad, including her brother, Raymond Brooks, to whom she dedicates the sequence. It begins with a quotation from a letter in which a soldier remarks on the state of men returning from the front, "crying" he writes, "trembling" (Brooks 1987, 64).[3] It is this understanding of war, culled from the "stuff of letters," as she writes in her autobiography (1972, 156), that will shape her imagining of the soldier's body.

While one might expect any socially conscious literature about war to include realistic depictions of wrecked and altered bodies, Brooks's willingness to invoke what Daryl Michael Scott calls "damage imagery" (qtd. in Baynton 2001, 41) in relation to the black male body is rare in the tradition of African American war literature. Part of the explanation for this omission, I will suggest, emerges from the dominant culture's conflation of discourses of disability and racial "otherness" within the United States; both are used to exclude bodies marked as "different," and therefore "damaged," from participation in the national body politic. Disability historian Douglas Baynton clarifies this relationship: "Disability has functioned historically to justify inequality for disabled people themselves[; however,] the concept of disability has been used to justify discrimination against other groups by attributing disability to them. . . . non-white races were routinely connected to people with disabilities, both of whom were depicted as evolutionary laggards or throwbacks" (34, 46). The notion of the black body as congenitally disabled—inherently defective, afflicted by deformity and disease—was merely compounded by the attribution of another form of (acquired) disability: the black body as irreversibly impaired by the violence of slavery.

THE RHETORIC OF WAR AND
THE REHABILITATION OF THE BLACK BODY

Within an ideological context that defined disability as deficiency, and blackness synonymously with disability, black American war writers' hesitance to represent the black body wounded by war becomes infinitely less mysterious: these images might unintentionally evoke other concepts of damage that are routinely ascribed to African Americans. This anxiety was exacerbated by the powerful cultural link between bodily and psychological injury. In post–Civil War literature particularly, it became imperative that the black body and the black "mind" be portrayed as uninjured by the injuring institution of slavery in order to disprove one of the main antiblack arguments that surfaced after emancipation—that slavery had made blacks "unfit" for citizenship. The desire to enact "damage control" by policing and correcting politically detrimental representations of blackness was generally shared within the African American writing community before Brooks's era. Arguably, "damage control" and issues of "correct" representation still affect black American literary and cultural production as we enter the twenty-first century. In black war writing, however, the absence of injury becomes more remarkable: in a literature about a violent enterprise, representation of bodily violation was rare.[4]

The dearth of references to black corporeal damage in African American war literature can be considered a literary version of bodily rehabilitation, mimicking the purposes of rehabilitative technologies used to reconstruct bodies disabled and altered by war. Although the purposes of those technologies might seem self-evident (i.e., to help the injured body regain its corporeal functions), disability scholarship has shown that the

goals of ontological restoration are all too frequently bound to ideological objectives that are little related to a disabled person's needs (including
the very real possibility that he or she might not deem bodily intervention necessary). Indeed, in *A History of Disability* French cultural critic
Henri-Jacques Stiker concludes that Western societies' rush to "fix" bodies labeled "disabled" stems from a growing unwillingness to acknowledge
circumstances (e.g., poverty or unsafe industries) that continue to create
socially produced (i.e., non-accidental, non-congenital) forms of disability (1999, 121–89).

Locating the emergence of this "new" rehabilitative imperative within
post–World War I France, Stiker claims the unprecedented numbers of
soldiers returning with permanent injuries prompted a shift in attitude
regarding the proper treatment of disabled veterans. Any genuine sense
of moral and ethical responsibility toward the injured individual, whose
wounds were viewed as lingering memorials to the epic disaster of the war,
was complicated by a competing desire to limit the impact of the conflict
on French society and to reduce, even deny, human culpability in its making. According to Stiker, what would prove an ultimately dangerous consensus began to take shape: the decision to view the injuries soldiers suffered as inevitable, "natural" occurrences rather than as the results of an
avoidable social calamity. Naturalizing disability in this manner, he writes,
required behaving as one would in the face of an earthly catastrophe, such
as a flood, an event for which no one can be held responsible and from
which complete recovery can be imagined: "we can and must repair . . . in
other words, efface, expiate" (124–25). Thus, the injured body was transformed into an "object of repair," something that could be returned to a
"prior, normal" state (124). To be most effective, this return also needed to
be wholesale. Consequently, in 1916 the National Office of the War Maimed
enacted a policy authorizing "the general use of prostheses" for all veterans
who presumably could benefit from them (123). The compulsion to physically "repair" the disabled body, to reverse corporeal "damage," was hence-
forth intertwined with the impulse to "redeem" society. Modern technology became indispensable to this project; the advanced prosthetic, unlike
its cruder and more apparent predecessors, "the crutch and wooden leg,"
could eradicate the physical signifiers of disaster, facilitating the forgetting
of a war that France wanted to purge from its collective memory (123).

Stiker's description of this intermediate step between fixing and forgetting is critical to understanding how rehabilitation operates in African
American texts. Successful rehabilitation permitted the "formerly" disabled body to be reintegrated into the nation's significant social structures,
such as work and family. Made "ordinary" again, "identical" to "normal"

citizens, the disabled would "disappear" within these institutions (129). I speculate that the presentation of an always already able-bodied masculinity unmarred by slavery and warfare acted as an attempt to "rehabilitate" the perception of black men as an argument for national and structural (re)integration. In other words, African American war writers wished for African men to be considered "normal" rather than aberrant or damaged. In this way, the specularity of a body marked "different" and the object of the condemning gaze could be eluded. There would no longer be a reason to stare, to categorize, to exclude. If the prospect of integration did in fact motivate textual modes of "damage control"—the conspicuous body disappearing into sameness—Brooks's detailed depictions of decidedly unrehabilitated black male bodies in "gay chaps at the bar," produced before the desegregation of the military, and in *Maud Martha*, written before the larger desegregation of the nation, would seem to undermine this aim.

The appearance of injured bodies at the close of *Maud Martha*, a work exploring a black woman's struggle to make her domestic life conform to the heteronormative ideals of marriage and family, continues to perplex the novel's readers. War is merely alluded to before this final chapter, seeming no more than a historical referent, and certainly not as central to Maud Martha's life or the novel's purpose. As many critics have noted, the semiautobiographical *Maud Martha* stands as Brooks's blunt response to blacks' subscription to the "second cult of true womanhood" of the 1950s. The "cult" emerged in part as a postwar backlash against women workers, who, after helping sustain the American economy, were nonetheless coerced, and sometimes forced, to relinquish their jobs to demobilized male veterans. The government-led campaign to return women to the home was further fueled by the specter of communism, that "other," "unnatural" way of being, lending new urgency to constructing oppositional ideologies of "Americanism." This incarnation of "Americanism" idealized a homogenous, patriarchal vision of the domestic that could resist internal and external disruptive political forces that threatened the foundation of American society: a capitalist economy dependent on gender, racial, and class stratification. Yet the domestic ideal reigning in the 1950s ran counter to African American familial configurations and labor patterns necessitated by economic exigencies. In his insightful reading of James Baldwin's rendition of the domestic space in his gay bildungsroman, *Go Tell It on the Mountain,* Roderick Ferguson explains that the question of whether a black heteronormative family was possible for African Americans (or, for that matter, desirable or "natural") was lost in sociological discourses that rescripted domestic variations in black communities as voluntary transgressions or signs of moral deficiency (2004, 140).

The "regulatory demands" of heteronormative families (140) had particular implications for black women. Because they were, from the onset of slavery, needed as both laboring machines and "sexual latrines" (hooks 1981, 33), the dominant culture generated an amalgam of cultural, medical, scientific, and sociological "evidence" declaring that black women's gender and sexual "abnormality" precluded them from fully inhabiting the category "woman."[5] Deemed physically malformed, genitally excessive, and sexually deviant, many black women sought to destigmatize their bodies by adopting the dominant culture's "feminine" paradigms, striving to present themselves as physically and morally fit for domesticity. Thus, much as the military (and war) had become a site where black men could "rehabilitate" their bodies, the domestic served as space where black women could also "rehabilitate" theirs. Indeed, Maud Martha, dismissed as an uncomely "old black gal" in the novel (Brooks 1993, 34), believes her worthiness as a woman can be validated through procuring a husband and a home, the prizes presumably offered only to those women considered desirable enough to deserve them.

Quite clearly, this model of black rehabilitation required that African Americans capitulate to a range of normalization processes espoused by white America. For black women, the most evident and detrimental concessions were corporeal in nature (e.g., skin lightening and hair relaxing). Noting that Maud Martha's mind turns to the "pale" female faces peering off the pages of "the Negro Press" just after she pictures the stream of wounded soldiers, Harry B. Shaw rightly interprets the novel as expressing "the specific war that black women wage with beauty" (1987, 264).

However, this battle with bodily image comprises only part of Maud Martha's struggle. Brooks paints a portrait of a woman whose psychic damage comes from both the "failure" of her body and the way her "gray" domestic life has stifled her autonomous desires and limited her world to her dingy kitchenette, leaving her "with her hungriest lack—not much voice" (Brooks 1993, 176). Two years before the novel's publication, the Negro Digest ran Brooks's editorial addressing the sources of black wives' domestic discontent, "Why Negro Women Leave Home" (1951). Her brief but biting commentary suggests that the economic independence wage work provided black women during World War II rendered them less equipped to submit to their husbands in household affairs. These newly empowered women, she writes, could "buy their child a new overcoat without planning an elaborate strategic campaign, or undergoing the smoke and tire of a semi-revolution" (28). The language Brooks chooses here is revealing, supporting an interpretation of Maud Martha as imagining black women's resistance to patriarchal norms as a form domestic warfare.

The "war with beauty" and the domestic "war" Brooks explores in *Maud Martha* and her editorial are obviously metaphorical, while the war she refers to in her novel and sonnet sequence is "actual." Still, the fact that the two "wars" are elided within *Maud Martha* suggests Brooks is inviting her audience to forge some form of comparison. Thus, rather than isolate *Maud Martha* as a novel about black women and the domestic, and "gay chaps at the bar" as poems about black men and war, I argue that the two should be read coextensively, as texts informing each other. More specifically, I suggest that Brooks uses both to explode the myth of racial "rehabilitation" and, thus, exposes as false the allegedly redemptive properties of the national and nationalist institutions black women and men had come to see as their salvation. Interpreted in this way, "gay chaps at the bar" and *Maud Martha* can be analyzed as an intervention into discourses that herald the military, warfare, and the domestic as means of black "normalization."

Brooks's distrust of normalization was well founded. As Stiker asserts, the most deleterious effects of positing social reintegration (or "normalization") as the outcome of rehabilitation were multiple and complex. First and foremost, it assumed a recognizable and objective "normality" to which all should strive. This tyranny of homogeneity was not content to reform bodies perceived as visibly or functionally "disabled"; it remade bodily interiors. As a result, an increasing number of people marked "different," from the poor to the unemployed, have been labeled "disabled," becoming targets of rehabilitative practices implemented across institutions to prod the "maladapted" into behaving like the "adapted" (Stiker 1999, 125–39). Refusing to characterize this coercion as simply domination in its most obvious form, Stiker notes that the Other will accept rehabilitation to gain whatever a given society markets as the benefits of sameness, colluding in a performance of assimilation that attempts to efface difference and the difficulties difference creates. More problematically, this cosmetic fix allows the inequities created by political, social, and ideological practices that relegate certain bodies to economic, gender, sex, and physical (and racial) alterity to conveniently recede from view. In short, Stiker believes that through "naturalizing" socially produced disability, naming all difference "disability" and claiming all "disabled" capable of "rehabilitation," preventive measures are judged unnecessary (174–75). Societal transformation halts; social destruction proceeds unimpeded.

I have detailed Stiker's assessment of Western culture's stance toward disability to illumine my penultimate claim that Brooks's war literature endeavors to correct this very posture. I invoke the language of rehabilitation here intentionally, for I believe that in the final analysis Brooks does forward an argument for rehabilitation's potential. Her version, however, neither begins nor ends with the reconstruction of bodies and minds violated by the destructive forces of racism, sexism, heteronormativity, capitalism or war. Instead, Brooks's highlighting of these forces and their debilitating effects on black Americans suggests a revisionary understanding of African American disability, what I will call a "black womanist politics of rehabilitation." Articulated through her deployment of "damaged" and imperfect figures in "gay chaps at the bar" and *Maud Martha*, Brooks's alternative set of politics accomplishes several aims. It forces socially produced disability into view (disallowing the disappearing acts that "normalization" encourages); takes society and its harmful institutional practices as the objects in need of repair; acknowledges the reality of specifically racial and gendered injury while resisting institutional rehabilitation as a "corrective"; envisions black male and female injury as bound; and refuses to exempt black Americans from the destruction done to self or other.

A HISTORY OF BLACK WAR WRITING

In order to fully elucidate how a black womanist politics of rehabilitation operates in her works, it is first necessary to situate Brooks within the broader literary context of black war writing to demonstrate how her World War II poetry and fiction mark an important turning point in the way war and the black body at war will function within that tradition. I study the author as part of a larger project on the African American war literature from the Civil War through World War II, wars before Truman's decision to issue Executive Order 9981 in 1948, mandating an end to segregation within all branches of the armed forces. Tracing the concerns of black war writing to William C. Nell's 1855 work, *Colored Patriots of the American Revolution,*[6] the first full-length history of black participation in warfare, I argue that many aspects of *Colored Patriots* are echoed in the literature that followed his publication, particularly his effort to include blacks in a public military history and to narrate acts of black patriotism and valor as irrefutable evidence that blacks had earned a place within the nation. As a whole, the early tradition of black war writing was a tool in the quest for black civil rights, reflecting African Americans' real and continued attempts to instrumentalize military service. Since the first militias were raised in the colonies, black men have envisioned military participation as an avenue toward liberation and citizenship, heeding the call for "able-bodied" men needed to fill military ranks, even when they were continually rejected.

The "able-bodied" criterion provided blacks with a more immediate and concrete reason to rebut theories of black corporeal debility. For instance, before black men were officially allowed to join the Union Army, Frederick Douglass published an editorial asserting that the powerful bodies of black men were needed to win the war (1990, 478). Douglass deploys black arms and hands as ready signifiers of ability and, importantly, as an ability cultivated in slavery rather than compromised by it. During a manpower crisis during the Revolutionary War, states such as New England and Maryland allowed "able-bodied" slaves to enlist with the permission of their masters, often in exchange for freedom. An "able body" could therefore directly translate into a liberated one. Just as often, however, the contention that the black body was inherently disabled prevented blacks from joining the military. During the Revolution, the Continental Congress decided not to enlist "Negroes, Boys unable to bear Arms nor Old men unfit to endure the Fatigues of the Campaign" (Quarles 1996, 15), placing black male bodies between the not completely formed bodies of children and the infirm bodies of the elderly. New Hampshire refused to accept "lunatics, idiots and Negros" (17), implying blackness was a similar mental deficiency.

The belief that the black body was impaired was undergirded by Western "scientific racialism" in the eighteenth and nineteenth centuries that characterized blacks as inferior and as subhuman. White abolitionist Thomas Wentworth Higginson, who commanded the first African American regiment officially raised for the Civil War, issued this progress report about his black subordinates: they "were growing more like white men— less grotesque" (Cullen 1992, 87). Another soldier marveled: "Put a United States uniform on his back and the chattel is a man" (85). These remarks suggest that black men's first task in demonstrating that they were worthy of citizenship lay in proving to whites that they were not "grotesques" or "chattel," but "men." Because whites could also imagine the black body "rehabilitated" by military service, African Americans seized opportunities to present their militarized bodies as reformed.

The investment in the military as a site of rehabilitation was neither unique to the United States nor to African Americans seeking elevation. Michel Foucault has suggested that by the time of the eighteenth century, the French army conceptualized the human body as a malleable form, an object that enters a "machinery of power that explores it, breaks it down and rearranges it" (1977, 138). The erect back, head held high, and chest thrown out are visible signs that the body has been "corrected," made pliant and docile; in short, they are signs that the body has been controlled, made something other, politically and physically, than it was upon entry.

The "peasant," Foucault observes, becomes "the soldier" (138). While it may be that the late nineteenth-century American military had yet to adopt the structure and rigor that would be its twentieth-century hallmark, the military was nevertheless thought to transform its members: it was a space where boys were made men and men made more manly—and, as Higginson declares, blacks could be made men.

Documents of African American military service abound with "before" and "after" photographs of black soldiers attesting to this radical reformation.[7] Serving as observable evidence of a rigorous and disciplined body, these photographs suggest that the reason many African American men joined the army was not to *be* "transformed" (as many understood they were already men) or "disciplined" (for many did not accept the nationalist ideologies that accompanied service), but rather to *display* a body the nation would accept as "corrected." The perfected body within African American war literature, particularly idealized representations of the black male soldier-citizen, contributed to a larger set of cultural images designed to refute characterizations of deficiency and offer evidence of bodily rehabilitation.

By World War I, the conception of American black men as naturally "afflicted" was so ingrained in military culture that after the war, some were denied disability compensation because government physicians argued that little distinction could be made between those injuries and disabilities caused by war and the typical disabilities of the African American race (Hickel 2001, 236–37). In 1944, when Brooks published her sonnets, racist notions of the deficient and subhuman body still persisted: to explain why black men could not be aviators, white soldiers circulated the preposterous myth that black soldiers had tails. In a sonnet titled "the white troops had their orders but the Negroes looked like men," Brooks exposes as absurd notions of black disability that rationalized military segregation:

They had supposed their formula was fixed.
They had obeyed instructions to devise
A type of cold, a type of hooded gaze.
But when the Negroes came they were perplexed.
These Negroes looked like men. Besides, it taxed
Time and the temper to remember those
Congenital inequities that cause
Disfavor of the darkness. Such as boxed
Their feelings properly, complete to tags—
A box for dark men and a box for Other—

Would often find the contents had been scrambled.
Or even switched. Who really gave two figs?
Neither the earth nor heaven ever trembled.
And there was nothing startling in the weather.

(1987, 70)

In an image both ironic and disturbing, black and white bodies are integrated as both are disabled, obliterated beyond recognition. Brooks's poem points to yet another irony, however, one beyond exposing the superficial nature of race. The political and social "recognition" that black men sought through service, a recognition they hoped might definitively negate racist characterizations of "congenital defects," is complicated by what their bodies could become in violent death—unrecognizable in relation to what they were before. Elaine Scarry (1985) has famously argued that a civilization embeds itself in the body; a handshake, a gait, a wave are signs of that civilization carried within an individual human form. The host of bodily rituals demanded by the military is a heightened demonstration of civilization manifested through the body. But death, Scarry claims, undoes all of that; the inherent contradiction in the idealized notion of "dying for one's country" lies within the deconstruction of the body slain on a battlefield. When "the chest is shattered," the nation is emptied from the body; "the civilization as it resides" in the body is unmade (122).

This "unmaking" is critical to Brooks's project. The unmaking of the black soldier's body, the focus on its ability to be disabled, is also the unmaking of the ideological assumptions that accompany those presentations of the black warring body as whole, able, heroic. If Brooks "corrects" many of the black war writers who preceded her, she also writes against visual military propaganda that used idealized constructions of the black male body as a recruitment tool and as a means of appeasing African Americans incensed both by policies that drafted blacks into segregated forces and by the scant acknowledgment they received for their services.

INCARNATING THE TRUTH OF WAR

In a longer poem from *Bronzeville*, "Negro Hero: To Suggest Dorie Miller," a "sonnet-ballad" (Brooks's own term), Brooks crafts an interior monologue for the famous black sailor who, during the attack on Pearl Harbor, gunned down at least two Japanese war planes as his ship was sinking and rescued his wounded captain (1987, 48). Miller was a mess attendant with no formal training on weaponry; at that time, black seamen were allowed to serve in only the most menial of capacities. The government did award his effort with the Navy Cross, but only after the black press expressed outrage over the military's negligence in refusing to recognize his heroism.[8] The War Department subsequently issued a poster depicting a brawny Miller, saluting, the slogan "above and beyond the call of duty" above his head.[9] The ability of his body, its size and strength, was afforded great attention in the press, although that same body had kept him from being legitimately introduced to military weaponry before the incident. In "Negro Hero" Brooks invests the sailor with an understanding of how beliefs in congenital difference/disability marred his achievement. "Still—am I good enough to die for them," he asks, "is my blood bright enough to be spilled, / Was my constant back-question—are they clear / On this?" (49).

In the experimental, off-rhyme, strained poems of "gay chaps at the bar" Brooks's exploration of these issues becomes more complex as she attempts to give voice to a range of "non-heroic" bodies: anonymous, "crying . . . trembling," and, most importantly, visibly physically broken. The decision to render the physically catastrophic potential of war in the sonnet, a form that is distinguished by the control the writer exercises over language, permits Brooks a space to consider the uses and limits of language, juxtaposing them against the uses and limits of the body. In her apparent attempt to bring war under the ordering properties of the sonnet, Brooks parallels how the official, mythologizing language of the state also tries to contain the destructive nature of war. This official rhetoric influences the language that most early African American war writers adopt to describe the black warring body (the soldiers are "courageous," "valiant"; they are "patriots" who "love their country") precisely because it encourages denial. But the truth of war, Brooks appears to say, will threaten any language—official or poetic—that seeks to regulate it. This is where the disabled body becomes central to Brooks's presentation of war. In choosing to "alter" the physical, human form of the black soldier, she is forced to alter the poetic form structuring the sequence.

The sonnet "still do I keep my look, my identity" demonstrates how deftly Brooks brings together the ideas of recognition, the body, language, and poetic form to rescript mythological presentations of war. Here, the speaker meditates on what might happen to his body during battle. It might easily be mistaken for a Shakespearean sonnet and indeed follows that rhyme scheme perfectly for the first eight lines:

Each body has its art, its precious prescribed
Pose, that even in passions droll contortions, waltzes

Or push of pain—or when grief has stabbed,
Or hatred hacked—is its, and nothing else's.
Each body has its pose. No other stock
That is irrevocable, perpetual
And its to keep. In castle or in shack.
With rags or robes. Through good, nothing or ill.

(65)

The last six lines allude to the Petrarchan sonnet:

And even in death a body, like no other
On any hill or plain or crawling cot
Or gentle for the lilyless pall
(Having twisted, gagged, and then sweet-ceased to
   bother),
Shows the old personal art, the look. Shows what
It showed in baseball. What it showed in school.

(65)

In merging the two forms, Brooks achieves a striking effect. The reader's expectations for the Shakespearean sonnet are ruptured at the precise moment when Brooks turns from the body's life to its death. In this poem, the "pose" struck before war becomes a posture of a different kind: a "twisted" one. Even though the speaker wishes to imagine his body unaffected, Brooks twists both the body and the form that "writes" that body, forcing both reader and sonnet to respond to war's ability to alter what it touches. The speaker's need to conceive of a death that does not transform him physically can be read as a somatic metaphor for the intended effects of American mythologies of war, which attempt to turn the nation away from the un-structuring or deconstructive aspects of war to war's ostensible capacity to "preserve" (e.g., ways of life) or to "save" (e.g., people or resources). If Brooks's poem seeks to remind us of the vulnerability of the body, it also asks us to note the fragility of rhetorical illusion. On its surface, her sonnet appears whole, undisturbed. Upon closer inspection, it is two fragments pieced together. Brooks's disability politics have given rise to a disability poetics.

A passage from *Maud Martha* further illustrates how the disabled body troubles claims made by governments about war's rectifying power. After Maud Martha finds her exhilaration disrupted by images of disfigurement, she meditates on the possibility of "man . . . completely succeed[ing] in destroying the world" (1993, 176). She then turns to flowers, assuring herself they would "come up again in the spring . . . if necessary, between or out of . . . the smashed corpses lying in strict composure, in that hush infallible and sincere" (179). Flowers growing out of corpses: Martha's insistence upon turning destroyed bodies into fertile, life-giving ones is more than a hopeful vision of regeneration. Rather, it seems Brooks alludes to the absurdity of narrating death wrought by war in any manner the living see fit. The "hushed" and silent dead, forced into the state of calm and decay that "composure" dually implies, have no choice but to cooperate in this reading. Similarly, in exploring representations of death in African American writing, Sharon Holland observes, "The ability of the emerging nation to speak hinges on its correct use of the 'dead' in the service of its creation" (2000, 28). The dead do not speak, but are "spoken for." The dead can be regulated.

However, the material existence of disabled bodies refuses the cooperation that memorializing so readily offers. David Gerber's examination of disability imagery in World War II films notes that many major "newsreels and newsmagazines, most significantly *Life,* had a policy against publishing images of dead, dying or severely wounded combat forces" (2000, 81). Gerber theorizes that these organizations believed the American public was unprepared to accept that warfare could produce such extraordinary disfigurement and such high rates of casualties.[10] An attendant anxiety stemmed from demobilization after World War II—that deformed, disfigured, disabled men would return "abnormal," their psyches as irrevocably altered as their bodies (the reflexive association that kept African American war writers from depicting images of damage). Inspiring even more fear in the public was the prevalent notion that these men no longer "fit" into society and would become disruptive: "menaces," operating in a realm outside of any proper social order. Gerber argues that many of the films produced after World War II are a recuperative response, focusing on the disabled veteran's successful reintegration into his community. As such, they depict disabled veterans as successfully rehabilitated, physically and emotionally. Emotional recovery signaled the veteran's readiness to reenter society, and that reentry was frequently finalized by marriage, a domestic space where heteronormative behavior is the ultimate signifier of masculine regeneration (74–75). Thus, Gerber argues, these films were meant to alleviate the fear that the veterans' losses might cause them to harbor anger and resentment toward the nation that sent them to war.

Gerber's analysis can be productively applied to recuperation narratives involving race. For demobilized African American soldiers, any anger emerging from their fractured bodies was reinforced by the racism they endured serving in a segregated, discriminatory army. Numerous letters from black servicemen document how physical disability and institutional racism operated in tandem, creating unbearable, often inhumane conditions. Disabled black men were frequently left unattended, made to work through injury, and punished for the failings of their bodies (McGuire 1993, 205–208). In a letter to one of the most prominent African American newspapers, *Pittsburg Courier,* one soldier pleaded: "I am a sick disabled man in the Army. If I don't get out of here alive very soon I'll end it all by killing myself. I am tired of suffering. . . . Since I've been here I've seen many cripple Negroes. . . . They keep our men in the army disabled until they die I know; it has happen here last week" (225). Another, claiming to write on "behalf of myself and 60 other men like me," complained, "the sick and disabled soldier is treated worse than a Jap. . . . The punishment we get for being disabled is extra duty" (217).

Brooks devotes several sonnets to the soldier's return, none of which ease society's worries about the mental or physical state of returning black veterans:

I bid, Be firm till I return from hell
. . . .
Hoping that, when the devil days of my hurt
Drag out to their last dregs and I resume
On such legs are left me, in such heart
As I can manage, remember to go home,
My taste will not turned insensitive
To honey and bread old purity could love.

(1987, 66)

In this sonnet, titled "my dreams, my works must wait till after hell," Brooks does what African American writers before her have not: she foregrounds pain and associates a failing body with a failing heart. Physical and psychological transformation are bound; damage to the body is damage to the mind. As her speaker acknowledges, physical and psychological transformation might make reintegration difficult, if not completely impossible; the soldier is not certain he can "remember to go home." Instead, he might do what was dreaded when demobilization began: become socially unmoored, unable to be regenerated by the comforts of the domestic space.

Brooks thus expressly challenges narratives that posit a completed reentry into society, leaving her soldier in transition, unhealed. By "disabling" the black bodies in her poetry without hint of the wishful recuperative sentiment Gerber describes, she creates an "othered" space where these bodies give voice to an alternative view of war.

I have argued that the goal of Brooks's politics of rehabilitation in her war writing is to prevent the repetition of the circumstances that make socially produced disability appear inevitable. Yet in "the progress" she ends her sonnet sequence with her soldiers' anticipation of war's psychic return in the form of a disordering posttraumatic "syndrome." Brooks is raising the probability that another war, "real" and material, will actually occur. In the final line the speakers conceptualize the warring body as "iron" ("The step / Of iron feet again. / And   again wild."), dehumanizing the soldiers as part of the war machine (75). To make war, in other words, soldiers must conceive of bodies as inanimate entities, an immunizing rhetorical maneuver that removes human beings from the discomfiting fact that they will both inflict and receive injury. In the last line there is a pause, a visual gap between the words "And" and "again." The speaker's verbal hesitation is followed by the vocalization of a radically opposing idea: the is body made "wild" by warfare, a being not "iron" at all, but who devolves into a state of utter savagery.

As much as we can praise Brooks's corrective, "realistic" constructions of human bodies and minds that are neither infallible nor inured, it must be acknowledged that there is danger in deploying images of disability in the service of a political agenda, a danger other than black war writers' anxiety that war damage and "congenital" racial damage could be conflated. No matter how "accurate" the "ableist's" representations might be, they may obscure disabled people's acts of self-representation. Further, as Rosemarie Garland-Thomson has claimed, the proliferation of "realistic" visual images of disability in the service of politics (e.g., "charity" photography) often invites false identification between the able-bodied viewer and the disabled subject (2001, 344). Any ensuing political or social action in such instances, Garland-Thomson argues, is motivated by a fear we could end up like the subject, a "warn[ing] . . . against becoming disabled" that reinscribes disability as a horrific condition without engendering an understanding of what the disabled person may feel (354). In addition, realistic images of disability that are meant to inspire action just as commonly rely on *dis*identification (345–46). We express "pity" for the poor "other" while distancing ourselves as we take comfort in our own good fortune. The act of representation, no matter how "authentic," aids in this estrangement precisely because the disabled are mediated. If we do act, it is frequently from a safe emotional, psychological, and physical proximity (e.g., a check in the mail).

Therefore, while Brooks enters potentially explosive territory by using disabled bodies as emblems of the catastrophe of war, her writing displays an acute awareness that simply exhibiting broken bodies is not enough for her readers to apprehend war's devastation or to compel them to preventive action. "Pity," an intellectual distancing reaction, must be supplanted by "sympathy," which, in Brooks's literary vocabulary, denotes a corporeal response that reduces the estrangement between the "able" self and the "disabled" other.

In the first of the three poems, grouped under the title "loose leaves from a loose-leaf war diary," Brooks implies there is a manner of visual apprehension that will inspire bodily sympathy in the able viewer—referred to alternately as "watch[ing] and "[see]ing" (1987, 110). Beginning with a quotation referencing the media ("thousands—killed in action"), she accuses "you" of refusing ways of looking that may lead to an appropriate response to war:

> You need the untranslatable ice to watch.
> You need to loiter a little among the vague
> Hushes, the clever evasions of the vagueness
> Above the healthy energy of decay.
> You need the untranslatable ice to watch,
> The purple and black to smell.
>
> Before your horror can be sweet.
> Or proper.
> Before your grief is other than discreet.
>
> The intellectual damn will nurse your half-hurt.
> Quickly you are well.
>
> But weary. How you yawn, have yet to see
> Why nothing exhausts you like this sympathy.

(110)

Here, "watch[ing]," "see[ing]," and subsequently feeling the emotions "proper" to warfare—"horror" and uncontained "grief"—are foreclosed by an intellectualism that permits the "you" to only "half-hurt." Brooks indicates that the clarity that comes with looking with "untranslatable ice" would inherently disallow "you" to become "well" so "quickly." This "loiter[ing]" manner of looking is also spatial, given the potential to bring "you" in closer proximity to war, forcing her to engage other senses: "The purple and black to smell." I am not proposing that Brooks has neatly solved the many problems arising from asking the able-bodied to "falsely" identify with disabled bodies or their circumstances. Yet her poem implicitly claims that identification, however fabricated, may be a necessary step in arousing a somatic correspondence. As Toni Cade Bambara once wrote of Brooks's own literary style, it "cause[s] internal bleeding."[11]

Although Brooks avoids specifying the gender of "you," I have sexed her as female because of Brooks's insistence in binding black male and black female injury in her later work *Maud Martha,* and because the writer critiques her character's inability to envision the connection between her own "feminine" debilities and the "masculine" wounds of disabled men. In large measure this incapacity emanates from Maud Martha's profound need to imagine herself unharmed (relatively) by the sexist and racist violence endemic to white heteropatriarchal culture. It is also due to a related need to believe she plays no part in abetting the culture's social dysfunction, particularly war, an event that asks women to see themselves outside of its primary functions. Maud Martha sees herself as neither "victim" nor "perpetrator."

HETERONORMATIVITY AND REHABILITATION

The ability to exempt herself from the world's "nasty, nasty mess" (151–52) is crucial to Maud Martha's self-perception; moreover, it is central to her method of survival as a black woman in a sexist, racist nation. Repeatedly, Maud Martha lauds herself for being "good." An early chapter, "you're being so good, so kind," finds a young Maud Martha feeling grateful that a white schoolmate will visit her home; accordingly, she scrambles to make her house look proper for her little guest, covering tears in the family sofa, even opening windows in case the rumor that "colored people's houses necessarily had . . . an unpleasant smell" (17) were actually true. He is "benefactor," she tells herself; she, "recipient" (18). Unveiling the depth of Maud Martha's double consciousness, "you're being so good, so kind" refers to how Maud Martha hopes the boy, whom she sees as a rudimentary embodiment of "the entire Caucasian plan" (18), will interpret her performance as graciousness.

As this episode foreshadows, the adult Maud Martha grows to meet the criteria for female "goodness" defined within the heteropatriarchal lexicon of the 1950s. She is chaste, clean, well-mannered; an exemplary homemaker; a dutiful (if discontented) wife and mother; a loyal daughter. She is, in other words, both compliant and constricted. A fully disciplined black female subject, she dares not behave in an unruly or "unfeminine" manner, a trade-off she makes to be considered "normal" and lead a "normal" life. However, Brooks shows us that her decision is hardly benign; the bargain Maud Martha strikes will inevitably affect more than her own dulled existence. In one of the most devastating and telling scenes in the work, her mother informs Maud Martha that her sister, the light-skinned, delicate, and ceaselessly envied Helen, is to be married (168). After a brief exchange Maud Martha and her mother move on to another subject— but not before exposing the institution of marriage as an economic transaction that permits men to prey on women who aspire to its ostensible comforts and "safety" (168). Though Maud Martha recognizes this, she nevertheless colludes in her mother's and father's passive acceptance of her sister's situation. Once more, her insights do not lead to action; Brooks reveals that the "good" Maud Martha is actually a very *bad* girl: complicit in another black woman's damage.

The mother's faulty logic demonstrates how the performance of heteronormativity is given (falsely) rehabilitative powers. If Helen is a "good girl" (like Martha), her marriage must also be a "good" one. The belief in the "normality" of Helen's marriage depends upon creating the illusion of wholesomeness; in turn, the illusion of wholesomeness rests upon the delusion that Helen herself is "whole." Any likely emotional and psychological problems are less important, it seems, than the tantalizing prospect of black upward mobility. Marrying "well," as it were, will miraculously remedy any of Helen's inner damage.

Similarly, Martha's investment in "donat[ing] to the world a good Maud Martha" (22) helps her to maintain her own illusion of psychic wholeness. Her self-named deficiency, "her hungriest lack—not much voice," recalls the confession a black soldier makes in one of Brooks's war sonnets: "I am very hungry. I am incomplete" (1987, 66). Both Maud Martha and the soldier may be superficially whole, bodily intact, yet they also feel an interior insufficiency, something missing within their invisible insides. Immediately before acknowledging her "lack" of voice, Maud Martha characterizes the emotions she is loath to exteriorize as a faceless entity (176). Brooks's decision to personify Maud Martha's hate is critical to the way disability functions in the novel, as it suggests that the unwhole person dwelling within Maud Martha is actually a repressed image of self—her "disabled" double—the woman she will not let anyone see. Whereas Maud Martha may consider the repression of her disabled self a private gesture, her desire to hide her disfigured "altered" ego parallels how disabled people were kept from public view (when not being made profitable spectacles) or rehabilitated into disappearing, normalized beyond recognition. That Brooks conceives of this figure without eyes or the capacity to smile underscores the social and political "danger" posed by visible disability. Maud Martha's disabled self is incapable of donning the mask so necessary to her "able" self's performance of the "good," the wholesome, the "normal."

Moreover, Maud Martha's physically and psychologically fragmented double can be read as a representation of the fragmentation inherent to feminine subjectivity, a concept Lennard Davis (1995) has provocatively interpreted within a disability studies framework. Following Lacan, Davis reminds us that the mistaken belief in our bodily integrity is requisite for proper socialization. This means we must first regulate ourselves, a process that begins by denying the original experiences of our bodies as infants, of our flailing arms and legs that feel disconnected from one another (Davis 1995, 134). Lacan theorizes that this correct apprehension of our physicality is interrupted when we see ourselves in a mirror and identify these refracted images as "self." Here, I will also point out that Lacan suggests our ability to look in the mirror at this stage is made possible only by a prosthetic: "Unable as yet to walk, or even to stand up, held tightly as he is by some support, human or artificial (what in France we call a 'trotte-bebe'), he overcomes" (Lacan 1977, 1).

Davis claims that "real" disabled bodies are therefore rejected as "the reminders of the whole" self "about to come apart at the seams" (1995, 132), a rejection arising from the fear that we, like the disabled, will be expelled from the social order. The need to avoid these reminders, like Maud Martha's repression of her double, partly explains Western culture's attraction to the idealized human form, artistic renderings of the female nude in particular. The perfected female form offers something beyond the repression of our "real" fragmentation; it allows us to suppress the effects of the violent and violating objectification of women, who are valued in terms of their individual parts: faces, legs, breasts. Davis theorizes that this valuation may explain the unlikely appeal of the Venus de Milo. As a representation of an amputated figure and of our own tentative state, she should inspire repulsion; yet she arouses desire as the spectator consumes a representation of a woman fixed in the submissive state that makes femininity both appealing and socially useful. At the same time, the viewer can defer acknowledging the pleasure he feels in consuming a "mutilated" female body by reconstructing her as "whole," imaginatively retrieving the body parts that were once present, what Davis calls her "phantom limbs" (134). This reconstitution enables the cultural fantasy that women are not, in fact, mutilated subjects and that society does not want them in this state.

BROOKS'S DISABILITY IDENTIFICATION

The fragmentation arising from female objectification is compounded by race; if women are reduced to "parts," black women are split even further as they are asked to pry the signs of blackness from their bodies and as blackness is ripped from their bodies and reshaped into a myriad of cultural signifiers. This leads me back to the images of disabled soldiers in "back from the wars!" that have jarred critics. Brooks employs stream-of-consciousness to maneuver Maud Martha's mind from "the men with two arms off and two legs off, then men with the parts of faces" to "the usual representations of womanly Beauty, pale and pompadoured" (1993, 179). The uncovering of male disability here is juxtaposed with representation that masks feminine fragmentation and rehabilitates female blackness into something desirable. That the disabled soldiers surface seemingly from nowhere and then quickly disappear can be explained in terms of Maud Martha's repression of her own "disabled" double. Maud Martha's unconscious begs her to make the crucial identification that her conscious mind will not—an identification that, if recognized, would destabilize the social order. Thus, the *conscious* identification with disabled bodies I referred to earlier (the "untranslatable watching" and somatic sympathy that precipitates social action) reveals its subversive potential. The somatic correspondence, both a sympathetic response to their condition and a brief suggestion of hers, is nonetheless promptly displaced by intellectualism. Although her body, like soldiers', is left in pieces, Maud Martha will not "loiter" among the wreckage long enough to "see."

Another soldier from the sonnets, exhausted by the apparent endlessness of the war, describes its perpetuity: "this morning men deliver wounds and death. They will deliver death and wounds tomorrow" (Brooks 1987, 73). Part of the reason Maud Martha diminishes the impact of war in thoughts of natural regeneration is rooted, we learn, in her pregnancy. "And in the meantime," she rhapsodizes, "she was going to have another baby" (1993, 180). The dichotomy is familiar. Men "deliver wounds"; women deliver life. I will nevertheless resist dismissing the conclusion of the novel as Brooks's reflexive capitulation to the ideologies attendant with gender inscription or as a simple need to tack on a "happy ending" to convince us that "another baby" will finally replenish Maud Martha's malnourished insides. All prior textual evidence points to the contrary. If Maud Martha romanticizes her first pregnancy, childbirth, and subsequent relationship to her daughter, Brooks does not offer Maud Martha a part within the cultural script her character fumblingly tries to follow.

Like the disabled soldiers' minds and bodies in "gay chaps in the bar," Brooks leaves Maud Martha's consciousness split at the novel's conclusion, a means of keeping matters open, unresolved. And like those poems, *Maud Martha* is a fractured text. We think we have been given Maud Martha's "whole" story, but important parts are missing: her nuptials, for example, and the fact that her brother, Harry, was sent to war. In spite of similarities, it bears repeating that black soldiers' "masculine" debilities caused by war are not the same as "feminine" debilities resulting from Maud Martha's "wars" with patriarchy, white supremacy, or heteronormativity. Also, the spectator/reader does not become disabled through "watching," "seeing," or somatic sympathy. There are no easy equivalents in Brooks's politics. But in closing the distances between masculine and feminine injury, the able-bodied and the disabled, Brooks uses her war writing to argue that very few (if any) escape the effects of a society whose structures engender destruction.

In thinking about Davis's claim about the powerful role Western art plays in denying disability, I find it interesting that Maud Martha is not only a repressed black female subject but also a repressed artist. The visual power Brooks gives her character, her gift of looking with an artist's eye, is nonetheless lost within Maud Martha's instinct to beautify what she apprehends. In "spring landscape: a detail," she remarks upon the "gray" sky, but notes the "sun was making little silver promises up there"; assessing the day as a "rather bleak" one for June; "still," she insists, "there were these little promises, just under cover" (1993, 4). The kind of artist Maud Martha would become, had she let herself become one, would probably be at odds with the writer who created her: the writer who allows herself to traverse a cultural and corporeal landscape marked by damage, to assess what she sees, and to offer us the parts other black war writers preferred to bury "in a hush, infallible and sincere" (173).

NOTES

1. Brooks's novel *Maud Martha* was originally published in New York by Harper and Row.

2. "Five Poems." Three of the "Soldier Sonnets" were first published in "Five Poems." Later, Brooks often would refer to "gay chaps" as her "soldier sonnets" when discussing the sequence.

3. Brooks republished *A Street in Bronzeville* in the 1987 compilation *Blacks* with several of her other publications, including *Annie Allen* (1949) and *Maud Martha*.

4. The tradition of fictional war writing actually began with a decapitation in William Wells Brown's 1867 novel *Clotelle; or, The Colored Heroine* (a revision of *Clotel; or, The President's Daughter* (1852). Although Brown's decision to allow Jerome to be injured and killed raised many questions, graphic descriptions of the wounded black male body and representations of the grotesque disappeared after Brown until the mid-twentieth century. Particularly within the black masculinist war novel, African American male writers created a brown-skinned, full-bodied, vigorous soldier-citizen that refuted the dominant culture's feminized construction of the black male body as degraded, passive, and weak.

5. Like other scholars of the period, bell hooks theorizes that women were "masculinized" as a justification for forcing black women to engage in "male" tasks (e.g., field labor). Conversely, they were employed in "feminine" roles (e.g., wet nurses). Black women were also ascribed "male" sexual appetites so that white men could claim they were victimized by a powerful sexual force. This alleged sexual appetite also figured in narratives that position women as sinful creatures whose lack of restraint leads to man's downfall, as in the biblical story of Eve. As a result of investing black women with both masculine and feminine characteristics, the black female body became an overdetermined cultural "grotesque," existing somewhere between the categories of "male" and "female." In addition, black women's genital excess was "confirmed" by images like those of the "Venus Hottentot," the name given to Saartjie Baartman, a South African woman whose genitals and buttocks were allegedly oversized. Baartman was exhibited in American freak shows during the second decade of the nineteenth century.

6. Nell's 1855 work, first issued in Boston by Robert F. Wallcut, expands his earlier pamphlet.

7. Marcus Woods (1991) and Maurice O. Wallace (2002) discuss these images.

8. In a series of letters, prominent black journalist Theodore Poston urged the Roosevelt administration to recognize Miller. The administration hired Poston, who became known by covering the famous Scottsboro trial, as a liaison to the black press.

9. Issued by the Office of War Information.

10. Similarly, the Bush administration's stance in the war against Iraq was to ban images of coffins containing dead soldiers being returned to the United States.

11. From a review printed on the back cover of *Maud Martha*.

REFERENCES

Baldwin, James. (1953) 1963. *Go Tell It on the Mountain*. New York: Dial Press.
Baynton, Douglas. 2001. "Disability and the Justification of Inequality in American History." In Longmore and Umansky, *New Disability History*, 33–57.
Brooks, Gwendolyn. 1945a. *A Street in Bronzeville*. New York: Harper and Brothers.
———. 1945b. "Five Poems." *Harper's Weekly* (February): 218–19.
———. 1949. *Annie Allen*. New York: Harper.
———. 1951. "Why Negro Women Leave Home." *Negro Digest* (March): 26–28.
———. 1953. *Maud Martha*. New York: Harper and Row.
———. 1972. *Report from Part One*. Chicago: Broadside Press.
———. 1987. *Blacks*. Chicago: Third World Press.
———. 1993. *Maud Martha*. Chicago: Third World Press.
Brown, William Wells. 1969. *Clotelle; or, The Colored Heroine, A Tale of the Southern States*. Miami: Mnemosyne.
Cullen, Jim. 1992. "'I's a Man Now': Gender and African American Men." In *Divided Houses: Gender and the Civil War*, edited by Catherine Clinton and Nina Silber, 76–96. New York: Oxford University Press.

Davis, Lennard J. 1995. *Enforcing Normalcy: Disability, Deafness and the Body.* London: Verso.

Douglass, Frederick. (1863) 1990. "Men of Color, To Arms!" In *A Documentary History of the Negro People in the United States,* Vol. 1, edited by Herbert Aptheker, 477–80. New York: Citadel.

Ferguson, Roderick A. 2004. *Aberrations in Black: Toward a Queer of Color Critique.* Minneapolis: University of Minnesota Press.

Foucault, Michel. (1977) 1979. *Discipline and Punish: The Birth of the Prison.* Translated by Alan Sheridan. New York: Vintage Books.

Garland-Thomson, Rosemarie. 2001. "Seeing the Disabled: Visual Rhetorics of Disability in Popular Photography." In Longmore and Umansky, *New Disability History,* 335–74.

Gerber, David A. 2000. "Heroes and Misfits: The Troubled Social Reintegration of Disabled Veterans of WWII in *The Best Years of Our Lives.*" In *Disabled Veterans in History,* edited by David A. Gerber, 70–95. Ann Arbor: University of Michigan Press.

Hickel, K. Walter. 2001. "Medicine, Bureaucracy, and Social Welfare: The Politics of Disability Compensation for American Veterans of WWI." In Longmore and Umansky, *New Disability History,* 236–67.

Holland, Sharon Patricia. 2000. *Raising the Dead: Readings of Death and (Black) Subjectivity.* Durham, N.C.: Duke University Press.

hooks, bell. 1981. *Ain't I a Woman: Black Women and Feminism.* Boston: South End Press.

Lacan, Jacques. 1977. *Écrits: A Selection.* New York: W. W. Norton.

Longmore, Paul K., and Lauri Umansky, eds. 2001. *The New Disability History: American Perspectives.* New York: New York University Press.

McGuire, Philip, ed. 1993. *Taps for a Jim Crow Army: Letters from Black Soldiers in WWII.* Lexington: University Press of Kentucky.

Nell, William C. (1855) 1986. *Colored Patriots of the American Revolution.* Salem, N.H.: Ayer.

Quarles, Benjamin. (1961) 1996. *The Negro in the American Revolution.* Chapel Hill: University of North Carolina Press.

Scarry, Elaine. 1985. *The Body in Pain: The Making and Unmaking of the World.* New York: Oxford University Press.

Shaw, Harry B. 1987. "*Maud Martha:* The War with Beauty." In *A Life Distilled: Gwendolyn Brooks, Her Poetry and Fiction,* edited by Maria K. Mootry and Gary Smith, 254–70. Chicago: University of Illinois Press.

Stiker, Henri-Jacques. 1999. *A History of Disability.* Ann Arbor: University of Michigan Press.

Wallace, Maurice O. 2002. *Constructing the Black Masculine: Identity and Ideality in African American Men's Literature and Culture, 1775–1995.* Durham, N.C.: Duke University Press.

Woods, Marcus. 1991. *Blind Memory: Visual Representations of Slavery in England and America.* New York: St. Martin's Press.

Seven

REVISING THE SUBJECT

Disability as *"Third Dimension"* in
Clear Light of Day *and* You Have Come Back

CINDY LACOM

In *Culture and Imperialism*, Edward Said states that the work of postcolonial scholars "should be seen as sharing concerns with minority and 'suppressed' voices within the metropolis itself: feminists, African-American writers, intellectuals, artists, among others" (1994, 54). Missing from his list, however—and, arguably, from too many analyses of the mechanisms of oppression and liberation—is a consideration of people with physical and/or mental disabilities.[1] To begin to address and fill in that gap, I examine characters in two texts, Anita Desai's *Clear Light of Day* (1980) and Fatima Gallaire-Bourega's *You Have Come Back* (1988), to argue that the disabled characters in each text serve critical political and ideological purposes during a particular postcolonial moment in their respective nations. It has become a theoretical commonplace to argue, as Frantz Fanon does, that Othering occurs on the basis of physical and verbal difference (1963).[2] To that end, narrative desire—the impulse to tell stories—"underlies the ways we construct the so-called normal and the aberrant, and the ways we explain the disjunctions between the two" (Epstein 1995, 19). Judith Butler reiterates this point in *Bodies That Matter* when she writes, "the subject is constituted through the force of exclusion and abjection, one which produces a constitutive outside to the subject, an abjected outside" (1993, 3). In a poststructuralist and post-Foucauldian world, we are familiar with the idea that we can conceive of normalcy only by conceiving of its opposite: deviance. And in traditional readings, the colonized body has been that *abjected outside* against which the British body—civilized, civilizing, normal—is constituted, at a both cultural and more literal level. Perhaps the best example of this is the so-called Hottentot Venus, whose enlarged labia and buttocks, circulated in the freak shows of Victorian England, marked her as savagely sensuous and measurably different from the English angel in the house.[3]

If the colonized body constitutes the abjected outside, and is part of what M. Jacqui Alexander and Chandra Talpade Mohanty call a "citizenship machinery which excludes and marginalizes particular constituencies on the basis of their difference," how are we to read the *disabled* colonized body (1997, xxxi)? How does it fit into this dialectic between colonizer and colonized and into the transaction of the postcolonial world? From a Bakhtinian perspective, one might argue that the very *grotesqueness* of disability has the potential to disrupt hegemonic paradigms and revise cultural norms. Donna Haraway considers such a possibility in "A Cyborg Manifesto," where she claims that the cyborg has the ability to transcend, transgress, and destroy boundaries (1998). Often, reading disability in terms of transgressive power provides a useful means for deconstructing the traditional paradigm of disability as tragedy.[4] However, in most literary texts that incorporate characters with disabilities, such liberatory and transformative potential is written in the margins and difficult to detect, if it is expressed at all.

THE "THIRD DIMENSION"

In order to do justice to the complex cultural and ideological work of disability and enrich my exploration of possible meanings of disability in postcolonial texts, I will incorporate Homi Bhabha's idea of the "third dimension" outlined in *The Location of Culture* (1994) in my readings of Desai's novel and Gallaire-Bourega's play.

The third dimension, as Bhabha describes it, exists in the moment of recognition that Self cannot be wholly contained within a Self/Other binary, a binary that is dependent upon fixed and static boundaries. In other words, as soon as we recognize that the chasm that divides *us* from *them* is artificial and reductionist, we move into a place where identity is ambivalent and mutable. As Bhabha notes, the very struggle to maintain that Self/Other binary articulates the possibility of slippage between the two categories and reminds us that "identity is never an a priori, nor a finished product; it is only ever the problematic process of access to an image of totality" (51).

In contemplating moments of potential slippage between identity categories, Bhabha develops the idea of the "evil eye," a figure that reminds us of what is missing or invisible in a text, a figure whose gaze "alienates *both* the narratorial I of the slave and the surveillant eye of the master" (53). The evil eye is the outside, the margin, the "structure of difference" that blurs the gap between slave and master by making *both* objects of observation and judgment. In this capacity, the evil eye has power because it unsettles the simplistic polarities of Self/Other, because it resists the *image of totality* that is so important in myths of both imperial and postcolonial worlds.

I want to use this image of totality to turn now to an examination of the disabled body that, almost universally perceived in terms of lack, comes to symbolize the impossibility of totality, acting as a sort of evil eye to remind us of what is absent. Harlan Hahn reads the cross-cultural and ahistorical recoil from those with disabilities as an expression of what he calls "existential angst" (1988). In considering the segregation of those with disabilities in ableist cultures—and he argues that most cultures are and have been ableist[5]—Hahn suggests that we seek to distinguish ourselves from disabled bodies because we understand the very real possibility that those bodies can become our own. At the most basic level, then, we Other those with physical and mental disabilities in order to shore up our own very temporal sense of able-bodiedness. After all, "No one is immune from becoming disabled" (Boyle 1991, 1).

Given this, I want to suggest that in critical ways the disabled body informs Bhabha's third dimension, that site where identity is negotiated. If, as Bhabha suggests, "the very question of identification only emerges *in-between* disavowal and designation" (1994, 50), then the disabled body multiplies the possible terms of disavowal for both the colonizer and the colonized; because disability can be a more evident signifier even than the color of one's skin, it becomes a visual means by which to define normalcy and, by extension, nation. And though Bhabha suggests that interstitial (in-between) spaces can foster those moments of recognition and connectedness that are essential to the creation of a heterogeneous nation (because difference itself is temporal and coexists with similarity), such moments are largely absent in the texts of Desai and Gallaire-Bourega, who, in a postmodern move, negate the hope of such synthesis.

DISABILITY AND THE DIALECTICS OF NATION-BUILDING

Acknowledging the prevalence of differentiation rather than synthesis in nation-building, Jean-Paul Sartre writes in his preface to Fanon's *The Wretched of the Earth*, "the European has only been able to become a man through creating slaves and monsters" (1963, 26). Similarly, I will suggest, the colonized are only able to "become men," to establish a national identity in the historical moment of decolonization, through the reification of a new category of *monsters*—the disabled, the deformed, the mad. To that end, disability *designates* a docile body upon which nationalist tensions can be arbitrated and against which a rationalist ideology can pull "a collection of disparate peoples into a self-identified nation" (Heng 1997, 31).

A second category that emerges in this moment of nation-building is *woman*. This is especially true in many Middle Eastern countries, where women's roles grow increasingly constricted as sharp gendered boundaries evolve in the chaos created by the colonizer's departure. As Deniz Kandiyoti notes, many Muslims draw a correlation between feminism and cultural imperialism, so the woman who resists culturally sanctioned behaviors in a postcolonial world comes to be understood as undermining the project of nationalism (1991, 5–8). Women become, as Amrita Chhachhi puts it, "the symbols and repositories of communal/group/ national identity . . . [so] threats to or the loss of control over their women . . . are seen as direct threats to manhood/community/family. It therefore becomes essential to ensure patriarchal controls over the labour, fertility, and sexuality of women" (1991, 163–65).[6]

In the two texts to which I now turn, I argue that the disabled body defines and delimits transformative possibilities and becomes a kind of repository for the anxiety that arises from mediation between old and new cultural norms. I also consider the meanings of a convergence between disabled and woman as identity categories.

Though Fanon has been critiqued for a too-simplistic understanding of the colonizer/colonized dynamic, his conception of the processes of decolonization and nation-building is useful here. He argues, "Decolonization unifies [a] people by the radical decision to remove from it its heterogeneity, and by unifying it on a national, sometimes a racial, basis" (1963, 46). Along with postcolonial feminist critics, I would add *gender* to the list.

If we look around, we can see that oppressive and homogenizing impulse in, for instance, the Islamic fundamentalism that is gaining such power in Iran and is becoming more of a force in certain other Middle Eastern cultures. The simplest reading of the disabled body in postcolonial cultures, then, might be that it provides the difference against which a homogenous national body is defined. Or as Rosemarie Garland-Thomson puts it in *Extraordinary Bodies,* reading the disabled body as Other supports the belief "that each citizen is a microcosm of the nation as a whole. A well-regulated self thus contributes to a well-regulated nation" (1997, 42).

Part of this *regulation* is the literal and symbolic regulation of the bodies of women and of people with disabilities. An imperative of homogeneity contributes to a social environment where bodies out of bounds are understood to have the potential to undermine the project of nationalism.

At such moments, individual bodies are often imbued with the metonymic power to represent the "social body," giving rise to a category of in/valid bodies that includes people with disabilities and women who refuse to enact "appropriate" behaviors. As Mary Poovey puts it, "The process by which a national identity is consolidated and maintained is . . . one of differentiation and displacement—the differentiation of the national *us* from aliens within and without" (1995, 55).

ANITA DESAI'S *CLEAR LIGHT OF DAY*

In the novel *Clear Light of Day,* Anita Desai explores the ambivalent role of characters with disabilities, both as sites of transgression and as repositories for cultural tensions in a postcolonial world. Desai uses the family as a microcosm for larger national concerns, as she does in many of her fictional explorations of postcolonial themes (for instance, in *Fire on the Mountain* [1977] and *Baumgartner's Bombay* [1988]). The novel traces the tensions of a Hindu family reunited in the family home, where one sister, Bim, who has stayed there caring for her brother, Baba, represents Indian culture while the other sister, Tara, represents more Western values. In essence, the family dynamics as the sisters confront their differences and struggle to balance old and new worlds become a microcosmic exploration of larger national concerns, establishing a "parallel movement between British withdrawal from India and the progressive emptying out of the Das home . . . [making] a distinct point about the erosion of cultural frames of reference" (Mohan 1997, 49).

In the midst of their negotiations exists Baba, who is developmentally disabled. At one level Baba represents the naive dream of detachment from postcolonial negotiations of power—that one can somehow remove oneself from such negotiations. He is literally left out of almost all arguments between his sisters and is thus exempt from the anguish caused by such altercations.

But the slippage of identity that occurs when the sisters struggle to understand each other's narratives is fostered by Baba's own fluid movement between symbolic identity categories. If on one hand he reflects Bim's passive resistance to change (he is addicted to order, ritual, to the known and familiar), he also embodies Tara's internalization of Western values, articulated in the American music to which he compulsively listens. As Rajeswari Mohan notes, "Brought to India by the American GIs and British Tommies, this music is coded as the monstrous and cosmic intrusion of Western popular culture" (1997, 51). On the surface, then, Baba's disability marks him as uniquely able to simultaneously participate in imperial standards and to reject them by escaping *reality*. Because of this dual role, he becomes the focus of his two sisters as they attempt to mediate between old and new cultural norms. At one point in the first part of the novel, Tara persistently asks Baba if he is going to go into the office to perform duties of which he is blatantly incapable; later that day, when one of his records develops a skip, he rushes off the property only to witness a man beating a horse and to return disoriented and deeply upset, "as if he were an amputee" (Desai 1980, 15). In many respects he is: that which is absent in him serves to justify why Bim has not changed and to explain why Tara recoils from "those silences and shadows" representative of "Old Delhi decadence" (15). Literally, then, it is through Baba's body (his silence, his compulsions, his ghostly presence) that the two sisters attempt to negotiate a balance between old and new India.

His "amputation" has gendered connotations as well. Baba is feminized by his disability in overt ways: he is not self-supporting, he does not participate in the public world, and he is very gentle. But Baba also lives in a semiotic world, resisting entry into the symbolic by means of his music and his mutterings. Graham Huggan suggests that "silence and music in several postcolonial texts can be seen . . . as providing alternative, nonverbal codes which subvert and/or replace those earlier, over-determined narratives of colonial encounter in which the word is recognized to have played a crucial role in the production of and maintenance of colonial hierarchies of power" (1990, 13). Like Baba, Aunt Mira, the alcoholic aunt who cared for the siblings when they were children, retreats into the semiotic and challenges social order with wildly transgressive acts—for instance, running naked and drunk in public. Aunt Mira does not fill a culturally sanctioned role, for she is not mother, wife, or worker. Rather, like Baba, she hovers at the edge of a "new" Indian society. Both characters act as constant irritants, refusing to fit neatly into either old or new cultural paradigms. In fact, their inability to fit in either category reminds us that such polarities (an old versus new world order) are simplistic, unrealistic, and unrealizable.

To that end, Baba and Aunt Mira have subversive potential; they function as the evil eye that observes and resists inclusion. Though Baba and Aunt Mira are in many respects passive figures upon which tensions are worked out, the novel itself resists resolution and instead suggests the process of negotiation will be ongoing. After one of her final outbursts of resentment, Bim comes to recognize, "It was Baba's silence and reserve and otherworldliness that she had wanted to break open and ransack and rob" (Desai 1980, 164). And yet Baba himself—whose story is never told firsthand, whose motives and memories remain a blank in his sisters' efforts to reconstitute their pasts and thus their present—remains silent, a third space, which is indeterminate and unrepresentable. He is that Stranger "whose languageless presence evokes an archaic anxiety and aggressivity" by highlighting the opacity of language in a story where language is all (Bhabha 1994, 166). Those who do not speak, or who do not speak with the dialect of the new nation, are dangerous, and their threat to nationhood must be contained. One means of containment is making static an "extraordinary body." This, I argue, is what happens with Baba: initially dangerous because of his fluid identity, he is neutralized when the sisters fix his identity as silent shadow, recipient of their dual care, lovable burden. Thus, together they situate him in a particular role as dependent and knowable. Toward the end of the novel, Desai momentarily reconsiders the idea of Baba as fixed in his difference from the sisters, offering a fleeting hope of connectedness in place of differentiation. In this scene, Bim brings Baba his tea and

> felt an immense, almost irresistible yearning to lie down beside him on the bed, stretch out limb to limb, silent and immobile together. She felt that they must be the same length, that his slightness would fit in beside her size. . . . Together they would form a whole that would be perfect and pure. She needed only to lie down and stretch out beside him to become whole and perfect.
>
> Instead, she went out. (1980, 166)

The opportunity of this moment—the impulse toward familiarity if not recognized similarity—is rejected, and the transformative power represented by Baba is negated. In the very next scene, Baba is absent while the sisters "paced the terrace" (166).

Given this absence, I am not convinced that the sisters accept him "as one of their own" (Huggan 1990, 15). Their tentative reconciliation is forged via acknowledgment of past memories and the articulation of shared familial bonds. But Baba's silence places him outside this reconciliation, and ultimately he serves as an Other, an abject outside by which the sisters establish their renewed ties. If, as Bhabha suggests, "the work of hegemony is itself the process of iteration and differentiation [which] depends on the production of alternative or antagonistic images that are always produced side by side and in competition with each other," then we can understand "a politics of struggle *as the struggle of identifications* and the war of positions" (1994, 29; emphasis in original). The struggle of identifications by the sisters occurs next to Baba's increasingly stable identity against which the sisters articulate a sense of unity.

Desai recognizes the temporal nature of that unity and reconcilia-tion—as Tara reminds Bim, "it's never over. Nothing's *over,* ever" (1980, 174). I agree with Trinh T. Minh-ha that "Silence as a refusal to partake in the story does sometimes provide us with a means to gain a hearing" (1989, 83), but in this novel, the "clear light of day," that sense of commu-nity and connectedness that Bim experiences during a musical gathering at the novel's climax, tends to elude Baba, whose "face was grave, like an image carved in stone" (Desai 1980, 182). Unlike his sisters, mobile, fluid, struggling to negotiate the changing nature of postcolonial India and their roles within it, Baba ultimately is cast in stone, fixed, excluded from the dialectic of nationhood.

FATIMA GALLAIRE-BOUREGA'S *YOU HAVE COME BACK*

M. Jacqui Alexander notes that the process of colonization demands a reconfiguration of identity and, by extension, women's sexuality (1991, 134). In the wake of liberation from imperial forces, the process of nation-building often demands a reconstitution of women's sexuality as part of the differentiation that occurs in the creation of a new national identity. Such differentiation is at the heart of Gallaire-Bourega's play *You Have Come Back,* in which the main character, Lella, returns to her Algerian home after leaving it twenty years earlier to marry a Frenchman (1988). Having learned of the death of her father, the man who disowned her upon her act of cultural betrayal, she comes back. Welcomed by her old servants and the younger women in the community, she is nonetheless warned to depart by Nounou, her old nurse, and by the Madwoman, an older woman despised and reviled in her community. The threat to Lella's safety is not initially articulated, but in the latter part of the play she is vis-ited by a group of older Algerian women, representing nationalist forces, who enact her father's will by killing her after she refuses to renounce her French, Christian husband.

I will focus on three of this play's characters: the Madwoman; the Crip-ple, an old man who appears midway through the play to add his warn-ing to the Madwoman's; and Lella herself. The first two characters enact a kind of chorus, commenting on the moral qualities of other characters and offering insights into the play's ethical and political dimensions.

The Madwoman does four things in the play: when one of the young women flatters Lella, she cries out, "Rock your pain"; when Lella describes her husband as a "pleasant companion and . . . a wonderful lover," the Madwoman cries "Brava!" twice (183). The third thing she does is dance madly until she falls into a faint after a woman begins a song of rejoicing;

and her final act is to interrupt by wildly howling a story of how one of the young women pleased her mother-in-law by having an operation that "opened [her] womb" (188). Each of the acts constitutes a cultural critique: in the first, the Madwoman's cry calls into question the sincerity of the young woman who praises Lella; in the second, she celebrates an act seen as traitorous by others; in the third, her wild dance ending in a transient death, a faint, undermines the celebratory ambiance of the luncheon; and finally, her howling initiates blood-thirsty anger among the young women, who say at this juncture things like "kill her" and "give her a blow to knock her out" (189). It is important to note that the Madwoman is hated, not only at the play's end by the older Algerian women representing nationalist forces, but also by these younger women who purportedly represent postcolonial evolution.

Their response to the Madwoman reinforces Fanon's argument that violence is an often necessary element in the development of a new nation and the destruction of colonial structures. Calling into question the idea of passive resistance, he suggests that change results from one of two causes: "either of violent struggle on the part of the people in their own right, or of action on the part of surrounding colonized peoples which acts as a brake on the colonial regime in question" (1963, 70).

Because the Madwoman defends Lella and transgresses national and cultural boundaries, the young women beats her into silence. Her silencing, reenacted at the end of the play when Lella is herself set upon by the older Algerian women and beaten to death, signals the power of the collective against the radical individual. But she also functions, I am suggesting, as the evil eye, that disruptive figure who does not fit anywhere and who, from the margins, refuses to allow the women to take refuge in myths of harmony and totality. Like Baba, the Madwoman uses the semiotic, in itself arguably subversive; her very inarticulateness enacts a hybridity of language "associated with vacillating boundaries—psychic, cultural, territorial" (Bhabha 1994, 59). Those vacillating boundaries negate the fixed world that the first part of this play so futilely attempts to maintain.

Ultimately, Lella cannot "come back," cannot import her hybrid identity into a culture whose nationalist fervor increasingly negates heterogeneity. Though the women attempt to make the Madwoman that Sartrean *monster* upon whom they might build a nation, they ultimately cannot. Their efforts fail and the tension between old and new norms reasserts itself. Thus, though the women attempt to inscribe the Madwoman's body as a repository for anxieties about national identity, to make it that Other against which they can define an Algerian identity, her disabled body cannot contain those anxieties. Failing to do so, it is expelled. The expulsion is only temporary, however, because the fluid nature of hegemonic paradigms means that subversive forces will also be changeable. Each new hegemonic paradigm is simultaneously in need of a monstrous figure against which to define a standard of normalcy and is disrupted by a new evil eye that threatens its borders. The disappearance of the Madwoman cannot guarantee against her reappearance as a different monster, a different re/presentation of that evil eye.

To that end, the Madwoman is replaced by the Cripple, another figure who disrupts the apparently joyous reunion with warnings of danger. Like the Madwoman, the Cripple's body is transgressive: he drags himself about with shoes worn on his hands; his posture is "twisted and ludicrous"; and he looks enough like a gargoyle to make the women scream and hide their faces when he appears. Lella dismisses him after he delivers his warning, but in the echo of "the sound of his thumping down the stairs," her heart is "suddenly filled with sadness and questions" (194). Too late, she recognizes that her desire to come back is nostalgic, unrealizable, and dangerous. In the play's last scene she is murdered, along with the Madwoman and the Cripple.

Like them, Lella has no place in a nation whose gendered categories are so sharply demarcated. Though her marriage to a Christian stigmatizes her in a Muslim country, her overtly expressed sexuality marks her perhaps even more fully in a nation where women are veiled and public expression of female sexuality is taboo. I agree with Evelyne Accad that sexuality is "central to social and political problems in the Middle East" (1991, 237), and there is literally nowhere in the new dialectic of nationhood for Lella's distinctly undocile body. Gayatri Spivak examines the problematic of where women fit in this historical moment in *A Critique of Postcolonial Reason*:

Between patriarchy and imperialism, subject-constitution and object-formation, the figure of the woman disappears, not into a pristine nothingness, but into a violent shuttling that is the displaced figuration of the 'third-world' woman caught between tradition and modernization, culturalism and development. (1999, 304)

Lella, who "shuttles" back and forth between the tenuous welcome of the younger women and the rigid judgment of the older, becomes a kind of disabled figure in the play, whose disability is marked by that physical body that resists "cultural authenticity expressed in Islamic terms" (Kandiyoti 1991, 3). I am arguing, in essence, that this collapse between the identity categories of woman and disabled suggests that those women who resist postcolonial patriarchal rules of behavior are stigmatized. Because of that stigmatization, they become partners with people with disabilities in the creation of a site where national identity is negotiated against and in opposition to their bodies.

Both the Madwoman and the Cripple embody subversive possibilities through their warnings to Lella and their refusal to be silenced as they challenge both class hierarchies and the scopic regime that seeks to regulate them. At the play's end, however, both fail to evoke overt or measurable transformation of their nation, and in that failure their disabilities become totalizing: the Madwoman is ignored *because* she is mad, while the Cripple's claim, "They will not get past my body," resonates ironically because of its complex truth; in fact, they never *do* get past his body. Though Gallaire-Bourega suggests that resistance to Islamic nationalist efforts is inherently disabling—the connections between Lella's and the misfits' identities becomes completely clear by the play's close—the exclusion and cultural dismissal of the disabled by both the new and the old Algerian cultural orders suggests that one's body limits one's role in either regime.

However, though the younger Algerian women do not reject Lella, they abandon her in the face of the more culturally sanctioned appearance of the older Algerian women, whose behavior is approved (and directed) by Lella's dead father, that most literal patriarchal figure. She, like the Madwoman and the Cripple, fails to transform or transcend this moment of deep cultural anxiety; she cannot come back to a nation and homeland that marks her as deviant and dangerous.

By emphasizing the similarities between Lella and those characters with disabilities, Gallaire-Bourega inscribes into the margins of her play the potential of those interstitial spaces where difference is renegotiated. In doing so, she opens the door to possible deconstruction both of disability and woman as fixed identity categories. But their exile by death limits that subversive potential. The in-between spaces created by interaction are fleeting, subsumed ultimately by a violent expulsion of difference that is understood as threatening to a hard-won national identity.

Gallaire-Bourega, personally invested in deconstructing a homogenous national identity that excludes difference, explores issues of oppression and hybridity in many of her plays. In *Madame Bertin's Testimony*, Madame Bertin speaks in a monologue of her life, her husband, and her suspicions of his pedophilia (1995). At the play's end she discloses herself as Monsieur Bertin, dressed as his wife. An example of hybridity and symbiosis but also of complex power negotiations, the play repeats certain themes of *You Have Come Back*. More generally, as an Algerian who has chosen to live in France and who writes and publishes her plays in French, Gallaire-Bourega has struggled to "integrate the two languages and cultures" (Temerson and Kourilsky 1988, 165). Recognizing that such efforts may be transitory, she nonetheless returns repeatedly to the subversive possibility of such moments.

Thus, some transgressive potential remains in the echo of the Madwoman's cries and in the shadow of the Cripple's halting figure. The recirculation of their disabled bodies suggests that, though temporarily exiled, other disabled bodies will reappear to disrupt the oppressive process of nation-building. Ultimately, the gaze of the evil eye can be only temporarily ignored. Thus, though the final stage directions show us the elder women bowing and kissing the male Elder's hand as they leave the murderous scene, the last image on stage pairs the Elder with Lella's body, which remains on stage. The ironic "call to prayer" that closes the stage directions, and the play, echoes just as does the sight of Lella's body: however still and silent, it remains before our eyes, a visual reminder that such subversive elements will not—cannot—simply disappear.

CONCLUSION

In both texts, physical, mental, and gender-based stigmas create and maintain a status quo where *normal* bodies do the necessary work of assimilating to new social patterns while arbitrating old power dynamics. To that end, the representation of disability, because it remains seemingly stuck in a subordinate relationship to able-bodiedness (which comes to include patriarchy) is problematic. In *Playing in the Dark,* Toni Morrison examines how Africanism historically has done the work of constructing whiteness in American literature and concludes, "Africanism is the vehicle by which the American self knows itself as not enslaved, but free; not repulsive, but desirable; not helpless, but licensed and powerful; not history-less, but historical; not damned, but innocent; not a blind accident of evolution, but a progressive fulfillment of destiny" (1990, 52). Similarly, the characters with disabilities in the two postcolonial texts I examine exist in a binary that excludes them even as it depends upon them to develop a status quo.

But we are reminded, as well, that that status quo is tentative, fluid, and subject to constant revision and that "out of bound" bodies foster that revisionary process in important, even radical, ways. Borrowing again from Morrison's argument that "A writer's response to American Africanism often provides a subtext that either sabotages the surface text's expressed intentions or escapes them through a language that mystifies what it cannot bring itself to articulate" (66), I want to suggest that similar mystifications occur in *Clear Light of Day* and *You Have Come Back*. Though Desai and Gallaire-Bourega might not be fully capable of articulating the transformative potential of disability, whether physical, mental, or gender-based, their respective representations nonetheless resonate with cultural and political implications. Both return repeatedly to figures of disability, and, in *You Have Come Back*, to the figure of the sexualized woman, to explore the unfixed nature of hierarchies, national identity, and power paradigms. For both, disability is an "echo, shadow, and silent force" that hovers at the margins of their texts (Gallaire-Bourega 1988, 48).

This presence, this shadow, always there, demands a closer reading and more careful consideration, because however concerted the endeavor to stabilize disability as the subordinate term in a normal/deviant binary, the potential of characters with disabilities to disrupt comfortable, comforting, and ultimately unreliable images of totality reminds us of their transgressive potential, however unarticulated, however mystifying—indeed, perhaps *because* it is unarticulated and mystifying. Such potential is certainly cause for further exploration in our quest to more fully understand and enrich the field of disability studies and its intersections with feminist and postcolonial applications.

NOTES

1. Many postcolonial scholars consider embodiment and its imbrication in power dynamics in terms of race, class, and gender, but none of the most important critics in the field—Edward Said, Homi Bhabha, Iris Young, Gayatri Spivak, Frantz Fanon, or Jacqui Alexander and Chandra Mohanty—consider disability. And a number of postmodern theorists writing on embodiment issues ignore *real* bodies, as David T. Mitchell and Sharon L. Snyder note (1997); for instance, in *Bodies That Matter*, Judith Butler (1993) only rarely considers lived bodies within concrete social locations.

In the field of disability studies, writers explore "the metaphorical and symbolic values that disability has represented," one of which is that of the Other (Mitchell and Snyder 1997, 12). In some instances, authors consider intersections of disability and race or ethnicity. For instance, in "Defining the Defective," Martin S. Pernick argues that two early films, *The Science of Life* and *The Black Stork*, "linked aesthetics, disability, and race" (1997, 95). And in "Disability and Ethnicity in Conflict," Marilynn Phillips interrogates the connections between disability and ethnicity in the transformation of a woman whose case study she discusses (1988). In a critique of similar studies of auto/biography, she notes, "The flaw in each theoretical framework is the dismissing or the disregarding of the weight that culture bears on those who are stigmatized and the extent to which the individual's coming to terms with a disability may necessitate first coming to terms with the inconsistencies in the cultural ethos" (200). The subject in her study at one point concludes that she would rather be "crippled than Polish" (205).

Clearly, more texts are being published that complicate the disabled/able-bodied or colonizer/colonized binary, but it would enrich the fields of disability studies, feminist theory, and postcolonial theory to consider more closely the role of disability in nation-building.

2. Fanon discusses linguistic colonization and the distrust it fosters in the process of nation-building. The mimicry of colonized people in positions of nominal power—dressing, speaking, and working with the Europeans—foments suspicion in the colonized and, according to Fanon, is used by the Europeans in "their struggle against the nationalist parties" (1963, 112). Other discussions of the subversive power of the semiotic can be found in the works of Julia Kristeva and Hélène Cixous.

3. In *Extraordinary Bodies*, Garland-Thomson discusses how visual difference in freak-show displays of white women next to black, "deformed"/savage women worked to reinforce racist ideologies in the first half of the twentieth century (1997). And in his study of eighteenth- and nineteenth-century shows in England, Richard Altick notes that the "displays of savages appealed to what was becoming [a] more and more openly and aggressively displayed aspect of the English character, its complacent assumption of racist supremacy" (1978, 279). Interestingly, as Altick notes, the display of such savages took place alongside displays of freaks—people with visible deformities or disabilities. In both cases, a white, ableist norm was established. See also Thomas Frost's *The Old Showmen and the Old London Fairs* (1971).

4. In *The Female Grotesque*, Mary Russo considers how transgressive bodies enact Bakhtin's carnivalesque, arguing that the body becomes a prototype of society; to that end, different and disabled bodies (the crone, for instance, but also the woman who breast-feeds in public) can offer "models of transformation and counterproduction situated within the social system and symbolically at its margins" (1994, 54). And in personal narratives like that of G. Thomas Couser's *Recovering Bodies* (1997), writers argue that disability can enrich self-exploratory narratives while revising the medical model of disability as tragic.

5. I am defining an ableist culture as one that uses able-bodiedness as a primary means of establishing cultural norms and standards and that, by extension, excludes those who are not considered able-bodied. Some examples in modern American culture might be negative attitudes toward aging and the elderly; cuts in state and federal monies for people with disabilities; and hostility toward changes in hiring practices, educational opportunities, and architectural structures demanded by the passage of the Americans with Disabilities Act of 1990.

Michael Oliver argues that cultural attitudes toward disability altered with the industrial revolution and the growth of capitalism. He suggests that in preindustrial, agrarian societies, even where people with disabilities "could not participate fully, they were still able to make a contribution. In this era disabled people were regarded as individually unfortunate and not segregated from the rest of society. With the rise of the factory . . . many more disabled people were excluded from the production process" (1990, 27). Because factory work demanded speed and regularity, people with disabilities were often unable to do the work and thus came to be seen as a burden on the state. As Oliver puts it, "Under capitalism . . . disability became individual pathology; disabled people could not meet the demands of individual wage labour and so became controlled through exclusion" (47).

6. See Michel Foucault's *Discipline and Punish* (1977) for a discussion on how categories of normalcy and deviance were formalized and his argument on how institutions increasingly came to manage "dangerous" individuals.

REFERENCES

Accad, Evelyne. 1991. "Sexuality and Sexual Politics: Conflicts and Contradictions for Contemporary Women in the Middle East." In Mohanty et al., *Third World Women*, 237–50.

Alexander, M. Jacqui. 1991. "Redrafting Morality: The Postcolonial State and the Sexual Offences Bill of Trinidad and Tobago." In Mohanty et al., *Third World Women*, 133–52.

Alexander, M. Jacqui, and Chandra Talpade Mohanty. 1997. Introduction to *Feminist Genealogies, Colonial Legacies, Democratic Futures*, edited by M. Jacqui Alexander and Chandra Talpade Mohanty, xiii–xvii. New York: Routledge.

Altick, Richard. 1978. *The Shows of London*. Cambridge, Mass.: Belknap Press.

Americans with Disabilities Act of 1990. http://www.usdoj.gov/crt/ada/pubs/ada .txt.

Bhabha, Homi K. 1994. *The Location of Culture*. New York: Routledge.

Boyle, Esther. 1991. *Women and Disability*. London: Zed Books.

Butler, Judith. 1993. *Bodies That Matter: On the Limits of Discursive Limits of "Sex."* New York: Routledge.

Chhachhi, Amrita. 1991. "Forced Identities: the State, Communalism, Fundamentalism, and Women in India." In Kandiyoti, *Women, Islam, and the State*, 144–75.

Couser, G. Thomas. 1997. *Recovering Bodies: Illness, Disability, and Life Writing*. Madison: University of Wisconsin Press.

Desai, Anita. 1977. *Fire on the Mountain*. London: Heinemann.

———. 1980. *Clear Light of Day*. New York: Penguin Books.

———. 1988. *Baumgartner's Bombay*. New York: Penguin Books.

Epstein, Julia. 1995. *Altered Conditions: Disease, Medicine, and Storytelling*. New York: Routledge.

Fanon, Frantz. 1963. *The Wretched of the Earth*. New York: Grove Press.

Foucault, Michel. 1977. *Discipline and Punish: The Birth of the Prison*. New York: Pantheon Books.

Frost, Thomas. (1881) 1971. *The Old Showmen and the Old London Fairs*. Ann Arbor, Mich.: Gryphon Books.

Gallaire-Bourega, Fatima. 1988. *You Have Come Back*. Translated by Jill MacDougal. In *Plays by Women: An International Anthology*, edited by Francoise Kourilsky and Catherine Termerson, 160–221. New York: Ubu Repertory Theater Publications.

———. 1995. *Madame Bertin's Testimony*. Translated by Jill MacDougall. In *Monologues: Plays from Martinique, France, Algeria, Quebec*, edited by Francoise Kourilsky. New York: Ubu Repertory Theater Publications.

Garland-Thomson, Rosemarie. 1997. *Extraordinary Bodies: Figuring Physical Disability in American Culture and Literature.* New York: Columbia University Press.

Hahn, Harlan. 1988. "Can Disability Be Beautiful?" *Social Policy* (Fall): 26–31.

Haraway, Donna.1998. "A Cyborg Manifesto: Science, Technology, and Socialist Feminism in the Late Twentieth Century." In *Contemporary Literary Criticism: Literary and Cultural Studies,* edited by Robert Con-Davis and Ronald Schleifer, 696–727. New York: Longman.

Heng, Geraldine. 1997. "'A Great Way to Fly': Nationalism, the State, and the Varieties of Third-World Feminism." In Alexander and Mohanty, *Feminist Genealogies,* 30–45.

Huggan, Graham. 1990. "Philomela's Re-Told Story: Silence, Music, and the Post-Colonial Text." *Journal of Commonwealth Literature* 25: 12–23.

Kandiyoti, Deniz, ed. 1991. Introduction to *Women, Islam, and the State,* 1–21. Philadelphia: Temple University Press.

Minh-ha, Trinh T. 1989. *Woman Native Other.* Bloomington: Indiana University Press.

Mitchell, David T., and Sharon L. Snyder, eds. 1997. "Disability Studies and the Double Bind of Representation." Introduction to *The Body and Physical Difference: Discourses of Disability,* 1–33. Ann Arbor: University of Michigan Press.

Mohan, Rajeswari. 1997. "The Forked Tongue of Lyric in Anita Desai's *Clear Light of Day.*" *Journal of Commonwealth Literature* 32: 47–66.

Mohanty, Chandra Talpade, Ann Russo, and Lourdes Torres, eds. 1991. *Third World Women and the Politics of Feminism.* Bloomington: Indiana University Press.

Morrison, Toni. 1990. *Playing in the Dark: Whiteness and the Literary Imagination.* New York: Vintage Books.

Oliver, Michael. 1990. *The Politics of Disablement: A Sociological Approach.* New York: St. Martin's Press.

Pernick, Martin S. 1997. "Defining the Defective: Eugenics, Aesthetics, and Mass Culture in Early-Twentieth-Century America." In Mitchell and Snyder, *Body and Physical Difference,* 89–110.

Phillips, Marilynn J. 1988. "Disability and Ethnicity in Conflict: A Study in Transformation." In *Women with Disabilities: Essays in Psychology, Culture, and Politics,* edited by Michelle Fine and Adrienne Asch, 195–214. Philadelphia: Temple University Press.

Poovey, Mary. 1995. *Making a Social Body: British Cultural Formation, 1830–1864.* Chicago: University of Chicago Press.

Russo, Mary. 1994. *The Female Grotesque: Risk, Excess, and Modernity.* New York: Routledge.

Said, Edward. 1994. *Culture and Imperialism.* New York: Knopf.

Sartre, Jean Paul. 1963. Preface to *The Wretched of the Earth,* by Frantz Fanon, 7–31. New York: Grove Press.

Spivak, Gayatri Chakravorty. 1999. *A Critique of Postcolonial Reason: Toward a History of the Vanishing Present.* Cambridge, Mass.: Cambridge University Press.

Temerson, Catherine, and Francoise Kourilsky. 1988. Introductory notes for "You Have Come Back." *Plays by Women: An International Anthology,* 160–221. New York: Ubu Repertory Theater Publications.

Eight

A HERITAGE OF ABLEIST RHETORIC IN AMERICAN FEMINISM FROM THE EUGENICS PERIOD

SHARON LAMP AND W. CAROL CLEIGH

In 2005 Terri Schindler Schiavo, a forty-one-year-old disabled woman, galvanized the nation's attention as her estranged husband fought for the right to terminate her life.[1] Ultimately, with court approval, Terri was starved and dehydrated until she died thirteen days later. The following year in Illinois, a disabled woman speculated about the possibility of a maternal role in the distant future. Her guardian reacted by initiating legal action to have her sterilized against her will. In 2007 we learned of the medical mutilation of a disabled girl known only as Ashley X, in order to prevent her physical maturation (Carlson and Dorfman 2007). While disability rights groups protested vigorously for these women's right to control their own bodies, mainstream feminist organizations remained aloof. How is it that feminists who claim to support all women's rights have seemingly abandoned disabled women?

When Charles Darwin declared, "Man is more powerful in body and mind than woman" (1874, 619), he echoed the sentiments of his nineteenth-century contemporaries as well as his predecessors. In Western culture women had always been stereotyped as biologically inferior to men (Golden 1992, 211). Portrayed as weak and "feeble-minded," with no legal rights, pre-suffrage women were vulnerable to being "legally kidnapped" and institutionalized by husbands, family, or community members who wanted to be rid of them, particularly when they strayed too far from socially acceptable "rules" (Geller and Harris 1994, 30–41, 59–67; Trent 1994, 72–77). The dominant cultural belief was that women who exerted mental energy, stepped outside the domestic sphere, or protested women's oppression were "defective."

As nineteenth-century scientific and social reformers sought to control so-called defective bodies by separating, institutionalizing, and eliminating people who were classified as idiots, imbeciles, and morons, American women fought for control of their bodies and fates. In this essay we will examine the lives and work of two influential feminists, Charlotte Perkins Gilman (1860–1935) and Margaret Sanger (1879–1966), and show how their use of eugenic language and ideology placed their feminist agenda in the ableist, eugenic mainstream.

In 1848 the Seneca Falls Convention produced the Declaration of Sentiments, asserting women's equality, including the right to participate in formulating laws. Reacting to characterizations of being weak or inferior as slander, feminists deflected such portrayals by distancing themselves from these categories and, consequently, disability. Using an ableist line of thinking, many feminist leaders agreed there was a category of "defectives" that should be subject to social control, but they argued against women being included in this "defective" class by virtue of their sex. For example, feminist Lucy Stone protested married women being ranked with "insane people and idiots" in the allocation of legal rights (Buhle and Buhle 1978, 67). The move by feminists to separate women from the devalued group of "defectives" without challenging the hierarchy that produced it served to make disability central to feminism as a negative trope.

Charlotte Perkins Gilman and Margaret Sanger are two well-known and still revered feminist leaders from the eugenics period whose work shows that support for eugenics, an ableist ideology, has been part of feminism from its early days. Because feminists continue to exemplify an ableist ideology that started with eugenics, they must face this history in order to include the more than one in five women who are disabled.

EUGENICS IN THE CONSTRUCTION OF FEMINISM: GILMAN AND SANGER

The ideology that one is better off dead than living with disability—and the concomitant argument that society is better off without its "defective" citizens—is as old as Western culture. We find instances of impaired children being murdered as long ago as the golden age of ancient Greece. During the late nineteenth century, Darwin's theory of evolution was used to reinscribe ableist ideology into a pseudo-science known as eugenics. Although feminists of the time took varying positions on eugenics, the majority of feminists incorporated the basic tenets of eugenics into their belief systems, making mainstream feminism an ableist enterprise.

Neither Gilman nor Sanger had a comprehensive understanding of either eugenic theories or the evolutionary theory grounding eugenics. Historians—feminist and otherwise—do not portray them as eugenically sophisticated. Still, both women participated in the popular scientific discourse of the time, and their works echo the common social appropriations of scientific vocabulary and topics. Using eugenic rhetoric to challenge the social construction of women and motherhood, they argued for reproductive and domestic freedom in order to improve the lives of women. Gilman and Sanger saw women's liberation from involuntary domestic and maternal roles as key to equality and progress.

While Darwin believed that evolutionary variation could move a species in any direction, Gilman and Sanger applied the term *evolution* in a popular sense, synonymously with *progress* and *improvement*. Linking women's progress to the progress of the race, they promised women's cooperation in regenerating the gene pool and claimed that emancipated women would realize their full evolutionary potential and develop superior maternal abilities that would include a role as eugenic enforcers. At a time when women were viewed as the inferior sex, Gilman and Sanger used maternalist rhetoric to assert women's "superior" biological and social value as bearers and nurturers of offspring (Gordon 1994, 55).

Distancing themselves from the "defective" category, Gilman and Sanger joined eugenists and pre-suffrage feminists in declaring female primacy in the regeneration of the human race. As early as 1886, black feminist educator Anna Julia Cooper argued, "There is material in [black women of the South] well worth your while, the hope in germ of a staunch, helpful, regenerating womanhood on which, primarily, rests the foundation stones of our future as a race" (Lemert and Bhan 1998, 61). Gilman echoes this sentiment: "If our human method of reproduction is defective, let the mother answer. She is the main factor in reproduction" (1898, 92). In the twentieth century, Margaret Sanger reiterates, "there are weighty authorities who assert that through the female alone come those modifications of form, capacity and ability which constitute evolutionary progress" (1922, 238).

Not only do Gilman and Sanger demand that women reject the misprisions of patriarchal culture, but they also assign to women full (and unrealistic) responsibility for producing superior offspring. Gilman declared, "Nothing the man has ever done or can do removes from motherhood its primal responsibility. Suppose the female . . . should mate with mangy, toothless *cripples-* and so produce weak, *malformed* young, and help exterminate her race. Should she then blame him for the result?" (1898, 100; emphasis added). An imperious eugenic enforcer, Gilman sets high standards for good motherhood, which, "like every other natural process is to be measured by results. It is good or evil as it serves its purpose. Human motherhood must be judged as it serves its purpose to the human race. Primarily, its purpose is to reproduce the race by reproducing the individual; secondarily, to improve the race by improving the individual" (88).

Sanger, in her most influential works, *Woman and the New Race* (1920) and *Pivot of Civilization* (1922), demonstrates a feminist ideology grounded in negative eugenics—the prevention of "defect." Sanger referenced findings of the Galton Laboratory for Great Britain linking high fertility rates and "feeble-mindedness" (1922, 47), and argued, "the most urgent problem of today is how to limit and discourage the over-fertility of the mentally and physically defective" (24). Tying birth control to eugenic ideology, she describes birth control as "nothing more or less than the facilitation of the process of weeding out the unfit or preventing the birth of defectives or those who become defective" (1920, 229). Predating the Nazi use of negative eugenics, which claimed more than 270,000 disabled lives (Mitchell and Snyder 2003), Sanger viewed the lives of disabled infants as not worth living. Describing eugenic killing as a feminist act of compassion, she declared, "It is her heart that the sight of the *deformed,* the *subnormal,* the undernourished, the overworked child smites first and oftenest and hardest" (1920, 97; emphasis added).

In contrast to the negative eugenics prominent in Sanger's campaign, Gilman promoted positive eugenics—encouraging "fit" families to have children. She deflected eugenicists' patriarchal arguments that changes in gender roles would be disastrous to the race by claiming that emancipated women would become "cooperative, superior" mothers who would produce "superior" offspring. Gilman combined feminist and eugenics ideologies and argued that sex discrimination prevented women's evolutionary progress and was the source of a plethora of social evils ranging from mental myopia to the ruin of the race.

Economics was one of the grounds of eugenics in popular discourse, and both Gilman and Sanger portrayed the economic independence of women as the key to sociopolitical and biological advancement. In 1898 Gilman gained international acclaim with the publication of *Women and Economics,* in which she declared women the moral superiors of men and asserted a liberated woman's potential economic value as regenerator of the human race (165). Gilman traced the historical development of gender roles and called for their radical revision, proclaiming that women's oppression is the result of arbitrary conditions and that "by removing these conditions, we may remove the evil resultant" (viii). She explained the crucial role of economic relations in evolution (12) and argued, "all the varied activities of economic production and distribution . . . should be common to both sexes" (27). She contended that women's economic dependence on men produces weakness in women and "defective" mothers who contribute to degeneration. Gilman complained that American men "have bred a race of women weak enough to be handed about like invalids" (Golden 1992, 93).

Both feminists and eugenicists wanted liberation: feminists from the "tyranny of male oppression" and eugenicists from the "tyranny of the weak." Gilman commiserated with eugenicists over the "burden" of "defectives," "always lurking in the back of your mind, the dreadful consciousness of other people's poverty, of the ghastly mill grinding out its product of *incapables, defectives, degenerates,* its swelling stream of disease and crime" (1935, 112; emphasis added). Merging popular economic, feminist, and eugenicist concern about race improvement, motherhood, and domesticity, she theorized that female oppression fed the "ghastly mill" by producing "defective" women and mothers "on whom the future of the race depends" (1898, 45). Gilman expanded pangenesis (heritability of environmental conditions) to include social factors. According to her, bad economic and sex relations cause disease and "makes us the sickly race we are" (13).

While Gilman's eugenic attention was directed primarily toward people who were already labeled "defective" and "feeble-minded," Margaret Sanger expanded the class of eugenically "unfit" to include the poor. Interestingly, Sanger's writings during her early activist years (1912–1916) emphasize Marxist themes rather than eugenics. Portraying birth control as a tool for working-class women to liberate and protect themselves from the burden of poor health and mortality caused by unwanted pregnancies, Sanger implored women to control their reproductive abilities. "Working women should not produce children who will become slaves to feed, fight and toil for the enemy—Capitalism," she declared (Kennedy 1970, 110). In October 1914, shortly after she began publishing in her feminist journal, *The Woman Rebel,* Sanger was charged with violating anti-obscenity laws. Seeking to delay her trial, she fled to England, where Havelock Ellis introduced her to eugenics (Reed 2003, 165). During this and later European trips, Sanger established relationships with eugenic-minded colleagues, including H. G. Wells and George Bernard Shaw, and attended secret meetings of neo-Malthusians, who supported sterilization, contraception, and abortion to reduce the numbers of the lower classes.

When Sanger returned to the United States in 1915, her campaign changed from a demand to free the poor from exploitation to a demand for social control of the poor. Historian Daniel Kevles found that eugenic supporters "were largely middle to upper middle class, White, Anglo-Saxon, predominantly Protestant, and educated" (1995, 64). Sanger's case for birth control changed emphasis from protecting poor people from becoming "unfit" to including poor people in the "unfit" category; from advocating birth control as a means to prevent maternal impairment and mortality among poor women to advocating birth control as a solution to a host of eugenically defined social problems: female oppression, poverty, disease, crime, war, "feeble-mindedness," and hereditary afflictions (Kennedy 1970, 109).

Sanger's campaign for birth control reached its height of influence during the heyday of eugenics (1920–1945), when nativist concerns over the supposed declining birth rate of white, Anglo-Saxon Protestants combined with economic and eugenic concerns about the "unfit." Two of her most widely read publications, *Woman and the New Race* (1920) and *Pivot of Civilization* (1922), were published after her indoctrination into eugenics. These texts compiled "every conceivable argument, emotional, rational, and polemical, in support of birth control" (89). Sanger exploited the fear of human degeneration in order to launch arguments for "voluntary motherhood" (birth control) as a remedy for a myriad of social problems.

In *Woman and the New Race* Sanger placed birth control within a feminist discourse of female sovereignty and reproductive rights and responsibilities. Medical teachings and social rhetoric of the time promoted the belief that overpopulation and poverty led to heritable impairments and "defects."[2] Despite the fact that her lived experience demonstrated little to no connection between large, poor families and "defective" offspring, she used the science of eugenics to attack the poor and claimed, "Everywhere we see poverty and large families going hand in hand. The least fit to carry on the race are increasing most rapidly. Many of the children thus begotten are diseased or *feeble-minded*; many become criminals" (Sanger 1922, 279; emphasis added).[3] Sanger argued that birth control would set mothers free and thereby accomplish eugenic goals. She wrote, "Motherhood, when . . . free to choose the time and number of children who shall result from the union, automatically works in wondrous ways. It refuses to bring forth *weaklings*, it refuses to bring forth slaves . . . it withholds the *unfit*, brings forth the *fit*" (1920, 45; emphasis added).

A primary eugenic theme in *Woman and the New Race* is the belief that "the feebleminded are notoriously prolific in reproduction" (41). Sanger contributed to public alarm over the fecundity of the "unfit" by referencing a host of other fears of the time: "Unwanted children, poverty, ill health, misery, death—these are links in the chain" (75). She blamed women for submitting to roles as "creators of over-population"; "unknowingly creating slums, filling asylums with insane, and institutions with other defectives" (4); and producing "defective" offspring "to perpetuate and multiply their ignorance, weakness and diseases" (65). Sanger presumed that poor women could break the chain of poverty, overpopulation, and degeneration by willfully taking control of their reproductive abilities.

If the evils wrought upon the family by uncontrolled pregnancies were not enough to convince "thinking women" to support her cause, Sanger expanded her analysis to the neighborhood, and the world. She portrays "weak" and "feeble-minded" offspring resulting from unwanted pregnancy as socially and economically threatening: "burdens and dangers to the intelligence of the community" (91). Sanger used Social Darwinism in her economic argument for birth control: "we see the funds that should be available for human development, for scientific, artistic and philosophic research being diverted annually, by hundreds of millions of dollars, to the care and segregation of men, women, and children who never should have been born" (100). In addition, she claimed that unwanted pregnancies contributed to overpopulation, which, in the struggle over limited resources, caused wars in which the strong and fit were killed, leaving the weak and helpless (161).

Some critics point to "The Dangers of Cradle Competition," a chapter in *The Pivot of Civilization* (1922), as evidence that Sanger has been unfairly portrayed as a eugenics advocate. That chapter's clearest criticism of eugenics is that "it has persistently refused to give any help toward extending the knowledge of contraceptives to the exploited classes" (183); however, Sanger's claim is not altogether true. She credited eugenicists for demonstrating the poor physical and mental condition of the human race (175). In fact, she accepted results of World War I army intelligence tests and used them to fuel public fear that those of lesser intelligence were overrunning the country. Citing the work of prominent eugenicist Dr. Karl Pearson for showing that "if fertility be correlated with anti-social heredity characters, a population will inevitably degenerate" (174–75), Sanger declared the "feeble-minded" the "great biological menace to the future of civilization" (176). She scoffed at the idea of judging the fitness of newborns. "Who shall say who is fit or unfit?" Sanger asked in seeming criticism of class and sex bias of eugenicists (181). Then, a few pages later, she answered the question crediting eugenics with pointing out the "network of *imbecility* and *feeblemindedness* that has been sedulously spread through all strata of society" (187; emphasis added).

Sanger steadfastly refused to support the positive eugenic argument that fit women were responsible for bearing more children, a concept she saw as antifeminist and oppressive to women. The primary tension between birth control and eugenic supporters was how birth control would be administered. While eugenicists were interested in developing methods of control over a public body, Sanger saw birth control as a method of an individual woman's control over her body. According to her, a woman's individual control must "come from within" (23) and not be imposed from without. "[M]otherhood must be made the responsible and self-directed means of human expression and regeneration" (280–81).

Sanger began her public career with the goal of improving poor women's lives by legalizing the dissemination of birth control information and freeing women from the "burden" of large families and poor health. As she cemented her own membership in the upper class, pleas for birth control to protect the poor from suffering waned. Instead, she came to portray birth control as a method of social control and demanded it in order to protect the wealthy from the prolific poor, whom she portrayed as intrinsically unfit and a national threat. Ultimately, Sanger incorporated eugenic ideology in the goals of the International Planned Parenthood Federation, established in 1952, which includes as its second objective "research institutions to be established by scientists classifying basic factors in eliminating harmful dysgenic births in the nation" (Reed 2003, 273).

THE PERSONAL IS POLITICAL

Gilman and Sanger were raised in poor families, and both experienced acquired and hereditary impairments and illnesses that, ironically, might have resulted in their being classified as "defective" or disabled. However, these two women became significant social actors in the feminist and eugenics movements and thereby circumvented that classification.

Gilman valued her independence and her work and despised weakness: "I am meant to be useful and strong, to help many and do my share in the world's work" (Golden 1992, 63). When her impairment interfered with her ability to work, she sought out and attacked the presumed source of her "defect"—women's subjugation. During her career, Charlotte Perkins Gilman wrote six full-length nonfiction books, several novels, and hundreds of articles, poems, and lectures. In addition, she wrote every article for a monthly magazine, the *Forerunner*, which she edited and published for seven years (123). Yet Gilman was unsatisfied with her achievements and estimated she had lost twenty-seven years of productivity as a result of her "nervous malady," which she described as "a constant dragging weariness miles below zero. Absolute incapacity. Absolute misery. To the spirit it is as if one were an armless, legless, eyeless, voiceless cripple" (1935, 91). Employing eugenic terminology, Gilman described herself as "weak, dark, and *feeble-minded,* limited of all usefulness" (110; emphasis added).

Working to cure socially induced female weakness and "defect" through women's liberation, Gilman addressed a painful aspect of her life, "the interminable *handicap* under which I lived" (210; emphasis added). To her, a "real defective" was one who could not work or be productive.

She abstracted herself from this category, struggling to pass as "normal." Gilman explained, "Since my public activities do not show weakness, nor my writings, and since brain and nervous disorder is not visible, short of *lunacy* or literal 'prostration,' this lifetime of limitation and wretchedness, when I mention it, is flatly disbelieved. . . . What confuses them is the visible work I have been able to accomplish. They see activity, achievement; they do not see blank months of idleness" (98; emphasis added). Because Gilman was deemed "normal" by the dominant culture, she did not see herself as a "real defective" and instead set up a hierarchy of "defect" that allowed her to distinguish herself from the category of "defectives" for whom she supported sterilization as a method of population control (1932).

Like Gilman, Margaret Sanger was no stranger to illness and impairment. Sanger was the sixth of eleven children born live to poor Irish American parents. Throughout her childhood she witnessed her mother become progressively weaker from tuberculosis. When her mother died at age forty-nine, Sanger attributed her death to the strain of eighteen pregnancies. Sanger's only daughter died of pneumonia at age five, two years after contracting polio (Sanger 1938, 54), and Sanger herself experienced a host of impairments, including tuberculosis, depression, a nervous disorder, a heart condition, alcohol and drug dependency, and leukemia (Reed 2003, 136).

Contrary to the prevailing eugenic belief that "defectives" produced more "defectives," Sanger described her siblings as having been born healthy and without impairments: "Mother's eleven children were all ten-pounders or more, and both she and father had a eugenic pride of race. I used to hear her say that not one of hers had a mark or blemish, although she had the utmost compassion for those who might have cleft palates, crossed eyes, or be 'born sick'" (1938, 29). Not only did Sanger consider her bloodline eugenically fit, but she also did not identify with the bottom of the class hierarchy. Raised in a shanty in the woods, she envied the rich households on the hill with their small, clean, and healthy families and disdained the rest of the working poor as dirty and sickly. Sanger was grateful that she was not "like the poor children in the flats" (17).

The link between poverty, large families, maternal impairment, and death that Sanger observed as a child resurfaced during her first career as a nurse in the impoverished immigrant neighborhoods of Lower East Side of Manhattan, where she treated poor women suffering and dying from health problems related to numerous pregnancies and self-abortions. When antipornography laws prevented her from sharing birth control information with her patients, she renounced her nursing career, resolving instead to "seek out the root of the evil, to do something to change the destiny of mothers whose miseries were as vast as the sky" (92). Sanger began her birth control campaign to reduce poor women's suffering, to protect them from a cycle of poverty and "defect."

Both Gilman and Sanger were diagnosed with "nervous prostration" (also called "hysteria"). Gilman's physician, Dr. S. Weir Mitchell, the foremost neurologist of his time (Golden 1992, 48) and an ardent eugenicist, prescribed a "rest-cure" treatment in the antifeminist tradition: "Live as domestic a life as possible. Have your child with you all the time.... Have but two hours intellectual life a day. And never touch a pen, pencil or brush as long as you live" (Gilman 1935, 95–96). Indeed, both of Gilman's great-aunts, Harriet Beecher Stowe and Catherine Beecher, were intellectuals and both had experienced nervous disorders. The prevalent hereditarian attitudes of the day might lead us to expect Gilman to have blamed her genetic makeup for her impairment. Yet Gilman, who sank into a deep depression after marrying reluctantly and giving birth to her only child a year later, attributed her malady to the unequal status of women and the gender-based discrimination of the time. In other words, it was the social oppression of being trapped in the unwanted institution of marriage and motherhood that caused her impairment rather than an inherent weakness in herself or in women generally. Additionally, her male-prescribed treatment of enforced inactivity and domestic confinement for "hysteria" was injurious instead of healing, leading to greater impairment. Gilman believed that she never fully recovered from the harm done to her by the rest-cure treatment, and the experience later served as the inspiration for one of her most renowned works, *The Yellow Wall-Paper* (1892).

Like Gilman before her, Sanger's "nervous prostration" was treated with the rest-cure. Sanger wrote, "At the end of eight months I was worse instead of better, and had no interest in living. . . . To every suggestion I was negative, I was not even interested in my baby" (1938, 60). "Once free from the horrors of *invalidism*" she regained an interest in life, although she would suffer periodically from what she described as a "nervous malady," which was exacerbated when she was confined in the domestic sphere (Gray 1979, 40; emphasis added).

Unlike Gilman, Sanger does not appear to have pondered the origins of her impairments. Gilman wrote about and came to understand the source of her disablement as socially constructed. Yet Gilman also blamed herself for not resisting the social pressure to marry and then for not having the willpower to overcome her impairment (Gilman 1935, 91–92). Her attempts to explore and "out" her mental illness were thwarted by her friends' denial of her impairment. Gilman wrote of her humiliation and frustration when her efforts to talk about her illness were met with "amiable laughter and flat disbelief" (104). Having no avenue for dialogue, she spent years in shame, discouragement, and misery.

Like Gilman, Sanger's self-perception as outside the category of "unfit" allowed her to appropriate eugenic tenets to feminist ideology. But just how was Sanger able to separate herself from the truly unfit? She escaped the ranks of the poor at age nineteen when she married William Sanger, a budding architect and artist. Her membership in the upper classes was cemented by her second marriage, to millionaire Noah Slee in 1922. Unlike her mother, Sanger would have only three planned pregnancies. While her mother's medical treatment consisted of doses of whisky administered by her father, Sanger's adult life took place in settings where health care and accommodations were readily available. During her nursing training, she was given a disability accommodation when her workday was shortened several hours so that she could take walks in fresh air, then the treatment for tuberculosis. Access to quality health care and rehabilitation services allowed Sanger to pursue a career in the public spotlight; she rose from the ranks of the poor, internationally acclaimed and welcomed by world leaders and thinkers.

Though Sanger promoted eugenic goals and used negative stereotypes of disability in her call for the elimination of "defectives," she was not threatened by the eugenic beliefs that she perpetuated or the associated methods of social control: "I am rich, I have brains, I shall do as I please" (1938, 121). Likewise, Gilman, who saw herself as a woman whose impairments were induced by social factors rather than heredity, did not seem to explore the obvious implication that she could become a eugenic target. A few years before her death, a New Jersey physician's testimony at the Third International Eugenics Conference (1932) endorsed the sterilization of the "feeble-minded" in cases where undesirable traits were not heritable. Gilman's self-descriptions ultimately placed her within this group, for whom mandatory sterilization had become medically and socially acceptable.

Sanger lived the last years of her life in a nursing home and ultimately succumbed to leukemia at age eighty-seven. Gilman declared herself "useless" at age seventy-five after being diagnosed with inoperable (but asymptomatic) cancer and ended her life by inhaling chloroform. In a final act of "social consciousness," Gilman claimed that her death was in support of euthanasia (Gilman 1935, 127). While Sanger does not appear to have been actively concerned with social reforms at the end of her life, Gilman may have seen her suicide as a way of redeeming herself in a world that had come to see "useless" people as toxic to the nation's health.

Gilman's and Sanger's efforts to empower women led to their own socio-economic rise. Both women tapped into the influence of patriarchal eugenics in order to gain improved social standing for themselves and other class-privileged women. They campaigned for the rights of a social group with which they identified: women. They did not, however, identify with the eugenic class of "defectives" as they might have done. As a result, while challenging notions of gender-based inferiority, they failed to challenge the very structure of oppression. Further, they did not recognize the social construction of the "true defective," nor did they reject eugenics. Although Gilman and Sanger disregarded the plight of other minority groups, they were able to believe that they were working in the best interest of humanity. In their view, the fit were vulnerable and in need of protection from the "tyranny of the weak," the "unfit." Gilman and Sanger succeeded in shifting eugenic targets, but they didn't question the need to construct a class of eugenically unfit people. Instead of challenging such social hierarchies, they, like many people today, struggled to "pass" or deny their own vulnerability in order to keep from slipping onto the bottom rung of the lethal social hierarchies they perpetuated.

Gilman and Sanger presented the public with new ideas that served to expand the range of women's choices. At the same time, they carried forward old ideas of mental and physical difference from the "norm" as a signifier of inferiority and thus kept these newly gained choices out of reach for disabled women. Eugenicists co-opted feminists such as Gilman and Sanger, who considered themselves compassionate and humane, into the role of eugenic enforcers, the ultimate exclusionists. Both devoted their careers to resolving social problems that caused them profound pain in their personal lives and contributed to raising women from the lowly social role of disempowered housekeepers to the powerful role of world-makers. In the process, however, they discriminated against people with disabilities and perpetuated negative stereotypes of disability that still have profound power in the twenty-first century. Thus, their feminist rhetoric rings hollow to the one in five women in the United States who are disabled.

MODERN FEMINISM AND THE DISABILITY RIGHTS MOVEMENT

There has been recent interest in the eugenic roots of modern feminism, but virtually all studies emphasize the racial or class bias inherent in eugenic ideology, often without acknowledging that disabled people are the primary eugenic targets. Meanwhile, a deep and seldom challenged project of creating bodily uniformity marches forward in practices such as genetic engineering, selective abortion, reproductive technology, so-called physician-assisted suicide, surgical normalization, aesthetic standardization procedures and ideologies of health and fitness. A kind of new eugenics that aims to regularize our bodies supports all of these practices. (Garland-Thomson 2004)

These practices inscribe themselves upon the bodies and souls of women and girls with disabilities, yet "mainstream" feminists, even those who deconstruct ideologies of race and class, continue to reinscribe ableist ideologies and ignore the impact of those ideologies on disabled women and girls.

Across the United States, the life chances of girls like Ashley X and women like Terri Schindler Schiavo are being medically and judicially destroyed, sometimes complete with national press attention, while feminists remain silent. Some have told us they consider such cases private or personal, apparently forgetting the basic feminist tenet that the personal is political. Feminists must not only examine the eugenic roots of feminism but also root out the ableist bias that now permeates their movement. In the twenty-first century will we finally have an answer for the lonely plea of Elizabeth Stone, whose religious differences with her family resulted in her incarceration in the McLean Asylum (Charlestown, Massachusetts) from 1840 to 1842? Stone pointed out that forced institutionalization is always unjust: "If I *had* lost my reason is it right to take advantage of a crazy person and destroy happiness?" (Geller and Harris 1994, 41; emphasis added).

We, as disabled women, scholars, and activists, challenge feminists to leave ableist bias behind and join us—outside of a hospice in Pinellas Park, Florida; at the American Medical Association's headquarters in Chicago; or wherever the "new eugenics" strikes next at the lives and hopes of disabled women. We will be there. Will you?

NOTES

1. This essay uses the word *disability* to describe a socially constructed category of people whose members have physical and mental impairments or differences deemed undesirable by "normative" standards. We refer to members of this class in both modern vernacular (e.g., disabled people or people with disabilities) and that of the eugenics period (e.g., "unfit," "feeble-minded," "defective," etc.). Quotation marks (or italics when contained within quotes) are used for eugenics-period labels in order to keep the rhetoric intact while highlighting language now considered slanderous.

2. For more detail, see Mary R. Melendy and Henry M. Frank (1992) and B. G. Jeffries and J. L. Nichols (1921).

3. Sanger's book *Woman and the New Race* (published by Brentano in 1920) was renamed *The New Motherhood* and published by Jonathan Cape in 1930.

REFERENCES

Buhle, M. J., and P. Buhle, eds. 1978. *The Concise History of Woman's Suffrage.* Urbana: University of Illinois Press.

Carlson, David R., and Deborah A. Dorfman. 2007. "Investigative Report Regarding the 'Ashley Treatment.'" Washington Protection and Advocacy System. http://www.disabilityrightswa.org/home/Full_Report_InvestigativeReportRegarding thcAshleyTreatment.pdf.

Darwin, Charles. 1859. *On the Origin of the Species.* New York: D. Appleton and Co.

———. 1874. *The Descent of Man and Selection in Relation to Sex.* New York: D. Appleton and Co.

Eng, Ruth Clifford. 2000. *Clean Living Movements, American Cycles of Health Reform.* Westport, Conn.: Praeger.

Galton, Francis. 1883. *Inquiries into Human Faculty and Its Development.* London: Macmillan.

———. 1869. *Hereditary Genius: An Inquiry into Its Laws and Consequences.* London: Macmillan.

Garland-Thomson, Rosemarie. 2004. "First Person." *Emory Report,* 6 July. http://www.emory.edu/EMORY_REPORT/erarchive/2004/July/er%20july%20 6/7_6_04firstperson.html.

Geller, Jeffrey, and Maxine Harris. 1994. *Women of the Asylum: Voices from Behind the Walls, 1840–1945.* New York: Doubleday.

Gilman, Charlotte Perkins. 1898. *Women and Economics: A Study of the Economic Relation between Men and Women as a Factor in Social Evolution.* Boston: Small, Maynard, and Co.

———. 1932. "Birth Control, Religion, and the Unfit." *Nation* 134 (27 January): 108–109. http://www.thenation.com/article/154433/birth-control-religion-and-unfit.

———. (1935) 1991. *The Living of Charlotte Perkins Gilman: An Autobiography.* Madison: University of Wisconsin Press.

———. 1999. *Herland, The Yellow Wall-Paper, and Selected Writings.* Edited by Denise D. Knight. New York: Penguin.

Golden, Catherine, ed. 1992. *The Captive Imagination: A Casebook on* The Yellow Wallpaper. New York: Feminist Press.

Gordon, Linda. 1994. *Pitied but Not Entitled: Single Mothers and the History of Welfare, 1890–1935.* Cambridge, Mass.: Harvard University Press.

Gould, Stephen Jay. 2002. *The Structure of Evolutionary Theory.* Cambridge, Mass.: Harvard University Press.

Gray, Madeline. 1979. *Margaret Sanger: A Biography of the Champion of Birth Control.* New York: R. Marek.

Haller, Mark. 1963. *Eugenics: Hereditarian Attitudes in American Thought.* New Brunswick, N.J.: Rutgers University Press.

Hasian, Marouf Arif, Jr. 1996. *The Rhetoric of Eugenics in Anglo-American Thought.* Athens: University of Georgia Press.

Irving, Katrina. 2000. *Immigrant Mothers: Narratives of Race and Maternity, 1890–1925.* Urbana: University of Illinois Press.

Jeffries, B. G., and J. L. Nichols. 1921. *Searchlights on Health: The Science of Eugenics.* Naperville, Ill: J. L. Nichols and Co.

Kennedy, David M. 1970. *Birth Control in America: The Career of Margaret Sanger.* New Haven, Conn.: Yale University Press.

Kevles, Daniel J. (1985) 1995. *In the Name of Eugenics: Genetics and the Uses of Human Heredity.* Cambridge, Mass.: Harvard University Press.

Kline, Wendy. 2001. *Building a Better Race: Gender, Sexuality, and Eugenics from the Turn of the Century to the Baby Boom.* Berkeley: University of California Press.

Larson, Edward J. 1995. *Sex, Race, and Science: Eugenics in the Deep South.* Baltimore: Johns Hopkins University Press.

Lemert, Charles, and Esme Bhan, eds. 1998. *The Voice of Anna Julia Cooper: Including A Voice from the South and Other Important Essays, Papers, and Letters.* Lanham, Md.: Rowman and Littlefield.

Melendy, Mary R., and Henry Frank. 1928. *Modern Eugenics for Men and Women.* New York: Preferred Publications, Inc.

Mitchell, David, and Sharon Snyder. 2002. *A World without Bodies.* VHS. Chicago: Brace Yourselves Productions.

———. 2003. "The Eugenic Atlantic: Race, Disability, and the Making of an International Eugenic Science, 1800–1945." *Disability and Society* 18 (7): 843–64.

Ordover, Nancy. 2003. *American Eugenics: Race, Queer Anatomy, and the Science of Nationalism.* Minneapolis: University of Minnesota Press.

Reed, Miriam. 2003. *Margaret Sanger: Her Life in Her Words.* Fort Lee, N.J.: Barricade Books.

Sanger, Margaret. 1920. *Woman and the New Race.* New York: Brentano's.

———. 1922. *The Pivot of Civilization.* Washington, D.C.: Scott Townsend Publications.

———. 1938. *Margaret Sanger: An Autobiography.* New York: W. W. Norton.

Trent, James W., Jr. 1994. *Inventing the Feeble Mind: A History of Mental Retardation in the United States.* Berkeley: University of California Press.

PART FOUR

SEXUAL AGENCY

AND

QUEER FEMINIST

FUTURES

Nine

DISABILITY, SEX RADICALISM,
AND POLITICAL AGENCY

ABBY WILKERSON

Beneath the moral stigmas attached to pathologized bodies lies fear: the fear of bodily alteration, and even death itself—and to the extent that the singular human body represents the body politic, the fear of social upheaval and chaos, the loss of all social order. Medical discourse has become one of the most powerful means of assuaging such fears by diagnosing and managing the bodily chaos that is indicative of social disorder. Because of its basis in biomedical science, medical discourse is presumed to be inherently objective and therefore an authoritative source of truth; because it represents the healing face of science and technology, its truths and their applications are presumed to be inherently benevolent.

Sexuality, for all of its uses in advertising, entertainment media, and other capitalist enterprises, is nonetheless a culturally feared aspect of the body, with especially serious implications for those whose bodies are perceived as falling outside a fairly narrow and rigid norm. Just as homosexuality, long considered an illness, was treated for years with drugs, castration, hypnotherapy, psychoanalysis, and aversion therapy, people with various kinds of disabilities have also faced medical denial of their sexualities.[1] A man and a woman who spent many years living in an institution for people with epilepsy wanted to marry and requested permission of a doctor at the institution. They were told "that they could get married, but they were not allowed to have sex" (Fegan, Rauch, and McCarthy 1993, 48). Those with cognitive disabilities have also been subjected to aversive therapies designed to stop behavior that is perceived as unnatural and otherwise inappropriate. A parent interviewed for *Sexuality and People with Intellectual Disability* mentions a young boy living in an institution who masturbated in the presence of others "by rubbing his thighs together when sitting down. So the staff at the institution attached sandpaper to the insides of his thighs" (9). Women with motor impairment also face medical obstacles to sexuality. Women with spinal cord injuries report being denied birth control by their doctors in a manner suggesting their sexual lives are over. Chris, who was paraplegic, had many questions during her initial seven-month hospitalization. When she asked about birth control pills, a nurse reported to her the doctor's response: "he said no because it would make you [Chris] bloat. Then he said you could just stick the pill between your knees and say no" (Becker 1978, 117). Elle Becker, also a paraplegic, had a similar experience: "About four days after I broke my back I asked my surgeon, 'I don't have my birth control pills with me. Is there something we can do about that?' He said 'Well, you don't need those anymore,' and walked out of my room" (255).

More recently, the *Washington Post* reported that Americans Disabled for Attendant Programs Today (ADAPT) shut down traffic at two locations in Washington, D.C., protesting the lack of attendant services that forces many people with disabilities into nursing homes (Fahrenthold 2000). What the *Washington Post* did not report was the failure of most nursing homes to respect residents' privacy and the resulting constraints on their sexual options—surely newsworthy in the U.S. city with the highest concentration of young people in nursing homes.[2] Sexuality is a vital means of pleasure, interpersonal connection, personal efficacy, and acceptance of one's body and of self more generally, all goods that might be especially useful to disabled persons in nursing homes. Furthermore, because one's autonomy is already compromised by residing in a nursing home, the violation of both sexual agency and personal security imposed by this loss of privacy should be recognized as a serious harm that needs to be rectified.

It must be understood, however, that medical authority over sexuality is not limited to such extreme cases. Medical discourse has a much broader socially recognized power that, even in its gentler manifestations, is nonetheless insidious in its ability to shape our sexual options, a sense of ourselves as sexual beings, and, ultimately, our very identities for ourselves and others. Even—perhaps especially—when this authority is used in benevolent ways, it accords the medical profession and related institutions an increasingly influential form of political power, which is too seldom acknowledged. Ann, a bisexual whose spinal cord was damaged in infancy, recognizes medical authority to reflect and reinforce cultural norms when she reviews the medical literature on sexuality in women with spinal problems and states, "I . . . find most of it is inadequate, condescending, restricted to the traditional middle class married view of sex, [and] still inherently male oriented (how to please the almighty male)" (Becker 1978,

112–13). Narelle, a woman with intellectual disability, states, "I left home when I was twenty-nine years old. I had a lot of pressure from my parents not to leave—I wanted to get married. I asked the doctor if I could get married because I had met a nice young man I wanted to marry" (Fegan et al. 1993, 39–40). Her experience reflects the widespread social reliance on medical discourse as a source of moral, not merely scientific, information. The challenge to the medical profession and to related institutions is to become self-critical of discursive practices in the field that undermine the status and the self-regard of particular groups. The challenge for society as a whole is to bear witness to these practices and to intervene in them.

These stories illustrate the political urgency of a radical politics of sex grounded in the experiences of all of those groups of people who are most socially marginalized. Any public articulation of sexuality as an aspect of life to which everyone should be entitled still remains almost unthinkable within mainstream discourse. Even less recognized is the strategic value of sexual stereotyping and other sexual harms as a significant force in perpetuating the inequality of *any* oppressed group. I contend, therefore, that sexual democracy should be recognized as a key political struggle, not only because of the importance of the basic human right to sexual autonomy but also because (as I will argue) a group's sexual status tends to reflect and reinforce its broader political and social status. I understand sexual agency not merely as the capacity to choose, engage in, or refuse sex acts, but as a more profound good that is in many ways socially based, involving not only a sense of oneself as a sexual being but also a larger social dimension in which others recognize and respect one's identity. We need a better understanding of the relationships between sexual agency and democracy. Sexuality must not be construed as one of many pursuits in life—like stamp collecting, bungee jumping, or orchid growing—in which autonomy, understood as a political good, affords one the freedom to make individual choices. Rather, we should consider whether sexual agency is far more central to political agency than has generally been acknowledged so far. In my view, the socially based aspects of sexual agency constitute a hierarchy in which those who are most socially privileged on various axes of social difference (including sexual orientation along with race, class, age, and gender expression, among others) are, other factors being equal, most likely to be considered respectable, and therefore worthy citizens. As I will discuss, if sexual deviance is understood entirely in terms of unorthodox sexual desires and practices, this obscures the impact of other axes of social difference on sexual identities of all groups, as well as sexual oppression related even to orthodox sexual practices and desires of heterosexual women.

Many people recognize that sexuality, as sexual identity, is one among a variety of axes of oppression, along with gender, race, class, and others. Feminists have also long viewed sexuality as one of several domains of experience in which women are disempowered; for radical feminists, it is the *key* domain that structures women's oppression. These lines of analysis have been enormously productive and have generated a great deal of healthy contention. What I wish to explore, however, is the role of sexuality in oppression more generally and the relationship between sexual agency and political agency.

History has provided us with repeated instances of efforts to constrain the political agency of social dissidents through efforts to constrain their sexual agency or depict them as sexual deviants. The Comstock Act of 1873 is an excellent example.[3] "It is no accident," writes public health professor Lynn P. Freedman, "that the public hysteria about sexuality stoked by the Comstock crusades followed the beginnings of the modern U.S. women's movement, which included among its central planks the advocacy of 'voluntary motherhood' and, somewhat later, of contraception itself" (1999, 157). These laws were enforced in a period of unprecedented social change, characterized by "growing labor unrest, the rise of socialist and anarchist movements . . . an increasingly vocal feminist movement . . . [and] huge waves of immigration" (157).

Another time of social and political upheaval was the civil rights era, which also saw the beginnings of the second wave of the women's movement. Objections to these movements also sometimes took the form of sexual moralizing or warnings. White southerner Minnie Bruce Pratt recalls the following incident:

> My father called me to his chair in the living room. He showed me a newspaper clipping, from some right-wing paper, about Martin Luther King, Jr.; and told me that the article was about how King had sexually abused, used, young Black teen-aged girls. I believe he asked me what I thought of this; I can only guess that he wanted me to feel that my danger, my physical, sexual, danger, would be the result of the release of others from containment. I felt frightened and profoundly endangered, by King, by my father. (1984, 36–37)

When social dissent thus becomes recast as sexual danger, a threat made to seem far more potent than the shortcomings of the status quo, it is not difficult to see how political agency is undermined at the same time.

Although queer theory's relevance for investigating the political dimensions of sexual agency should be clear, disability studies' role in this context may be less understood. Queer perspectives have helped us understand and resist regimes organized around controlling various sexual identities and practices. Disability perspectives reveal the broad array of cultural norms that privilege an illusory ideal mind and body at the expense of actual bodies of all shapes and sizes, that are subject to a host of contingencies and are all too fragile, yet capable of a vast array of thoughts, movements. Together, queer and disability perspectives help reveal why sexual agency must be understood as an important and, in some ways, key component of the liberation struggles of all disenfranchised groups rather than a luxury to be addressed after achieving goals that might be perceived as more basic. Working toward this end requires disability studies to engage in sustained dialogue not only with the critical framework of sex radicalism but also with feminism and critical race theory in order to understand how sexual hierarchies are always simultaneously gendered and racialized. It also requires serious critical engagement with the ageism that renders both youth and the elderly as less than fully human and the infantilization that denies agency to adult members of some groups, such as people with disabilities.

All of these politically engaged critical frameworks help illuminate how marginalized groups come to be perceived as deviant bodies; how actual or perceived differences in these bodies are taken as demonstrating particular forms of inferiority; and how these associations become articulated in the pathologized erotic "natures" attributed to each group. It is not surprising that queer and disability movements have displayed similarly flamboyant and defiant political and aesthetic sensibilities (as indicated by the Not Dead Yet disability action group or the *Diseased Pariah* newsletter created by gay men living with AIDS). First I will look at one of the founding documents of queer theory, assessing its relevance for current and future conjunctions of disability studies, queer theory, and other frameworks. I will go on to examine the political implications of erotophobia as it affects oppressed groups more generally, then take up the role of sexual shame in oppression based on sexuality and gender, and return to medical constructions of the sexuality of people with disabilities and others. Finally, I will consider the important role of counter-discourses and coalition politics in a movement for inclusive sexual liberation.

SEXUAL DEMOCRACY, FEMINISM, AND EROTOPHOBIA

Gayle Rubin's "Thinking Sex: Notes for a Radical Theory of the Politics of Sexuality," which first appeared in 1984, is widely regarded as providing both the impetus and the justification for queer theory (1993). In her essay, Rubin attempts to lay the groundwork for a "democratic morality" of sex (15), "challeng[ing] the assumption that feminism is or should be the privileged site of a theory of sexuality" (32). The concept of sexual perversion, for example, is in her view a cultural judgment whose operations are not reducible to those associated with the cultural categories of gender. Rubin contends:

> Sex is a vector of oppression. The system of sexual oppression cuts across other modes of social inequality, sorting out individuals and groups according to its own intrinsic dynamics. It is not reducible to, or understandable in terms of, class, race, ethnicity, or gender. Wealth, white skin, male gender, and ethnic privileges can mitigate the effects of sexual stratification. A rich, white male pervert will generally be less affected than a poor, black, female pervert. But even the most privileged are not immune to sexual oppression. (22)

Rubin concludes, "In the long run, feminism's critique of gender hierarchy must be incorporated into a radical theory of sex, and the critique of sexual oppression should enrich feminism. But an autonomous theory and politics of sexuality specific to sexuality must be developed" (34).

I think Rubin is correct in claiming that feminism cannot be the "privileged site of a theory of sexuality" (32)—that is, sexual oppression is not finally reducible to gender oppression, even though the two are generally intertwined in various ways. This important insight (which at one time surely startled many feminists, myself included) allows us to recognize sexual oppression as it affects many groups, an insight that could be (and to a limited degree has been) very fruitful for feminism at the same time. However, conceptualizing sexual politics as autonomous overlooks the multifaceted, interactive nature of oppression. Instead, I would like to suggest a conceptualization of sexual oppression as an integral aspect of the oppression experienced by any group. Rubin is certainly correct that "a rich, white male pervert will generally be less affected [by sexual stratification] than a poor, black, female pervert" (22), but what also needs to be addressed is that to be constituted as poor, black, and female in this society means already being a pervert, with one's sexuality constructed as inherently disorderly, even dangerous, in need of monitoring by others (Roberts 1997). As I hope to illustrate, being considered "other" in any way almost always renders an individual's or group's sexuality socially problematic, which itself should be considered a hallmark of oppression. Sexual democracy, then, will require not only opposing the political forces that stigmatize some sexualities as perversions, but also dismantling oppressive social relations, including racism, ableism, capitalism, sexism, and ageism, which cause some groups' sexuality to be scrutinized in the first place.

To be sure, vectors of oppression other than gender have been taken up within feminism for some time now, thanks to women of color and others who challenged the exclusionary nature of "hegemonic feminism" (Sandoval 1991). For as Barbara Smith noted in the closing session of the 1979 conference of the National Women's Studies Association (NWSA), "Feminism is the political theory and practice to free *all* women: women of color, working-class women, poor women, physically challenged women, lesbians, old women, as well as white economically privileged heterosexual women. Anything less than this is not feminism, but merely female self-aggrandizement" (qtd. in Moraga and Anzaldúa 1981, 61). This recognition that feminism itself provides the ground for a multifaceted analysis of, and response to, oppression has met with a great deal of resistance, especially from white middle-class heterosexual feminists who mistakenly believed they could speak "as women" and for all women (Alarcón 1990; Spelman 1988).

Lesbian feminist Minnie Bruce Pratt writes of the complex process by which she began to recognize her own racial and class privilege and its coexistence with her oppression in other respects. She was forced to reexamine her own place in the world, and the place of others, when coming out as a lesbian stripped her of the "protection" extended to her as a white southern married (read "good and pure") woman. If Pratt's lesbianism brought the loss of both a "protection" (which she came to see as control) and a moral innocence (later revealed as ignorance) that had seemed hers by birthright, it was also the force that motivated her to undergo a painful transformation:

> I am trying to speak from my heart, out of need, as a woman who loves
> other women passionately, and wants us to be able to be together as
> friends in this unjust world; and as a woman who lives in relative security
> in the United States, and who is trying to figure out my responsibility and
> my need in struggles against injustice in a way that will lead to our friend-
> ship. (1984, 15)

Pratt "set out to find out what had been or was being done in [her] name" (35), focusing initially on a regional history that included Klan marches and lynchings, and a familial history that included slave ownership, before eventually turning to current U.S. military interventions, "protection" on an international scale, and the place of the military buildup in the U.S. economy. In this process the illusion of her good standing in the world, and the rightness of many features of that world, was destroyed. Ultimately, Pratt rejects narrow notions of womanhood and the politics deriving from them while noting how privileged women may lose a (false) sense of self yet stand to gain in opposing social hierarchies other than those based on gender. For example, she notes, "The real gain in our material security as white women would come most surely if we did not limit our economic struggle to salaries of equal or comparable worth to white men in the U.S., but if we expanded this struggle to a restructuring of this country's economy so that we do not live off the lives and work of Third World women" (55). Thus, Pratt exemplifies a sense of feminism expanded beyond early notions of gender as both independent variable and ultimate influence in women's lives.

Gloria Anzaldúa, a Chicana lesbian and Tejana, writes from her vantage point as a multiple border dweller:

> As a *mestiza* I have no country, my homeland cast me out; yet all countries are mine because I am every woman's sister or potential lover. (As a lesbian I have no race, my own people disclaim me; but I am all races because there is the queer of me in all races.) I am cultureless because, as a feminist, I challenge the collective cultural/religious male-derived beliefs of Indo-Hispanics and Anglos; yet I am cultured because I am participating in the creation of yet another culture, a new story to explain the world and our participation in it, a new value system with images and symbols that connect us to each other and the planet. (1987, 80–81)

For Anzaldúa, as for Pratt, lesbianism and feminism, as well as her mestiza, or mixed blood, identity, are the ground of an inclusive politics that rejects narrow conceptions of identity in favor of a complex notion of oppression, privilege, and resistance. In her version of *mestizaje*, Anzaldúa finds opportunity to see and move beyond reductive cultural boundaries and categories.

While Anzaldúa and Pratt, in the company of many others, have worked to move feminism beyond earlier notions of gender as trump card, such important insights for feminism and other efforts to undermine oppression have not resulted in any general awareness of sexual harms as a link connecting many oppressed groups. Cultural erotophobia is a likely factor in the failure to recognize this commonality, as I hope to demonstrate in this essay. Locating herself within the "sexual unorthodoxy," which includes the recent body of queer theory, cultural studies scholar Cindy Patton defines erotophobia in the following way:

the terrifying, irrational reaction to the erotic which makes individuals and society vulnerable to psychological and social control in cultures
where pleasure is strictly categorized and regulated. Each component of
sexuality—sexual practice, desire, and sexual identity—constitutes a particular type of relationship between the individual and society, providing gripping opportunities for different forms of erotophobic repression.
(1985, 103)

Patton uses this concept primarily in a discussion of social policies and
sexual politics, but she also extends it to the politics of medical knowledge. Erotophobia (like homophobia) involves not only explicit declara-
tions of pathology, but also other practices and attitudes that more subtly
reflect cultural taboos against sexual practices, desires, and identities.

Michael Warner argues that erotophobia is an even more fundamental cultural value than the hierarchy of sexual deviance might suggest: it
is not merely unorthodox sexuality but sex itself that is the problem. "It
might as well be admitted," he says, "that sex is a disgrace . . . the possibility
of abject shame is never entirely out of the picture" (1999, 2). He notes that
it is quite possible for deeply erotophobic attitudes to coexist with overtly
sexualized environments, as in the United States, where it is difficult to get
through the day without being bombarded by sexualized images in advertising and entertainment. Erotophobic attitudes are manifested in "thousands of ways for people to govern the sex of others . . . directly, through
prohibition and regulation, and indirectly, by embracing one identity or
one set of tastes as though they were universally shared, or should be"
(1). Warner's recognition of the fundamental shamefulness of sex provides
a useful jumping-off point for exploring the intersection of erotophobic
judgments and prohibitions with other cultural practices that stigmatize
and otherwise harm members of oppressed groups.

In recent years important work has been done to expose the sexual
stereotyping to which various groups have been subjected (and I will turn
to examples of this shortly). This work's limitation is that it has largely
been carried out in reference to one group at a time. Surprisingly, it is seldom noted that oppressed groups generally tend to share the experience
of being particularly subject to erotophobic judgments of their sexual
behaviors or "natures," restrictions against practices associated with them,
sexual violence and harassment, and other constraints on their sexuality. If sexual harms, including stereotyping, are one of the hallmarks of
oppression, then cultural associations of a group with specific sexual tendencies or ways of being are (for all but the most privileged) connected
to significant material and psychological harms inflicted on its members

differentially. This suggests, furthermore, that erotophobia is a central tool of inequality.

Although these sexual images and harms, and their political significance for particular groups, have received a great deal of attention, their connection to one another and their status as a hallmark of oppression have not. The perspectives of feminism, queer theory, disability studies, and critical race theory are among those now making it possible as well as strategically important to begin an analysis that would connect each group's sexual oppression to that of other groups while attending carefully to the specifics of each group's experiences, sexual images, and their relation to material practices. Cultural erotophobia is not merely a general taboo against open discussions of sexuality and displays of sexual behavior, but also a very effective means of creating and maintaining social hierarchies: of sexuality, and those of gender, race, class, age, and physical and mental ability.

CULTURAL EROTOPHOBIA AND OPPRESSED GROUPS

The experience of powerlessness is a central aspect of oppression and strikingly evident in the context of sexuality. According to political philosopher Iris Young, power in contemporary U.S. society resides at least in part in the social norm of "respectability" associated with the middle and upper classes (1990). In the arena of sexuality, I understand powerlessness in terms of interference with the sexual agency of an individual, constituted as a member of a particular social group. Oppressed groups differentially face restrictions, penalties, and coercion and are denied access to important information, all in relation to their sexuality. The "erotic segregation" imposed by social taboos on interracial relationships may exert less power than was formerly the case, yet it continues to separate racial and cultural groups, limit individuals' sexual agency, and stigmatize those couples who defy the taboo (Twine 2002). While some of the following examples may be familiar as indications of a particular group's status and well-being, their place in the larger pattern I am drawing is worthy of new attention.

Feminists, of course, are quite familiar with sexuality as a ground of oppression, having brought social attention to a variety of problems women face, such as young women's elevated risk of sexual assault and abuse compared to all other groups. And it is feminists who have noted that "protection" for young women more likely involves coercive or paternalistic measures, such as restrictions on abortion through parental consent or notification provisions, rather than serious efforts to transform the rape culture that targets young women. President George W. Bush's imposition of abstinence-only programs (surely we can't call them "sex education") made it more difficult for young women (and men) to make responsible, informed decisions and avoid pregnancy, HIV, and sexually transmitted diseases; while the Obama administration changed these policies, their legacy is still with us in many ways.

We should also notice striking correlations between the experiences of people with disabilities and those of other groups who have been treated as if their sexualities exceed the bounds of respectability. Many people with disabilities, whether physical or cognitive, have been and continue to be sterilized without their consent, or under less than fully voluntary conditions, as have poor women, especially those of color.[4] Feminists as well as disability and antiracism activists have not only opposed coercive sterilization as a violation of individual rights, but have also expressed their uneasiness with the genocidal implications of the practice.

The hypersexualized image of African American and Latino men is by now all too familiar, subjecting them historically and in the present to a range of sanctions, including hate crimes such as lynching, criminal penalties for consensual sex (miscegenation laws), and higher conviction rates and stricter sentencing for sex crimes such as rape (hooks 1992). Such images continue to flourish all too easily. News coverage of the sexual assaults after New York's 2000 Puerto Rican Day parade frequently relied on "racist notions of men of color as animalistic predators" and, as Jennifer Pozner points out, tended to focus "on the few white women victimized in the park, while sidelining the experiences and voices of women of color—even though black and Latina women suffered the majority of assaults" (2001, 15). People with developmental disabilities have also been regarded as hypersexual, and in some cases as predators of (nondisabled) children, or as inherently and inevitably victimized—but in any case as possessing a sexuality requiring monitoring and control by others. These cases sharply contrast with the "boys will be boys" attitude that often characterizes cultural views of the normative white, middle-class, heterosexual male's sexual behavior (Midzian 1991).

Lesbian, gay, bisexual, and transgender people face a well-known array of legal obstacles to sexual agency, of which sodomy laws and legislation restricting marriage and its benefits to heterosexuals are just the beginning. People with cognitive disabilities often face obstacles to marriage and various aspects of sexual agency as well; marriage is still illegal for people with mental retardation in some states, despite the many couples who have functioned successfully with this disability. Another barrier is access to information. Parents, educators, politicians, and librarians deprive queer youth of power by denying them access to information, as reflected in a host of legal battles over sex education curricula, as well as debates over internet decency standards and restricting access to various materials in libraries.[5] Similar obstacles to information apply for people with cognitive impairments—in part due to the perception that, like queers, they are all too capable of being sexual creatures—and for those with physical disabilities, because supposedly they are asexual yet in need of protection from others. The message to a young person who is marginalized based on his or her sexual identity, disability, or both: your sexuality—a fundamental aspect of personhood—is inappropriate.

One reason for this denial of sexuality is that regardless of age, people with intellectual disabilities are considered children, incapable of forming substantive life preferences, learning the skills necessary to negotiate sexual choices, or making meaningful decisions in general. The vast majority of intellectually disabled people are "only mildly disabled and have the potential to lead largely independent lives" (Fegan et al. 1993, 18). They have demonstrated their ability to respond to sexual counseling that is nonjudgmental, affirms a range of sexual choices in relation to an individual's own values, and utilizes techniques designed for a variety of cognitive abilities about how to weigh consequences, recognize various options for satisfying one's desires, negotiate activities with others, and avoid unsafe or nonconsensual sex. Similar principles apply to issues such as menstruation, contraception, and reproduction. I do not want to minimize the complex, challenging issues at stake in sexual education for cognitively disabled people, but rather I seek to highlight both the possibility and the moral necessity of an approach that respects their sexual agency as a basic aspect of human dignity. (Moreover, similar considerations apply for people with physical disabilities, who have no difficulty understanding sexual information but are nonetheless infantilized in ways that also contribute to their desexualization [Clare 1999, 103–22; Finger 1985, 302; Garland-Thomson 1997, 285].)

Because of the belief that homosexual acts cannot be the result of rational choice, nondisabled queer youth are also treated as if their sexual orientations and sexual behaviors, unlike those of (nondisabled) heterosexual youth, do not reflect meaningful or legitimate choices or decisions in any way.[6] Thus, they, too, are seen as needing protection from themselves. Yet in every case, people should have access to the kind of counseling I have described, in a manner appropriate to their individual circumstances and intellectual capacity, so that they can make pleasurable and responsible decisions for themselves with the support of adults.

For young people (and some adults), both queerness and disability heighten vulnerability to violence and harassment, which is compounded by the failure of institutions (schools, medical staff, hospitals, nursing homes) and families to protect them, and an increased risk of being victimized at home.[7] For queer youth, these harms are overtly attached to their stigmatized sexuality or unconventional gender identity, while the victimization of people with disabilities, especially women, often takes sexual forms. Information designed to foster sexual agency is vitally important for queer and disabled youth in order to promote self-respect, pleasure, and safety in every sense of the word. Far too often, however, information about sexuality is treated as dangerous in itself, perhaps even a cause of victimization, while the social powerlessness that marks members of these groups as vulnerable targets gets little attention.

SEXUAL SHAME, FEMININITY, AND POLITICAL AGENCY

One Saturday morning on the George Washington University campus, a young woman exits Adams Hall after spending the night in a young man's room. Whether this was a night of pleasure for her, or something else, her return to her own dorm is known in campus parlance as "The Walk of Shame"—a locution somehow never applied to *his* journey back to his room if he stays with her.

The notion of shame, and the basis of shame in sexuality, figures prominently in Sandra Bartky's (1990) account of patriarchal domination as well as in Michael Warner's account of queer oppression and politics (1999). For both theorists, shame is not so much a psychological state of individuals as such (even though it may shape individual subjectivity), but rather a socially based harm that oppressed groups are subject to in particular ways.

The picture of queer oppression emerging from *The Trouble with Normal* involves the overt stigmatization of unorthodox sexual practices, desires, and identities through such means as sodomy laws, the restriction of marriage to heterosexuals, medical pathologization of queerness, overt moral proscriptions against queerness, and a broad array of cultural practices. This stigma results in a profound shame (and here I'm using this term in a slightly different way than Warner) with significant political implications. Shame is deployed as a "political resourc[e] that some people use to silence or isolate others" (Warner 1999, 12), and sexual deviants are considered a "danger to the body politic" (19).

Because of the extreme stigma associated with queerness, one becomes alienated from one's own sexuality. Warner argues that what he calls the "official queer movement" has attempted to overcome this shame and alienation through a bid for respectability, pursued through such means as the campaign for gay marriage (and one might also add the failure of some of these organizations to include transgender concerns in their efforts). Such efforts are misguided, according to Warner, because they fail to address the fundamental problem of marriage as an official enforcement of the hierarchy of sexual deviance, creating a two-class system in which the conventional sexuality of the monogamous couple (whether straight or gay) is upheld as the fundamental unit of society, at the expense of unconventional family units and those who are not monogamous or whose sexuality is unconventional in other ways. In short, the norm of respectability reinforces unjust social hierarchies.

As Bartky's *Femininity and Domination* indicates, shame and alienation connected to sexuality are similarly fundamental constituents of subjectivity for heterosexual women, through a variety of means (1990). One aspect of femininity is attractiveness to the male gaze, a norm that involves women in a lifelong project against the forces of chaos, and imposes "what is in effect a prohibition or a taboo on the development of her other human capacities. In our society, for example, the cultivation of intellect has made a woman not more but less sexually alluring" (42). The affective dimension of femininity as nurturance that is central to the behavioral and psychological norms of heterosexuality mandates continual care for the feelings and general well-being of men and children. This activity requires a relinquishing of epistemic and ethical agency (which includes the ability to recognize and act on behalf of one's own interests). In terms of sexual practice and identity, Bartky notes that "sexual objectification is one way of fixing disadvantaged persons in their disadvantage" (27) and recognizes a colonized sexual imagination as one of the destructive consequences of patriarchal domination (60). All of these aspects of femininity, which are tied to heterosexuality, involve alienation as estrangement from oneself, one's humanity, and one's interests.

In terms of shame, heterosexual women's situation differs from that of queers in significant ways. Because supposedly there is nothing "abnormal" in being a woman, at least not in any way that is explicitly acknowledged, unlike the case of queerness, the social causes of heterosexual women's shame and alienation are far less clear and overt, subjecting them to murkiness and contradiction. Moreover, while queer desire exists in clear opposition to the norm of heterosexuality, cultural forces influence heterosexual women to desire the very norms of femininity that dehumanize women and mark them inferior. Both nurturance and the desire for and pursuit of beauty, which Bartky calls narcissism, typically become fixed as fundamental aspects of the self very early in life. Thus, heterosexual women are made, and make themselves, complicit in hierarchies that systematically disadvantage them. Feminine narcissism, for example, on these grounds is rendered "infatuation with an inferiorized body" (40). Through such means, femininity becomes fundamentally an occasion for shame, which Bartky characterizes as "the distressed apprehension of the self as inadequate or diminished," requiring "if not an actual audience . . . then an internalized audience with the capacity to judge me" (86). Bartky's analysis reveals how "women . . . are made to feel shame in the major sites of social life. . . . [I]n the act of being shamed and in the feeling ashamed [it is] disclosed to women who they are and how they are faring within the domains they inhabit" (93). While moral philosophers have generally come to accept the "ontologically disclosive" nature of emotion, "constitut[ing] a primordial disclosure of self and world," shame has been conceptualized primarily in cognitive terms (89). Yet Bartky demonstrates how shame as a condition of women's subjectivity is not a cognitive attribute, but consists in socially imposed *feelings* of inadequacy that are likely to be in direct contrast to women's conscious beliefs about themselves. As Bartky notes, "the corrosive character of shame . . . lies in part in the very failure of these feelings to attain to the status of belief" (95). This explains the functions of shame persisting over time, as opposed to other accounts that focus on particular instances of shame.

Bartky concludes, "Under conditions of oppression, the oppressed must struggle not only against more visible disadvantages but against guilt and shame as well" (97). Warner would concur. They successfully demonstrate shame's connection to sexuality in multiple ways, and in particular ways in particular social locations, and moreover, that shame's interference with sexual agency constitutes an interference with political agency.

MEDICAL DISCOURSE AND SEXUAL POWERLESSNESS

Earlier, I suggested that sexual agency crucially involves the social dimension of mutual recognition of and respect for people's sexual identities. The absence of this good for particular groups, then, constitutes a significant aspect of sexual powerlessness. People who are marginalized based on disability, sexuality, or both know all too well that one of the main cultural influences for the perception of some bodies as different, and ultimately morally degenerate, is medical discourse. I will briefly examine specific ways in which medical discourse neglects sexuality as an aspect of health, displays sexist and heterosexist values, fails to address other aspects of social group difference, relies on ultimately conservative reproductive norms, focuses on the pathological at the expense of healthy states and processes, and conceptualizes the body and human life in biological terms that are abstracted from social relations. All of these failings not only reflect broader social values, but provide powerful reinforcements for them as well. Medicine is thus a major force in the social relations of sexual powerlessness and the shaming which so often accompanies it.

Nancy Mairs writes that throughout the many years she has lived with multiple sclerosis, "Not one of my doctors . . . has ever asked me about my sex life" (1996, 51). In general, many health care providers are unwilling or unable to interview patients and provide information about sexuality and related health concerns. The *Journal of the American Medical Association* reported in 1996 that "only 11% to 37% of primary care physicians routinely take a sexual history from their new adult patients" (Keen 1996, 19). As a result, "doctors often fail to screen, diagnose, or treat important medical problems," particularly in gay and lesbian patients (19), and in heterosexuals with disabilities as well, many of whom are not integrated into disability communities and may thus have no other source but their physicians for sexual information related to their conditions.

Medical failure includes avoidance of sexually related issues and also research programs shaped in ways that harm people with disabilities. Barbara Faye Waxman identifies several aspects of "scientific indifference" to women's sexuality: failure to address differences such as gender, sexuality, race, or class; inattention to disability as socially constructed; focus on men with spinal cord injuries, emphasizing the promotion or maintenance of "normal" penile erectile function, and excluding women and men with other disabilities; a focus on the pathological, reflecting "a societal view that disabled women are not whole women; rather, they are seen as defective women" (1996, 182); and finally, values associated with eugenics and cultural fears about disabled people reproducing (181–83).[8]

These problematic medical concepts, omissions, and emphases both reflect and reinforce broader cultural values, such as notions of sexuality based on a normative heterosexual male perspective, a penis-centered, intercourse-based, goal-oriented view of sex. As Billy Golfus wryly notes in "Sex and the Single Gimp,"

> Everybody knows that the punch line is when Old Faithful goes off. That's the point of chasing them in the first place, isn't it? . . .
>
> Look, everybody's been taught that sex is about put tab A in slot B. . . . So what do you do when you can't feel slot B? Forget it? If it's not acrobatic and aerobic, then it's not real sex. How big and how many times is what counts to most people. Then you don't even have to feel much, just keep counting and measuring. (1997, 420)

Such notions deny the actual polymorphousness of human sexuality. Both men and women with spinal cord injuries, for example, report their experiences of a diffuse sensuality, including orgasms centered in earlobes, nipples, sensitive areas of the neck, and elsewhere (Panzarino 1994; Whipple, Richards, Tepper, and Komisaruk 1996); "portions of the body that retain feeling may become more highly eroticized than they were before injury" (Keller and Buchanan 1993, 229). If heterosexual vaginal intercourse is taken as the norm, the sexual practices of many will not seem to count as sex at all. Knowledge of diffuse male sexualities may be culturally suppressed, or even incomprehensible, because they are perceived as incompatible with masculinity, while for women such pleasures are perceived as outside the domain of legitimate heterosexual experiences. The repercussion for those with physical disabilities, like many others, may be silence and unintelligibility, their sexualities rendered incoherent, unrecognizable to others or perhaps even to themselves, a clear instance of cultural attitudes profoundly diminishing sexual agency and the sense of self- and personal efficacy that are part of it.

Moreover, sociobiological notions of sexual pleasure as an innate incentive to reproduce, rather than a legitimate and meaningful human need in itself, typically underlie medical notions of sexuality, contributing further to the unintelligibility of sexual desire and practice as many people experience it. These notions are particularly problematic for women. After author Suzanne Berger's severe back injury, her doctor attempted to elicit her sexual concerns by asking brusquely, "So how are things with your husband?" (1996, 61). Such language inadvertently reveals the standard medical principle of subsuming women's sexuality into that of their presumed male partners, a tendency that becomes even more pronounced for women with physical disabilities. This medical inability to address women as sexual subjects is also evident in a study of women with spinal cord injuries. Beverly Whipple and her colleagues asked participants:

> to comment on the extent and quality of their postinjury sexuality education by health professionals. The overall quality was considered poor. Generally included with information on bowel and bladder functioning, the materials that were distributed were of poor quality, outdated, and usually targeted for men. The focus of female sexuality education was on giving, rather than receiving, sexual pleasure and on reproductive issues, such as fertility and conception. (1996, 79)

Gynecologists are less likely to ask women with disabilities whether they are sexually active (Welner 1996, 81), and when they do, they are likely to assume heterosexuality (O'Toole 1996, 138), thereby failing to address the concerns of lesbians and bisexuals. In a National Institutes of Health study of women with disabilities, a number of participants reported that their physicians "did not know how their disabilities affected sexual functioning, said nothing at all, or provided inaccurate information" (Nosek 1996, 25).

Such medical ignorance and negativity persist despite studies that suggest possibilities that are far more hopeful. In reviewing research on women with spinal cord injury, Beverly Whipple and her colleagues found "most of the current literature is not concerned with whether women with spinal cord injury have any sexual desire or response" but with whether they can "'satisfy [a husband's] needs'" (1996, 71). Yet their own work, based on the principles of participatory action research, yielded distinctly different results, providing evidence of greater genital sensitivity and capacity for orgasm than the literature suggested. Significantly, their study was based in part on participants' self-stimulation, a methodology unlikely to be employed in more typical research shaped by male-centered norms. Whipple and her colleagues found that after injury, women often experience a common "sexual trajectory" moving eventually from a period of "sexual disenfranchisement" to "sexual rediscovery" (79).

Surely, it is clear that these problematic trends in medicine are strongly connected to broader cultural values, not merely by passively reflecting the culture that surrounds it. In part, medical discourse gains authority from biology, construed as largely independent of social relations, with specific consequences for people with disabilities. This medical epistemology views illness or disability as an individual organism's departure from biological normalcy rather than a condition that always develops in relation to a particular social context, the significance of which has been amply illustrated by the women's health, AIDS, and disability rights movements. Michelle Fine and Adrienne Asch note, "There is an assumption that disability is located solely in biology, and thus disability is accepted uncritically as an independent variable" (1993, 52). Medical discourse thus underpins social practices that marginalize people with disabilities while presenting these social practices as the inevitable consequence of biology.

One of the most important influences of medicine—and the reason it has received so much critical attention in disability studies—is its active shaping of cultural perceptions of disability identity itself, which thereby structures how the nondisabled interact with people with disabilities. Philosopher Eva Feder Kittay and her husband were struggling to come to terms with their infant daughter Sesha's severe cognitive disability when they were sent to consult with a pediatric neurologist, who told them "after a five-minute exam—that our daughter was severely to profoundly retarded and that we should consider having other children because 'one rotten apple doesn't spoil the barrel'" (1999, 6). Kittay's writing suggests that what she and her husband needed was to begin to consider how they could help Sesha develop the capacities she possessed that made her human, capable of affectionate relationships with her parents and others. Yet the neurologist's remarks (which contained no new information about Sesha's disability) made this crucial time all the more difficult for them. Kittay and her husband were able to resist the brutally insensitive suggestion that their daughter was disposable, less than fully human, and, as Kittay points out, that they were fortunate to have a variety of financial and other resources, which aided them in recognizing and facilitating the development of their daughter's personhood. How many parents of disabled children have neither the strength nor the resources to resist similar medical messages, with their ring of objective and even therapeutic truth? Medical dehumanization of disabled children can even contribute to parental violence against them. Dick Sobsey, primary researcher for the University of Alberta Abuse and Disability Project, writes, "Health care personnel . . . are usually among the first to discuss a child's disability with the child's family. Negative and discouraging attitudes on the part of the physician can interfere with the bonds between parents and their children, and in doing so, increase the child's risk for abuse" (1994, 363).

The social presumption that medicine apprehends the fundamental truths of disability is thus enormously damaging. Medical pathologization of disability, particularly as it manifests itself in negativism regarding the sexuality of people with disabilities, is thus a major contributor to the sexual powerlessness and shaming of members of this group.

CONCLUDING REFLECTIONS: COUNTER-DISCOURSES AND COALITIONS

Nancy Mairs, a self-described "crip," writes, "The fact that the soundness of the body so often serves as a metaphor for moral health, its deterioration thus implying moral degeneracy, puts me and my kind in a quandary. How can I possibly be 'good'?"—a statement of shame if ever there were one (1996, 57). It is, of course, medical discourse to which we usually turn in order to decide which bodies are sound and even what bodily soundness is, and this discourse's reliability is seldom questioned. Disability as presently constructed in the United States manifests as a central defining characteristic of a personhood that is rendered less than ideal (Gauthier 1983; Wilkerson 1998, 88–93). This lesser status appears to be incontestable because it is medically certified, with medical evidence regarded as utterly objective, detached from values, emotions, and particular human interests.

Yet neither medical fatalism nor medical relegation of some to a lesser status or a life without sexuality is fully deterministic in the end, nor are other oppressive cultural norms. Alternative possibilities for politics and pleasures are being imagined and enacted individually and collectively. Often it has been noted, after all, that being regarded as outside the norm gives one less stake in upholding it, particularly when it turns out to be punitive, unjust—or impossible. And when one experiences a break with the past, as in the case of people who are suddenly disabled, the loss of "how things used to be," though undeniably traumatic, can sometimes open the door to new possibilities. For example, some (although not all) of the participants in Elle Becker's early study of women with spinal cord injury report eventually becoming more sexually assertive after their injury, due to the need to actively reconstruct their sexual desires and practices rather than passively enact what they had been led to expect of themselves and their partners (1978). Nondisabled women have much to learn from these responses to an extremely challenging circumstance, just as everyone can learn more from paraplegics and quadriplegics about the extensive possibilities of human sexualities that depart from heterocentric and phallocentric norms.

If these arguments have been convincing, the political importance of overcoming shame will be quite clear. There are many ways to try to overcome or avoid shame, and perhaps one of the most common involves bids for respectability, but as Warner warns us, this strategy poses significant risks for queers. Perhaps respectability poses similar dangers for feminism. If the "official queer movement" is pursuing respectability through marriage and thereby solidifying the outsider status of those who don't jump on the marriage bandwagon, national feminist organizations may be pursuing the same illusory and problematic goal when they defend "reproductive choice" as the right to avoid unwanted pregnancy while at the same time they fail to defend women's right to sexual pleasure.

Warner argues that an accessible sexual culture is necessary for sexual autonomy. Bartky warns of the harms to women of what might be called a patriarchal sexual monoculture. Their arguments suggest we must attend to the material conditions that make it possible to access sexual culture and work to transform those that make it unimaginable. We must consider, for example, the war against terrorism upheld as protecting American lives and helping to liberate Afghan women while they and other women are allowed to die all over the world in childbirth or from unsafe abortions. In 2002 President Bush withheld $34 million in congressionally approved funds to the United Nations Population Fund because of false allegations that the money could be used to promote abortions. This could jeopardize delivery of supplies to Afghan women, since the fund provides "clean underwear, sanitary napkins, and sterile delivery kits—soap, a string, and a clean razor blade" (Cocco 2002).

Overcoming shame and undermining the moral influence of medicine (which comes both from direct pronouncements and omissions and from its cultural status as a source of knowledge and order) will require the creation of powerful counter-discourses. One resource for these are the experiences of creating new pleasures that disabled people exemplify, or the specific forms of resistance to sexual vilification or victimization demonstrated by other groups. This task of constructing counter-discourses has been central to the women's health, disability rights, LGBT, and AIDS movements. I believe it also will become increasingly recognized as strategic for other social change movements and must be understood as fundamental to the struggle for sexual democracy, which in turn must be recognized as a vital and necessary component of all struggles for democracy and inclusion. But in order for individuals and groups to succeed in fostering their own sexual agency, they must seek and in some measure gain others' mutual recognition and respect. These responses from others are not primarily emotions or attitudes (although attitudes are important); they are more broadly political responses. In other words, the success of counter-discourses requires not only that they persuade others but also that they act in solidarity. Audre Lorde asked us to imagine "an army of one-breasted women descend[ing] upon Congress" (1980, 16). We might imagine diverse groups struggling together for sexual democracy. What if NWSA sat with ADAPT at the American Medical Association for medical support for attendant services, enabling disabled women and men to live in their own communities rather than in nursing homes? What if the NAACP (National Association for the Advancement of Colored People) marched with PFLAG (Parents, Friends, and Families of Lesbians and Gays) protesting the firing of educators who are willing to answer young people's questions about queer sexuality? What if a million mothers marched on Washington, D.C., to demand comprehensive sex education for all children? This dream of fighting for the sexual agency of oppressed groups requires us to think the unthinkable, to sacrifice comfort and abandon respectability to work for genuine inclusion. Perhaps the first step is to face the challenge of asking, when such coalitions have not materialized, why they have not and to begin the hard work necessary to make them possible.

NOTES

Thanks to editor Kim Hall, anonymous readers for the *NWSA Journal*, and Roger Gottlieb for their many useful suggestions, as well as audiences at the University of

North Carolina at Asheville Gay and Lesbian Studies Conference, the Radical Philosophy Association, the Society for Disability Studies, the National Women's Studies Association, and "*Femininity and Domination* Twelve Years Later: A Conference to Honor Sandra Bartky," where I presented somewhat different versions of this essay. Kudos to Shannon Wyss and other students in my sexualities seminar at George Washington University for lively discussion of issues in the section on Rubin's work. More than anyone, Cindy Newcomer has consistently modeled for me a vision of the moral importance of sexual agency. I am deeply grateful to Bob McRuer and our other comrades in the Queer Theory and Disability Studies groups at George Washington University, as well as Melissa Burchard, Cayo Gamber, Peg O'Connor, and Lisa Heldke for their friendship and inspiration, which enriched this essay. As always, Patrick McGann's support exceeds even his amazing insight and editing skills.

1. See Wilkerson on the pathologization of homosexuality (1998, 44–48).

2. Many participants in Becker's study (1978) encountered this problem. Also see Shin (2000).

3. The Comstock Act outlawed representations or objects considered "'obscene, lewd, or lascivious,'" including all devices used for contraception or abortion (Freedman 1999, 157).

4. See Held (1993, 2557) and Hubbard (1997, 190) on the sterilization of disabled women, and Corea (1985), A. Davis (1981), Dreifus (1977), and Poirier (1990) on that of poor women and women of color.

5. O'Bryan (2000) gives an account of a conference organized by the Boston chapter of the Gay, Lesbian, and Straight Education Network (GLSEN) that included a confidential workshop in which educators took questions about sexuality from queer youth. A right-wing organizer attended the session incognito, secretly taping it and then publicizing the content in print, on the radio, and at a Washington, D.C., press conference, replete with sensationalized commentary on the sexual practices mentioned. As a result, "one workshop facilitator has been fired, another has resigned, [and] some state legislators have expressed a desire to curtail state funding of programs to help Gay youth" (28).

6. I speak of *choice* here as interpreting and acting on one's desires, regardless of whether those desires should themselves be considered voluntary in some sense.

7. See Sobsey (1994). Also see Wyss (2001), whose groundbreaking original study on high school experiences of gender-variant youth offers a chapter on violence and harassment by peers, as well as a brief overview of the literature on violence against queer youth.

8. Given that people seek medical remedies when they have specific physical complaints, it may seem unremarkable that the focus of medical practice tends to the pathological. However, it is worth examining the larger picture in which the structure of Western medical knowledge is itself grounded in pathology (indeed, as Michel Foucault [1975] reminds us, modern Western medicine has its foundations in death, in the examination of corpses), what goes wrong in the body and how, rather than alternative frameworks that begin from a standpoint of health and how it is maintained, within and across particular social contexts.

REFERENCES

Alarcón, Norma. 1990. "The Theoretical Subject(s) of *This Bridge Called My Back* and Anglo-American Feminism." In *Making Face, Making Soul/Haciendo Caras: Creative and Critical Perspectives by Women of Color,* edited by Gloria Anzaldúa, 356–69. San Francisco: Aunt Lute.

Anzaldúa, Gloria. 1987. *Borderlands/La Frontera: The New Mestiza.* San Francisco: Aunt Lute.

Bartky, Sandra Lee. 1990. *Femininity and Domination: Studies in the Phenomenology of Oppression.* New York: Routledge.

Becker, Elle Friedman. 1978. *Female Sexuality Following Spinal Cord Injury.* Bloomington, Ill.: Accent Press.

Berger, Suzanne E. 1996. *Horizontal Woman: The Story of a Body in Exile.* Boston: Houghton Mifflin.

Clare, Eli. 1999. *Exile and Pride: Disability, Queerness, and Liberation.* Cambridge, Mass.: South End Press.

Cocco, Marie. 2002. "Afghan Women Get Caught in U.S. Abortion Politics." *Newsday,* 22 January. http://www.commondreams.org/views02/0122-03.htm.

Corea, Gena. 1985. *Hidden Malpractice: How American Medicine Mistreats Women.* New York: Harper and Row.

Davis, Angela. 1981. *Women, Race, and Class.* New York: Vintage Books.

Davis, Lennard J. 1997. *The Disability Studies Reader.* New York: Routledge.

Dreifus, Claudia. 1977. *Seizing Our Bodies: The Politics of Women's Health.* New York: Vintage Books.

Fahrenthold, David A. 2000. "Disability Group Makes Point." *Washington Post,* 20 June, B3.

Fegan, Lydia, Anne Rauch, and Wendy McCarthy. 1993. *Sexuality and People with Disability.* 2nd ed. Baltimore: Paul H. Brookes.

Fine, Michelle, and Adrienne Asch. 1993. "Disability beyond Stigma: Social Interaction, Discrimination, and Activism." In Nagler, *Perspectives on Disability,* 49–62.

Finger, Anne. 1985. "Reproductive Rights and Disability." In *With the Power of Each Breath: A Disabled Women's Anthology,* edited by Susan E. Browne, Debra Connors, and Nanci Stern, 293–307. Pittsburgh: Cleis Press.

Foucault, Michel. 1975. *The Birth of the Clinic: An Archaeology of Medical Perception.* New York: Vintage Books.

Freedman, Lynn P. 1999. "Censorship and Manipulation of Family Planning Information: An Issue of Human Rights and Women's Health." In *Health and Human Rights,* edited by Jonathan M. Mann, Sofia Gruskin, Michael A. Grodin, and George J. Annas, 145–78. New York: Routledge.

Garland-Thomson, Rosemarie. 1997. "Feminist Theory, the Body, and the Disabled Figure." In L. Davis, *Disability Studies Reader,* 279–93.

Gauthier, David. 1983. "Unequal Need: A Problem of Equity in Access to Health Care." In *Securing Access to Health Care: The Ethical Implications of Differences in* the *Availability of Health Services*. Vol. 2, *Appendices: Sociocultural and Philosophical Studies*, 179–205. Washington, D.C.: U.S. Government Printing Office.

Golfus, Billy. 1997. "Sex and the Single Gimp." In L. Davis, *Disability Studies Reader*, 419–28.

Held, K. R. 1993. "Ethical Aspects of Sexuality of Persons with Mental Retardation." In Nagler, *Perspectives on Disability*, 255–59.

hooks, bell. 1992. *Black Looks: Race and Representation*. Boston: South End Press.

Hubbard, Ruth. 1997. "Abortion and Disability: Who Should and Who Should Not Inherit the World?" In L. Davis, *Disability Studies Reader*, 187–200.

Keen, Lisa. 1996. "AMA Urges Doctors to 'Recognize' Gay Patients." *Washington Blade*, 11 September, 27.

Keller, Sandra, and Denton C. Buchanan. 1993. "Disability and Sexuality: An Overview." In Nagler, *Perspectives on Disability*, 227–34.

Kittay, Eva Feder. 1999. "'Not *My* Way, Sesha, *Your* Way, Slowly.'" In *Mother Troubles: Rethinking Contemporary Maternal Dilemmas*, edited by Julia E. Hanigsberg and Sara Ruddick, 3–27. Boston: Beacon Press.

Krotoski, Danuta M., Margaret A. Nosek, and Margaret A. Turk, eds. *Women with Physical Disabilities: Achieving and Maintaining Health and Well-Being*. Baltimore: Paul H. Brookes.

Lorde, Audre. 1980. *The Cancer Journals*. San Francisco: Aunt Lute.

Mairs, Nancy. 1996. *Waist-High in the World: A Life among the Nondisabled*. Boston: Beacon Press.

Midzian, Miriam. 1991. *Boys Will Be Boys: Breaking the Link between Masculinity and Violence*. New York: Anchor Books.

Moraga, Cherríe, and Gloria Anzaldúa. 1981. *This Bridge Called My Back: Writings by Radical Women of Color*. Watertown, Mass.: Persephone Press.

Nagler, Mark, ed. 1993. *Perspectives on Disability*. Palo Alto, Calif.: Health Markets Research.

Nosek, Margaret A. 1996. "Wellness among Women with Physical Disabilities." In Krotoski et al., *Women with Physical Disabilities*, 17–33.

O'Bryan, Will. 2000. "'Obviously, Privacy Was Breached.'" *Washington Blade*, 16 April, 1.

O'Toole, Corbett Joan. 1996. "Disabled Lesbians: Challenging Monocultural Constructs." In Krotoski et al., *Women with Physical Disabilities*, 135–51.

Panzarino, Connie. 1994. *The Me in the Mirror*. Seattle: Seal Press.

Patton, Cindy. 1985. *Sex and Germs*. Boston: South End Press.

Poirier, Suzanne. 1990. "Women's Reproductive Health." In *Women, Health, and Medicine in America*, edited by Rima D. Apple, 217–45. New Brunswick, N.J.: Rutgers University Press.

Pozner, Jennifer L. 2001. "*Dateline* Plays the Blame Game." *Bitch* 13: 15–16.

Pratt, Minnie Bruce Pratt. 1984. "Identity: Skin Blood Heart." In *Yours in Struggle: Three Feminist Perspectives on Anti-Semitism and Racism*, edited by Elly Bulkin, Minnie Bruce Pratt, and Barbara Smith, 9–63. Ithaca, N.Y.: Firebrand Books.

Roberts, Dorothy. 1997. *Killing the Black Body: Race, Reproduction, and the Meaning of Liberty.* New York: Pantheon.

Rubin, Gayle. 1993. "Thinking Sex: Notes for a Radical Theory of the Politics of Sexuality." In *The Lesbian and Gay Studies Reader,* edited by Henry Abelove, Michele Aina Barale, and David M. Halperin, 3–44. New York: Routledge.

Sandoval, Chela. 1991. "U.S. Third World Feminism: The Theory and Method of Oppositional Consciousness in the Postmodern World." *Genders* 10: 1–24.

Shin, Annys. 2000. "Before Their Time." *Washington City Paper,* 17 October, 26ff.

Sobsey, Dick. 1994. *Violence and Abuse in the Lives of People with Disabilities.* Baltimore: Paul H. Brookes.

Spelman, Elizabeth V. 1988. *Inessential Woman: Problems of Exclusion in Feminist Thought.* Boston: Beacon Press.

Twine, France Winddance. 2002. Comments on Bartky's "Race, Complicity, and Culpable Ignorance." Paper presented at *"Femininity and Domination* Twelve Years Later: A Conference to Honor Sandra Bartky," University of Illinois at Chicago, 15 February.

Warner, Michael. 1999. *The Trouble with Normal: Sex, Politics, and the Ethics of Queer Life.* Cambridge, Mass.: Harvard University Press.

Waxman, Barbara Faye. 1996. "Commentary on Sexual and Reproductive Health." In Krotoski et al., *Women with Physical Disabilities,* 179–92.

Welner, Sandra. 1996. "Contraception, Sexually Transmitted Diseases, and Menopause." In Krotoski et al., *Women with Physical Disabilities,* 81–90.

Whipple, Beverly, Eleanor Richards, Mitchell S. Tepper, and Barry R. Komisaruk. 1996. "Sexual Response in Women with Complete Spinal Cord Injury." In Krotoski et al., *Women with Physical Disabilities,* 69–80.

Wilkerson, Abby. 1998. *Diagnosis: Difference: The Moral Authority of Medicine.* Ithaca, N.Y.: Cornell University Press.

Wyss, Shannon Elaine. 2001. "'Blue Coconuts': Youth Doing Transgender and Genderqueer in U.S. High Schools." MA thesis, George Washington University.

Young, Iris. 1990. *Justice and the Politics of Difference.* Princeton, N.J.: Princeton University Press.

Ten

DEBATING FEMINIST FUTURES

Slippery Slopes, Cultural Anxiety, and the Case of the Deaf Lesbians

ALISON KAFER

In 2001 I served as a teaching assistant in an Introduction to Women's Studies course at a liberal arts college in Southern California. One of the assigned texts was Marge Piercy's novel *Woman on the Edge of Time* (1976), chosen by the instructor in order to spark discussion about what a feminist future might look like. Published more than three decades ago, the novel continues to be popular among feminists for its representation of an egalitarian society. Students responded enthusiastically to Piercy's book, finding it hopeful and compelling reading. As a disability studies scholar, however, I found the novel troubling for its erasure of disability and disabled bodies, an erasure never debated or discussed in the novel. *Woman on the Edge of Time* simply takes for granted that a feminist future is one without disability and disabled bodies. As I will argue, this assumption is not limited to Piercy's novel, but is pervasive in contemporary medical practice and public discourse.[1] Using Piercy's novel as a springboard, I examine the highly publicized—and highly criticized—decision by two Deaf lesbians to choose a Deaf sperm donor for their children.[2] As in *Woman on the Edge of Time*, cultural critics and commentators took for granted the idea that a better future is one without disability; "common sense" allegedly dictates that disabled bodies have no place in the future and that such decisions merit neither discussion nor dissent.

Woman on the Edge of Time is a feminist utopia/dystopia chronicling the experiences of Connie Ramos, a poor Chicana who is involuntarily institutionalized in a New York mental ward. The novel moves back and forth among three settings: mental institutions and Connie's neighborhoods in 1970s New York; Mattapoisett, a utopian village in 2137; and a future, dystopic New York City, inhabited by cyborgs and machines, in which all humans have been genetically engineered to fulfill certain social roles.[3] While incarcerated in the violent ward of a mental institution in 1976, Connie develops the ability to travel mentally into the future, interacting with a woman named Luciente who lives in the utopian Mattapoisett community. During one attempt at mental travel, Connie's attention is diverted and she finds herself in the dystopic future Manhattan, but the rest of her time travels involve Mattapoisett.

Piercy lovingly describes Mattapoisett. She has clearly thought a great deal about difference in constructing this world, trying to articulate what a thoroughly feminist, antiracist, socially just, and multicultural community might look like. All sexual orientations and identities are present and respected in her vision of Mattapoisett; everyone possesses equal wealth and resources; and all have access to education according to their interests. People in Mattapoisett have developed harvesting and consumption patterns intended to redress the global imbalance of wealth, resources, and consumption wrought during Connie's era. The world is viewed holistically, with Mattapoisett's inhabitants aware of how their actions affect others both within the borders of their community and beyond.

Luciente explains to Connie that Mattapoisett's communal harmony has been achieved through radical changes in the system of reproduction. All babies are born in the "brooder," a machine that mixes the genes from all the population's members, so that children are not genetically bound to any two people. Three adults co-mother each child, a task that is undertaken equally by men and women. Through hormone treatments, both men and women are able to breast-feed, exemplifying the community's belief that equality between the sexes can be engineered through technological intervention and innovation. By breaking the traditional gendered nature of reproduction, explains Luciente, the brooder has eliminated fixed gender roles and sexism within the community. It has also eradicated racism by mixing the genes from all "races," thereby rendering everyone mixed-race and making it impossible to maintain notions of "racial purity." Cultural histories and traditions have been preserved but have been separated from the concept of "race." Luciente's friend Bee tells Connie that the community has recently decided to create more "darker-skinned" babies in order to counteract the historical devaluation of people of color, resulting in a village inhabited by people of all skin tones: "we don't want the melting pot where everybody ends up with thin gruel. We want diversity, for strangeness breeds richness" (96).

All decisions concerning the community are publicly debated during open meetings. Decisions are made on the basis of consensus, and every community member is allowed and expected to participate. People volunteer to serve as representatives to inter-community meetings at which decisions affecting a larger population are debated. No decisions are made for others. Every person has the right to speak out on issues that affect him or her.

To illustrate the way this participatory democracy works, Piercy gradually introduces Connie, and the reader, to a conflict being played out in Mattapoisett. The "Mixers" and the "Shapers" are involved in a heated disagreement about the next direction the brooder should take. The Shapers want to program the brooder to select for "positive" traits, while the Mixers are interested only in eliminating genes linked to birth defects and disease susceptibility, which the brooder already does. Luciente and her friends are on the side of the Mixers, arguing that it is impossible to know which traits will be necessary or valued in the future. Piercy makes it clear that Luciente's perspective mirrors her own; her dystopian vision of a future New York's genetically engineered inhabitants suggests the logical—and undesirable—result of a Shaper victory. Piercy refuses, however, to simply impose a Mixer victory on Mattapoisett; she depicts a continuing process of respectful dialogue and public debate between the two groups, creating a vision of a feminist community in which all people participate equally in the decisions that affect them. The Mixer/Shaper debate is never resolved in the novel, illustrating Piercy's notion of the importance of open-ended dialogue and group process.

It is this description of democratic decision making, of a community debating publicly how it wants technology to develop in the future, that has made *Woman on the Edge of Time* such an attractive text to feminist scholars of science studies and political theory. Decades after its initial publication, the novel continues to inspire feminist thinkers with its image of an egalitarian future in which all people's voices are heard, respected, and addressed. A quick glance at women's studies syllabi collected on internet databases reveals the continued popularity of the book in conversations about "feminist futures," "feminist utopias," and "ecofeminisms"; *Woman on the Edge of Time* is often taught in introductory women's studies classes to initiate discussion about feminist worldviews.[4] Several feminist political theorists and science studies scholars cast the book as a vital exploration of political and technological processes influenced by feminist principles. José van Dijck, for example, praises Piercy for depicting science as "a political and democratic process in which all participants participate," a depiction that recognizes genetics "as a political, rather than a purely scientific," practice (1998, 86–87). Political theorist Josephine Carubia Glorie shares Van Dijck's assessment, asserting that Piercy's novel features a society in which all community members are able to engage in social critique (1997, 158). Even those who disagree with Piercy's pro-genetic engineering and assisted reproduction stance, such as ecofeminists Cathleen and Col-leen McGuire, find *Woman on the Edge of Time* to be a compelling vision of a world without social inequalities (1998).[5] As these comments sug-gest, thirty years after its initial publication *Woman on the Edge* remains a powerful, productive text for feminist theorists concerned with the role of technology in the lives of women and committed to envisioning an egali-tarian, just world. Indeed, in an era of corporate, profit-driven genomic medicine, bioengineering, and assisted reproductive technologies (ART), Piercy's imagined world of democratic and feminist technology is com-pelling. Her articulation of the "Mixers vs. Shapers" debate—Do we breed children for desired traits?—seems prescient in the early twenty-first cen-tury as bioethicists and genetic specialists debate the morality and feasi-bility of allowing prospective parents to create or select embryos on the basis of such traits as gender, hair color, or height.[6]

What has gone unnoticed in these praises of Piercy's novel, however, is the place of disability, and specifically disabled bodies, in her imagined utopia. In a world very carefully constructed to contain people of every skin tone and sexual orientation, where people of all genders and ages are equally valued, people with disabilities are markedly absent. This absence cannot simply be attributed to oversight or neglect; it is not that Piercy forgot to include disability and disabled people among her cast of charac-ters and life experiences. On the contrary, the place, or rather the absence, of disability in Piercy's utopia cuts to the heart of the Mixers/Shapers debate praised by some feminist theorists. Both the Shapers and the Mix-ers agree on the necessity of screening the gene pool for "defective genes" and "predispositions" for illness and "suffering." It is taken for granted by both sides—and by Piercy and (presumably) her audience—that everyone knows and agrees which genes and characteristics are negative and there-fore which ones should be eliminated; questions about so-called negative traits are apparently not worth discussing.

Thus, disabled people are not accidentally missing from Piercy's utopia; they have intentionally and explicitly been written out of it. Mattapoisett, an influential feminist fictional utopia, has wiped out congenital disability. The apparent lack of any physically or cognitively disabled inhabitants of Mattapoisett, coupled with the genetic screening of all congenital disabili-ties, suggests that even disabilities acquired through age, illness, or acci-dent are lacking in this utopia; presumably medicine has advanced to such a degree that all impairments can be cured or prevented. At first glance, mental illness seems to be an exception to this absence. Unlike the stigma and forced institutionalization Connie faced in 1970s New York, the inhab-itants of Mattapoisett recognize mental illness as part of a normal course of life, with people "dropping out" of their communities as needed to tend to their mental and emotional needs. But this requirement to drop out, to separate oneself from the community until one's functioning returns to "normal," enacts another version of this erasure of disability. People with disabilities apparently have no place in this feminist future; indeed, it is their very absence that signals the utopian nature of this future.

Neither Piercy, writing in the mid-1970s, nor theorists like Van Dijck and Glorie, writing in the late 1990s, seem to have noticed that the entire Mixers/Shapers debate rests on profound assumptions about whose bodies matter. Van Dijck and Glorie praise Piercy for articulating a vision of science as a democratic process in which all voices are heard, yet the assumptions underlying the Mixers/Shapers debate suggest that the perspectives of an entire class of people, those with congenital disabilities, are ignored. Never once do the nondisabled members of Mattapoisett debate the decision to eliminate ostensibly defective genes or question how one determines which genes are labeled "defective" or what "defective" means. Van Dijck highlights Piercy's recognition that genetics is political—contested and contestable, subject to debate and disagreement—but fails to realize that screening the gene pool for allegedly negative traits is also political. In both the novel and interpretation of the novel, it is assumed that disability has no place in feminist visions of the future and that such an assumption is so natural, so given, that it does not merit public debate.

What does it mean that disability appears in Piercy's utopia only as an unwanted characteristic in a debate over genetic engineering, a debate itself used to illustrate her ideas about democratic science? What does it mean that feminists writing and teaching about the United States in the 1990s and 2000s use this novel, specifically the Mixers/Shapers debate, as an example of ideal democratic decision making and public critique, and of a political community grounded in feminist principles of egalitarianism and democracy? What can be inferred about disability from the fact that contemporary feminists highlight a debate in which both parties assume from the beginning that "negative" traits are self-evident, natural, and therefore outside the scope of discussion? What can a feminist disability studies reader learn from the fact that feminist theorists have offered no critique of a debate in which people with disabilities do not participate, presumably because they have already been removed from this (allegedly) diverse, multicultural, egalitarian landscape?

I suggest that Piercy's depiction and, more importantly, feminist theorists' praise of it mean that disability in the United States is often viewed as an unredeemable difference with no place in visions of the future. Disability and the disabled body are problems that must be solved technologically, and there is allegedly so much cultural agreement on this point that it need not be discussed or debated. "Everyone" agrees that disabled bodies would not exist in a just world, that disability and justice are mutually opposed. Disability, then, plays a huge, but seemingly uncontested, role in how Americans in the 1990s and 2000s envision the future. Utopian visions are founded on the elimination of disability, while dystopic, negative visions of the future are based on its proliferation; both depictions are deeply tied to cultural understandings and anxieties about the proper use of technology.

In this essay I focus on one particular case of the alleged misuse of technology: the decision by a Deaf lesbian couple to use a Deaf sperm donor in their quest to have children. The story of Sharon Duchesneau and Candace McCullough is consistently described in both popular media and academic scholarship in terms of "the future," articulations that rely on a model of disability as an unacceptable problem that must be fixed or eliminated. I am less interested in arguing for or against these women's decision than in detailing how critics of the couple utilize dystopic rhetoric in their condemnations, presenting deafness and disability as traits that obviously should be avoided. Indeed, responses to the Deaf couple's decision take for granted the idea that a world free of disability should be our goal as a nation and that a world that includes disability is dystopic and antithetical to progress. As with *Woman on the Edge of Time,* a world free of impairment is portrayed as a goal shared by all, a goal beyond question or analysis, a goal that is natural rather than political.

DEAF/DISABLED: A NOTE ON TERMINOLOGY

For most hearing people, to describe deafness as a disability is to state the obvious: Deaf people lack the ability to hear, and therefore they are disabled. For some people, however, Deaf and hearing alike, it is neither obvious nor accurate to characterize deafness as a disability and Deaf people as disabled. Rather, Deaf people are more appropriately described as members of a distinct linguistic and cultural minority, more akin to Spanish speakers in a predominantly English-language country than to people in wheelchairs or people who are blind. Spanish speakers are not considered disabled simply because they cannot communicate in English without the aid of an interpreter, and, according to this model, neither should Deaf people who rely on interpreters in order to communicate with those who cannot sign. Drawing parallels between Deaf people and members of other cultural groups, supporters of the linguistic-cultural model of deafness note the existence of a vibrant Deaf culture, one that includes its own language (in the United States, American Sign Language [ASL]), cultural productions (e.g., ASL poetry and performance, publications by and for Deaf communities), residential schools, and social networks, as well as high rates of intermarriage (Padden and Humphries 1988; Van Cleve and Crouch 1989). As Deaf studies scholar Harlan Lane explains, "The preconditions for Deaf participation [in society] are more like those of other language minorities: culturally Deaf people campaign for acceptance of their language and its broader use in the schools, the workplace, and in public events" (1997, 161).[7] This linguistic-cultural model of deafness shares a key assumption of the social model of disability—namely, that it is societal interpretations of and responses to bodily and sensory variations that are the problem, not the variations themselves.

Everyone Here Spoke Sign Language, Nora Groce's study of hereditary deafness on Martha's Vineyard from the early eighteenth century to the mid-twentieth century, provides an example of this perspective. Groce discovered that genetic deafness and deaf people were so interwoven into the population that almost every person on the island had a deaf relative or neighbor (1985). As a result, everyone in that community signed, a situation that proves it is possible for hearing people to share the responsibility of communication rather than simply expecting deaf people to lip-read and speak orally or alleviate their hearing loss with surgeries and hearing aids.[8] Groce's study challenges the idea that deafness precludes full participation in society, suggesting that the barriers deaf people face are due more to societal attitudes and practices than to one's audiological conditions. For those who subscribe to this worldview, deafness is best understood as a distinct culture in which one should feel pride rather than a disability one should attempt to ameliorate through hearing aids and cochlear implants (CI).

Although some Deaf people are averse to the label *disabled*, either because of their immersion in Deaf culture or because of an internalized ableist impulse to distance themselves from people with disabilities, others are more willing to explore the label politically. This kind of exploration is based on making a distinction between being labeled as "disabled" by others—especially medical or audiological professionals and the hearing world in general—and choosing to self-identify as disabled. Deaf people who choose to take up the label of disability do so for strategic reasons. For some, the decision stems from a desire to ally themselves with other disabled people. They recognize that people with disabilities and Deaf people share a history of oppression, discrimination, and stigmatization because of their differences from a perceived "normal" body. As a group, Deaf and disabled people can work together to fight discrimination, and they have done so since the birth of the modern disability rights movement in the late 1960s. Thus, while some Deaf people may be opposed to (or at the very least ambivalent about) seeing deafness as a disability, they may simultaneously be willing to identify themselves as disabled or to ally themselves with disabled people in order to work toward social changes and legal protections that would benefit both populations (Lane 1997).[9]

Recognizing this affinity between disability and deafness is particularly important for analyzing cure narratives and utopian discourse, because it is precisely the image of deafness as disability that animates these narratives. What makes the actions of parents who express a preference for a Deaf baby so antithetical to the larger culture is the refusal to eradicate disability from the lives of their children. Within mainstream culture, deafness is not seen as a cultural difference to be celebrated, but as a medical problem to be eradicated, or at least ameliorated.

In the literature of reproductive technologies and their "proper" use, heterocentrism and homophobia intersect powerfully with ableism and stereotypes about disability. These stories reveal a profound anxiety about reproducing the family as a normative unit, with all of its members able-bodied and heterosexual. At sites where disability, queerness, and reproductive technologies converge, marginalized people are often criticized and condemned for their alleged failure to use technology properly to reproduce the family. I turn now to one such story in which ableism and heterocentrism combine, a situation in which parents were widely condemned for failing to protect their children from both disability and queerness.

REPRODUCING CULTURAL ANXIETY: THE CASE OF THE DEAF LESBIANS

In November 2001 Sharon Duchesneau and Candace (Candy) McCullough, a white lesbian couple living in Maryland, had a baby boy named Gauvin, who was conceived by assisted insemination. Both Duchesneau, the birth mother, and McCullough, the adoptive mother, are Deaf, as is their first child, Jehanne. Jehanne and her new brother, Gauvin, were conceived with sperm donated by a family friend, a friend who also is Deaf. Duchesneau and McCullough had originally intended to use a sperm bank for the pregnancies, but their desire for a Deaf donor eliminated that option: men with congenital deafness cannot become sperm donors. Reminiscent of the eugenic concern with the "fitness" of potential parents, deafness is one of the conditions that sperm banks and fertility clinics screen out of the donor pool.[10] Several months after he was born, Gauvin underwent an extensive audiology test to determine if he shared his parents' deafness. To the delight of Duchesneau and McCullough, the diagnosis was clear: Gauvin had "a profound hearing loss" in one ear and "at least a severe hearing loss" in the other (Mundy 2002).[11]

Duchesneau and McCullough's decision to select a Deaf sperm donor arose out of their belief that deafness can more accurately be described as a cultural identity rather than a medical disability. Duchesneau and McCullough chose to use a donor from their cultural community, and thereby to increase their chances of having a child who would be able to share more fully in their cultural experiences and identity. They envision a future that includes deafness, a characteristic that many want to eliminate through cochlear implants and genetic testing. The women are very clear that they would accept and love a hearing child, but they refuse to accept the ableist standards of mainstream culture that assumes Deaf men's sperm, and thus congenital deafness, must not be allowed. "A hearing baby would be a blessing," Sharon explains, "a Deaf baby would be a special blessing" (Mundy 2002).

Liza Mundy covered Duchesneau and McCullough's story for the *Washington Post Magazine* in March 2002. Her essay made quite a splash, and the story of the Deaf lesbian couple was picked up by many other newspapers and wire services. Papers across the United States and England ran versions of and responses to the story, and cultural critics from across the ideological spectrum began to weigh in. The Family Research Council, a Washington-based organization that "champions marriage and family as the foundation of civilization," issued a press release in 2002 with comments from Ken Connor, the group's president.[12] Describing Duchesneau and McCullough as "incredibly selfish," Connor berates the pair for imposing on their children not only the "disadvantages that come as a result of being raised in a homosexual household" but also the "burden" of disability. Connor links disability and homosexuality, casting both as hardships these women have "intentionally" handed their children. The Family Research Council's press release closes with a quote from Connor that not only continues to link homosexuality with disability but also depicts both as leading toward a dystopic future: "One can only hope that this practice of intentionally manufacturing disabled children in order to fit the lifestyles of the parents will not progress any further. The places this slippery slope could lead to are frightening" (Family Research Council 2002). The use of the term *lifestyles*—a word frequently used to refer derisively to queers and our sexual/relational practices—effectively blurs together deafness and queerness, suggesting that both characteristics are allegedly leading "us" down the road to ruin. As Robert McRuer has noted, the "dream of an able-bodied future is . . . thoroughly intertwined with the heterosexist fantasy of a world without queers" (2003, 154–55).

The Family Research Council was not alone in discussing these women's desire for a Deaf baby in the context of their sexuality. Indeed, even queer commentators seemed to find something troubling, and ultimately dystopic, about the idea. Queer novelist Jeanette Winterson seems to suggest that it was precisely these women's queerness that made their decision anathema:

> If either of the Deaf Lesbians in the United States had been in a relationship with a man, Deaf or hearing, and if they had decided to have a baby, there is absolutely no certainty that the baby would have been Deaf. You take a chance with love; you take a chance with nature, but it is those chances and the unexpected possibilities they bring, that give life its beauty. (2002)

It is worth noting that Winterson appears concerned only about the loss of certain possibilities—namely, the possibility of having a hearing child. Screening out deaf donors from sperm banks *also* removes the chance of "unexpected possibilities," at least in terms of genetic deafness, but apparently the denial of that chance does not trouble her.

Winterson condemns Duchesneau and McCullough for removing the element of "chance" from their pregnancy and guaranteeing themselves a Deaf baby, a guarantee that could not happen "with nature." However, her remarks obscure the fact that the women's use of a Deaf donor provided no such guarantee. It was no more certain that their child would be born Deaf than it would be if Winterson's imagined genetically Deaf heterosexual couple had a child. The odds would be exactly the same, yet Winterson finds no fault with the imagined heterosexual conception. She appears to believe that it is acceptable, if perhaps regrettable, for heterosexual Deaf couples to have Deaf children, because such an act is "natural"; bearing Deaf children becomes "unnatural," and thereby dangerous, when it is done outside the bounds of a "normal, natural" relationship—an odd position for a queer writer to take and one that certainly has been influenced by dominant ableist culture. It is these women's queerness that has led them to use assisted insemination, but it is their deafness, and their belief that deafness is desirable, that has made them the targets of criticism.

Winterson echoes Connor's evocation of a "slippery slope" leading to a dangerous, unknown future when she suggests that these women's actions will lead to other, allegedly even more troubling futures, such as blind women claiming the right to have blind babies. It is perhaps no accident that she refers to "blind women" rather than "blind people," again implying that it might be "natural" for a heterosexual blind couple to reproduce, but not a lesbian one. She even draws on this image for the title of her essay "How Would We Feel if Blind Women Claimed the Right to a Blind Baby?"[13] The tone and content of Winterson's essay answers this question for her readers, making clear that "we" would feel justifiably outraged.

This rhetorical move—shifting from an actual case involving deafness to a hypothetical situation involving a different disability—is a popular strategy to convince a disabled person that her decision to choose for disability, either by having a disabled child or by refusing technological fixes, is misguided, illogical, and extreme. By decontextualizing the situation, removing it from a Deaf person's own sphere of reference, it is assumed that she will be able to recognize her error in judgment. This practice suggests that some disabilities are worse than others, that eventually one can substitute a particular disability that is so "obviously" undesirable that the disabled person will change her mind. Cross-disability alliances are presumed to be nonexistent, and all Deaf people are portrayed as believing it would be best to eliminate the birth of "blind babies" or people with x disability.

This story is complicated by the fact that Winterson's stance is not without basis. In the *Washington Post* story, McCullough does express a preference for a sighted child. According to Mundy,

> If they themselves—valuing sight—were to have a blind child, well then, Candy acknowledges, they would probably try to have it fixed, if they could, like hearing parents who attempt to restore their child's hearing with cochlear implants. "I want to be the same as my child," says Candy. "I want the baby to enjoy what we enjoy." (2002)

McCullough and Duchesneau's position that Deaf babies are "special blessings" does not mean they are not also simultaneously implicated in the ableism of the larger culture; their desire for deafness does not necessarily extend to a desire for any and all disabilities. (It is worth noting in this context, however, that McCullough does not express a desire for genetic testing and selective abortion.) What interests me about this story is how commentators from across the political spectrum take for granted that "everyone" views these women's behavior as reprehensible, suggesting it is a "simple fact" that life as a Deaf person is inferior to life as a hearing person. Even McCullough subscribes to this view regarding blindness, taking it for granted that a blind child is in need of medical intervention. Deaf and disabled people are not immune to the ableist—or homophobic—ideologies of the larger culture.

Indeed, even some disabled queers mirrored the blend of heterocentrism and ableism circulating through mainstream responses to Duchesneau and

McCullough's reproductive choices. A participant on the QueerDisability Listserv, for example, found their decision to choose a Deaf donor troubling, partly because of the hardships and social barriers their children would face, partly because of the alleged financial burden their children would place on the state. Echoing Winterson, the Listserv member drew a distinction between the "naturally" Deaf children who result from a heterosexual relationship and the "unnaturally," and therefore inappropriately, Deaf children who result from queer relationships. We are left to wonder how this community member would view the choice by an infertile heterosexual Deaf couple to use a Deaf sperm donor, whether that choice would be deemed more natural and therefore acceptable.[14] These comments lead me to believe that the Listserv member would, like Winterson, find less fault with the imagined heterosexual couple than with the real homosexual one: either deafness or homosexuality in isolation would be permissible, but the combination is too abnormal, too disruptive, too queer, even for some gays and lesbians and people with disabilities.

These kinds of responses to the use of assisted insemination by Deaf queers support Sarah Franklin's argument that while reproductive technology "might have been (or is to a limited extent) a disruption of the so-called 'natural' basis for the nuclear family and heterosexual marriage, [it] *has instead provided the occasion for reconsolidating them*" (1993, 30; emphasis in original). With few exceptions, Franklin explains, the state has taken little action to guarantee queers and/or single parents equal access to assisted reproductive technologies, and prominent people in the field of reproductive medicine have been outspoken in their belief that these technologies should not be available to same-sex couples or single parents.[15] Assisted insemination may make it easier for queers to bear children, thereby "unsettling the conflation of reproduction with heterosexuality," but heterocentric/homophobic attitudes may prevent, or at least hinder, their use of this technology (Franklin 1993, 29).

Dorothy Roberts notes that racism also plays a role in access to assisted reproductive technologies, as doctors are far less likely to recommend fertility treatments for black women than for whites (1998, 254). Although clinics cannot legally discriminate against potential patients on the basis of race, they can neglect to inform people of color about all possible treatments. This trend is only the latest in a long history of marginalization, discrimination, and abuse; African American, Latina, and Native American women have undergone forced and coerced sterilization, medical experimentation, and coerced abortion at the hands of medical professionals and government employees who deemed them unfit (Ordover 2003; Roberts 1998).

It seems probable that ableist attitudes pose similar barriers to disabled people's use of assisted reproductive technologies. Many disabled women report being discouraged by their doctors and families from having children, a fact that suggests they might not receive all the fertility assistance they need (Litwinowicz 1999). The policing of these technologies serves to reinforce the dominant vision of a world without impairment and to perpetuate the stigmatization of the queer, disabled, nonwhite body.

The case of Kijuana Chambers deserves attention here, as her experience with a Colorado fertility clinic illustrates the kind of policing reconsolidation to which Franklin refers. Chambers went to the Rocky Mountain Women's Health Care Center (RMWHCC) for alternative insemination. After three cycles of treatment the clinic informed Chambers that they could no longer work with her. Chambers is blind, and the clinic believed her blindness posed a direct threat to the welfare of any future child (Hughes 2003). Until she could provide an assessment from an occupational therapist attesting to her ability to raise a child, the clinic would no longer treat her. Chambers sued the RMWHCC under the Americans with Disabilities Act and Section 504 of the Rehabilitation Act, claiming the clinic illegally discriminated against her on the basis of her disability. Sighted women, her supporters noted, were not required to provide documentation of their ability to childproof their homes or raise their children. In November 2003 a U.S. District Court jury in Denver found in favor of the defendants, deciding that the clinic behaved appropriately in questioning Chambers's fitness. The Tenth Circuit Court of Appeals decided in the summer of 2005 not to rehear her case, letting the lower court's decision stand.

Chambers's race (African American) and her sexual orientation (lesbian) may well have factored into the clinic's decision, but the clinic's spokespeople and legal staff, and the media, have focused primarily on her status as a single disabled woman. An article in the *Denver Post,* for example, makes no mention of her race or sexual orientation, and other news reports on the case followed suit. Given disability's long history in the United States of being seen as more medical than political, the exclusive focus on her blindness guaranteed that this case would be understood by the public as a matter of common sense and child protection rather than discrimination. This is not to suggest that race played no role in Chambers's treatment; during the hearing, she was portrayed in almost animalistic terms, with witnesses testifying to her dirty underwear, disheveled appearance, and emotional outbursts, claims that at least implicitly drew on histories of racist claims about African and African Americans' allegedly primitive and uncivilized nature. (By contrast, Duchesneau and

McCullough, white, middle-class, professional women, were depicted as "selfish.") I want to suggest that discrimination on the basis of disability, in this case blindness, is often seen not as discrimination at all and therefore as having no place in the political arena. It is assumed to be self-evident that blind women cannot parent safely or appropriately, and there is nothing discriminatory or political about asking them to prove otherwise to a medical expert (as Chambers was required to do).

Chambers challenged the clinic's assertion that medical professionals were the best judge of her ability to raise a child, and she disputed their suggestion that an occupational therapist could provide a more accurate assessment of her assistance needs than she herself could. The jury agreed with the clinic's position, however, that they were justified in requiring "expert" documentation of her parenting abilities. Unfortunately, explains Carrie Lucas of the Colorado Cross-Disability Coalition, presumptions of incompetence are common for parents and potential parents with disabilities (Hershey 2003). The Chambers case provides a powerful example of how the use of reproductive technologies by certain people—such as disabled people, queers, single parents, or, as in this case, a disabled queer single parent—is patrolled and restricted, with "nontraditional" users brought under strict surveillance. This surveillance is cast, then, not as a political decision, or a potentially discriminatory one, but as common sense, self-evidently necessary for a better life.

None of the articles tracing the reproductive choices of Sharon Duchesneau and Colleen McCullough questioned the assumption that a future without disability and deafness is superior to one with them. As in Piercy's fictional debate between the Mixers and the Shapers, no one recognized the screening out of Deaf sperm donors as a *political* decision; only the Maryland women's selection of a Deaf donor was seen as political. The vast majority of public reactions to these women's choices tell a story about the appropriate place of disability/deafness in the future; it is assumed that everyone, both hearing and Deaf, disabled and nondisabled, will and should prefer a nondisabled, hearing child.

News coverage of these women's stories reveals profound anxieties about the proper use of technology in imagining the future. Duchesneau and McCullough are described as "manufacturing" their children, a depiction that suggests something diabolical and decidedly unnatural about selecting for deafness. Although Mundy's original article makes clear that the Deaf sperm donor only increased the women's chances of having a Deaf baby to 50 percent, wire reports and stories in other papers describe the women as manipulating nature and technology to "guarantee" a Deaf baby, a misrepresentation that depicts the women as meddling with the future.

Even essays in medical journals followed this pattern, referring to the use of the donor as "guaranteeing" and "ensuring" a Deaf child (Anstey 2002; Levy 2002). Critics condemned these women for failing to do everything in their power to prevent disability, a failure that, in the ableist worldview, sentenced their children to a negative, imperfect future.[16]

The *queerness* of this future had everything to do with its portrayal as negative and imperfect. Although Ken Connor and the Family Research Council probably would not celebrate the use of a Deaf sperm donor by a heterosexual couple, it is highly unlikely that they would condemn it as aggressively and publicly as they did here, casting such a move as the first step on a slippery slope into the unknown. (They have not gone on record, for example, condemning Deaf heterosexuals who have children.) The case of the Deaf lesbians acquired the mileage that it did because of its evocation of a *queer* disabled future; heterosexism and ableism intertwine, each feeding off and supporting the other.

Indeed, the case of the Deaf lesbians has been presented to the public almost exclusively in terms of what the future can, should, and will include. Duchesneau and McCullough do not describe their reproductive choices in terms of a future vision, but others do. Whether warning of a slippery slope, other disabled people "manufacturing" disabled children, or "unnatural" lifestyles, commentators see their selection of a Deaf sperm donor as a sign of a dangerous future. The future allegedly invoked by their actions is dangerous because it advocates an improper use of technology; technology should be used only to *eliminate* disability, not to *proliferate* it. Such a goal is *natural,* not *political,* and therefore neither requires nor deserves public debate.

OPEN TO DEBATE? DISABILITY AND DIFFERENCE IN A FEMINIST FUTURE

Conceptualizing disability as a problem to be eradicated is reminiscent of how Marge Piercy addresses disability and other differences in *Woman on the Edge of Time.* In her utopian vision of a future Mattapoisett, diversity is highly valued, with the village's inhabitants rejecting the idea of a "thin gruel" in which everyone is the same. I want to suggest, however, that the community is actually founded on an *erasure* of difference. Sexism is rooted out not through the passing of antidiscrimination laws or a changing of attitudes, but by erasing reproductive differences, rendering both sexes able to breast-feed and neither able to give birth. Similarly with racism: Mattapoisett uses the brooder to mix races together; different skin tones may result, but the practice is founded on the idea that racism can never be eliminated until everyone is, essentially, the same. Piercy removes the stigma of mental illness but stipulates that those who are unwell voluntarily remove themselves from the community until they are back to "normal." Other disabilities she eliminates entirely from her vision of the future. In Piercy's utopia the problem is not ableism, the problem is disability itself; and it is best solved by segregating people with mental illnesses and eradicating "defective" genes from the brooder. Moreover, eliminating disability takes place without debate or discussion; the whole community apparently supports it. In Mattapoisett the problem of disability is best solved through its eradication, segregation, and erasure.

Philosopher Erin McKenna suggests that although *Woman on the Edge of Time* provides a compelling vision of a feminist future, with its focus on gender equality, interconnectedness, and participatory democracy, it is, in the end, problematic. McKenna explains that Piercy has failed to articulate a "process of transition . . . a convincing method for changing values, beliefs, and habits." (This lack is evident in Piercy's use of the brooder—not attitudinal change or consciousness-raising—to solve the problems of racism and sexism.) Consequently, diversity within the community is at risk, because some people may begin to "feel threatened by the freedom someone has to be different . . . [and] the community may fall back on the techniques of shame, gossip, ostracism, expulsion, or eugenics to remove those who are perceived as a threat or challenge" (McKenna 2001, 79–80).

Nowhere is this possibility more clear than in Piercy's treatment of the difference of disability. The mentally ill, as noted above, are expected to engage in self-segregation until their "difference" has passed, allowing them to rejoin the community. Even more troubling, those with other disabilities have been bred out of the community, cured not only of their disabilities but of their very existence. Even McKenna fails to notice that Mattapoisett has built "ostracism, expulsion, [and] eugenics" into its very foundations; in breeding out allegedly defective traits, the brooder has been practicing eugenics all along. In erasing difference through the brooder, Piercy moves away from "the process model" of utopia, which thrives on uncertainty and openness, in favor of an "end-state model," which proffers a fixed, specific model of the future. End-state models, explains McKenna, are problematic because they are, by definition, exclusive. By establishing a fixed vision of the future—in this case, a feminist utopia where all disabilities have been eradicated or segregated—Piercy casts certain people, ideas, and ways of being out of the range of possibility. For all its attention to diversity and inclusion, Mattapoisett allows only one type of body: a nondisabled one.

Woman on the Edge of Time and the furor surrounding McCullough and Duchesneau's reproductive choices both represent disability as a difference with no place in the future. Disability is a problem to be eliminated, a hindrance to one's future opportunities, a drag on one's quality of life. Indeed, concerns about "quality of life" are often used to justify the selective abortion of "defective" fetuses, the use of cochlear implants in young children, and the drive toward "a cure" for disability. Cultural commentators worrying over the "manufacture" of Deaf or blind babies question their quality of life. Bioethicists typically frame questions about the removal of life support or the use of life-saving measures in terms of quality of life. Similar claims are made opposing same-sex parenting: critics argue that children raised in queer households will have a lower quality of life than children raised in heterosexual ones. However, each of these situations assumes not only that disability inherently and irreversibly lowers one's quality of life, but also that there is only one possible understanding of "quality of life" and that everyone knows what "it" is without discussion or elaboration.

In *The Trouble with Normal*, Michael Warner condemns "quality of life" rhetoric, arguing that this terminology masks dissent by taking for granted the kinds of experiences the term includes (1999, 183). Although he is challenging the use of quality-of-life arguments in public debates about pornography and public sex, Warner's argument resonates with cultural constructions of disability.[17] *Woman on the Edge of Time* and critics of Duchesneau, McCullough, and Chambers assume that disability destroys quality of life, that a better life precludes disability, and that disability can and should be "fixed" through technological intervention. They make no room in their future visions for other perspectives on disability; they allow no real debate. Disability and deafness "obviously" should be cured and eliminated, relegated to the history books, for there is no place for them in the utopic future, only in the dystopic one.

Bioethicists such as Dena Davis condemn parents' refusal to fit their children with cochlear implants; others query how any responsible potential parent could knowingly bring a disabled child into the world. These discussions often revolve around the need for an "open future"; Davis, for example, argues that the refusal to "cure" deafness through CI limits the future choices of children and that such a refusal is thereby a "moral harm" (2001, 63–65). But what Davis and her colleagues fail to recognize is that CI, prenatal testing, and selective abortion also limit children's future choices. Children with CI are often discouraged from using sign language or engaging with Deaf culture, taboos that limit their future signing abilities and their comfort in Deaf culture.

Davis's insistence on an open future without disability echoes Piercy's portrayal of a utopia in which all disabilities can be cured through breakthroughs in medical technology. Casting disability only as a difference to be eradicated or cured in the future, Piercy and Davis remove disability from visions of a desirable future and foreclose the possibility of thinking about disability differently. In other words, not only do they cast disability out of their personal visions, but they also suggest that no moral vision of the future can include disability; we can never see disability as simply part of "normal" human variation. But to eliminate disability is to eliminate the possibility of discovering alternative ways of being in the world, to foreclose the possibility of recognizing and valuing our interdependence. The future no longer appears so "open" after all. Indeed, in the drive to eliminate disability through technology, asks Susan Wendell, "what else . . . might we lose in the process?" (1996, 84).

Wendell suggests that living with disability or illness "creates valuable *ways of being* that give valuable perspectives on life and the world," ways of being that would be lost through the elimination of illness and disability (2001, 31). For example, adults who require assistance in the activities of daily life, such as eating, bathing, toileting, and dressing, have opportunities to think through cultural ideals of independence and self-sufficiency; these experiences can potentially lead to productive insights about intimacy, relationship, and interdependence. "If one looks at disabilities as forms of difference and takes seriously the possibility that they may be valuable," argues Wendell,

> it becomes obvious that people with disabilities have experiences, by virtue of their disabilities, which non-disabled people do not have, and which are [or can be] sources of knowledge that is not directly accessible to non-disabled people. Some of this knowledge, for example, how to live with a suffering body, would be of enormous practical help to most people. . . . Much of it would enrich and expand our culture, and some of it has the potential to change our thinking and our ways of life profoundly. (1996, 69)

To eliminate disability is to eliminate the possibility of discovering alternative ways of being in the world, to foreclose the possibility of recognizing and valuing our interdependence.

I want to stress that not only are Davis, Piercy, and the critics of the Deaf lesbian couple lobbying for an eventual (and allegedly inevitable and attainable) end to disability, either through technological aids, cures, or genetic tests, they are also suggesting that such a goal is so obviously appropriate that it neither requires nor deserves debate. Or, rather, they suggest that any debate would always already be determined in advance; there is simply nothing to discuss, because we all agree. There is no need, for example, for public debate over the exclusion of deaf donors from sperm banks because no reasonable person would choose such a donor. To do otherwise would be construed as selfish and shameful, as we have seen.

To be clear, no decisions have been made as to which "defects" should be eliminated or about what constitutes a "defective" gene; with few exceptions, assisted reproductive technology remains largely unregulated in the United States. As a result, public discussions of these technologies have lagged far behind their use and development, and they rarely include the perspectives of disabled people. As H-Dirksen L. Bauman argues, "Presumptions about the horrors of deafness are usually made by those not living Deaf lives" (2005, 313). The Prenatally and Postnatally Diagnosed Conditions Awareness Act (2008) is a step in the right direction, mandating that women receive comprehensive information about disability prior to making decisions about their pregnancies, but it remains unclear how well this policy will be funded or enforced. Moreover, as the debate surrounding Duchesneau and McCullough's reproductive choices makes clear, selecting for disability remains a highly controversial position, and hypothetical disabled children continue to be used to justify genetic research and selective abortion. "Curing" and eliminating disability—whether through stem cell research or selective abortion—is almost always presented as a universally valued goal about which there can, and should, be no disagreement.

I want to suggest that stories of Deaf lesbians intentionally striving for Deaf babies be read as counter-narratives to mainstream stories about the necessity of a cure for deafness and disability, about the dangers of non-normative queer parents having children. Their story challenges the feasibility of technological promises of an "amazing future" in which genetic and medical intervention cures impairment; it resists a compulsory able-bodied heterosexuality that insists upon normal bodies. This challenge is precisely what has animated the hostile responses to this family. Their choice of deafness suggests that reproductive technology can be used as more than a means to screen out alleged defects, that disability cannot ever fully disappear, that not everyone craves an able-bodied future with no place for bodies with limited, odd, or queer movements and orientations, and that disability and queerness can indeed be desirable both in the future as well as now.

The story of the Deaf lesbians, Candace McCullough and Sharon Duchesneau, is only one among many. An ever-increasing number of memoirs, essays, and poems about life with a disability, as well as theoretical analyses of disability and able-bodiedness, tell other stories about disability, providing alternatives to the narratives of eradication and cure offered by Marge Piercy in *Woman on the Edge of Time*. There are stories of people embracing their bodies, proudly proclaiming disability as sexy, powerful, and worthy; tales of disabled parents and parents with disabled children refusing to accept that a bright future for our children precludes disability and asserting the right to bear and keep children with disabilities; and narratives of families refusing to accept the normalization of their bodies through surgical interventions and the normalization of their desires through heterocentric laws and homophobic condemnations. These stories deserve telling, and the issues they raise demand debate and dissent. It is not that these tales are any less partial or contested than the others in public circulation; they, too, can be used to serve multiple and contradictory positions.[18] But they challenge the paired assumptions that disability cannot belong in feminist visions of the future and that its absence merits no debate.

NOTES

I would like to thank Susan Burch, Rosemarie Garland-Thomson, Kristen Harmon, Sujatha Jesudason, Cathy Kudlick, Dana Newlove, Sara Patterson, Ranu Samantrai, Ellen Samuels, Zandra Wagoner, and Peggy Waller for their assistance and feedback.

1. Susan Merrill Squier (1994; 2004) makes a case for literature, specifically science fiction, in analyzing biomedicine and reproductive technology. Fascinated by representations of reproductive technology in feminist fiction, she urges cultural critics to attend to the "ideological construction . . . being carried out through the production and dissemination" of these texts (1994, 19).

2. The use of *Deaf*, with a capital *D,* is intended to signal pride in one's Deaf identity and in the cultural practices and historical traditions of Deaf people. *Deaf* with a capital letter signifies community identity and pride, whereas *deaf* with a small *d* simply connotes being unable to hear or hard-of-hearing. In her discussion of the rhetoric of deafness, Brenda Jo Brueggemann explains that the term *hearing impaired* is seldom used by Deaf or hard-of-hearing people themselves; "the term . . . is purely audiological" (1999, 141n29).

3. Piercy does not specify the year of the dystopic New York, suggesting only that it is another possible future, an alternative to the one found in Mattapoisett.

4. For more extensive listings, see "Women's Studies Syllabi," University of Maryland, http://www.mith2.umd.edu/WomensStudies/Syllabi; and Center for Women and Information Technology, "Women's Studies Syllabi," University of Maryland, Baltimore County, www.umbc.edu/cwit/syllabi.html.

5. See also Huckle (1983) and Davis (1997). Even feminist theorists who take a more critical stance toward Piercy's vision of utopia, finding fault with its use of

violence or its reliance on small communities, praise Mattapoisett's system of participatory democracy. See, for example, McKenna (2001).

6. For discussion of these issues, see, for example, Andrews (2001), Davis (2000), Franklin and Roberts (2006), McGee (2000), Mundy (2007), and Plotz (2001). A wide range of disability studies scholars and feminist thinkers have addressed the issue of prenatal testing and selective abortion, analyzing the impact these practices have on women and people with disabilities and deconstructing the assumptions about gender and disability that support them. For examples of this work, see, among others, Rapp (1999), Finger (1990), and Parens and Asch (2000).

7. Lane acknowledges there are differences between Deaf people and other linguistic minorities. He notes, "Deaf people cannot learn English as a second language as easily as other minorities. Second and third generation Deaf children find learning English no easier than their forbears, but second and third generation immigrants to the U.S. frequently learn English before entering school. . . . Normally, Deaf people are not proficient in this native language [sign language] until they reach school age. Deaf people are more scattered geographically than many linguistic minorities. The availability of interpreters is even more vital for Deaf people than for many other linguistic minorities because there are so few Deaf lawyers, doctors, and accountants, etc." (1997, 163–64).

8. Unfortunately, there is an extensive history of requiring Deaf people to do precisely that: learn to lip-read, speak orally, abandon signing, and undergo painful surgeries and medical treatments in order to "correct" their hearing loss. Scholars of Deaf studies have traced histories of Deaf people being punished, often brutally, for engaging in sign language, and of the campaigns waged against residential schools and Deaf communities. In spite of such treatment, the Deaf community continued to use and fight for sign language (Buchanan 1999; Burch 2002).

9. Lane (1997) stresses that part of recognizing the "great common cause" between culturally Deaf people and people with disabilities is respecting how culturally Deaf people understand their own identities. For more recent examinations of the relationship between deafness and disability, see essays in Bauman (2008) and Burch and Kafer (2010).

10. Deafness is not the only trait screened out of the gene pool. Sperm banks exclude male donors who have family histories of cystic fibrosis, Tay-Sachs disease, alcoholism, and other conditions deemed problematic or undesirable. Under guidelines established by the FDA, most sperm banks exclude gay men and men who have had sex with men in the last five years.

11. Sadly, Gauvin died suddenly and unexpectedly from an inherited condition (unrelated to his deafness). In contrast to his birth, his passing met with little public reaction.

12. See "Marriage and Family," Family Research Council, http://www.frc.org/marriage-family.

13. For an essay on a blind woman reflecting on her desire for a blind child, see Kent (2000). Kent movingly describes her internal struggles in realizing that her parents and her husband, all sighted, do not share her understanding of blindness

as a "neutral trait" and are concerned about the possible blindness of her future children.

14. These comments were not left unaddressed by other members on the Listserv. Participants questioned the assumptions about the "burdens" caused by disability and about the inappropriateness of Deaf women choosing a donor that reflected their own lives, a choice nondisabled couples make regularly. They also challenged the contention that Deaf children pose a financial strain on the state, arguing that economic arguments about the "strain" caused by people with disabilities have often been used to justify coerced and forced sterilization, institutionalization, and coerced abortion.

15. Patrick Steptoe, known as the "father of in vitro fertilization," remarked that "it would be unthinkable to willingly create a child to be born into an unnatural situation such as a gay or lesbian relationship" (qtd. in Franklin 1993, 31). Dorothy Roberts (1998) and Elizabeth Weil (2006b) add that many fertility clinics require proof of a "stable" marriage before initiating treatment, an open-ended requirement that can be used to block the treatment of queers, women of color, and poor people. California prohibits discriminating against queers in fertility treatments, but as Elizabeth Weil argues, such discrimination can hide under other names. Guadalupe Benitez lost her case against the North Coast Women's Care Medical Group when they argued that they had refused to treat her not because she was a lesbian, but because she was unmarried; in an earlier case, which the clinic lost, Benitez was able to prove that treatment had stopped because of her status as a lesbian (Weil 2006b).

16. I do not mean to suggest that criticisms of the couple would have been justified if the use of a Deaf donor had increased the odds to more than 50 percent. In fact, I doubt critics would have left the women alone if the odds were less than 50 percent.

17. Ellen Samuels examines the limits of analogy, arguing that there often is an imprecision in meaning and an effacement of specificity when *disability* is used in place of *sexuality*, an argument I find persuasive and compelling (2002). At the same time, in this case I think the substitution points to important parallels between disability and queerness. Both queerness and disability have been cast as entities to be avoided, as drains on a child's quality of life; moreover, as I have argued here, their combination has proved especially threatening.

18. Lennard Davis argues that we need to question whether these kinds of reproductive decisions—choosing deafness and disability—are "radical ways of fighting against oppression" or "technological fixes in the service of a conservative, essentialist agenda" (2008, 319). I would only add that the two are not mutually exclusive; the same choice can serve both agendas. What is needed then are examinations of how particular choices function in particular contexts; such explorations are impossible as long as selecting for disability remains largely inconceivable.

REFERENCES

Andrews, Lori B. 2001. *Future Perfect: Confronting Decisions about Genetics*. New York: Columbia University Press.

Anstey, K. W. 2002. "Are Attempts to Have Impaired Children Justifiable?" *Journal of Medical Ethics* 28: 286–89.

Bauman, H-Dirksen L. 2005. "Designing Deaf Babies and the Question of Disability." *Journal of Deaf Studies and Deaf Education* 10 (3): 311–15.

Bauman, H-Dirksen L., ed. 2008. *Open Your Eyes: Deaf Studies Speaks*. Minneapolis: University of Minnesota Press.

Brueggemann, Brenda Jo. 1999. *Lend Me Your Ear: Rhetorical Constructions of Deafness*. Washington, D.C.: Gallaudet University Press.

Buchanan, Robert M. 1999. *Illusions of Equality: Deaf Americans in School and Factory, 1850–1950*. Washington, D.C.: Gallaudet University Press.

Burch, Susan. 2002. *Signs of Resistance: American Deaf Cultural History, 1900 to World War II*. New York: New York University Press.

Burch, Susan, and Alison Kafer, eds. 2010. *Deaf and Disability Studies: Interdisciplinary Perspectives*. Washington, D.C.: Gallaudet University Press.

Davis, Dena S. 2001. *Genetic Dilemmas: Reproductive Technology, Parental Choices, and Children's Futures*. New York: Routledge.

Davis, Kathy. 1997. "'My Body Is My Art': Cosmetic Surgery as Feminist Utopia?" In *Embodied Practices: Feminist Perspectives on the Body*, edited by Kathy Davis, 168–81. Thousand Oaks, Calif.: Sage Publications.

Davis, Lennard J. 2008. "Postdeafness." In *Open Your Eyes: Deaf Studies Speaks*, edited by H-Dirksen L. Bauman, 314–325. Minneapolis: University of Minnesota Press.

Family Research Council. 2002. "*Washington Post* Profiles Lesbian Couple Seeking to Manufacture a Deaf Child." PR Newswire Association, 1 April.

Finger, Anne. 1990. *Past Due: A Story of Disability, Pregnancy, and Birth*. Seattle: Seal Press.

Franklin, Sarah. 1993. "Essentialism, which Essentialism? Some Implications of Reproductive and Genetic Technoscience." In *If You Seduce a Straight Person, Can You Make Them Gay? Issues in Biological Essentialism versus Social Constructionism in Gay and Lesbian Identities*, edited by John P. DeCecco and John P. Elia, 27–40. Binghamton, N.Y.: Harrington Park.

Franklin, Sarah, and Celia Roberts. 2006. *Born and Made: An Ethnography of Preimplantation Genetic Diagnosis*. Princeton, N.J.: Princeton University Press.

Glorie, Josephine Carubia. 1997. "Feminist Utopian Fiction and the Possibility of Social Critique." In *Political Science Fiction*, edited by Donald M. Hassler and Clyde Wilcox, 148–59. Columbia: University of South Carolina Press.

Groce, Nora Ellen. 1985. *Everyone Here Spoke Sign Language: Hereditary Deafness on Martha's Vineyard*. Cambridge, Mass.: Harvard University Press.

Hershey, Laura. 2003. "Disabled Woman's Lawsuit Exposes Prejudices." The Ragged Edge. http://www.raggededgemagazine.com/extra/hersheychamberstrial.html.

Huckle, Patricia. 1983. "Women in Utopias." In *The Utopian Vision: Seven Essays on the Quincentennial of Sir Thomas More*, edited by E. D. S. Sullivan, 115–36. San Diego: San Diego State University Press.

Hughes, Jim. 2003. "Blind Woman Sues Fertility Clinic: Englewood Facility

Halted Treatments after Questions about Her Fitness as a Parent." *Denver Post,* 7 November.

Kent, Deborah. 2000. "Somewhere a Mockingbird." In Parens and Asch, *Prenatal Testing and Disability Rights,* 57–63.

Lane, Harlan. 1997. "Constructions of Deafness." In *The Disability Studies Reader,* edited by Lennard J. Davis, 153–71. New York: Routledge.

Levy, Neil. 2002. "Deafness, Culture, and Choice." *Journal of Medical Ethics* 28: 284–85.

Litwinowicz, Jo. 1999. "In My Mind's Eye: I." In *Bigger Than the Sky: Disabled Women on Parenting,* edited by Michele Wates and Rowen Jade, 29–33. London: Women's Press.

McGee, Glenn. 2000. *The Perfect Baby: Parenthood in the New World of Cloning and Genetics.* Lanham, Md.: Rowman and Littlefield.

McGuire, Cathleen, and Colleen McGuire. 1998. "Grassroots Ecofeminism: Activating Utopia." In *Ecofeminist Literary Criticism: Theory, Interpretation, Pedagogy,* edited by Greta Gaard and Patrick D. Murphy, 186–203. Urbana: University of Illinois Press.

McKenna, Erin. 2001. *The Task of Utopia.* Lanham, Md.: Rowman and Littlefield.

McRuer, Robert. 2003. "Critical Investments: AIDS, Christopher Reeve, and Queer/Disability Studies." In *Thinking the Limits of the Body,* edited by Jeffrey Jerome Cohen and Gail Weiss, 145–64. Albany: State University of New York Press.

Mundy, Liza. 2002. "A World of Their Own." *Washington Post Magazine,* 31 March.

———. 2007. *Everything Conceivable: How Assisted Reproduction Is Changing Men, Women, and the World.* New York: Knopf.

Ordover, Nancy. 2003. *American Eugenics: Race, Queer Anatomy, and the Science of Nationalism.* Minneapolis: University of Minnesota Press.

Padden, Carol, and Tom Humphries. 1988. *Deaf in America: Voices from a Culture.* Cambridge, Mass.: Harvard University Press.

Parens, Erik, and Adrienne Asch, eds. 2000. *Prenatal Testing and Disability Rights.* Washington, D.C.: Georgetown University Press.

Piercy, Marge. 1976. *Woman on the Edge of Time.* New York: Fawcett Crest.

Plotz, David. 2001. "The 'Genius Babies,' and How They Grew." *Slate.* http://www.slate.com/id/100331.

Rapp, Rayna. 1999. *Testing Women, Testing the Fetus: The Social Impact of Amniocentesis in America.* New York: Routledge.

Roberts, Dorothy. 1998. *Killing the Black Body: Race, Reproduction, and the Meaning of Liberty.* New York: Vintage.

Samuels, Ellen. 2002. "Critical Divides: Judith Butler's Body Theory and the Question of Disability." *NWSA Journal* 14 (3): 58–76.

Squier, Susan Merrill. 1994. *Babies in Bottles: Twentieth-Century Visions of Reproductive Technology.* Brunswick, N.J.: Rutgers University Press.

———. 2004. *Liminal Lives: Imagining the Human at the Frontiers of Biomedicine.* Durham, N.C.: Duke University Press.

Van Cleve, John Vickrey, and Barry Crouch. 1989. *A Place of Their Own: Creating the Deaf Community in America.* Washington, D.C.: Gallaudet University Press.

Van Dijck, José. 1998. *Imagenation: Popular Images of Genetics*. New York: New York University Press.

Warner, Michael. 1999. *The Trouble with Normal: Sex, Politics, and the Ethics of Queer Life*. New York: Free Press.

Weil, Elizabeth. 2006a. "A Wrongful Birth?" *New York Times Magazine*, 12 March.

———. 2006b. "Breeder Reaction." *Mother Jones* 31 (4): 33–37.

Wendell, Susan. 1996. *The Rejected Body: Feminist Philosophical Reflections on Disability*. New York: Routledge.

———. 2001. "Unhealthy Disabled: Treating Chronic Illnesses as Disabilities." *Hypatia* 16 (4): 17–33.

Winterson, Jeanette. 2002. "How Would We Feel if Blind Women Claimed the Right to a Blind Baby?" *Guardian*, 9 April.

PART FIVE

INCLUSIONS,

EXCLUSIONS,

AND

TRANSFORMATIONS

Eleven

DISPARATE BUT DISABLED

Fat Embodiment and Disability Studies

APRIL HERNDON

At a 2002 conference on race, a prominent but controversial white male academic presented a paper on buckshot skull studies, noting comparisons between Caucasian and African skulls.[1] Well known for his race/ist scholarship, this scholar concluded that such studies represent facts that cannot be ignored, implying that racism, at least on some levels, can be biologically and scientifically justified. During the discussion of his paper, I posed a question about feminist-standpoint epistemology, his obvious belief in science as purely objective, and his recalcitrance to situate himself, as a white male, within the context of his own study and scientific epistemology. After replying with the tiresome argument that only scientists can criticize science and stating that feminist-standpoint epistemologists needed to build a rocket that made it to the moon before he would take their criticisms seriously, he continued to argue for pure objectivity, stating he could "show [me] studies that empirically prove women's hips are wider than men's."

Unpacking his choice of example exposes the liability I faced as a woman of size in a culture that values thinness. First, his example reminded me of my body size (while I was standing in the front of a crowded room) lest I forget that I am a large woman violating the ideal figure of womanhood. I often out myself as a Fat woman, meaning I use *Fat* to indicate a politicized identity similar to *Deaf* when expressed as a cultural and political identity that moves away from impairments and medical conditions and toward a politics of embodiment, but the politics of this situation certainly erased my ability to define myself and articulate my own identity in meaningful ways.[2]

Second, this scholar's comment drew attention to the fact that I am a large *woman* and therefore have sinned not once but twice. Thus, he hailed me on two different but conjoined levels of subjectivity. His emphasis on gender distinctions and his marking of me as both a woman and as fat with large hips served to elicit shame on two levels. First, I should be ashamed because a powerful, older, academic male marked me as an undesirable woman by gesturing to the breadth of my hips, assuming I would be invested in what he as an established male academic thought of my hips (or perhaps all women's hips). In this sense, his comment reflects both patriarchal power and heteronormativity. Finally, pointing out body size publicly can injure the psyche enough to impose silence. The cultural script reads that once called out on being fat, a woman reassumes her proper place and remains quiet.

Perhaps the final observation to be gleaned from such condescension and marginalization is an obvious inability to understand the complex relationship between empirically proven data, the influence of questions on resulting data, and the relevance accorded data. Yes, it might be true that women's hips, on average, are larger than men's. This observation alone, however, is not particularly problematic. The problem is that the questions posed about fatness, within both medical and sociocultural realms, indicate a profound bias. Like inquiries launched to find the causes of homosexuality, the search for medical and/or psychological origins of fatness reveals the place of fatness, fat embodiment, and fat people within current epistemological rubrics. The issue is how this information is used to support social decisions; in the case of the aforementioned scholar, it can be argued that his deployment of the empirical fact of the size of women's hips publicly pathologized and discredited a fat woman.

Physically discernible "imperfections" such as fatness manifest as further evidence of women's pathologies. Particularly unfortunate is the evocation and acceptance of these pathologies without investigation of political commitments spurring such studies onward. Initiating inquiries from the lives of fat women raises hosts of questions about how it is that fatness features in the lives of women and whether or not fatness is best understood within the context of disability studies. What consequences emerge when women, already facing sexual discrimination, are also large? How do discussions about socially and/or physically disabled bodies both echo and expand feminism's long battle over natural and socially constructed bodies? Can examining the contours of fat embodiment and medical models of fatness help us better understand how we can usefully frame such inquiries? How does gender feature in these struggles, and why might examining the specific construction of the female body in conjunction with disability be particularly revealing? This essay will explore these questions and others by mapping the terrain of feminism, disability studies, and fatness alongside mainstream medical paradigms most often used to describe fatness. By exposing and illustrating why these medical rubrics cannot usefully account for the stigma associated with fat embodiment, this essay seeks to set the stage for political commitments that recognize disability as a diverse social category that can meaningfully incorporate fat embodiments.

WHY DISABILITY STUDIES?

The Americans with Disabilities Act of 1990 (ADA) defines impairment as "[any] physiological disorder, condition, cosmetic disfigurement, or anatomical loss affecting one or more of the following systems: neurological, musculoskeletal, special sense organs, respiratory (including speech organs), cardiovascular, reproductive, digestive, genito-urinary, hemic and lymphatic, skin and endocrine" (Solovay 2000, 135). Following disability scholars such as Simi Linton and Susan Wendell, I aim to dislodge disability from its origins in impairments and medicalized physical conditions. This is not to suggest physical impairments are unimportant; certainly there is physical suffering endured by many. Rather, I am interested in how such impairments feature in people's lives and divulge cultural values about bodies and normativity.

Similarly, Wendell encourages readers to defamiliarize the most common notions about disability by looking for social and environmental factors. She writes:

> One of the most crucial factors in the deconstruction of disability is the change of perspective that causes us to look in the environment for the source of the problem and the solutions. It is perhaps easiest to change perspective by thinking about how people who have some bodily difference that does not impair any of their physical functions, such as being unusually large, are disabled by the built environment—by seats that are too small . . . doors and aisles that are too narrow . . . the unavailability or expense of clothing that fits. (1996, 46)

Examining the terrain of disability from the perspective that problems inhere, not within particular individuals, but rather within social contexts, social expectations, and built environments allows us to map disability as a socially constructed phenomenon rather than a physical trait.

For both Wendell and Linton, disability studies must move beyond studying physical impairments and toward a study of group politics. In other words, the distinction between impairments and disabilities must be understood as both theoretically and epistemologically important. Linton's germinal text, *Claiming Disability* (1998), maintains the distinction between impairment and disability in order to articulate and theorize differentiations between medical and cultural, individual and group. Thus, she characterizes *impairment* as related more closely to medicalized individuals while *disability* refers to disabled people as a culturally recognized and defined group. Linton argues that "we should . . . utilize the term *disability studies* solely for investigations of disability as a social, cultural, and political phenomenon" (149). Thus, while understanding there are fat people who suffer impairments because of their size, I choose to focus on disability studies in terms of Linton's use of the concept. While physical impairments surely cause personal struggles, the treatment of fat/disabled people as social pariahs must be addressed first and foremost. The reliance upon biological truths about bodies, as I will discuss and argue more intensely later in the paper, serves only to further pathologize individuals. I will use feminist theory and disability studies to criticize culturally embedded values about fat people as a group.

Resistance to seeing fatness as a disability and fat people as a politicized group situates itself within medical epistemological frameworks that focus mostly on the biology of individuals. In a striking comparison between the politics of the supposed biological categories of race and disability, Wendell states, "The belief that 'the disabled' is a biological category is like the belief that 'Black' is a biological category in that it masks the social functions and injustices that underlie the assignment of people to these groups" (1996, 24). Echoing the problems with individualization and medicalization, Sondra Solovay writes that the battle between those who choose to see weight as a disability and those who discredit any attempt to do so stems from the belief that weight constitutes a problem with an impaired individual (2000, 135). For weight in particular, dominant definitions of impairment and disability are entangled in cultural debates about medicalization, group and individual autonomy, cultural decisions and consequences of pathologizing certain bodies, demanding corrective action on the part of individual people rather than collective social action.

Yet another resistance to thinking of fatness as a disability is the fact that fatness is not specifically named in the ADA. If we stop to consider the numerous policies written to protect one group then later extended to others, it becomes painfully obvious that there is inherent *fatphobia* in the very decision to deny weight explicitly. Sexual harassment policies, for example, were originally aimed at protecting women from unwanted sexual attention and harassment proffered by men. However, recent cases have, rightfully, moved beyond the original purpose and dated language of such policies to protect men who are sexually harassed by same-sex colleagues. Thus, interpretations of sexual harassment policies acknowledge dynamic cultural shifts. Similarly, those interpreting the ADA and state legislation passed for similar purposes have also remained open to considering newly proposed forms of disability. When members of the medical community began to cite scientific studies suggesting that alcoholism was a disease, in the sense that those suffering from it shared similar physical traits and characteristics, courts adopted similar views. As a result, alcoholism, although not explicitly named under the ADA as a disabling condition, is often legally recognized as a disability. Thus, courts clearly do engage in considering shifting paradigms of disability—but often not where fatness is concerned. There is far more at stake in locking out obese individuals than merely being true to the original nomenclature or intention of antidiscrimination legislation; closing the door on disability claims is far more about the pervasive and perverse fatphobia of our culture.

The frequent dismissal of fatness as a disability lodges itself in an intense cultural fear of frivolous ADA claims and what it might mean to accommodate larger bodies. *The Simpsons*, a television sitcom, provided a classic episode that exemplifies this fear. Titled "King Size Homer," the episode consisted of Homer, one of the lead characters, getting another wacky idea to escape work; he decided to purposefully gain enough weight so that he would be accommodated, able to work at home (1995). His goal weight, which he eventually exceeded, was 316 pounds. To surpass this weight, Homer stuffed his face with hamburgers, ice cream, and in the end, Play-Doh. At his desired weight, Homer was depicted as a muumuu-wearing fat man who loafed all day and changed television channels with a broomstick. Recounting familiar narratives of fatness as a voluntary condition resulting from poor eating habits and a sedentary lifestyle and of disabled people as dangerous to the American purse because accommodation must be suffered by the public writ large, the episode stripped the issues down to elemental fears of Otherness. "King Size Homer" underscored the role of volition in dominant understandings of both fatness and disability.

Sadly, fears of frivolous claims are not restricted to media satire or speculation. The most serious consequences of the panic generated by disability claims are "negative decisions . . . based on unfounded fears" (Solovay 2000, 36). The U.S. Department of Justice is also concerned and attempting to allay the public's fears. On the ADA website, the section titled "Myths and Facts about the Americans with Disabilities Act" addresses questions concerning weight and the ADA, facts and myths about the frivolity of ADA cases, and abuse of legislation by those with "emotional problems"

(1990). In essence, facts and myths included on the site address people's fears about the government being bamboozled into providing accommodations for those who are undeserving, such as fat people who are "eating up" more than their share of funds. Discussions of weight and disability seem perpetually freighted with issues of choice and frivolity.

MEDICAL CONSTRUCTIONS OF FATNESS

In addition to fears of frivolous claims, many people fear that accepting fatness as a disability, and thus a protected category under the ADA, condones fatness at a time when obesity is considered a public health crisis of epidemic proportions. Medicalization presents fatness as a disease epidemic and strips away humanity, focusing solely on a medical condition and ignoring the people involved. While a majority of people in the United States believe that fat is unhealthy, immoral, and often downright disgusting, medical opinions on weight are actually quite mixed. Even well-respected members of the medical community are beginning to understand that such assertions display a woefully fatphobic and misguided understanding of obesity that damages fat people in very tangible ways

For example, in January 1998 Dr. Jerome Kassirer and Dr. Marcia Angell published an editorial in the *New England Journal of Medicine* that succinctly stated the reasons why any New Year's resolution to lose weight was doomed. Citing the well-known fact that 95 percent of diets fail, Kassirer and Angell ask that the medical community stop pushing for weight loss. In addressing the issue of "health" so often used to justify fatphobia, they write:

> Given the enormous social pressure to lose weight, one might suppose there is clear and overwhelming evidence of the risks of obesity and the benefits of weight loss. Unfortunately, the data linking overweight and death, as well as the data showing the beneficial effects of weight loss, are limited, fragmentary, and often ambiguous. (1998, 52)

Thus, there is very little compelling evidence that losing weight equals a step toward health or that losing weight is even really possible for the vast majority of folks, putting claims about volition and the possible consequences of the epidemic of obesity to rest.

Despite the efforts of doctors such as Kassirer and Angell, misinformation continues to circulate, further confusing the American public about fatness. In 1993 the *Journal of the American Medical Association* published a brief statement titled "Actual Causes of Death in the United States." This short piece contained the statement that three hundred thousand people had died in the previous year due to factors such as poor eating habits and sedentary lifestyle (2208). Weight was never specifically mentioned. In the following months, however, weight was all that was mentioned. Exhibiting the power of fatphobia—even where supposedly objective medicine is concerned—this information suddenly appeared in other sources, but subsequent citations failed to indicate that sedentary lifestyle and poor eating habits *contributed* to these three hundred thousand deaths; instead, obesity was cited as the *cause* of these deaths, conflating poor eating habits and sedentary lifestyles with a particular embodiment.[3]

My own experience with doctors resonates with these examples of fatphobia and the overwhelming cultural narratives of fatness, which are constructions fueled far more by the drive toward normative bodies than by solid medical evidence. I have many times been reminded that despite the fact that my blood pressure, cholesterol, and pulse are within acceptable ranges, I am unhealthy, for no other reason than my weight. Although it is difficult to find scientific studies that suggest fatness is in and of itself the catalyst behind diseases such as atherosclerosis or high blood pressure, it seems that many medical practitioners feel quite comfortable telling patients that regardless of any other aspect of their lifestyle or health, they are ill. The doctors who have confronted me have offered a litany of possible impairments they see in my future, ranging from heart disease to arthritis in my knees.

These hypothetical corporeal futures are based in stereotypes of people of size, laying bare the stigma associated with larger-than-average bodies. A careful and complete review of scientific studies does not, as many assume, reveal direct ties between fatness and the diseases we so closely associate with it.[4] Steeped in both the creation and reflection of popular narratives about fatness, many medical accounts (despite confounding scientific evidence) dramatize negative aspects of obesity, further stigmatizing fat people. It is this stigma, these cultural narratives about fatness, the black cloud of misunderstanding and hatred that heavily hangs around the shoulders of people of size (our albatross, if you will), that medicalized accounts and those focusing on impairments alone fail to address. Medical narratives of fatness and the language of impairment often cannot usefully address alternative accounts offered by those embodied as fat and/or disabled. Alternative accounts, especially those that resist popular accounts of suffering and self-hatred, disrupt expectations of what it means to be fat and/or disabled. Linton writes, "We [disabled people] further confound expectations when we have the temerity to emerge as forthright and resourceful people, nothing like the self-loathing, docile, bitter, or insentient fictional versions of ourselves the public is more used to" (1998, 3). As Wendell explains in *The Rejected Body*, the stigma associated with certain bodies and abilities can sometimes be as disabling as physical impairments themselves: "the distinction between the biological reality of a disability and the social construction of a disability cannot be made sharply, because the biological and the social are interactive in creating disability" (1996, 35). Further, Wendell states, "being identified as disabled also carries a significant stigma in most societies and usually forces the person so identified to deal with stereotypes and unrealistic attitudes and expectations that are projected onto her/him as a member of a stigmatized group" (12). When medical narratives of disability maintain such firm footing within cultural imaginations, little room is left for political self-definition.

GROUP IDENTITY? THE CASES OF DEAF CULTURE AND FATNESS

Although medicine's analysis of weight assumes it is the individual's responsibility to control her body, it is also clear that medicine finds little room for individual analyses of fat people as individuals. Instead, almost anyone who is considered obese by medical standards will be given the same list of possible conditions and complications. Having previously argued that fat people are not usually treated as individuals, even (or especially) during medical exams, I would like to move on to examining the contours of what granting fat people group status might entail.[5] Historically, civil rights legislation has been informed by the belief that certain groups have been oppressed via social structures such as racism, sexism, and nationalism; however, people who are fat remain largely unprotected by such legislation. In addition to fears about frivolous claims, the belief that fat people do not constitute a cohesive social group hinders progress toward protection. Yet, many of the criteria for politicized group identities are met by fat people because they inhabit a similar stigmatized social location.

In character with medical narratives previously discussed, *the obese* are often referred to as a group, particularly when they are accused of emptying our national health care budget and driving up insurance rates for healthy Americans (Gaesser 1996, 60; Albrecht and Pories 1999, 149). Psychoanalysis is another branch of medicine that refers to *the obese* and *the disabled* as groups. One particularly interesting study, supposedly conducted to better understand "the morbidly obese patient," states that "depression is the hallmark of the obese" and that many of us are very "angry people" (Fox, Taylor, and Jones 2000, 479).[6] Familiar with such strategies, Simi Linton notes a trend in psychological and psychoanalytical studies of disabled people of casting personality traits as pathologies related to embodiments (1998, 99). Thus, the stigma and pathology surrounding both fat and disabled people are conceived around the notion that both are cohesive groups. Unfortunately, the group *Fat* is often evoked for the purposes of pathology rather than activism.

There are many other shared experiences among fat people, despite our diversity. First, we are constantly told to change our bodies, regardless of how we might feel about such proposals. Second, we are repeatedly told to lose weight even though mounting evidence shows weight loss as a false panacea. Third, our bodies are held up as public spectacles on a daily basis. Pitted against one another, particularly in the case of women, we are often represented as warning signs for those who are currently thin as well as those who are already heavy. Watching *The Jerry Springer Show* on any given day provides ample evidence of many women's ability to chastise other women about weight. Thin women castigate fat women, and women who are themselves large play the game of "at least I'm not that fat." Despite conflict and differentiation within the group, these experiences remain similar across such lines; suggesting that Fat is a shared political identity while regarding Fat as a viable political identity might encourage protection for fat people as a class. However, resistance to such proposals is quite strong. Why? What specifically makes the proposition of acknowledging fat persons as a group so threatening? How are notions of individual responsibility and "choice" implicated here?

As disparate as the identities Fat and Deaf might seem, critically reading recent debates about deafness and what is now being referred to as "elective disability" is especially helpful in thinking through these questions. As a quick review, both Fat and Deaf people are often considered morally blameworthy when they choose not to adopt recommended treatment. Similarly, both fatness and deafness are routinely recognized as medical conditions but seldom as the counter-hegemonic identities of Fat and Deaf, especially within the contexts of law and medicine. These are only a few of the comparisons we should examine if our goal is to better understand the current criteria and narratives necessary for qualifying for civil rights protection. Doing so enables us to better understand both Fat and Deaf identities as well as the political commitments and values that underpin the representations of both as mutable, curable conditions.

Beginning with current debates between those who believe cochlear implants can and should be used to cure deafness and those who believe these implants are pieces of genocidal quackery, a careful analysis of fatness and deafness reveals similar strategies for eliminating both physiological traits despite the fact that medical interventions produce neither thin nor hearing people. While cochlear implants are touted as cures for deafness, members of Deaf culture fight to be recognized as a legitimate social group, a group that should not be forced to assimilate into a mainstream hearing culture. As Bonnie Poitras Tucker explains in "Deaf Culture, Cochlear Implants, and Elective Disability," Deaf culture is based on several practices believed to create cultural autonomy:

> The theory of Deaf culture is primarily premised on a shared language—American Sign Language (ASL). Individuals who communicate via ASL clearly *do* speak a different language. . . . [I]n addition, some members of the Deaf cultural community claim to be part of a separate culture as a result of attending segregated . . . schools for Deaf children, or as a result of their participation in Deaf clubs or wholly Deaf environments in which they socialize or work. (1998, 6–7)

Additionally, most individuals who identify as members of Deaf culture take great pride in their deafness (7). Those inside and outside Deaf culture, who both acknowledge and wish to support this culture and pride, refuse to view Deaf people as flawed individuals who should be "cured."

Despite protestations, support for mandatory cochlear implants and demands for responsible self-correction are intensifying. Is it the responsibility of the Deaf to assimilate? First we must elaborate on what assimilation entails when achieved via cochlear technology. Proponents of cochlear implants, such as Tucker, describe the technology as "a surgically implanted device that is capable of restoring hearing and speech understanding to many individuals who are severely or profoundly deaf" (1998, 6). Supporters of cochlear implants often view the surgical insertions of the devices as Deaf culture's responsibility to larger society, especially when deafness is discovered in children.

Furthermore, cochlear implant advocates consider Deaf individuals as impaired *individuals,* failing to consider Deaf as a legitimate cultural group identity. From this perspective, the presence of a "cure," and Deaf people's refusal of it, amounts to choosing disability, which of course angers both advocates of cochlear technology and people who worry about frivolous disability claims for supposedly volitional conditions. While I'm not making an argument for Fat culture, I want to suggest, as Rosemarie Garland-Thomson has, that "the shared experience of stigmatization creates commonality" (1997, 15). Similarly, Harlan Lane, Robert Hoffmeister, and Ben Bahan maintain that because many Deaf people grow up in hearing homes, physically and culturally distanced from one another, common

experiences, such as time spent in schools for the Deaf, are more generative of the "DEAF-WORLD" than "any single locale" (1996, 124–25). Hence,
the experiences and status of being Fat and being Deaf are what bind individuals in these groups together, and the groups Fat and Deaf are then
bound together by their struggles against mainstream culture's treatment
of people thought to have abnormal embodiments.

Many opponents of cochlear implants are concerned about both the
possible coercive power involved with this technology and its questionable success rate. Some members of the Deaf culture might persuasively
argue that there is no "choice" of disability because cochlear implants simply do not create hearing people. For example, Robert A. Crouch, who is a
staunch opponent of cochlear implants, believes there are serious limitations to cochlear technology. Crouch asserts that we must reconsider the
"miracle" of technology, especially given the limited results the technology often produces: "in a . . . study that measured the speech intelligibility
of prelingually deaf children who had used their cochlear implants for
three and a half years of more, only approximately 40 percent of the words
spoken by these children were understood by a panel of three persons"
(1997).

Likewise, bariatric surgeries, which often reduce stomach capacity to
around two tablespoons and bypass sections of bowel, are encouraged
despite questionable outcomes.[7] The National Association to Advance Fat
Acceptance (NAAFA) maintains a staunch position against such surgeries: "the National Association to Advance Fat Acceptance condemns gas-
trointestinal surgeries for weight loss under any circumstances" ("NAAFA
Policy: Weight Loss Surgery" 2002). NAAFA opposes these surgeries due
to a lack of follow-up studies, the performance of new surgeries without
adequate testing, and a host of surgical complications, including death.
Most similar to cochlear implants, however, is the fact that weight loss
surgeries simply do not produce thin people. NAAFA states, "Currently,
the most frequently performed procedure, vertical banded gastroplasty,
results in weight loss of about 20% within 18–24 months. Because weight
regain is common within two to five years after operation, doctors plan
'staged surgery.'" In spite of the limited success and serious complications
accompanying weight loss surgery, the IRS offered tax deductions for
those who pay for their own bariatric surgeries ("Taxpayer's Guide" 2000).
In sum, both fatness and deafness are represented as mutable and ideally
curable despite the mixed outcomes of medical technologies designed for
carrying out the task.

When Fat and Deaf people are not recognized as disabled, fatness and
deafness are depoliticized. For Fat people, who are often already isolated

from both mainstream culture and other disabled people, nonrecognition further breaks down group bonds, isolates us as discrete individuals, and severely hinders the forming of politically conscious Fat politics. Linton states, "The material that binds us [disabled people] is the art of finding one another, of identifying and naming disability in a world reluctant to discuss it" (1998, 5). This "art" can be severely hindered by the isolation of disabled people into discrete individuals who, because of the diverse nature of their impairments, are thought to share no common experiences. The experiences of Fat and Deaf people reveal commonalities between seemingly disparate groups of people and can form the basis for new and perhaps previously untapped political alliances.

WEIGHT, FEMINISM, AND DISABILITY

Flipping through the pages of the morning paper or perusing magazines while standing in checkout lanes, women are constantly reminded that to be overweight—especially to be obese—is not only a medical emergency but also an affront to dominant aesthetic values of female embodiment, both of which constitute ripe ground for further discrimination of women. Hence, the social positioning of fat women demands careful and thoughtful analysis within the framework of disability studies. As legal scholar Sondra Solovay argues, young women and girls are much more likely to fall prey to the self-deprecation of "internalizing anti-fat discourses" (2000, 36). In short, already socially disadvantaged by the nature of female embodiment, fat women find themselves in a difficult position that requires an analysis of fatness as a central component in shaping their lives.

Given all the attention feminist scholarship has rightly given to issues of weight (particularly the fear of fatness), why are some feminist scholars still resistant to Fat as a group identity? Why is fatness depicted as an individual attribute rather than a significant point in constellations of identity? In her study of standpoint epistemology, *What Can She Know?* Lorraine Code maintains that fatness, hair color, and eye color are all individual attributes that do not produce their own unique social locations or group identities. Code writes:

> It is not necessary to consider how much Archimedes weighed when he made his famous discovery, nor is there any doubt that a thinner or fatter person could have reached the same conclusion. But in cultures in which sex differences figure prominently in virtually every model of human interaction, being male or female is far more important to the construction of subjectivity than are such attributes as size or hair color. (1991, 11–12)

Code makes two false assumptions in this statement. First, while I would agree there are instances where gender might very well be more important, to say that gender is always more important is to make a false and sweeping generalization. Perhaps Denise Riley best explains why such generalizations prove false when she writes, "there are always different densities of being sexed in operation" (1998, 6). As Riley reminds us, these "densities" are dynamic, which means that gendered constructions feature differently and incorporate various co-constructing elements at different contextual moments. Code assumes gendered constructions will trump others and that gendered constructions do not include body size.

Second, Code forgets that what she considers insignificant "attributes," such as size, co-construct gendered norms and subjectivities. As corporeal theorists and the host of studies about eating disorders and women's relationships to their bodies suggest, it is nigh impossible to cleave gender norms from corporeal norms. Code, however, indicates such attributes are often unimportant when examining gendered subjectivities. For Code, gender operates almost (if not completely) independent of attributes such as body size. The violence of cleaving femininity and fatness negates how often women's experiences of femininity are filtered through their bodies and vice versa. Furthermore, it is a profound instantiation of the mind/body split that feminism has so often struggled against.

For many women and/or feminist scholars, fat is particularly scary and threatening, often evoking contradictory desires and troubling realizations. Fat tests the boundaries between individual desires for certain embodiments and larger feminist goals of resisting corporeal ultimatums precisely because so many women and/or feminists struggle with their own physical identities.[8] Complexities surrounding fatness, women's bodies, and the possibilities of fatness as a transitory and fluid embodiment also work on another level. In addition to possibly negating the identity of women for whom fatness is not a transitory condition, the notion of fatness as fluid is dangerous and threatening because it serves as a reminder that our bodies are dynamic rather than fixed. Thus, the female body, already thought to be flawed, is at risk of being further pathologized by fatness. As Margrit Shildrick points out in Leaky Bodies and Boundaries, "the body is a fabrication that mimics material fixity" (1997, 13). Our bodies are forever in the process of undeclared construction, and once we dislodge fatness from biology and begin to think of who is categorized as fat as a social decision (in the same way categorizing who is disabled is a social decision), solid categories surface as fluid boundaries.

In my experience, even the most enlightened friends and colleagues tend to be fatphobic, partly because biologically based cultural narratives are so pervasive and because, in some sense, the boundaries of who is fat and who is not are recognized as contextual. Any woman who has walked down a street to hear the word (and insult in this case) *fat* hurled from a passing car understands that no particular female embodiment provides safe haven from such comments. Part of the power of "fat," when used as an insult, is lodged in the fact that no standard definition exists. There are, of course, the weight charts referred to in medical accounts, but, cultur-ally, "fat" can mark any woman, referencing body size in general, a jiggle of a thigh, or the slight swell of a tummy. As Solovay reminds us, negative associations with fatness are far-ranging and difficult to pin down to any one body type: "all gradations of fat, even slight to moderate, have been regarded by government agencies and popular culture as mutable, voli-tional, and dangerous conditions that are synonymous with physical and moral shortcomings" (2000, 151). Thus, the lack of firm cultural defini-tions of fatness exposes all women to the danger of discrimination.

Fatness and disability also remind us that bodies are subjected to changing sociocultural contexts as well as physiological changes. While always casting Fat as a transitory identity is problematic, the physical con-ditions of both fatness and disability can be usefully understood as fluid. Recognizing this fluidity moves away from ideas of inherently flawed individuals and toward accounts of dynamically situated bodies and iden-tities. Many women have times in their lives when they gain weight and/ or become disabled. Regardless of whether either is permanent or tempo-rary, the existence of these possibilities removes bodies from solid ground and acknowledges once again that bodies are unstable. As Susan Bordo notes in *Unbearable Weight,* femininity is both empowering and disem-powering, an argument clearly played out in the fear of fatness and/or dis-ability (1993). The approximation of ideal femininity can offer social capi-tal to women, albeit social capital that is, as Bordo points out, ultimately disempowering. The prospect of having one's body read as a text about slovenly behavior, inherent flaws, and abnormality—all narratives associ-ated with fat people and disabled people in general—robs many women of what they think of as a significant source of power. With *normal* and *ideal* always defined by what is pathologized and classed as abnormal, the pos-sibility of the slippage between these categories and the contingent power involved can prove divisive to women as a social group.

REVOLUTIONARY FATNESS

In *Fat? So! Because You Don't Have to Apologize for Your Size,* Fat activ-ist Marilyn Wann succinctly describes the position in which feminist scholars dedicated to fully understanding the lives of all women find themselves: "once you become aware of the system, it's your choice, your responsibility, to choose how you will relate to it" (1998, 33). Wann's statement provides direction for Fat women and disabled people, as well as political theorists who attempt to illuminate marginalized identities. The "system" Wann speaks about works to silence Fat women and their status as disabled, but scholarship that initiates inquiries from the lives of Fat women—not as biologically categorized by weight and impairments but as socially situated—can break this silence in profound ways.

I am the Fat woman pointed out during academic conferences. I am the person who is disabled by seats in auditoriums that don't accommodate my body. I am the woman Susan Powter swears can and should be thin, and I am the tragic woman over whom Richard Simmons sheds tears. I am also the Fat woman whose identity and narration of fat embodiment resists fatness's cultural moorings in sadness and despair but whose story is seldom represented. Unfortunately, representations of disabled people most often focus on pain and suffering: "Particularly noteworthy for its absence is the voice that speaks not of shame, pain, and loss but of life, delight, struggle, and purposeful action" (Linton 1998, 113). Representations of women, and especially representations of women characterized as fat and/or disabled by popular media, often focus on pain and suffering rather than the possibilities of such embodiments. One such possibility rests in demystifying fatness and disability, making it possible for fat women; disabled men and women; non-fat, nondisabled men and women; and those living at multiple conjunctions of these identities to work together around shared goals rather than pitting themselves against one another in struggles for power. While Fat and Deaf people may seem so disparate that political alliances would be strained, common experiences and shared goals of social justice have the potential to bind these diverse groups to one another in meaningful ways.

Nomy Lamm, in her essay "It's a Big Fat Revolution," shares her frustration with what she sees as a refusal to deal with fatness and fat oppression as a political issue: "maybe we should be demystifying fat and dealing with fat politics as a whole. And I don't mean maybe, I mean it's a necessity" (1995, 91). Lamm's urgency stems from what she sees as a general lack of scholarship that deals with fatness and women in a productive way. Rather than sidebarring discussions of fatness within scholarship, the lives of Fat women should be catalysts for analyses of fatphobia and oppression. When scholars initiate thinking from the lives of Fat women, it becomes apparent that body size does matter. Fat women's social location affords them a view of fatphobia and weightism from which feminist scholars can learn a great deal. Subjected to medicalization and stigmatization, fat women's bodies must also be represented as sites of power, entitlement, and freedom rather than of fear, misunderstanding, and pity. Situating fatness and Fat women within the context of disability studies and feminist standpoint epistemology can proffer resistant accounts of marginalized embodiments and identities.

NOTES

1. Since I first published this essay in the *NWSA Journal* special issue on feminist disability studies (2002), precious little has changed regarding the politics of weight discrimination. Court cases about fatness and disability other than those discussed here have produced an assortment of rulings, but the social treatment of fat people remains problematically static. Although "morbid obesity" is now generally covered under ADA legislation because "extreme" fatness is thought almost always to affect one or more major life activities, all fat people suffer from inadequate protection from rampant social discrimination, with slightly to moderately fat people seldom finding suitable protection under ADA legislation. As the war on obesity has intensified, so have questions of how we might understand weight as a social issue and Fat people as a social group. Toward the goal of reimagining weight and Fat people, I still believe that disability studies and disability legislation offer the best route to a richer understanding of fatness and a prompt remedy to discrimination.

2. The concept of "outing" oneself as a Fat woman is discussed by both Marilyn Wann (1998) and Eve Kosofsky Sedgwick (1990). Both authors understand that although fatness is very visible, it is often ignored, both by fat people themselves and by thin people, because it can be difficult to discuss. Additionally, the concept of "coming out" as a Fat woman resists the idea that "I am just like everyone else" or desire to be so by directly confronting people with my weight and my difference and deviance from the standard body.

3. Here I am greatly indebted to Dr. Jon Robison. During the summer of 1998 I took a summer class with Jon, which turned out to be germinal to my work. Jon's refusal to settle for the easy explanations of obesity and his desire to offer socially just accounts of fatness that took into account both medical and cultural narratives were both inspiring and informational. It was during Jon's class that I first heard about the misquotation of this particular statistic.

4. For a comprehensive review of scientific studies, see Glen Gaesser's *Big Fat Lies* (1996).

5. At times, I use *fat* and *fatness*, usually when speaking about the medicalized understandings of these terms. Finally, I use *obesity* and *obese*, terms that are rightfully controversial, when speaking within the framework of medicine where those are the terms of choice.

6. The trend of characterizing the "obese" as psychologically damaged is rampant throughout texts encouraging bariatric surgeries. Two examples are Norman B. Ackerman's *Fat No More* (1999) and Michelle Boasten's *Weight Loss Surgery* (2001).

7. In addition to the Ackerman and Boasten texts mentioned in the previous note, Carnie Wilson (1998) offers a particularly honest account of the process involved in such surgeries. Although Wilson's account is an endorsement of such procedures, it presents bariatric surgeries as both painful and problematic procedures. The NAAFA website also contains detailed descriptions of various procedures housed under the general heading of bariatric surgeries.

8. I also struggle with ambiguous desires where my embodiment is concerned. Some days I feel wonderful, and other days I wonder why I don't just go on a diet. Acknowledging and working through these disparate feelings and the contradictions between my personal feelings and my political commitments is an integral part of my scholarship and my lived experience as a Fat woman. Duncan Woodhead, a colleague from the history department at Michigan State University, tells me I am in "full possession of my fatness." For me, being in "full possession of my fatness" means dealing with these contradictory feelings and political commitments. Thus, my intent is not to chastise women who find fatness problematic but rather to suggest that these are issues that must be recognized and engaged.

REFERENCES

"A Taxpayer's Guide on IRS Policy to Deduct Weight Control Treatment." 2000. American Obesity Association Home Page. www.obesity.org/taxguide. (URL no longer active.)

Ackerman, Norman B. 1999. *Fat No More: The Answer for the Dangerously Overweight*. New York: Prometheus.

Albrecht, Robert J., and Walter J. Pories. 1999. "Surgical Intervention for the Severely Obese." *Balliere's Clinical Endocrinology and Metabolism* 13 (1): 149–72.

Americans with Disabilities Act. 1990. U.S. Public Law 101–336. 101st Cong., 2nd sess., 26 July.

Boasten, Michelle. 2001. *Weight Loss Surgery: Understanding and Overcoming Morbid Obesity*. Akron, Ohio: FBE Service Network and Network Publishing.

Bordo, Susan. 1993. *Unbearable Weight: Feminism, Western Culture, and the Body*. Berkeley: University of California Press.

Code, Lorraine. 1991. *What Can She Know? Feminist Theory and the Construction of Knowledge*. New York: Cornell University Press.

Crouch, Robert A. 1997. "Letting the Deaf Be Deaf: Reconsidering the Use of Cochlear Implants in Prelingually Deaf Children." *Hastings Center Report* 27 (14): 21.

Fox, Katherine M., Susan L. Taylor, and Judy E. Jones. 2000. "Understanding the Bariatric Surgical Patient: A Demographic, Lifestyle and Psychological Profile." *Obesity Surgery* 10: 477–81.

Gaesser, Glenn A. 1996. *Big Fat Lies: The Truth about Your Weight and Your Health*. New York: Fawcett Columbine.

Garland-Thomson, Rosemarie. 1997. *Extraordinary Bodies: Figuring Physical Disability in American Culture and Literature*. New York: Columbia University Press.

Kassirer, David, and Marcia Angell. 1998. "Losing Weight: An Ill-fated New Year's Resolution." *New England Journal of Medicine* 338 (1): 52–54.

"King Size Homer." 1995. *The Simpsons*. www.thesimpsons.com/recaps/season7.

Lamm, Nomy. 1995. "It's a Big Fat Revolution." In *Listen Up: Voices from the Next Generation*, edited by Barbara Findlen, 85–94. Seattle: Seal Press.

Lane, Harlan, Robert Hoffmeister, and Ben Bahan. 1996. *A Journey into the Deaf-World*. San Diego, Calif.: Dawnsign Press.

Linton, Simi. 1998. *Claiming Disability: Knowledge and Identity*. New York: New York University Press.

McGinnis, J. Michael, and William H. Foege. 1993. "Actual Causes of Death in the United States." 1993. *Journal of the American Medical Association* 270 (18): 2208.

"Myths and Facts about the Americans with Disabilities Act." 1990. U.S. Department of Justice home page. http://www.ada.gov/archive/mythfact.htm.

"NAAFA Policy: Weight Loss Surgery." 2002. National Association to Advance Fat Acceptance Online. http://www.naafaonline.com/dev2/about/Policies/WEIGHT LOSSSURGERY.pdf.

Riley, Denise. 1998. *Am I That Name? Feminism and the Category of "Women" in History*. Minneapolis: University of Minnesota Press.

Sedgwick, Eve Kosofsky. 1990. *Epistemology of the Closet*. Berkeley: University of California Press.

Shildrick, Margrit. 1997. *Leaky Bodies and Boundaries: Feminism, Postmodernism, and (Bio)ethics*. New York: Routledge.

Solovay, Sondra. 2000. *Tipping the Scales of Justice: Fighting Weight-Based Discrimination*. Amherst, N.Y.: Prometheus Books.

Tucker, Bonnie Poitras. 1998. "Deaf Culture, Cochlear Implants, and Elective Disability." *Hastings Center Report* 28 (4): 6–14.

Wann, Marilyn. 1998. *Fat? So! Because You Don't Have to Apologize for Your Size*. Berkeley, Calif.: Ten Speed Press.

Wendell, Susan. 1996. *The Rejected Body: Feminist Philosophical Reflections on Disability*. New York: Routledge.

Wilson, Carnie, with Mick Kleber. 1998. *Gut Feelings: From Fear and Despair to Health and Hope*. Carlsbad, Calif.: Hay House.

Twelve

CHRONIC ILLNESS AND EDUCATIONAL EQUITY

The Politics of Visibility

KAREN ELIZABETH JUNG

Living with the fundamental conditions of an ill body does not merely involve the experience of contingency, lack, and limitation in activity and role performance; it also inaugurates consignment to an identity category that signifies disadvantage and oppression (Garland-Thomson 1998): those who are *disabled*. While chronic illnesses, such as rheumatoid arthritis and encephalomyelitis, do not fit the more taken-for-granted understanding of disability—usually because they are less visible or *invisible*—they still comply with the criteria set forth by the United Nations' definition of *disability*, because they restrict the ability of a person to perform the activities of daily living in ways that result in economic and social disadvantages. According to the United Nations' definition, disability is grounded in the inability to perform personal, social, or occupational activities, and it can result from genetic defects, accidents, or the sequelae of chronic illness (Albrecht 1992; Wendell 1996; Williams 1998). It bears remembering that there is no precise or universally accepted definition of *disability*: defining *disability* is a practice of power wherein the category can be contracted or expanded in accordance with the vested interests of the definer (Albrecht 1992; Wendell 1996).

In this essay I take up the experiences of women who are disabled by chronic illness and are pursuing postsecondary education. I use an institutional ethnographic approach (D. Smith 1987, 1999) to integrate two areas of study: the embodied experience of illness and the systemic inequities that can be produced by both disability and illness. Institutional ethnography, like other forms of ethnography, relies on interviews, documents, and observation-participation as data (Campbell 1998; D. Smith 1987). Unlike most other ethnographic approaches, however, institutional ethnography uses this data to look beyond the actualities of individual women's lives to the outside forces that structure and regulate local and particular experience. By starting with chronically ill women's own accounts of their experiences in the academy, this analysis sheds light on how a university's disability policy is implemented in the concrete circumstances of their everyday lives. It is important to note that I do not use these accounts in a way that implies any transparent or unmediated relationship to truth. Experience bears traces of the social relations that determine the conditions and purposes of our actions. Thus, a critical consideration of the experience of chronic illness provides an entry point into the social relations that organize it.

This ability to close the gap between the subjective experience of illness and the unequal relations of power in which chronically ill women are embedded is of particular importance for feminist disability studies. Feminist disability studies scholars have long criticized more mainstream disability studies scholarship that neutralizes the subjective experience of pain and struggle and that obscures the material and historical effects of differences of gender, ability, and impairment (Morris 1992; Garland-Thomson 1998; Wendell 1996). These omissions in disability studies are typically grounded in the pragmatic attempt to "identify and address issues that can be changed through collective action" (Oliver 1996, 38). However, the insistence that there is no necessary causal relationship between impairment and disability, which reflects the need to *break the link* between a person's body and a person's social situation, makes it difficult to incorporate and understand the personal experience of pain and impairment (Morris 1992; Oliver 1996). Feminist disability studies scholars argue for analyses of disability that take into account the materiality of the disabled or chronically ill body and that incorporate analyses of other axes of difference, such as gender, sexuality, age, level of ability, type of disability, race, and ethnicity (Morris 1992; Garland-Thomson 1998; Wendell 1996, 1998).

In this analysis I attempt to unsettle the understanding of disability as a fixed or homogeneous category by exploring the implications of chronic illness for women who are pursuing postsecondary education. I argue that while chronically ill women depend crucially on some form of academic accommodation to remain engaged in their studies, the requirement that they make themselves visible or *known* as disabled within institutional contexts subjects them to a range of normative, prognostic, diagnostic, and other judgments and assessments that may disorganize and disrupt their future student and career opportunities.

The problem of being chronically ill while pursuing a postsecondary education is crucial for women. Often characterized by pain, fatigue, inflammation, limitation in mobility, and inability to perform the activities of daily living, chronic illnesses such as rheumatoid arthritis (RA) and myalgic encephalomyelitis (ME) affect mainly women and are not always readily visible to and identifiable by others as disabilities (Wendell 1996). Far from being medical conditions that affect only a small proportion of the population, these kinds of chronic disease conditions are typical of twentieth-century industrial society and are sufficiently prevalent to be described by writers in the field of medical sociology as the "new morbidity" (Russell 1989; Williams 1998; Zola 1994).

Education, which provides the means to well-paid, flexible, and more professional employment, has been identified as an especially important social determinant of health (Lippman 1998) and as a crucial component in resisting the accumulation of disadvantage and downward mobility that is common to the onset and progression of chronic, "incurable" illness (Esdaile 1989; Lock 1998). Given that women are particularly vulnerable to the more negative economic consequences of disability (Roeher Institute 1995), it is essential that policies providing accessibility and accommodation foster the inclusion, participation, and success of women with visible and invisible disabilities in postsecondary education.

Finally, postsecondary education provides the means through which women with disabilities are eventually able to participate in the production of a body of knowledge that reflects their own experiences, interests, and ways of knowing. Feminist disability scholars note that there are few genuine attempts to include disability and that most feminist analyses of the intersections of identity categories are confined to the familiar recitation of gender, race, and class (Meekosha 1998; Morris 1992; Wendell 1996, 1998). Even within the ranks of those who favor a more democratic curriculum that would accurately represent the perspectives and experiences of different, often excluded, groups, some debate whether disability is sufficiently central to the liberal arts or social sciences to be integrated into the existing curriculum (Linton 1998; Garland-Thomson 1998). In part, "the persistent assumption that disability is a self-evident condition of bodily inadequacy and private misfortune whose politics concern only a limited minority" inhibits scholarly engagement with issues relating to illness and disability (Garland-Thomson 1998, 282).

Even feminist research has been slow to recognize disabled women's issues and failed to identify that the same logic ranking people according to ability is also present in discussions about gender (Linton 1998; Meekosha 1998; Garland-Thomson 1998). Feminist disability scholars note it is disappointing that there is little, if any, engagement with disability as an axis of difference that is also related to the sexed body (Asch and Fine 1998; Linton 1998; Garland-Thomson 1998; Wendell 1996). This essay represents a small step toward remedying the infrequent engagement of both sociology and women's studies with illness and disability as problems of discrimination and oppression.

BIOMEDICAL AND SOCIAL APPROACHES TO DISABILITY

Disability rights activists have argued, since at least the 1960s, that the biomedical model (which works in the interests of the medical system, health care professionals, social welfare workers, charitable fund-raising organizations, etc.) is a limited way of understanding and managing disability. The biomedical model, they argue, has become intertwined with and part of the discrimination and oppression experienced by disabled individuals (Lane 1998; Linton 1998; Lupton 1997; Oliver 1992). In the introduction to *The Disability Studies Reader,* for example, Lennard Davis notes, "People with disabilities have been isolated, incarcerated, observed, written about, operated on, instructed, implanted, regulated, treated, institutionalized, and controlled to a degree probably unequal to that experienced by any other minority group" (1998, 1). These interventions and practices are rationalized by the biomedical approach to disability.

In contrast to the medical model, people with disabilities have argued for a social model of disability, a model shifting the obligation for change from the body and activities of the person with a disability to the built environment and social arrangements that are organized around norms of *able-bodiedness* (Barnes 1998; Davis 1998; Oliver 1996; Shakespeare 1998). If the organization of the social actually generates the barriers and problems associated with disability, then the negative economic, social, and personal consequences following from disability are neither natural nor inevitable. From the perspective of the social model, exclusion and marginalization are not consequences of an individual's impairment. Rather, they are the consequences of social discrimination (Davis 1998; Morris 1992; Oliver 1992, 1996). Likewise, *disability* does not refer to bodily impairments and limitations; it is the naming of the experience of oppression (Linton 1998). Rather than focus on "fixing" people with disabilities, disability rights activists and feminist disability studies scholars direct attention to the disabling effects of a normalizing society.

THE SOCIAL ORGANIZATION OF
KNOWLEDGE AND INSTITUTIONAL ETHNOGRAPHY

In keeping with the spirit of the disability studies commitment, I use an institutional ethnographic approach to explore the broader social relations in which women disabled by chronic illness are embedded. Although Dorothy Smith has not directly addressed the problem of disability in her own work, her theoretical approach to the social organization of knowledge shares similar origins and insights with the emerging discipline of feminist disability studies (1987, 1990a, 1990b, 1999). For example, Smith's approach originates in the feminist movement's discovery that, as women, they had been consciously and deliberately excluded from participating in the formation of the intellectual, cultural, and political worlds in which they were living (1987). Feminist disability studies, likewise, is both an area of political activity and an academic field of inquiry: contesting the oppression and exclusion of disabled people from the mainstream of social life and working to assemble a body of knowledge that reflects their own experiences and interests (Davis 1998; Linton 1998; Morris 1992). Both feminism and the disability rights movement are part of broad cultural struggles that emerged in the 1960s and provoked new sites of conflict in academia around issues of difference—such as gender, race, sexuality, and class. Similarly, feminist and disability studies scholars agree that objectivist and scientific approaches to knowledge production suppress and silence those who are marginalized or excluded. These silences in the academy, they argue, are integral to the reproduction of unequal relations of power in the social world.

Smith's distinctive theoretical approach provides a unique advantage: an ontology of the social as "a concerting of activities that actually happens . . . in time and in actual local sites of people's bodily existence" (D. Smith 1999, 97). This directs the researcher's attention not only to the activities and routines of ordinary individuals in their everyday settings, but also to the way their activities are coordinated with, oriented to, and co-determined by the activities of others. Power, according to George Smith, is a product of the coordination of ordinary everyday activity with broader generalized and generalizing social relations. Texts are constituents of these social relations, and they play an important role in conceptually coordinating and temporarily concerting general forms of social action (1995). Their materiality and reproducibility also offer analysts entry into the social relations they organize (Campbell 1998; D. Smith 1999). Examples of texts that are salient in this study include the university's disability policy and dominant cultural understandings of disability.

The official university policy is situated within a framework of human rights legislation, and it is designed to provide *otherwise qualified* disabled students with reasonable opportunities to access resources and participate as members of the university community. Typically, a disability is institutionally recognizable only if it results in problems of access, requires modifications in regular teaching and evaluation practices, and is medically verifiable.[1] This policy, like other kinds of text-mediated relations, accomplishes a particular coordination of knowledge and action that introduces a *ruling* structure into the local setting of the academy and into the concrete circumstances of chronically ill women's lives.

Just as formal institutional texts can be used to explicate the socially organized activities that produced them, personal accounts also reveal how individual choices and courses of action become bound up in organizational practices and wider social relations. Recognizing that "local events are often controlled by forces beyond the purview of those acting at that site" (Linton 1998, 35), institutional ethnography provides a way to start with everyday experience in order to show "how power is exercised, in what official or unofficial activities, by whom and for what purposes" (Campbell 1998, 96). It is important to note that in institutional ethnography, experience is not the object of the research; experience, in and of itself, is not treated as knowledge or as truth. Experience provides a place to begin the inquiry. Beginning with the premise that individuals contribute to the production of the social relations in which they live, an exploration of people's everyday worlds can show what they say and do, how they coordinate and plan their activities, and actually "contribute to and are articulated with the relations that overpower their lives" (D. Smith 1990a, 204). In my analysis of the implications of university disability policies for chronically ill women, I rely on data gathered from interviews, observation, and documents, such as the university's disability policy, to explicate some of the broader societal processes in which the experiences of chronically ill women are embedded.

DISABILITY, GENDER, AND POSTSECONDARY EDUCATION

The disability rights movement continues to stress the need for a social, rather than biomedical, model of disability as the basis for antidiscrimination policies within the legal, educational, health care, economic, and other social systems in North America. Current human rights legislation affords all individuals the same protection from discrimination and provides equitable access for people with disabilities in all the systems and core services in which other members of society are entitled to participate. In principle, people with disabilities should have equal access to and be able to participate fully in postsecondary educational opportunities.

In North America the social approach to disability has taken the form of a disabilities apparatus organized around the concepts of accessibility and accommodation. In postsecondary education, *accessibility* refers to the institution's legal obligation to create genuine opportunities for people with disabilities to participate in all aspects of university life. The duty to *accommodate,* as one aspect of the duty not to discriminate, requires the institution to take an active part in modifying those practices, facilities, or services that prevent the inclusion and participation of otherwise qualified students who are disabled.

Improving accessibility includes making changes in the built environment and providing specialized adaptive equipment to disabled students. Accommodation usually involves procedural changes and modifications in teaching and academic evaluation practices. For chronically ill students, it is this latter category that is of greatest import. Exactly what constitutes an accommodation is a matter of law: courts have the ultimate authority to define the meaning of the term and the extent of the institution's responsibility to provide it.

Within a university, disability policies are part of the discursively elaborated process wherein human rights legislation impacts people's everyday lives to ensure that people with disabilities are not discriminated against. While disability policy is the textual means through which the university recognizes its *moral and legal duty* to provide accommodation, it is also designed to protect the university from unreasonable expense or "undue hardship" and from lowering or otherwise compromising academic standards. In other words, the formal rules and procedures of disability policy—which instruct students to identify themselves as disabled, supply appropriate medical documentation, and negotiate accommodations with individual instructors—are intended to reconcile the interests of the law; of disabled students, faculty, and staff; and of the academy.

It is also important to note the context within which accessibility and accommodation are delivered in postsecondary education. Since the economic crisis of the 1980s there has been a reduction in government revenues along with a reordering of social and economic priorities in the United States and Canada (Bellamy and Guppy 1991). In the context of new economic realities restricting resources and budgets for postsecondary education, there are also perceived limits to the objectives of openness and accessibility. Critics of the more liberal educational system have questioned the usefulness and necessity of a policy of openness and accessibility when, at the same time the cost of maintaining the current system continues to rise, benefits to its graduates can be seen to decline (Bellamy and Guppy 1991; Fortin 1987). Increasingly fierce competition among students for limited funding and enrollment restrictions in particular courses of study give weight to the argument that chronically ill or disabled students unnecessarily drain or waste scarce educational resources. This is especially problematic where chronically ill women's full participation in the labor force or ability to complete a program of study is perceived to be questionable.

In the face of shrinking resources and the restructuring of education along the lines of the market system, productivity and accountability have more weight than openness and accessibility. In the current economic reality, the legal obligation to promote equitable access is seen as inherently incompatible with maintaining a quality of education that emphasizes such ideals as excellence, competition, and selection (Fortin 1987). Organized in relation to the merit principle, these ideals are achieved through the application of increasingly stringent academic entrance criteria, higher standards of evaluation, and the imposition of quotas that, for the most part, fail to recognize any concomitant responsibilities to disadvantaged people (Hanen 1991). Nonetheless, universities are required to demonstrate compliance with the relevant human rights legislation.

As universities are required to formulate and implement policies that foster the inclusion of previously excluded groups, and as instructors are required to modify practices of teaching and evaluation, there is a concomitant rise in resistance to the changes that such initiatives entail (Breslauer 1991; Tancred 1991). Although the abstract criteria of social justice may be embraced, there are contradictions and difficulties that arise wherever such ideals must be implemented as a coherent set of tasks within the concrete circumstances of people's lives. Accessibility and inclusiveness also disrupt the existing institutional order of the university, which is an intrinsic part of those generalized and generalizing social relations that continue to disadvantage and exclude people on the basis of class, gender, race, ethnicity, sexuality, and ability. The resistance to including previously excluded groups is connected to what feminist and antiracist critiques call the *backlash* discourse that seeks to protect the privileged, usually male and white, academic status quo.

There are varieties of ways in which this backlash discourse or resistance to inclusiveness and diversity can be framed. For example, the changes and initiatives entailed by policies providing academic accommodation can be seen as the encroachment of political and administrative concerns into a domain usually reserved for academics and, thus, as a threat to a faculty's autonomy and control over curricular content and evaluative methods in its various disciplines (Blackburn 1991). Epithets such as *politically correct* are often used to disparage the active implementation of particular initiatives, and arguments about the problem of censorship and the freedom to teach as one sees fit may be used to resist legislated or juridically imposed remedies (D. Smith 1999). Questions about standards in canons of scholarship may be raised, reflecting the assumption that procedural changes required to accommodate disabled students may inadvertently erode and undermine the quality of education (Blackburn 1991; Hanen 1991; Tancred 1991).

As with other affirmative remedies seeking to correct and compensate for past failures, disability policies providing accessible and accommodating education usually also succeed in calling attention to and supporting group differentiation (Fraser 1997). That is, they mark a particular disadvantaged group "as inherently deficient and insatiable," as "recipients of special treatment and undeserved largesse" (25). While policies and procedures that provide services, assistance, and accommodation for people with disabilities are aimed at correcting inequitable outcomes of social arrangements, the process of accommodation—which involves providing special exceptions to the ordinary rules—also contributes to the ableism that singles out disabled people as targets of resentment. The framing of academic accommodation as an unfair advantage that discriminates against the student majority presents chronically ill students with a dilemma: making use of disability policies means being dependent on practices deemed to be inherently incompatible with "fair play" and academic excellence.

Thus, for women who are chronically ill and are pursuing an education, material disadvantage will be experienced in combination with social stigma based on the perception that disabled students are inherently different from "ordinary" students, pose an unnecessary burden on scarce educational resources, and are needy and flawed individuals. It is within this climate that the measures adopted by universities across North America to ensure the fair and consistent treatment of people with disabilities must be understood.

EVERYDAY EXPERIENCE AND CHRONIC ILLNESS

While it is not my intention to scrutinize chronically ill women as a group or as deviations from the norm, but to explore those social relations that regulate and organize their experience as students, it is useful to briefly describe the background conditions of their lives and the varieties of their social situations. Of the six women I interviewed, three were graduate students, two had completed undergraduate degrees, and one was working her way toward her first degree; all attended the same university. Although other differences such as race, ethnicity, sexuality, and socioeconomic background are crucial in understanding the experiences of people with disabilities, I focus mainly on the problems presented by chronic illness.

My decision to focus on chronically ill women was prompted by the call in feminist disabilities studies for analyses that disrupt the homogeneity of the category of *disability* by including other axes of difference—that is, of the meaning of "invisible" disabilities within feminist analyses of disabilities (Morris 1992; Wendell 1996). All but one of the women I interviewed applied for university admission during or after the onset of illness. All but one returned as mature students (in their mid- to late twenties, thirties, and forties), times when most women expect to be independent and established. Two interview informants lived at home with parents, two lived with partners, and two lived alone. The women who lived at home did so out of necessity rather than choice, aware that autonomy and privacy had been forfeited in exchange for social and economic support. For the women living with partners, social isolation and poverty were similarly mitigated; however, a whole new dimension of negotiation of roles—especially gendered roles—and the actual work required to sustain a relationship were added to the work of being a student. The experience of living alone was characterized by frequent expressions of loneliness and worries about money.

For all the women interviewed, the onset and course of illness disrupted their participation in the paid labor force; none were engaged in regular, full-time, paid work. All the interviewees, however, performed modified work of some kind. Because alternate forms of labor-force participation often do not lead to financial self-sufficiency, the women in my study relied on supplemental or alternate sources of income—from disability pension benefits (set at the social minimum), student loans, spousal and parental support, scholarships based on academic achievement, and grants from vocational rehabilitation programs for expenses such as tuition, books, and equipment. For all of these women, the experience of chronic illness either occasioned their return to the university or influenced their chosen course of study.

Each woman provided multiple examples of the experience of requesting and obtaining accommodation. The formal institutional process requires students to identify themselves as "disabled" to the university's administrative apparatus and to supply appropriate medical documentation of the disability. These two steps constitute a process of application for the university's assistance and services. Where documentation is deemed acceptable, the disability services office provides the instructor with sufficient information, in accordance with rules designed to protect the student's confidentiality, to confirm the receipt of appropriate medical documentation. Finally, the student is required to individually negotiate and arrange the accommodation with the instructor.

In an informal process, students still identify as disabled, provide documentation of their disabilities, and negotiate the accommodation with the individual instructor. They do not use the services of the university's formal administrative apparatus, however, and they may not supply the same kind of authoritative medical documentation of disability. For example, some students provided notes from their doctors; others displayed those parts of their bodies that had become swollen, inflamed, or immobile. In this study, one of the informants had never submitted to either the formal or informal institutional process for receiving accommodation; another had only identified as disabled occasionally and informally, when assistance or accommodation was deemed absolutely necessary.

While each informant had her own particular understanding of the aims and uses of the disability policy and had experienced accommodation in different ways, all depended on some form of accommodation to remain engaged in their studies, and they all referenced the university's policies and procedures in ordinary talk about their university experiences. For these women, academic accommodation included extensions of time to complete assignments and exams, alternate media for assignments, attending full-time programs on a part-time basis, and taking leaves of absence from programs of study.

Despite their dependence on accommodation, all the women expressed discomfort with being identified as disabled in the institutional context. Indeed, even though they participated voluntarily in the interview process, all expressed fears and anxieties that they would be inadvertently identified in the research findings. Ironically, the same incidents that the research informants believed to be unique to themselves were shared by the other informants. This is an important point: chronically ill women express ambivalence about disclosing their disabilities and submitting to the scrutiny that disclosure entails. They know that being defined as disabled, and judged as properly eligible for accommodation in the institutional context, has ambiguous and contradictory consequences. Their shared conviction that the experiences and struggles of illness are unique to themselves as individuals illustrates their social isolation from others who are similarly disabled. It also demonstrates that chronic illness as a disability is largely invisible in the organizational context of the university.

THE SOCIAL RELATIONS OF ACCESSIBILITY AND ACCOMMODATION

When chronically ill students activate the university's disability policy, they activate the relevant human rights legislation in relation to themselves and their own bodily experience. A request for accommodation also enters the disabled student into a social relation where her need for some alteration in the instructional setting or process confronts the needs, views, and teaching practices of her instructors. The excerpts below suggest some of the features of this particular social relation:

> So first of all, I went to the grad adviser and appealed to her on the basis of my disability. What I said was, "I have a chronic illness; I'm older than most of the other students; I have a disability of pace, and I need you to recognize that and treat me equitably." And what I got back was a line about "well, we need to create a level playing field for all of the students." And I said to her, "When you live with a disability, there is no level playing field; most of the time we're not even on the field." And I said, "I don't want fairness; I want equity." And she didn't understand the difference. She kept falling back on "we have to treat everyone the same; we have to be fair to the other students as well."

> There are some teachers who are really fair, and then there are others that aren't. And they constantly use the rhetoric of having to do what is fair for the other students. You know, they keep saying that. And I would say, "Well, those other students don't have a disability, and those other students don't face this whole mess, you know." And they still come back to the same issue of fairness, you know. They just don't understand; the awareness isn't there.

> The problem of getting accommodation always seems to be weighed against the need to instill competitiveness and toughness in the students. And the nagging suspicion that accommodations somehow undermine the quality of education, like you're getting something for nothing.

In each of the above excerpts, the informants provide a glimpse of those social relations that organize the university's disability policy. The most striking feature of their responses is the recurrence of the notion of unfair advantage: the belief that accommodation may result in an unfair advantage for the disabled student; that accommodation may thwart efforts to maintain a "level playing field" for all students; and, finally, that accommodation may lower academic standards.

The preoccupation with avoiding unfair advantages and maintaining a level playing field—which was repeated in all of the interviews with students, faculty, and administrative staff—are part of the social relations of instruction where academic achievement is organized in terms of competitiveness and comparison among students. Here, demonstrating skill, speed, logic, calculation, mastery of a particular body of knowledge, and other competencies needs to be evaluated under the same conditions and at the same time in order to produce verifiable results that can be ranked hierarchically and used reliably to infer the level of student achievement in the course.

Meeting institutional standards and demonstrating individual merit are crucial in decision-making processes that pertain to allocating funds, awarding scholarships, and determining student eligibility for entrance into particular programs of study. Meeting standards is also fundamental to the credentialing of labor power. Because many students generally struggle financially, academically, and physically to complete their programs of study, procedural changes and exceptions to the ordinary rules for one group of students—especially those whose disabilities may not be visible or otherwise obvious—may call into question both the fairness of the accommodation and the legitimacy of the student's claim.

The disability services coordinator at the university where I conducted the study speaks about this explicitly:

> Any non-visible disability is more of a problem. That's true. And I guess somebody comes in and, well, you know, that person looks perfectly normal and a lot of people will be surprised. And the person comes in and says, "I have a disability, I can't put my paper in on time." And from the point of view of the professors—who are thinking, okay, they'd like to trust you, but they would like a bit more evidence or something like that—there's always the issue of fairness to the other students that comes into play. And unfortunately, people are there who are cheating, in terms of trying to play the system. But it's not a perfect world, so you will always have people who are trying to take advantage of the system.

In the excerpt above, the coordinator takes for granted that accommodation provides an advantage for the student and that it lowers the academic standard to which other students, without disabilities, are held.

THE PROBLEM OF THE BODY AS A CULTURAL TEXT

In addition to the notion of unfair advantage to which both the informants and the coordinator refer, their comments also show how less-obvious or invisible disabilities are more likely to activate assumptions that students may fraudulently claim disability in order to take advantage of the system and thus gain access to advantages that accommodation is believed to confer. This suspicion is structured into the social relations that govern and organize the process of application. When students apply for university services and privileges, they set in motion practices of assessment, evaluation, and judgment. These practices subject chronically ill women to normative judgments that assess the worthiness and legitimacy of their claim of disability.

The fact that students may cheat means instructors and administrators must assume what Don H. Zimmerman calls "an investigative stance" in which "being 'skeptical' is a way of displaying a hard-headed commitment to establishing the 'facts of the matter' (as against the [individual's] mere *claims*)" (1969, 331; emphasis in original). The coordinator understands that the process of inquiring further may reveal information that is counter to the student's own account of the situation. Fierce competition for grades and scarce funding increase the likelihood that students may attempt to gain an advantage over their peers. Claiming disability is one way students may be granted extended deadlines, allotted additional time to write an exam, permitted to use particular types of equipment, and so forth. This understanding justifies displaying the "active assumptions of the investigative stance" as evidence of "a recognizably adequate" process for ensuring the fairness of requested accommodations to other students and the conformity of accommodations to academic principles (331). Regardless of the veracity of the assumptions made by the instructor or the administrative office, the investigative stance always informs the daily, routine practice of deciding who is *really disabled* and thus eligible for accommodation and what kinds of accommodation should be provided.

The skeptical or investigative stance is particularly relevant for students who are disabled by chronic illness, because chronic health conditions fail to properly fit the institutional framing of disability. Unpredictable periods of exacerbation and remission and the experience of pain and fatigue—all characteristics of chronic diseases such as RA and ME—are difficult to gauge and measure objectively. Changing symptoms disrupt more prevalent understandings of disability as fixed or constant physical conditions. Even people with serious chronic illnesses that impose significant restrictions on their lives may appear *perfectly normal*. For example, when asked to talk about some of the more difficult aspects of their illnesses, the women in my study explained:

> I think the whole issue [is] around understanding the change of it, how it changes all the time. The volatility of symptoms makes it so different today than the next day. You know, when I hear

comments—"Well, do you really need those crutches? Because yesterday you weren't using any, so are you sure you need those?"—those kinds of things show to me a lack of understanding, in general, of the complexity of it, in terms of the lengths people with chronic illness must go to, to manage everyday.

I know I don't look like I need it, and in class I know that the professor really watched me, you know, to see if I could write, or how much I wrote, which made it really awkward for me.

Being constantly ill like this is very unpredictable. You know, you may start out all healthy and gangbusters, and then part way through you find your energy bottoming out . . . and then you're flat on your back sleeping ten or fifteen hours a day. Unless you look very closely, I look very healthy, and why would I need to get an extension, or why would I even need to use any of the services for disabled students?

In the above excerpts, the women reveal how others' reactions to their claims of disability are organized by how closely their bodies approximate the concept of normal. Dominant cultural understandings of disability are particularly important in organizing how legitimate instances of disability are recognized. These cultural understandings, in which the production of images plays a central role, do not arise spontaneously. Images and understandings of illness and disability, like culture in general, are socially organized.

Images of people with disabilities may be used by charitable organizations, health care professionals, and entertainment and news media to elicit contributions, entertain, inform, warn, inspire fear or caution, and so on. Because disabled or chronically ill people tend to lack the opportunities to produce their own images and understandings of disability, the images and forms of thought that dominate do not necessarily represent the whole range of experiences of people with disabilities (Morris 1992). Nonetheless, images and dominant cultural understandings regulate how we ordinarily recognize disability and how we distinguish between those cases that are legitimate and those that are fraudulent.

A visibly damaged or disordered body is more likely to be read as incontrovertible proof of disability than the body of a chronically ill person. In the absence of visible signs of impairment, chronically ill bodies are not as easily *read* as disabled: those who are chronically ill are required to identify themselves as disabled in each request for accommodation, and they must provide proof of their claim's genuineness.[2] Even when they supply appropriate medical documentation, chronically ill women find they must revalidate and re-explain their claim to faculty members in each and every course requiring accommodation.

Assessing the legitimacy of a disability claim is not unique to the academy. Suspicion is not a characteristic of a misguided or uninformed individual, but a built-in feature of the disability policy, and suspicion and skepticism are structured into the procedures used to guide the interpretation of human rights codes. Not all physical attributes and conditions upon which unfair treatment may be based are included in human rights legislation. Protection covers only those physical attributes or conditions that cannot be changed and that—with due accommodation—would not be relevant to the individual's overall functioning (Bickenbach 1994).

The assumption of what Jerome Bickenbach calls "voluntarism" holds that there can be no discrimination where the social response to the physical attribute or condition is not unwarranted, irrational, and unfair. In other words, "the moral and political foundation of social policy for people with disabilities" can be characterized as a matter of determining when the disadvantages a person with a disability experiences are socially produced handicaps and when they are "unavoidable concomitants of disability that fall outside the range of misfortunes to which society has an obligation to respond" (114).

Where an individual is seen to have control over the disability or where the disability is not seen to be immutable, the social obligation to satisfy those needs is diminished. Indeed, as the reasoning from this assumption follows, to satisfy the needs of those who are malingering, fraudulent, undeserving, or who have brought particular conditions upon themselves is to "dilute or pervert the benefits provided by anti-discrimination legislation" and to trivialize the human rights protections for those who are "truly disabled, but genuinely capable" (119).

The preoccupation with "capturing the true 'target population'—those whose conditions of dysfunctioning are biomedically verifiable and 'substantial' enough to disqualify the fraudulent and malingering"—always legitimates a skeptical stance in relation to the claims of chronically ill women (120). Ironically, once questions of dishonesty and fraud are resolved, other practices of assessing, evaluating, and judging are set in motion.

CHRONIC ILLNESS AND ADDITIONAL JUDGMENTS AND ASSESSMENTS

Other judgments accompanying disability policies include assessments of the disabled individual's "deservingness" of accommodation, valuations of the severity and implications of the visible symptoms of the disease, predictions of whether or not chronically ill women will be capable of productive or full employment in the future, and appraisals of their suitability for their chosen professions. Although these kinds of assessments and other judgments are not intended to be part of the provision of services and accommodation, they nonetheless construct the conditions of the student's subsequent progress through the educational system. And they are all set in motion when one identifies as disabled.

The process of application for accommodation is regulated within the context of the policy. Formal rules and processes must be followed. However, even when the request for accommodation proceeds in a less formal and more personal way, the applicant must still prove she is what the institution defines as disabled. The applicant can find herself allocated to a stereotyped group, such as *disabled*, "which suffers from the imposition of prejudice but which is inescapable to the very extent that application and access are worthwhile" (Schaffer and Lamb 1981, 107). While chronically ill women depend on some form of accommodation to remain enrolled and engaged in their studies, the process of requesting and obtaining accommodation makes them peculiarly visible in unanticipated ways. For example,

> I was in my third year and I had good grades, . . . and I was actually not asked but told that I had to go and see the acting dean of my department. . . . She proceeded to ask why I thought I would make a good [professional in my field]. And for fifteen minutes she grilled me. . . . And it was, "How do you think you're going to cope? Do you really think you can do this job?" And I really question whether or not anybody else got that kind of treatment.

> When I applied for grad school and I got to the interview stage, I had this distinct impression that he'd made the decision before I got in the door, that I would get in, because I just felt so comfortable, and I basically sat there and talked about my life. . . . Anyway, he revealed at one point—much later—that he had wondered whether or not I was physically up to being a graduate student and had some serious doubts about my ability to complete the program because of that.

The above comments reveal the vulnerability of chronically ill women in practices of scrutiny, evaluation, and judgment that go beyond the original determination of disability. In the first instance, the woman's disability is interpreted as a contraindication to her future professional goals. In the second, the interviewee discusses how her graduate supervisor's prognosis of her health almost foreclosed her educational opportunities. While it is generally accepted that medical practitioners should be accorded greater authority in recognizing and describing the condition and limitations of the student's body, faculty members may believe that they, too, have diagnostic and prognostic authority over students disabled by chronic illnesses.[3]

The problem of diagnostic and prognostic judgments is not confined to the academy: references, student records, and practicum reports all leave a paper trail of evidence that leads back to the diagnosis of chronic illness. The informants were all aware of the possible consequences of the documentation of their disabilities. For example:

> Say you're applying for jobs at a later stage and if they see something that triggers a rejection of some kind. I suppose I do wonder about that, and I do have concern about keeping that trail of records. . . . Sometimes I feel very paranoid, very cautious about all that documentation being out there. I mean, if the mobility problem becomes particularly bad, and obviously visible, then worrying about the documentation is pointless. The disability is obvious. But when things are on the mend. . . .

Once institutionally visible, chronically ill students lose the ability to control how they will be identified in other contexts. In social contexts where disabilities are believed to make an individual's full-time and consistent involvement in a particular program or employment opportunity uncertain, or where requirements to provide accommodation may be perceived as onerous, it is impossible to ensure that knowledge of an existing medical condition will be either suspended or not taken into account in decision-making processes.

While the original judgment about whether or not students meet the institutional definition of disability always take place in accordance with strict rules (i.e., the rules and procedures of the policy), these other types of diagnostic and prognostic assessments and judgments do not. And though they are not intended to be punitive, they are the kinds of practices in which discrimination and exclusion are grounded. Informal diagnostic and prognostic judgments represent a definite and concrete set of organizational courses of action in which the informant's eligibility for particular opportunities may be called into question.

"UNFAIR ADVANTAGE" AND SELF-ASSESSMENT

Accommodation is crucial in allowing chronically ill women to remain engaged in their studies; however, the advantage it confers is offset by the disadvantage of becoming identified as disabled. Indeed, where chronically ill students critically reflect on the concept of unfair advantage, they recognize that this thinking is flawed: they point to the selective way it treats the material conditions of their lives and how it conflates accommodation with actual benefits and educational gains.

The informants also speculate about the causes of this mistaken assumption—that is, the inability to differentiate between fairness and equity, preferences or biases of particular instructors, lack of awareness of disability issues, and so on. Even though they explicitly identify the faulty logic behind this reasoning, the notion of unfair advantage nonetheless finds its way into the talk of chronically ill women who use this same concept to interpret their own experiences and activities. For example:

> A lot of times during my B.A., there was a lot of guilt. Like, "Why would I need an extension [of time]?" A lot of it, a lot of issues like feeling lazy came up. Like, did I really need it? . . . Having come from a family that, you know, we've worked hard for where we're at. So these are really confusing times, too. Like even now, I guess it's been diagnosed for about seven years and it's still difficult; there's still denial in that. There's part of me that doesn't want to use those concessions unless it's absolutely necessary.

> I do this thing, you know, where I'm always asking myself, "Could I have gotten up earlier? Could I have stayed up typing longer? Am I really that tired?"

> I think when I was receiving support and getting assistance, there was this constant feeling of, okay, should I be doing this? You know, those kinds of guilt issues where you're not doing anything out of the ordinary, you're certainly not taking advantage, but you're feeling that your life is not your own right now. I think that was an issue for me. And it wasn't worth it.

These excerpts show that even chronically ill women organize themselves in relation to the concept of accommodation as unfair advantage. Fully aware of the disadvantages they face in the classroom and on campus, the informants still experience guilt and anxiety about using any form of assistance or accommodation. They adopt a skeptical stance in relation to themselves to scrutinize their motives and discipline their activities. Their bodily limitations and impairments are not interpreted as consequences of unequal relations of power or oppressive ideologies, but as personal inadequacies. One's experience of chronic illness—along with the pain, struggle, and limitation it entails—is shaped by the "truths" of disability that circulate in and are produced by institutions. When they speak about accommodation, the women in my study take up a subject position from within the ruling relations of the university, one that invariably limits their use of the policy and that may undermine their full participation in the academy.

CONCLUSION

An institutional ethnographic approach provides a unique way to illustrate the disjuncture between the stated intentions of the university's disability policy and the actual experience of its implementation in the lives of chronically ill women. For the university, self-identification of disability is the entry point to an institutional process that is designed to actively accomplish the university's legal obligation not to discriminate against students with disabilities. For chronically ill students, self-identification of disability opens the door to normative, prognostic, and diagnostic judgments that are inescapable to the extent that academic accommodation is deemed to be worthwhile.

Disability is not a category of a natural kind; it is a means by which an idiosyncratic and personal experience of illness or impairment can be made visible to the administrative bodies of the university for the purpose of activating an organizational course of action. The university's disability policy, along with the assumptions and social relations that structure it, provides an interpretive schema through which legitimate instances of disability can be recognized and acted upon. The failure of chronic illness to properly fit the ideological framing of *disability* means suspicion and skepticism structured into the policy are routinely activated when chronically ill women seek to obtain accommodation. Chronically ill students themselves use this schema to interpret and act on their own experiences and activities. At the same time that it subordinates and subsumes their embodied experience of pain and limitation, it also represents an institutional course of action that counts on the university's public display of good citizenship.

Paradoxically, if they choose not to identify as disabled and to limit their use of the disability policy, chronically ill women contribute to their own social invisibility. With their experience thus isolated and individualized, chronically ill women find few opportunities to represent their own experiences within the general culture, or even within the disability rights and feminist movements (Morris 1992). This absence, or lack of a voice, makes it difficult to incorporate the realities of chronic illness into both mainstream disability and feminist disability research, effectively reinforcing mistaken beliefs that people with disabilities are unable to make significant contributions to traditions of learning in the academy (Davis 1998).

The argument that disadvantage and discrimination may be consequences of institutional measures designed to produce fairness for disadvantaged groups contradicts the assumption that lofty ideals can be legislated and that good rules always will have good effects. As the above analysis demonstrates, the abstract criterion of social justice always must be understood as a set of coherent tasks enacted in the actual local settings and circumstances of people's lives. Even though they are organized and implemented in the interest of producing fairness for disadvantaged groups, disability policies are necessarily bound up in practices of power. As my study reveals, even beneficial practices may have negative or unintended consequences. As such, this analysis provides a point of departure for oppositional work. It allows professionals, and those who are ordinarily objects of others' professional practices, to choose what course of action to follow, to disorganize the "ruling project as originally conceived" (Campbell and Manicom 1995, 11).

NOTES

1. See the University of Victoria, Policy on Providing Accommodation for Students with a Disability, Section 4.2, in *Accessing the University of Victoria*.

2. The issue of providing appropriate medical documentation is both complex and contentious. On one hand, it represents the student's responsibility to act and attests to their *actual need*. It is also perceived to resolve the problem of ensuring that only properly eligible students receive accommodation. On the other hand, disabled students experience this requirement as a violation of privacy and an unnecessary burden of time and effort. More importantly, even though the accommodation is a social measure designed to alleviate the problem of discrimination and exclusion, it is legitimized by individualistic biomedical understandings of disability. In other words, implementing university policy is both dependent upon and coordinated with medical practices. Even at the heart of a social response to the problem of discrimination, medical practitioners still have authority over the bodies, knowledge, and experiences of chronically ill women. Instead of moving away from the biomedical model, practices of accommodation reinforce and sustain the resiliency of medical ways of knowing about disability.

3. Within the context of health care, women and women's health care needs are often discounted or ignored (Lock 1998). Because pain and fatigue—the most common symptoms of illnesses like RA and ME—cannot objectively be measured, these kinds of complaints are often disregarded or subordinated to visible evidence that physicians can observe. "The subjective experience of illness does not stand in a one

to one relationship with measurable pathology," and the process of diagnosis is often protracted and complex (56).

REFERENCES

Albrecht, Gary. L. 1992. *The Disability Business: Rehabilitation in America*. London: Sage Publications.

Asch, Adrienne, and Michelle Fine. 1998. "Nurturance, Sexuality, and Women with Disabilities." In Davis, *Disabilities Studies Reader*, 241–59.

Barnes, Colin. 1998. "The Social Model of Disability: A Sociological Phenomenon Ignored by Sociologists?" In Shakespeare, *Disability Reader*, 65–78.

Bellamy, Leslie Andres, and Neil Guppy. 1991. "Opportunities and Obstacles for Women in Canadian Higher Education." In *Women and Education*, 2nd ed., edited by Jane Gaskell and Arlene McLaren, 163–92. Calgary, Alberta, Canada: Detselig Enterprises.

Bickenbach, Jerome E. 1994. "Voluntary Disabilities and Everyday Illnesses." In Rioux and Bach, *Disability Is Not Measles*, 109–25.

Blackburn, Susan Stone. 1991. "The Culture of Universities: The Nature of Academe." In *Equity in Universities*.

Breslauer, Helen. 1991. "Hiring and Recruitment: Strategies for Designated Groups." In *Equity in Universities*.

Campbell, Marie. 1998. "Institutional Ethnography and Experience as Data." *Qualitative Sociology* 21 (1): 55–73.

Campbell, Marie, and Ann Manicom. 1995. Introduction to *Knowledge, Experience, and Ruling Relations: Studies in the Social Organization of Knowledge*, 3–17. Toronto: University of Toronto Press.

Davis, Lennard J., ed. 1998. *The Disabilities Studies Reader*. New York: Routledge.

Equity in Universities: A Challenge for the Decade. Proceedings of the First Conference on Employment Equity, May 6–8, 1991. Ottawa, Canada: Ontario Universities Employment and Educational Equity Network.

Esdaile, John. 1989. *Social Support and Social Networks as Promoters of Physical and Psychological Well-Being in Persons with Arthritic and Rheumatic Conditions*. Ottawa, Ont.: Health Services and Promotion Branch.

Fortin, Michele. 1987. *Accessibility to and Participation in the Post-Secondary Education System in Canada*. Ottawa, Ont.: National Forum Committee.

Fraser, Nancy. 1997. *Justice Interruptus: Critical Reflections on the "Post-Socialist" Condition*. New York: Routledge.

Garland-Thomson, Rosemarie. 1998. "Feminist Theory, the Body, and the Disabled Figure." In Davis, *Disability Studies Reader*, 279–94.

Hanen, Marsha. 1991. "The Culture of Universities: The Nature of Academe." In *Equity in Universities*, 1–4.

Lane, Harlan. 1998. "Constructions of Deafness." In Davis, *Disabilities Studies Reader*, 153–71.

The Roeher Institute. 1995. *Disability and Vulnerability: A Demographic Profile*. North York, Ont., Canada: Roeher Institute.

Linton, Simi. 1998. *Claiming Disability: Knowledge and Identity.* New York: New York University Press.

Lippman, Abby. 1998. "The Politics of Health: Geneticization Versus Health Promotion." In Sherwin et al., *Politics of Women's Health,* 64–82.

Lock, Margaret. 1998. "Situating Women in the Politics of Health." In Sherwin et al., *Politics of Women's Health* 48–63.

Lupton, Deborah. 1997. "Foucault and the Medicalization Critique." In *Foucault: Health and Medicine,* edited by Alan Peterson and Robin Bunton, 94–110. New York: Routledge.

Meekosha, Helen. 1998. "Body Battles: Bodies, Gender and Disability." In Shakespeare, *Disability Reader,* 163–80.

Morris, Jenny. 1992. "Personal and Political: A Feminist Perspective on Researching Physical Disability." *Disability, Handicap, and Society* 7 (2):157–66.

Oliver, Michael. 1992. "Changing the Social Relations of Research Production." *Disability, Handicap, and Society* 7 (2): 101–14.

———. 1996. *Understanding Disability: From Theory to Practice.* London: Macmillan.

Rioux, Marcia, and Michael Bach, eds. *Disability Is Not Measles: New Research Paradigms in Disability.* North York, Ont., Canada: Roeher Institute.

Russell, Susan. 1989. "From Disability to Handicap: An Inevitable Response to Social Constraints." *Canadian Review of Sociology and Anthropology* 26 (2): 276–92.

Schaffer, Benjamin B., and Geoff Lamb. 1981. *Can Equity Be Organized? Equity, Development Analysis and Planning.* Farnborough, UK: Gower Publishing.

Shakespeare, Tom, ed. 1998. *The Disability Reader: Social Science Perspectives.* London: Cassell.

Sherwin, Susan, and Feminist Healthcare Network, eds. 1998. *The Politics of Women's Health: Exploring Agency and Autonomy,* Philadelphia: Temple University Press.

Smith, Dorothy E. 1987. *The Everyday World as Problematic: A Feminist Sociology.* Toronto: University of Toronto Press.

———. 1990a. *The Conceptual Practices of Power: A Feminist Sociology of Knowledge.* Toronto: University of Toronto Press.

———. 1990b. *Texts, Facts and Femininity: Exploring the Relations of Ruling.* London: Routledge.

———. 1999. *Writing the Social: Critique, Theory, and Investigations.* Toronto: University of Toronto Press.

Smith, George. 1995. "Assessing Treatments: Managing the AIDS Epidemic in Ontario." In *Knowledge, Experience and Ruling Relations: Studies in the Social Organization of Knowledge,* edited by Marie Campbell and Ann Manicom, 18–34. Toronto: University of Toronto Press.

Tancred, Peta. 1991. "Hiring and Recruitment: Strategies for Designated Groups." In *Equity in Universities.*

University of Victoria: Office for Students with a Disability. 1997. *Accessing the University of Victoria: A Handbook for Persons with a Disability* (rev. June 1997).

Wendell, Susan. 1996. *The Rejected Body: Feminist Philosophical Reflections on Disability.* London: Routledge.

———. 1998. "Toward a Feminist Theory of Disability." In Davis, *Disability Studies Reader,* 260–78.

Williams, Gareth. 1998. "The Sociology of Disability: Towards a Materialist Phenomenology." In Shakespeare, *Disability Reader,* 234–44.

Zimmerman, Don H. 1969. "Record-Keeping and the Intake Process in a Public Welfare Agency." In *On Record: Files and Dossiers in American Life,* edited by Stanton Wheeler. New York: Russell Sage Foundation.

Zola, Irving Kenneth. 1994. "Towards Inclusion: The Role of People with Disabilities in Policy and Research Issues in the United States—A Historical and Political Analysis." In Rioux and Bach, *Disability Is Not Measles,* 49–66.

Thirteen

RES[CRIP]TING FEMINIST THEATER
THROUGH DISABILITY THEATER

Selections from the DisAbility Project

ANN M. FOX AND JOAN LIPKIN

MAN: Was I too healthy? Was that it? Did some secret-society deity decide
I should be given a handicap to even up the race?
WOMAN: Well, that is an interesting conjecture.

—MYRNA LAMB

One of the pieces in Myrna Lamb's classic, early feminist and episodic
play, *Mod Donna and Scyklon Z,* "But What Have You Done for Me
Lately?" features a man who is impregnated so that he might experience
the dilemma of an unwanted pregnancy in an anti-choice culture. Here,
disability metaphorically represents the female body within a patriarchal
society as "handicapped" (as the above quote suggests) and looms as the
potential punishment for women denied reproductive choice:

> WOMAN: There is a woman who unwittingly took a fetus-deforming drug
> administered by her physician for routine nausea, and a woman who
> caught German measles at a crucial point in her pregnancy, both of whom
> were denied the right to abortion, but granted the privilege of rearing
> hopelessly defective children. (Lamb 1971, 164–65)

As Lamb's play suggests, feminist theater is in a curiously ambiguous
position with regard to disability. For the conscientious reader, it quickly
becomes apparent that disability images are as ubiquitous in the literary
and theater landscapes as their live counterparts are in a society more
inclined to either politely overlook their presence or mark it in highly controlled ways. Indeed, as disability theater scholar Victoria Ann Lewis has
noted, "It is not that the nondisabled theater world knows nothing about

disability and is waiting to be enlightened. To the contrary, the depiction of disability is over-represented in dramatic literature" (2000, 93). This is no less true for the American feminist playwrights who have been writing women into theater for the contemporary stage. Consider many of the plays following Lamb's that are otherwise lauded for their feminist sensibilities, and you will discover that they emulate, rather than challenge, that early and essentialist female icon of disability in theater, *The Glass Menagerie*'s Laura Wingfield, Tennessee Williams's heroine impaired by a limp (1972). Prominent figures of this kind include paraplegic Julia in Maria Irene Fornes's *Fefu and Her Friends* (1990); the severely depressed MaGrath sisters in Beth Henley's *Crimes of the Heart* (1988); and paraplegic Skoolie in Kia Corthron's *Come Down Burning* (1996).[1] "Feminists today," notes disability studies scholar Rosemarie Garland-Thomson, "often invoke negative images of disability to describe the oppression of women," and that theoretical use finds its artistic corollary with great regularity in feminist playwriting (1997, 279). Lamb's example, while an early one, continues the use of disability as a metaphor for female oppression that is present in characters as early as the neurasthenic Young Woman (whose mental disorder emerges as she is battered by gender expectations) in Sophie Treadwell's *Machinal* (first performed in 1928, last published in 1993), or as recent as brain-damaged Sara, beaten in a gay bashing in Diana Son's *Stop Kiss* (1999). A similar use of metaphor persists today, in plays like Lisa Loomer's *The Waiting Room* (first performed in 1993, published in 1998), in which the impairments of the three female protagonists become a way to signal their oppression as women, or Eve Ensler's *The Good Body* (2004), in which fat is pathologized as both cause and symbol of female self-loathing.

It is certain that the use of physical difference as a metaphor, one that does not represent disability experience for its own sake, is deeply at play in theater. Disability studies scholars David T. Mitchell and Sharon Snyder have labeled this process as it occurs in literary fiction "narrative prosthesis" (2000). That it is as pervasively present within feminist playwriting, which ostensibly rejects the socially constructed value systems embraced by more canonical theater (more on this in a moment), seems at first something of a paradox. Disability theater scholar Carrie Sandahl points to several examples of this seemingly ironic state of affairs:

> Consider the use of epilepsy as unbearable stigma in Marsha Norman's
> '*Night Mother*; or paralysis as a perverse, grotesque burden in Maria Irene
> Fornes's *Mud*. Even "positive" metaphors (as in Jane Wagner and Lily
> Tomlin's use of mental illness as inspiration in *Search for Signs of Intelligent*

Life in the Universe) ignore the actual material conditions of the disabled people portrayed. (1999, 15)

Sandahl's list can easily be extended; the plays mentioned above are also works where "the use of disability as a dramaturgical device tends to erase the particularities of lived disability experiences" (15). Paraplegia, for example, operates as a metaphor for the punitive nature of patriarchal structures in *Fefu*. Each of the MaGrath sisters' depressive episodes contributes to the larger image of southern eccentricity and repression that Henley creates. And in Corthron's play, the poverty circumscribing its women throughout is embodied in Skoolie, as she is compelled to wheel herself about in a crudely fashioned cart.

This is not meant to negate the power and worth of these plays and the importance of their roles in challenging assumptions about class, race, gender, and sexuality. It is also not meant to imply that only feminist playwrights have invoked images of disability in this way; for example, plays ranging from August Wilson's *Fences* (first performed in 1985, published in 1986) to David Feldshuh's *Miss Evers' Boys* (1989) also use disability to embody experiences of racial and economic oppression. Furthermore, the move from the page to the stage, informed by a feminist sensibility, does not always necessarily follow old patterns; indeed, "when feminism and disability politics are taken into consideration together, they can productively inform and complicate one another" (Sandahl 1999, 12). Metaphor, which is at the heart of theatrical language, need not be rejected completely, but might likewise be enhanced in just this fashion. Cherríe Moraga's *Heroes and Saints* (1996), for example, is a feminist work that powerfully interweaves metaphor and the lived experience of disability. The play's main character, Cerezita, born without a body as a result of her mother's drinking from the pesticide-ridden community water supply, embodies the outcome of the environmental racism leveled against her Latino/a community. But Moraga also creates Cerezita as a desiring, desirable human being whose disability is very much part of her identity, not merely a personal tragedy. Cerezita resists her mother's attempts to hide her from the stares of strangers, insisting on her own visibility; indeed, her disability later makes it possible for her to actively lead her community, not just passively inspire them. Still, there is no avoiding the fact that in much feminist theater, we see reflected the tensions and questions that have already emerged from the movement to place disability studies and feminist thought in conversation with one another. Given feminist theater's relative inattention to the presence of disability beyond its more troublesome metaphorical uses, to what end might the feminist practitioner of theater concern herself with disability culture? What in feminist practice lends itself to creating theater centered on disability and to redirecting the power of metaphor in representation? And what, in turn, does a "disability aesthetic" have to offer by way of expanding and interrogating feminist theater?[2]

Before engaging these questions it is important to define what is meant by *feminist theater* and *disability theater,* respectively. For the purposes of this essay, *feminist theater* will be defined as that which also seeks to effect social change through questioning the traditional apparatus of theatrical representation and, by extension, calls attention to the social construction of identities upon which privilege is based. In other words, as feminist theater and performance scholar Jill Dolan points out, it is a theater whose theoretical perspective "is concerned with more than just the artifact of representation—the play, film, painting, or dance. It considers the entire apparatus that frames and creates these images and their connection not just to social roles but also to the structure of culture and its divisions of power" (1993, 47). This is a category of feminist theater typically defined as materialist. Engaging psychoanalytic, poststructuralist, and Marxist theories, it seeks to challenge not only traditional forms of spectatorship but all elements of theatrical creation and presentation. The playwright is not assumed to be literally or figuratively the solitary producer of meaning (and presumably male), the theatrical space is not presumed to be a proscenium arch, and the representational style is not presumed to be mimetic or that of theatrical realism. Dolan also allies materialist feminism with "a postmodernist performance style that breaks with realist narrative strategies, heralds the death of unified characters, decenters the subject, and foregrounds the conventions of perception" (1996, 97). This challenges conventional uses of representation, history, and language that, conversely, place women either at the periphery or in the center as objectified and gazed-upon entities.

Because a definition of *disability theater* has not been as extensively theorized as feminist theater, to speak of disability theater is instantly to raise questions that point to the elusiveness of defining the thing itself and that have yet to be fully explored by critics. Does any work by a disabled playwright automatically count, regardless of subject matter? Should such a category include images of disability in canonical theater? Should it include long-established theatrical traditions within communities where the label of "disabled" is met with much more contention, such as Deaf theater? Should it include art made with disabled populations that primarily emphasizes the therapeutic or cathartic effects for those involved as performers?

It is no more accurate to assume all work by disabled playwrights or performers is necessarily disability theater than to surmise all work by women playwrights is feminist. The most innovative and productive disability theater, for the purposes of this essay, does not include disability's more traditional theatrical manifestation—that is, the tokenized presence of the disabled character in isolation—as a metaphor for insidiousness or innocence, or as a heroic overcomer. This does not mean we should ignore the historical representation of disability in theater or not ask questions about the kinds of cultural dialogues it alternately reflects and invokes around deviations from bodily normalcy. Because this kind of representation of disability experience is more widespread in popular literature and the mass media, to analyze these characterizations is a monumental, important task awaiting disability studies scholars.

Nevertheless, to speak of disability theater as an entity is to speak of a self-conscious artistic movement of roughly the last three decades during which, particularly since the passing of the Americans with Disabilities Act in 1990, writers and performers within disability culture have moved to create art that is as multifaceted as the community from which it emerges. Victoria Ann Lewis's article "The Dramaturgy of Disability" has been crucial for identifying some of the important writers of disability theater for an academic audience and has also initially delineated the dramaturgical strategies that underpin disability writing for the stage (2000). Lewis points to artists whose approaches to theater run the gamut from writing plays (Mike Ervin, the late John Belluso, Susan Nussbaum) to conducting performance workshops (Lewis's own Other Voices Project, a disability performance workshop based at the Mark Taper Forum in Los Angeles) to creating solo performance work (Cheryl Marie Wade). To her initial list we can add significant other forays into the performance of disability, including playwrights such as Katinka Neuhof; community-based theater workshops like the DisAbility Project (based in St. Louis, Missouri), Actual Lives (based in Austin, Texas), and Our Time (based in New York City); theaters featuring disabled professional actors such as Blue Zone (based in Los Angeles); and solo performers like Lynn Manning, Terry Galloway, Julia Trahan, and David Roche. Lewis's landmark anthology, *Beyond Victims and Villains: Contemporary Plays by Disabled Playwrights* (2005), published works by Nussbaum, Manning, Ervin, Belluso, and Lewis herself, as well as playwrights such as Charles Mee Jr. and David Freeman.

In her study Lewis locates two prominent directions in disability theater: one focuses on exposing disability as a social construction and the other "celebrates the difference of the disability experience, what is called 'disability culture' or 'disability cool' in the disability community" (2000, 102). The former emphasis produces theater that advocates for disability rights, contravenes familiar stereotypes, questions definitions of bodily normalcy, resists essentializing disability into one kind of physical experience, and foregrounds how disability intersects with other identity categories. The latter direction emphasizes representing the experience of disability and disability culture. Kathleen Tolan locates the work of disabled theater artists along slightly different lines: "There are artists and groups whose main interest is social/political, who perceive their main work as critiquing society, changing perceptions, forging communities . . . there are others whose greatest interest is in artistic and aesthetic exploration and expression" (2001, 17).

As useful as Lewis's and Tolan's definitions may be, they suggest polarized categories of creation we might begin to think beyond. How might we begin to imagine a definition of disability theater that negotiates these divisions between art and activism in a more synthesized fashion, producing something we might label a *disability aesthetic* of theater? In the process of doing so, disability theater can not only expand its own artistry in dialogue with feminist theater, but can also in turn problematize feminist theater's potential reification of the metaphorical use of disability as a sort of *dramaturgical prosthesis*. Through the interrelationship of these approaches, we might in turn contribute to the call Rosemarie Garland-Thomson has made for feminism and disability studies to productively inform one another.

The DisAbility Project is a useful company through which to investigate the question of a disability aesthetic of theater. As artistic director Joan Lipkin points out, "I always say to my ensemble . . . that we are equal parts art and advocacy. And the minute we fail to delight, surprise, move or mystify in *how* we say things as well as *what* we say, we've lost our focus" (Tolan 2001, 19). The DisAbility Project is thus consciously at the intersection of the artistic and activist strains of disability theater and is part of the burgeoning discourse about disability and performance engaged by recent studies such as Petra Kuppers's *Disability and Contemporary Performance: Bodies on Edge* (2003) and Carrie Sandahl and Philip Auslander's *Bodies in Commotion: Disability and Performance* (2005).

The scripts that follow, "Facts and Figures," "Employment," and "Go Figure," exemplify how we might begin to answer the questions raised above and further explore how feminist and disability theaters can inform and enhance one another. They are three of an expansive and growing repertoire of theater pieces created by feminist playwright and director Joan Lipkin and the members of the DisAbility Project, a grassroots theater ensemble that creates and performs work centered on disability culture. Founded in 1997, the DisAbility Project is comprised of actors with and without disabilities, embodying a diverse (although by no means complete) representation of performing experience, age, race, gender, class, sexuality, *and* disability. The disabilities represented at varying times within the group include paraplegia, quadriplegia, AIDS, multiple sclerosis, cerebral palsy, stroke, blindness, bipolar disorder, cancer, spina bifida, muscular dystrophy, spinal cord injury, asthma, polio, epilepsy, amputation, depression, Down syndrome, cognitive disability, schizophrenia, and alcoholism. Under Lipkin's direction, the members of this community-based theater meet weekly in workshop sessions to share experiences, create, and rehearse work. Originally, as conceived, the DisAbility Project was intended to build toward a single theater event in the fall of 2000. It evolved, however, into an ongoing ensemble that as of this writing has performed for over 85,000 people. They continue to create theatrical work and take award-winning performances out into the greater St. Louis area (although they have traveled as far west as Las Vegas, increasingly receive requests for performances throughout the country, and are making their work available to global audiences through internet broadcast).[3] Given their mission and interest in societal transformations, they have found that their work can have the greatest impact by focusing on audiences of two kinds: those in educational institutions and business environments.[4] At any given performance, the company draws from a repertoire of approximately thirty pieces to assemble a production tailored to the individual audience. The pieces cover a range of disability experiences, including disability history, transportation, parking, pain, employment, attendant care, sexuality, health care, architectural accessibility, and social interaction. In addition to depicting some realistic situations, there are also several pieces that are primarily visual in nature, in which the innovative movement and stage images that can be created by disabled bodies are the primary focus. The company plans to continue this emphasis on dance and movement as a way to diversify the kinds of performance with which it can engage the community and to show what kinds of movement are possible and exciting to contemplate. While the movement work that they create in collaboration with, for example, the Missouri School for the Blind explores a specific disability identity, other pieces like "Stop the Violence" also suggest the fuller engagement of disabled people with larger civic issues. They also have created work that ensures disabled people are part of ongoing policy conversations (such as their performances presented within diversity training sessions) and cultural projects (such as "The Assorted Short Adventures of Tom, Huck, and Becky," presented in conjunction with the National Endowment for the Arts' Big Read programming).

The creative process from which these scripts emerge begins to suggest how feminist theater practice and disability theater might engage each other. Although the weekly workshops take place under Lipkin's direction, the resulting work resists privileging a single view; instead, it is collaborative, multi-perspectival, and constructed in concert with Lipkin, the performers, guest artists, and the audience (whose feedback has given rise to new pieces). Because the ensemble cast contains a range of performers with and without disabilities, no one kind of bodily experience is reified as the disabled or nondisabled norm. Likewise, the presence of disabled actors emphasizes the importance of their performing their own stories or those emerging from their own community. And while there are significant and material differences in the lived identities of nondisabled and disabled people, integrating this company underscores there are concerns relevant to the disabled community that have real implications for nondisabled individuals as well. It would be rare to find someone who does not have a family member, friend, neighbor, or co-worker without a disability. Furthermore, one can become disabled at any time, and we are all on our way to becoming disabled by virtue of the aging process. Certainly our body-phobic culture includes a wide range of physical shapes, sizes, and capabilities for which there is little tolerance.

A playwright whose own principles of feminist playwriting and directing embody poststructuralist and materialist thought, Lipkin has long interrogated socially constructed categories of race, class, gender, and sexuality that are typically regarded as cohesive and natural. She has informed her work on the DisAbility Project with similar innovations in theme and style, confounding traditional audience expectations and viewing habits. Each of the following three scripts links to concerns and methodologies advanced by feminist theater but likewise infuses those ideas and dramaturgical strategies with a disability perspective.

For example, "Facts and Figures" extends a feminist critique of history and language; both are systems of meaning from which disability has usually been erased, except as a disembodied expression of derision ("You are so ADD").[5] In a personal interview, Lipkin emphasized that in performing this piece the company wants to "awaken the audience to attend to language differently and have their experience of the performance to be grounded in a sense of history." "Facts and Figures" at once presents an audience with the realities of the disability experience while simultaneously exposing how that experience is co-opted and portrayed negatively within everyday language. This piece foregrounds the lived experience of those with disabilities, past ("Freak shows exhibiting the bodies of disabled men and women were common entertainment in the Victorian period") and present ("People with disabilities are the largest minority in the United States"). Through the revelation of these facts, disability is moved out of the world of the "private, generally hidden, and often neglected" (Wendell 1997, 266). The included facts link the experience of female and disabled bodies ("During witch trials, many of the women who were tried for witchcraft had disabilities"), foregrounding for an audience how female and disabled bodies have simultaneously occupied sites of marginalization.

But these facts also remind us there is a specific disability experience to be articulated. Disability studies scholar Susan Wendell, in calling for a feminist theory of disability, confirms this necessity and suggests the opportunity arising from it:

> Emphasizing differences from the able-bodied demands that those differences be acknowledged and respected and fosters solidarity among the disabled. It challenges the able-bodied paradigm of humanity and creates the possibility of a deeper challenge to the idealization of the body and the demand for its control. (1997, 272)

The reconsideration of social history that feminist theater seeks to re-create is therefore deepened by acknowledging other categories through which communities are marginalized, including disability. The figures of speech interwoven with the piece's facts confirm this. Using disability negatively ("He gave me such a lame excuse!" "That is so retarded"), these expressions at once appropriate and reconfigure physical difference solely as lacking. By questioning the dismissive assumptions behind our use of language that addresses disability ("She is psycho"), the piece invites each audience member to become aware of and thus accountable for her or his own use of metaphor and language. Incorporating such a consciousness of language can only help practitioners of feminist theater examine their own use of disability with as much care as they would language marking race, class, sexuality, and gender, for example.

One of the facts with which "Facts and Figures" presents audience members concerns disabled workers: "People with disabilities are the most under-employed population in the country. Mostly because our transportation systems make it difficult for them to get jobs, or employers won't hire them." More specifically, as Heather Gain and Lisa Bennett point out, the disabled have "the highest unemployment rate of any group—somewhere between 72 and 90 percent" (2002, 16). The piece titled "Employment" comically and pointedly expands on this fact by performing the assumptions about ability that underlie employer willingness—or, rather, unwillingness—to consider disabled job applicants. The characters in "Employment" challenge the seeming impasse that results when a disabled person applies for a job but is quickly turned down on the grounds that she might "turn off the customers," not be up to the rigors of "a pretty demanding job," and is only suited for "the sheltered workshop." "Can this situation be saved?" asks the job seeker, turning to the audience for resolution. In some settings the audience is given the opportunity to create potential solutions to the dilemma, imagining how the workplace and workers' roles could be reimagined to include the disabled person. Members of the DisAbility Project have also constructed alternate endings that can be presented if an audience is less inclined to participate, endings in which they, along with the manager, are invited to open their minds. Lipkin and ensemble tweak the social assumptions about what disabled workers can and cannot do and offer a further pointed comment: in an age when disabled people are unemployed in such large numbers and employers are in need of reliable workers, ableist attitudes serve no one. Linking gender to economic inequity is not new in feminist theater, but the attention paid to the particular link between disability and unemployment enhances that critique of economic privation based on social identity.

"Go Figure," the story of Katie Rodriguez Banister's reimagining of her sexual identity after becoming disabled, allies constructions of gender and disability and also speaks importantly to unquestioned assumptions in our society that disabled persons are asexual, undesirable, and undesiring. What is immediately striking about this piece is that even as Banister revels in remembering her sexuality before her accident ("You may not be able to tell, but I used to be quite the Barbie girl"), that memory is tinged with the recollection of worry about what people would think of her. We, as audience members, are reminded that Banister's change in experience underscores that the female body, in both its nondisabled and its disabled identities, is policed as the site of potential transgressions away from normalcy, whether the standard be one of beauty, sexual propriety, or physical wholeness. Banister's life transition from nondisabled to disabled is therefore not a shift from normalcy to abnormalcy so much as a movement from being the object of one kind of spectatorial look to another. As Garland-Thomson reminds us, "If the male gaze informs the normative female self as a sexual spectacle, then the stare sculpts the disabled subject as a grotesque spectacle" (1997, 285). In our society both female bodies and disabled bodies find themselves literally and figuratively marginalized because of their supposed deviation from an idealized norm, whether that model is a particular gender, a standard of femininity or heterosexuality, or some illusory construction of wholeness. Garland-Thomson specifically points out the parallels:

> Both the female and the disabled body are cast within cultural discourse as deviant and inferior; both are excluded from full participation in public as well as economic life; both are defined in opposition to a valued norm which is assumed to possess natural corporeal superiority. (279)

This is comically, but pointedly, illustrated when Banister remembers, "I placed a personal ad in the singles paper: 'Petite, professional, independent woman on wheels seeks male,'" and "one man," unable to imagine a disabled woman placing a personal ad, "thought I drove around a lot." But Banister's experiences, while distinct, are perhaps not as removed from those of nondisabled women as might be imagined, since "female bodies, like bodies of color, homosexual bodies, *and* disabled bodies, are positioned culturally so as not to forget their embodiment" (Miner 1997, 293).

Banister powerfully reclaims her own particular sexuality, breaking down the illusion that the "temporarily able-bodied" watching her performance are somehow removed from these issues. Equally important is her assertion that she is having "the best sex of my life"; hers becomes not an overcoming narrative on how to learn to do without, but an invitation to the audience to learn to do *with* differently. "Go figure!" she exclaims, but that expression of surprise can simultaneously be read as an invocation to the audience, disabled and nondisabled spectators alike, to figure out how to move beyond the narrow confines of how society defines sexual roles. For this reason, it is particularly fitting that Banister trade off telling her story with Rich Scharf, an openly gay male member of the company. This destabilizes the expectation that feeling circumscribed by normativity is only *her* story and that it is one grounded only in a presumption of heterosexuality.

As Nancy Mairs explains in *Waist-High in the World,* "Most people, in fact, deal with the discomfort and even distaste that a misshapen body arouses by disassociating that body from sexuality in reverie and practice" (1996, 51). "It was like I was a virgin again," Banister exclaims about her sexual identity after becoming disabled, and in a sense she is "like a virgin." She and the audience have to reimagine her sexuality and desirability as manifested in ways beyond what society deems normal or acceptable. In this way, Banister is one of those quadriplegics who, as Wendell asserts, "have revolutionary things to teach about the possibilities of sexuality" (1997, 274). The materiality of Banister's life as a sexual being is acknowledged, celebrated, and also the means by which a reimagining of sexuality can occur *through* disability.

Dramaturgically, the pieces discussed here all sustain aesthetic challenges to traditional theater practice that are familiar to those historically adapted by feminist playwrights. The episodic nature of the performance, juxtaposing, for example, monologic pieces with more nonrepresentational ones, makes for a nonlinear viewing experience, echoing movement within feminist theater to resist conventionally realistic representation and progressive plots.[6] A resistance to these more traditional forms can likewise inform a disability aesthetic that resists social constructions of physical evolution, progress, and normalcy by resisting Western theatrical convention. In form and content, these pieces invite the nondisabled members of the audience to consider new ways to perceive space, time, and the body while not denying the materiality of those same bodily experiences as lived by disabled people.

More specifically, both "Go Figure" and "Employment" rely on Brechtian interventions into the theatrical viewing experience, including direct address to the audience and disrupting conventionally realistic representation. In "Go Figure," for example, two actors become a split subject to pass the single story back and forth; while it is Banister's experience, Scharf's presence suggests its connection to others. The readable physical and gender difference between Scharf and Banister at once prevents us from universalizing Banister's experience and simultaneously compels us to consider how Scharf might have felt his own body similarly circumscribed by ideals of male beauty and masculinity. In "Employment," rolling back the scenes to invite audience members to "replay" them in a different, more activist manner, works to create a similar alienation of the audience from a passive viewing experience. This referencing of fast-forward and rewind is a product of the age of television and video, pointing to the manner in which the DisAbility Project also uses references to popular culture. Deconstructing the assumption that theater is only high culture, these references, like the comedy of the pieces, invite audience members to link their own experience and vernacular with those used by the disabled characters, thus further establishing a connection.

One final note about the performance context for these scripts: the scripts are typically performed in concert with other pieces created by members of the DisAbility Project; in a typical performance, anywhere from eight to twelve pieces are performed, depending on the audience, size of the ensemble, venue, and amount of time available. While other pieces might be performed in between them, when all three are part of a performance, the scripts included here are generally presented in the following order: "Facts and Figures," "Employment," and "Go Figure." The order is purposeful; as Lipkin observed in a personal interview, "the experience of any performance is an emotional, spiritual, intellectual, and visceral journey. The arc of that journey is crafted carefully." As a result, "Facts and Figures" and "Employment" both come early in the performance. "Facts and Figures" foregrounds a history with which audience members may be unfamiliar, while "Employment" simultaneously embodies the concrete reality of job discrimination while solidifying an audience's connection through humor. "Go Figure," as one of the most intimate and emotionally challenging pieces, comes later in the performance.

Rosemarie Garland-Thomson has called for disability to become a "universalizing discourse," invested in

> asserting the body as a cultural text which is interpreted, inscribed with meaning, indeed *made,* within social relations of power. Such a perspective advocates political equality by denaturalizing disability's assumed inferiority, casting its configurations and functions as difference rather than lack. (1997, 282)

Toward that end, and as these pieces demonstrate, an emergent disability theater can simultaneously build upon and complicate the thematic and aesthetic interrogations feminist theater initiates with regard to other kinds of social identities. This might further encourage feminist theater to avoid the subtle reinscriptions of normalcy encoded in a too-commonly well-intentioned, albeit superficial, use of disability in theater. Go figure: crip culture can rescript feminist theater in ways that contribute to establishing disability and feminism as powerful allies in imagining a more expansive view of reality, onstage and off.

FACTS AND FIGURES
Joan Lipkin and the DisAbility Project
Two groups of the ensemble
Odd numbers on stage left, even numbers on stage right. This piece can be done with as many as sixteen people, each taking their own line, or a smaller group with a doubling up on lines. There should be varying heights and levels among the groups. Each person has her or his factoid written on a piece of paper, preferably memorized. After the reading of the line, the paper is discarded in whatever way possible (crumbled, thrown to the floor, etc.).
  ENSEMBLE MEMBER ONE: That is so retarded.

ENSEMBLE MEMBER TWO: In medieval times, disabilities were seen as a curse from God.

THREE: The industry has been crippled.

FOUR: During witch trials, many of the women who were tried for witchcraft had disabilities.

FIVE: He's a lame duck.

SIX: Court jesters with physical disabilities were common entertainment through much of European history.

SEVEN: Those kids are such freaks.

EIGHT: Freak shows exhibiting the bodies of disabled men and women were common entertainment in the Victorian period.

NINE: He gave me such a lame excuse.

TEN: People with disabilities are the largest minority in the United States.

ELEVEN: Hey, four eyes!

TWELVE: In China, many children with visible disabilities are killed or abandoned at birth.

THIRTEEN: He/she is psycho.

FOURTEEN: People with disabilities are the most under-employed population in the country. Mostly because our transportation systems make it difficult for them to get jobs, or employers won't hire them.

FIFTEEN: You are so ADD.

SIXTEEN: Most people with disabilities live below the poverty line.

[*At the word "below," the ensemble begins to bend over in whatever way possible. Then they begin to slowly rise up, with a collective hum, getting increasingly louder as they rise. When they are fully upright again, those people in the ensemble who can, begin to wave their fists in the air and emit a sustained roar. This comes to a collective stop. The ensemble takes several moments to breathe and transition. They move slowly into a brief contact improvisation with each other, touching and connecting in various places on their bodies.*]

[*Beat.*]

ALL: [*to audience, with outstretched hands and arms where possible*] Welcome to our world!

EMPLOYMENT
Joan Lipkin and the DisAbility Project
Salesperson
Manager

Job Seeker (A woman using a wheelchair)
Wild Shoppers (As few as three, as many as you like)
Wild Shopper #1
Wild Shopper #2
Wild Shopper #3 (At least one of the shoppers should be someone who uses a wheelchair)
Salesperson is found amid the Wild Shoppers. The roar of the shoppers pushes the Salesperson from among their midst. S/he runs into the Manager's office excited and flustered.

SALESPERSON: It's a jungle out there! [*Wild Shoppers writhe, pull at various items, improvise comments and roar.*] I'm putting in for combat pay.

MANAGER: You're just a little tired.

SALESPERSON: I won't go back in there. [*Wild Shoppers roar and improvise comments again. Items of clothing go flying.*] I won't. [*S/he starts to sob.*]

MANAGER: There, there . . .

SALESPERSON: Have *you* ever worked the post Christmas sale? [*More frenzy from the Wild Shoppers. Perhaps more roar. Salesperson sobs.*] Post Christmas. Pre-Christmas. Columbus Day?!!! I need more help.

MANAGER: We're doing all we can. But in this economy, it isn't easy. They're paying $8.50 an hour plus benefits at Taco Bell on Manchester. And $9.00 at Triple A Dry Cleaning.
[*Salesperson continues to sob. In rolls Job Seeker in a wheelchair.*]

JOB SEEKER: Excuse me. I'm here about the job.

MANAGER: Oh, you must be looking for the sheltered workshop. It's at the other end of the mall.

JOB SEEKER: No, I meant the job here. The one that was listed in the paper.

MANAGER: Oh. There must be some mistake. We sell clothes.

JOB SEEKER: Yes, I can see that. And I wear them. That's why I'm here. I live to accessorize.

SALESPERSON: Fantastic! I love what you're wearing.
[*Manager pulls Salesperson aside to talk with her/him privately.*]

MANAGER: Excuse me. We can't hire her. It'll turn off the customers.

SALESPERSON: Oh, I don't know. She's more enthusiastic than most of the people we have working on the floor. And perky. You did say that perky was part of the job description. And she obviously loves clothes.

JOB SEEKER: [*to audience*] I love clothes. I never wear white after Labor Day.

MANAGER: It's not just that. The aisles are too crowded. She couldn't get through.

[*Wild Shoppers roar.*]

JOB SEEKER: I'd really like to work here. Really, I would.

SALESPERSON: And I'd like to do something but my hands are tied.

JOB SEEKER: [*to audience*] Can this situation be saved?

[*Everyone hums theme song from* Jeopardy. *A Wild Shopper breaks away from the group to offer an alternative scenario.*]

WILD SHOPPER #1: Excuse me. I have an idea. Could we roll this scene back a little?

[*The Wild Shopper, Salesperson, and Manager mime rolling back of time with hand gestures and vocalization. The scene resumes.*]

JOB SEEKER: I'd really like to work here. Really, I would.

SALESPERSON: And I'd like to do something but my hands are tied.

WILD SHOPPER #1: I have been here for an hour and a half and no one has offered to help. Or even said hello. What you need around here is more friendliness. Why couldn't she work as a greeter?

JOB SEEKER: [*to audience*] Hi. Hi. How ya doing? Thank you for coming. Welcome.

WILD SHOPPER #1: See? She's great.

MANAGER: I don't know. I'm not sure that something like that is in our budget.

WILD SHOPPER #1: Sheesh. Even Wal-Mart has a greeter. I'm not shopping here anymore!

[*Wild Shopper #1 goes back to crowd. Everyone hums the* Jeopardy *song again, this time a little faster. Wild Shopper #2 interrupts it before it ends.*]

WILD SHOPPER #2: I know! I know! You say the aisles are too crowded? I agree. It is way too crowded in here. How about if she was a cashier? [*to audience*] How about that?!

JOB SEEKER: [*to audience*] Cha-ching! Cha-ching!

[*The Wild Shoppers roar.*]

SALESPERSON: We need to open up another register.

MANAGER: I don't know. It's a pretty demanding job. How do I know that she is responsible?

JOB SEEKER: Oh, I'm very good with money. You have to be when you love clothes as much as I do.

MANAGER: I'm sure you are. [*to Salesperson*] But we'd have to make special arrangements for her. You know, with the equipment and all. It could be expensive.

WILD SHOPPER #2: How expensive could it be? She already has her own chair. Good luck, lady!

[*Manager is clearly noncommittal so Wild Shopper #2 goes back to crowd. At this point, Salesperson could ask the audience if they have any ideas and then bring them up to discuss them. Improv is involved. Job Seeker remains enthusiastic and Manager is uncomfortable and unconvinced.*]

Alternate Ending #1

[*Depending upon the audience's mood, a final suggestion could be taken from Wild Shopper #3*]

WILD SHOPPER #3: You know, anyone who loves clothes as much as she does (and I must say, you look mahvelous) . . .

JOB SEEKER: Thank you, dahling.

WILD SHOPPER #3: Anyone who loves clothes as much as she does should be a personal shopper.

JOB SEEKER: Oh, yes. I'd love it! And I would love to spend somebody else's money for them.

[*The Wild Shoppers roar.*]

MANAGER: How would she get around?

JOB SEEKER: I got here, didn't I?

MANAGER: I don't know.

WILD SHOPPER #3: Well, I do. [*to Job Seeker*] Here's my card. [*to Manager*] I'm with that little department store down the street.

MANAGER: Not blah-blah-blah?!

WILD SHOPPER #3: The very one.

MANAGER: And are you blee-blee-blee?!

WILD SHOPPER #3: Indeed, I am.

MANAGER: Oh no!

WILD SHOPPER #3: And I know talent when I see it. [*to Job Seeker*] My car is out front. Shall we discuss the details over lunch? [*S/he leaves, and she follows.*]

JOB SEEKER: Cha-ching, Cha-ching, Cha-ching!

[*Wild Shoppers roar, Salesperson and Manager look at each other in disbelief.*]

Alternative Ending #2

JOB SEEKER: I could be a greeter, a cashier, a personal shopper and more. Maybe you've just never worked with someone like me before. Please think about it. You know, open your mind?

MANAGER: You're right. And I really will.

SALESPERSON: Just do it soon, please?!

[*The Wild Shoppers roar.*]

SALESPERSON: I need help fast!

Alternate Ending #3

[*After the audience has come up to propose several endings, the ensemble needs to bring the scene to a strong close.*]

SALESPERSON: [*to Manager*] So, what do you think?

MANAGER: I'm not sure.

JOB SEEKER: Look, I could be a greeter, a cashier. [*Mention all of the other things that have been proposed.*] Maybe you've just never worked with someone like me before. Please think about it. You know, open your mind?

MANAGER: You're right. And I really will.

SALESPERSON: Just do it soon, please?!

[*The Wild Shoppers roar.*]

SALESPERSON: I need help fast!

GO FIGURE

Katie Rodriguez Banister, Joan Lipkin, and Rich Scharf

Rich: a gay man

Katie: a woman using a wheelchair

Rich is alone on stage.

RICH: You may not be able to tell, but I used to be quite the Barbie girl. Oh yeah, I always was a traditional little girl at heart. I enjoyed dressing up and all that went with it. From my first pair of panty-hose to my bouffant hair, shellacked in place with half a can of Aqua-net. Remember how popular big hair was in the 80's? The bigger the hair, the closer to God. And with the makeup to match. The trick was to go to that borderline Barbie look without being sickening; I'm not sure I always succeeded. God, I can remember my college girlfriends and I dressing up to go out for the night with the boom box blaring, "no parking, no parking on the dance floor, baby."

[*Rich starts to turn stage left as he says the following line.*]

RICH: My favorite outfit was this gray cashmere sweater . . .

[*Katie comes out from stage left as the following line is said in unison, the two of them facing each other.*]

KATIE AND RICH: . . . with my black leather mini-skirt and four-inch gray snakeskin pumps.

KATIE: That outfit said . . .

RICH: . . . look at me.

[*Rich and Katie face back toward audience.*]

KATIE: Why, I even won a wet T-shirt contest once at a bar, and the girl next to me dropped her drawers.

RICH: . . . and I still won!

KATIE: My first kiss was in sixth grade at the Kirkwood ice rink. After the rink closed, John, this absolute doll, called me over, put his lips on mine and then ran off. It was so cool!

RICH: I was stunned! When my dad came to pick me up, I felt like throwing up because I was sure he knew what I had done, that he could read it on my face!

KATIE: [*wryly*] And it's a good thing that Dad didn't always know what I did as an adult. If there was a man I was attracted to . . .

RICH: [*Rich starts to move behind Katie*] . . . with whom I wanted to be sexual . . .

KATIE: I just went for it. I liked being sexual,

RICH: . . . and I certainly didn't have any problems finding willing partners.

KATIE: I figured . . .

[*Rich is behind Katie by this time and they look at each other while saying the following in unison.*]

KATIE AND RICH: . . . God gave us our sexuality to be enjoyed, right?

[*Rich returns to Katie's right side and faces her.*]

KATIE: Well, I did worry about what people thought about me . . .

[*They face each other during the following lines.*]

RICH: Tramp.

KATIE: Slut.

RICH: Hussy.

KATIE: Trollop!

[*Beat.*]

RICH: Intern!

[*They face the audience.*]

KATIE: And sometimes I would feel worse afterward, after I'd had sex with someone . . .

RICH: . . . even though I got what I wanted!

[*Rich starts to kneel at Katie's side.*]

KATIE: But I had fun, too, you know?

[*Rich is kneeling at Katie's side so that their heads are level with each other as the following line is said in unison.*]

KATIE AND RICH: It felt powerful to be attractive!

KATIE: Then an auto accident brought my life to a screeching halt. I became a quadriplegic, and my life changed—ha—to say the least. I remember the first time I saw myself in the mirror at the hospital.

[*Rich has sunk onto his knees by this point.*]

RICH: I was devastated. I didn't look like me. I didn't even look like a female anymore. I felt more like an it.

KATIE: And I fought for my womanhood. I told my occupational therapist that I'm not leaving rehab until I can put on my own lipstick!

[*Rich steps in front of Katie to face audience, as Katie turns to face upstage.*]

RICH: An old boyfriend from high school came to visit me in the hospital. We had been a very active couple. He walked up to the bed, leaned over, and gave me a rose. Then we engaged in a major lip-lock session. I was in heaven. Thank God my hormones weren't paralyzed! But when we met again after I got out of the hospital, it was a disaster. It just didn't work. I was devastated again. And it was at that point that I realized that the life I had was no longer.

[*During the following lines said in unison, Rich and Katie will rotate, lazy-Susan style, with Katie ending up facing the audience and Rich behind her facing upstage by the end of the lines said in unison.*]

KATIE AND RICH: No more wet T-shirts. No more pumps. And I miss my pumps, damn it. And no more sex.

KATIE: It's funny. You think there are certain things in life that you'll never accept. And then those things happen to you. And somehow you accept them or bust, I guess. So I slowly accepted the fact that this chair had become my world. My life. And a part of who I am. And somehow I refused to give up. That's when I placed an ad in the singles paper: "petite, professional, outgoing, independent woman on wheels seeks male." I got over 30 letters! Although one man thought I drove around a lot.

[*Again, Katie and Rich rotate as above; by the end of the following line said in unison, Rich will face the audience and Katie will be behind him, facing upstage.*]

KATIE AND RICH: I did date two men, but they were disasters. So I just gave up.

RICH: So imagine my surprise, a few years later, when I met someone. And he expressed interest in me. And I said, "Oh no. You don't understand. I don't do that anymore. I can't date you. It's just not possible." Well, let me tell you, this man is patient. And over the course of a year and a half, he became my best friend, and I began to trust him, and I could no longer fight my feelings of attraction for him. So one day we were in the kitchen, and I said, "Pull up a chair, and come sit by me." And we kissed. And kissed. For an hour and a half we kissed. Hey, I had to make up for lost time!

[*By the end of the line Katie has turned to face the audience, even with Rich and to his right.*]

KATIE: But I still kept my guard up. I mean kissing was fine, but obviously it couldn't go any further than that. Well, about a month later, we're at a friend's wedding, our sixth of seven that summer! And the good ole preacher was preaching . . .

RICH: "If you love someone, and you know it, grab a hold of them, and let them know it, too!"

[*During Katie's line below, Rich will step upstage away from Katie and look at her; this has now briefly become Katie's story alone.*]

KATIE: So I did. We didn't make the reception. Instead, we went back to my place and I let him know in no uncertain terms that I wanted to be with him. But as he was removing my tray, and foot pedals, and my shoes, I started crying,

RICH: "Oh God, what if this doesn't work? What if you're not satisfied? What if I can't do it?"

[*By this time Rich has come up behind Katie.*]

KATIE AND RICH: It was like I was a virgin again!

[*The following lines will overlap slightly.*]

KATIE: Well, I told you this guy was patient.

RICH: And he lifted me to the bed.

KATIE: And would position my legs, you know.

RICH: Move my leg if he needed to.

KATIE: And even though I'm paralyzed from the chest down . . .

RICH: . . . I could feel the pressure of his hands on my breasts.

KATIE: And I could feel him inside me . . .

RICH: . . . kind of like a distant pressure.

KATIE: I could feel it in my head . . .

RICH: . . . like the tingling of a limb that has fallen asleep.

KATIE: And it was the same:

KATIE AND RICH: "Oh my God, oh my God, oh my God!"

KATIE: Just in different places now.

[*Rich comes out from behind Katie and stands to her left.*]

RICH: It's funny. Don't get me wrong—I'm still pissed to be in this chair. But instead of becoming a permanent wall, this chair has helped to teach me about true love.

KATIE: And I'm having the best sex of my life.
[*Katie and Rich look at each other, then look at the audience.*]
KATIE AND RICH: Go figure!

NOTES

1. The plays mentioned here cover a wide range of feminist playwriting. Understandably, not all scholars would agree on their being classified as such. However, what is suggested by their use is that across the spectrum of feminist theater, however that enterprise is defined, there exists a pervasive use of disability images.

2. Daniel J. Wilson articulated this definition of a "disability aesthetic" during the National Endowment for the Humanities Summer Institute on Disability Studies at San Francisco State University in the summer of 2000.

3. Joan Lipkin and That Uppity Theatre Company have been recognized with numerous honors, including: a Focus St. Louis "What's Right with the Region" Award for Improving Racial Equality and Social Justice, a Missouri Governor's Council on Disability Community Enhancement Award, a Missouri Arts Council Missouri Arts Award, a John Van Voris Award for Community Service, an Arts for Life Special Lifetime Achievement Award, a Human Rights Campaign Organizational Equality Award, a Distinguished Alumni Award from Webster University, a Woman of Worth Award, a Frederick H. Laas Memorial Award, a Visionary Award from Grand Center, Inc, a Brotherhood/Sisterhood Award from the National Conference for Community and Justice, and the James F. Hornback Ethical Humanist of the Year Award. Artifacts from the DisAbility Project are also included in the permanent collection of the Missouri History Museum.

4. For example, they created work about disability and employment for the Social Security Administration in Kansas City in summer 2006.

5. "Facts and Figures" was originally developed by students at Davidson College working with Lipkin during a weeklong residency in March 2001.

6. We might think here of plays ranging from *Fefu and Her Friends* (Fornes 1990) to Ntozake Shange's *Spell #7* (1979).

REFERENCES

Banister, Katie Rodriguez, Joan Lipkin, and Rich Scharf. 1999. "Go Figure." Unpublished manuscript.

Corthron, Kia. 1996. *Come Down Burning*. In *Contemporary Plays by Women of Color: An Anthology*, edited by Kathy A. Perkins, 90–105. New York: Routledge.

Davis, Lennard J., ed. 1997. *The Disability Studies Reader*. New York: Routledge.

Dolan, Jill. 1993. *Presence and Desire: Essays on Gender, Sexuality, Performance*. Ann Arbor: University of Michigan Press.

———. 1996. "In Defense of the Discourse: Materialist Feminism, Postmodernism, Poststructuralism . . . and Theory." In *A Sourcebook of Feminist Theatre and Performance*, edited by Carol Martin, 94–107. New York: Routledge.

Ensler, Eve. 2004. *The Good Body.* New York: Villard.

Feldshuh, David. 1995. *Miss Evers' Boys.* New York: Dramatists Play Service.

Fornes, Maria Irene. 1990. *Fefu and Her Friends.* New York: PAJ Publications.

Gain, Heather, and Lisa Bennett. 2002. "The Faces of Social Security." *NOW Times* 34 (1): 16.

Garland-Thomson, Rosemarie. 1997. "Feminist Theory, the Body, and the Disabled Figure." In Davis, *Disability Studies Reader,* 279–92.

Henley, Beth. 1979. *Crimes of the Heart.* In *Plays from the Contemporary American Theater,* edited by Brooks McNamara, 227–91. New York: Mentor.

Kupper, Petra. 2003. *Disability and Contemporary Performance: Bodies on Edge.* New York: Routledge.

Lamb, Myrna. 1971. "But What Have You Done for Me Lately?" *The Mod Donna and Scyklon Z: Plays of Women's Liberation,* 143–66. New York: Pathfinder Press.

Lewis, Victoria Ann. 2000. "The Dramaturgy of Disability." In *Points of Contact: Disability, Art, and Culture,* edited by Susan Crutchfield and Marcy Epstein, 93–108. Ann Arbor: University of Michigan Press.

———. 2005. *Beyond Victims and Villains: Contemporary Plays by Disabled Playwrights.* New York: Theatre Communications Group.

Lipkin, Joan, and the DisAbility Project. 2001a. "Employment." Unpublished manuscript.

———. 2001b. "Facts and Figures." Unpublished manuscript.

Loomer, Lisa. 1998. *The Waiting Room.* New York: Dramatists Play Service.

Mairs, Nancy. 1996. *Waist-High in the World: A Life among the Nondisabled.* Boston: Beacon Press.

Miner, Madonne. 1997. "'Making up the Stories as We Go Along': Men, Women, and Narratives of Disability." In *The Body and Physical Difference: Discourses of Disability,* edited by David T. Mitchell and Sharon Snyder, 283–95. Ann Arbor: University of Michigan Press.

Mitchell, David T., and Sharon Snyder. 2000. *Narrative Prosthesis: Disability and the Dependencies of Discourse.* Ann Arbor: University of Michigan Press.

Moraga, Cherríe. 1996. *Heroes and Saints.* In *Contemporary Plays by Women of Color: An Anthology,* edited by Kathy A. Perkins, 230–61. New York: Routledge.

Sandahl, Carrie. 1999. "Ahhhh Freak Out! Metaphors of Disability and Femaleness in Performance." *Theatre Topics* 9 (1):11–30.

Sandahl, Carrie, and Philip Auslander, eds. 2005. *Bodies in Commotion: Disability and Performance.* Ann Arbor: University of Michigan Press.

Shange, Ntozake. 1978. *Spell #7.* In *Nine Plays by Black Women,* edited by Margaret B. Wilkerson, 243–91. New York: Mentor.

Tolan, Kathleen. 2001. "We Are Not a Metaphor." *American Theatre* (April):17–21, 57–59.

Treadwell, Sophie. 1993. *Machinal.* London: Nick Hern Books.

Wendell, Susan. 1997. "Toward a Feminist Theory of Disability." In Davis, *Disability Studies Reader,* 260–78.

Williams, Tennessee. 1972. *The Glass Menagerie.* New York: Signet.

Wilson, August. 1986. *Fences.* New York: Plume.

Contributors

W. Carol Cleigh is a disability rights activist and author. In addition to a number of published articles, she has led several direct-action campaigns and served on boards and committees to promote the rights of disabled people, including the Not Dead Yet national board. Although she is now retired to the mountains of western North Carolina, she continues to advocate for access and against the ableist belief that one is better off dead than disabled.

Elizabeth J. Donaldson is Associate Professor of English at the New York Institute of Technology, where she teaches courses in American literature. Her primary research interests include medicine and literature, disability studies, and cultural studies of mental illness. She serves on the board of the *Journal of Literary and Cultural Disability Studies* and has co-edited a special issue on "Disability and Emotion" with Catherine Prendergast. Her reviews and essays have appeared in *Disability Studies Quarterly, Teaching American Literature, NWSA Journal, Atenea, Interdisciplinary Humanities, Metapsychology,* and the collection *Amy Lowell: American Modern.*

Nirmala Erevelles is Associate Professor of Social Foundations of Education and Instructional Leadership at the University of Alabama. Her research and publications are in the areas of disability studies, multicultural education, feminism, and sociology of education. She has published articles in several journals such as *Educational Theory, Studies in Education and Philosophy, Journal of Curriculum Studies, Disability and Society,* and *Journal of Literary and Cultural Disability Studies,* among others. Her book, *Disability and Difference in Global Contexts: Towards a Transformative Body Politic,* will be published by Palgrave MacMillan in 2012.

Ann M. Fox is Associate Professor of English and Gender Studies Coordinator at Davidson College in Davidson, North Carolina. Her early scholarship traced the rise of feminist sensibilities in American commercial theater. An American Association of University Women American Postdoctoral Fellow for 2003–2004, her current scholarship focuses on disability and theater. She is particularly interested in rereading twentieth-century American drama from a disability studies perspective and has published work on the subject in *Gendering Disability, Journal of Literary and Cultural Disability Studies,* and *Disability Studies Quarterly.* With Jessica Cooley, she has also co-curated two gallery exhibitions centered on disability and art: RE/FORMATIONS: Disability, Women, and Sculpture, and STARING.

Rosemarie Garland-Thomson is Professor of Women's Studies at Emory University in Atlanta, Georgia. Her fields of study are feminist theory, American literature, and disability studies. Her scholarly and professional activities are devoted to developing the field of disability studies in the humanities and in women's studies. She is the author of *Staring: How We Look* (2009) and *Extraordinary Bodies: Figuring Physical Disability in American Literature and Culture* (1997); editor of *Freakery: Cultural Spectacles of the Extraordinary Body* (1996); and co-editor of *Disability Studies: Enabling the Humanities* (2002). She is currently writing a book called *Cure or Kill: The Cultural Logic of Euthanasia,* which traces eugenic thought through American literature.

Kim Q. Hall is Professor of Philosophy and a faculty member in the Women's Studies and Sustainable Development programs at Appalachian State University. She is the guest editor of the *NWSA Journal* special issue on Feminist Disability Studies (2002) and co-editor of *Whiteness: Feminist Philosophical Reflections* (1999). Her recent published essays focus on gender, identity, and embodiment through the lens of queerness, feminism, and disability. She is currently working on a book titled *Making Our Bodies Our Selves.*

April Herndon is Assistant Professor of English at Winona State University. Her scholarship has been published in the *NWSA Journal* and *Social Semiotics.* She is currently working on a book about the childhood obesity epidemic.

Jennifer C. James is Associate Professor of English and Director of the Africana Studies Program at George Washington University. Her recent work includes *A Freedom Bought with Blood: African-American Literature of War, the Civil War–World War II* (2007), and chapters in two forthcoming collections, "Ecomelancholia: Slavery, Terror, War, and Black Ecological Imaginings" in *Environmental Criticism for the 21st Century* and "Blessed Are the Warmakers: Martin Luther King, Vietnam, and the Black Prophetic Tradition," in *Writing War across the Disciplines.* Professor

James also edited a special issue of *MELUS* on the intersections of race, ethnicity, and disability with Cynthia Wu (2006).

Karen Elizabeth Jung teaches in the sociology department at Trent University in Peterborough, Ontario, Canada. Her current research brings together the disparate areas of women and disability, chronic illness, and equity in organizational contexts.

Alison Kafer is Associate Professor of Feminist Studies at Southwestern University. She was the 2006–2007 Ed Roberts Visiting Scholar in Disability Studies at the University of California, Berkeley. Her work on gender, sexuality, and disability has been published in several journals and anthologies, including *Journal of Women's History, Gendering Disability, Feminist Interventions in Ethics and Politics,* and *That's Revolting: Queer Strategies for Resisting Assimilation.* She is the co-editor of *Deaf and Disability Studies: Interdisciplinary Perspectives* (2010), and she is working on a manuscript about feminist queer crip futures.

Cindy LaCom is Professor of English and Director of Women's Studies at Slippery Rock University. In graduate school, she discovered the then new field of disability studies while working on a dissertation chapter that analyzed the interplay between female invalidism and female sexuality. She has since published essays on the gendered and ideological meanings of physical disabilities in *Discourses of Disability, PMLA,* and *Disability Studies Quarterly* and in books on disability history and liberatory pedagogy. A past member of the Modern Language Association Committee on Disability Issues in the Profession, she is currently working on a book that examines the social, gendered, and ideological meanings of physical disability in Victorian literature and culture.

Sharon Lamp is a Chicago-area disability rights activist and scholar and is currently enrolled in the Disability Studies PhD program at the University of Illinois, Chicago. Her academic and activist interests are in the areas of disability identity and culture, social policy, and bioethics. She received the Society for Disability Studies Irving K. Zola award for her essay "It Is for the Mother: Feminist Rhetorics of Disability during the American Eugenics Period," an earlier version of the essay published in this volume. She is also the recipient of an award from the Council for Disability Rights and the Gnawing Gargoyle for Public Policy Advocacy award. She is interested in sustaining connections between her disability rights activism and disability studies scholarship and is a founding member of community-based and graduate student organizations that include the Suburban Access Squad, Disabled Students Union, and the Disability History and Culture Collective.

Joan Lipkin is the Producing Artistic Director of That Uppity Theatre

Company, where she cofounded the DisAbility Project with occupational therapist Fran Cohen. The DisAbility Project is one of the oldest and only projects in the United States to create and tour work about the culture of disability featuring participants with and without disabilities. She specializes in creating work with marginalized populations, including women with cancer; LGBTQ youth, adults, and their families; adolescent girls; people with Alzheimer's and early stage dementia; and blind and at-risk youth. An educator, writer, and social activist, her work has been published and presented throughout the United States, Canada, and the United Kingdom. She is the recipient of numerous awards, including the James F. Hornback Ethical Humanist of the Year, Visionary, Healthcare Hero, Human Rights Campaign, Community Enhancement, What's Right with the Region for Improving Racial Equality and Social Justice and National Conference for Community and Justice, among others.

Susannah B. Mintz is Associate Professor of English at Skidmore College in upstate New York. She is the author of *Threshold Poetics: Milton and Intersubjectivity* (2003) and *Unruly Bodies: Life Writing by Women with Disabilities* (2007), and the co-editor, with Merri Lisa Johnson, of *On the Literary Nonfiction of Nancy Mairs: A Critical Anthology* (2011). She has written extensively in the fields of seventeenth-century poetry, autobiography and creative nonfiction, and disability in literature. Her creative work has been published in literary journals including *Michigan Quarterly Review* and *Ninth Letter,* and she is currently at work on a study of literary representations of pain.

Ellen Samuels is Assistant Professor of Gender and Women's Studies and English at University of Wisconsin, Madison. She was a 2006–2007 Ed Roberts Postdoctoral Fellow in Disability Studies at University of California, Berkeley. Her critical work on disability has appeared in *GLQ: Gay/ Lesbian Quarterly, MELUS: Multi-Ethnic Literatures of the United States, Leviathan: A Journal of Melville Studies,* and is forthcoming in *Signs: A Journal of Women in Culture and Society.* She is the 2011 recipient of the Catherine Stimpson Prize for Outstanding Feminist Scholarship awarded by *Signs.*

Abby Wilkerson is the author of *Diagnosis: Difference: The Moral Authority of Medicine* (1998) and co-editor with Robert McRuer of "Desiring Disability: Queer Theory Meets Disability Studies" (a special issue of *GLQ: Gay/Lesbian Quarterly,* 2003). Her articles have appeared in such publications as *Hypatia: Journal of Feminist Philosophy, Radical Philosophy Review, Food, Culture and Society, Transformations,* and a number of anthologies. She is a philosopher teaching in the University Writing Program at George Washington University.

Index

asylum, 92, 93, 100, 102, 109n15, 130, 180.
See also mental illness
autobiography, 8, 69–89
Autobiography of a Face, 88n12

Baartman, Saartjie, 6, 19, 157n5, 159
Bahan, Ben, 254
Baldwin, James, 139
Bambara, Toni Cade, 152
Barbie, 30–32, 296, 304
Bartky, Sandra, 5, 205, 206
Bauman, H-Dirksen L., 236
bearded woman, the. See Pastrana, Julia
beauty, 16, 24, 26, 39; and femininity, 30,
    32, 206; gender, race, and, 140–141,
    155; ideals or standards of, 39, 71, 96,
    296, 298
Beauvoir, Simone de, 3, 19, 51
Becker, Elle, 194, 212, 214n2
Beecher, Catherine, 184
Bennett, Lisa, 295
Berry, Halle, 93
Bérubé, Michael, 48–49, 69
Bhabha, Homi, 160, 161, 164–165, 167,
    171n1
Bickenbach, Jerome, 278
birth control, 196; and eugenics, 178,
    179–182, 194. See also contraception
"black Atlantic," the, 130
blindness, 49, 70, 76, 81, 83, 87, 88,
    109n16, 231; in film and literature,
    74–75, 77; and gender, 71, 76, 85; in
    Jane Eyre, 101–103; myths and narra-
    tives of, 69, 71, 74–75, 83, 88, 89n14;
    and passing, 87–88; and reproductive
    choice, 227–228; and right to parent,
    230–231, 238, 239n13
body, the, 22, 24, 84, 119, 136, 149, 245,
    260n2, 263, 287; black, 136, 137, 142,
    143, 145, 159; cultural history of, 16, 17;
    docile, 24, 34, 143–144, 161; and iden-
    tity, 25, 34; politics, 22, 118
Bordo, Susan, 21, 34, 258
Braille, Louis, 82–83
braille, 80–83
breast: Breast Cancer Fund, 25, 35; can-
    cer, 24–26; female, 25
Brontë, Charlotte, 91
Brooks, Gwendolyn, 8, 136–157

Brown, William Wells, 156n4
Brueggemann, Brenda Jo, 237n2
Bush, George W., 202–203, 212; Bush
    Administration, 157n10
Butler, Judith, 6, 7, 33, 34, 48–64, 106,
    159, 171n1
Bynum, Caroline Walker, 33

Caminero-Santangelo, Marta, 93
capitalism, 38, 39, 120, 127, 142, 179
Carlson, Licia, 4
Cather, Willa, 61
Chamberlin, J. Edward, 129
Chambers, Kijuana, 230–231, 234
Chesler, Phyllis, 92
Chhachhi, Amrita, 162
Cho, Julia, 52–53, 61
chronic illness, 263–283. See also illness
Chronicle of Higher Education, The, 42
Cibber, Cauis Gabriel, 100–101
citizenship, 120–122, 127, 130, 131, 195,
    282; discourses of, 7, 107; and race, 8,
    122, 137, 142–143
civil rights, 29–30, 32, 105, 142, 252–253;
    movement, 13, 15, 35, 37, 196
Clare, Eli, 3
class, 92, 96, 119, 139, 169, 179, 181, 182,
    183, 186, 199, 202
cochlear implants, 224, 226, 228, 234,
    253–255
Code, Lorraine, 256–257
cognitive disability, 69, 105, 125, 129,
    187n1, 203–204, 210–211, 221; and race,
    143, 203; and sexuality, 203–204. See
    also feeblemindedness
colonialism, 120–123, 132n1; colonizer/
    colonized binary, 161, 172n1; decoloni-
    zation, 161, 162
coming-out narrative, 88, 199, 260n2;
    and disability, 34–35; and fatness,
    260n2
Communism, 139
Comstock Act, 196, 214n3
conjoined twins, 26, 53
Connor, Ken, 226, 232
Continental Congress, 143
contraception, 179, 196, 204, 214n3. See
    also birth control
Cooper, Anna Julia, 177

Corker, Mairian, 64
cosmetic surgery, 23–24
Couser, G. Thomas, 87
"crip," 211
cripple, 35, 101; eugenics discourse and, 177, 211; in *You Have Come Back*, 166–170
cult of true womanhood, 139
cyborg, 21, 59, 120, 124–125, 160, 218

DALY (disability-adjusted life years), 127–128, 131
Darwin, Charles, 175, 176, 177; Social Darwinism, 181; sociobiological interpretation of, 130, 176–177
Davis, Dena, 234, 235
Davis, Lennard, 34, 51, 59, 103–105, 107, 109n10, 119, 132n2, 154, 239n18, 266
Deaf, 218, 223, 224, 232, 238nn8,9; culture, 234, 254–255; distinction between deaf and, 237n2; linguistic-cultural model of deafness, 223–225, 238n7
Declaration of Sentiments, 176
dehumanization, 125, 211
dependency, 29, 75, 80, 118, 132n2
Desai, Anita, 159–161, 163–166; *Clear Light of Day*, 159, 163–166, 170–171
disability: ability/disability system, 15–17, 19; and abortion, 28, 50; aesthetic, 9, 290, 292, 298, 308n2; and children, 227–228; congenital, 145, 146, 150; and critical race theory, 197; as defect, 221–233, 236; and discourse of cure, 8–9, 27–28, 234, 236; and ethnic studies, 34–35; fatness as, 248–249, 258–259; and femininity, 30, 32, 55–56; and illness, 60, 87; and impairment, 64, 104–105, 109n9, 247–248, 264; invisible/visible, 69, 263, 264, 273, 275; as lack, 161; in literature, 159–173; medical model of, 8, 88, 106, 172n4, 266, 283n2; medical pathologization of, 211, 252; metaphor for oppression, 288; overcoming narrative, 3, 32–33, 71; and passing, 35, 39; and quality of life argument, 28; and queerness, 204–205, 225, 228–229, 232, 239n17; and queer theory, 34–35, 197; and

reproductive choice, 227–228, 232; and right to parent, 230–232, 238n13; rights movement, 2, 29–30, 105, 175, 225, 266, 268; and sexuality, 32–33, 193–214, 226; social model of, 5, 8, 109n9, 187n1, 208, 224, 266; theater, 290–291; universalizing versus minoritizing view of, 17 (*see also* Sedgwick, Eve Kosofsky); and the university, 263–283; and veterans, 118, 139
DisAbility Project, 9, 205, 291–294, 299–308
disability studies, 1, 50, 52–54, 58, 63
disease, 56, 110n21, 122, 129, 131, 137, 250–251
disidentification, 150
Dolan, Jill, 290
"Don't Ask, Don't Tell," 123
Douglas, Frederick, 143
Dreger, Alice, 2, 5–6
Duchesneau, Sharon, 225–226, 228–229, 231, 234, 236

Eiseland, Nancy, 36
Ellis, Havelock, 179
Ensler, Eve: *The Good Body*, 288
eugenics, 2, 8, 21, 28–29, 118, 129–131, 175–176, 180, 183, 185–187; and feminism, 178–179, 180, 185–186; and poverty, 179–180, 183–184
euthanasia, 2, 6, 29, 50, 130, 185, 187. *See also* physician-assisted suicide
evolution, 79, 177–178

family, 122, 163, 225, 229
Family Research Council, 226–227, 232
Fanon, Frantz, 159, 161, 162, 167, 171n1, 172n2
Fatness, 246, 250, 253, 260n5, 288; cultural narratives of, 249–250, 251; and Deafness, 245, 253–255; as disability, 9, 248–249, 258, 259; fatphobia, 248, 250, 251, 257–258; and gender, 246–247, 249, 257; medical views of, 246, 250, 251
feeblemindedness, 129, 175, 178, 179, 185, 187n1
Feldshuh, David, 289; *Miss Evers' Boys*, 289

Whitman, Walt, 109n11
Wilchins, Riki Ann, 62
Williams, Tennessee, 288
Wilson, Carnie, 261n7
Wilson, Daniel J., 308n2
Wilson, James, 110n20
Winfrey, Oprah, 93
Winterson, Jeanette, 227–229

womanism, 8, 142
World Bank, 126, 127, 128

Yates, Andrea, 94, 108n7
Young, Iris Marion, 3, 18, 25, 202

Zimmerman, Don H., 276
Žižek, Slavoj, 73

Printed and bound by CPI Group (UK) Ltd, Croydon, CR0 4YY

25/03/2025

14647348-0002